JEWISH FOOD

The World at Table

HarperCollinsPublishers

JEWISH FOOD

Matthew Goodman

For information, address HarperCollins Publishers Inc., 10 East 53rd Street, New York, NY 10022.

HarperCollins books may be purchased for educational, business, or sales promotional use. For information, please write: Special Markets Department, HarperCollins Publishers Inc., 10 East 53rd Street, New York, NY 10022.

FIRST EDITION

Designed by Cassandra J. Pappas

Printed on acid-free paper

Library of Congress Cataloging-in-Publication Data.

Goodman, Matthew.
Jewish food : the world at table/[Matthew Goodman]—1st ed.
p. cm.
Includes bibliographical references and index.
ISBN 0-06-052128-7
1. Cookery, Jewish. I. Title.

TX724.G666 2005
641.5'676—dc22 2004047535

05 06 07 08 09 ❖/RRD 10 9 8 7 6 5 4 3 2 1

For Cassie and Ezra

Contents

Acknowledgments

All books are really the products of a community, and this one more than most. I am deeply indebted to many, many people for their contributions to its making. First among them is my agent, Bill Clegg, whose tireless efforts on behalf of my work are both humbling and inspiring. My editor at HarperCollins, Susan Friedland, offered sharp-eyed comments and thoughtful criticism from which this book has benefited enormously. Evie Righter's copyediting, so careful and precise, was the sort that any writer would treasure. Excellent translations were cheerfully provided by Chana Pollack and Géraldine de Haugoubart, and likewise, recipe testing by Irma and Marty Shore.

Some of the material in this book originally appeared in the *Forward*, where, as the "Food Maven" columnist, I have had the good fortune to work with three talented editors: Erica Brody, Aliza Phillips, and Ellen Umansky.

I am deeply grateful to my parents, Burton and Joellyn Goodman, and my in-laws, Steve and Nancy Schwerner, for their enthusiastic support.

Over the past several years, innumerable people have generously shared with me recipes, personal stories, and historical information. I thank them all, and especially: Bea Gitlin Abrams, Gail Agasi, Molook Ahdoot, Rita Arditti, Nesrin Bakkaloglu, Riva Ben-Ezra, Alegria Bendelac, Ana Bensadón, Eva Bertoin, Vivian

Beyda, Liliana Brown, Selma Cherkas, Lea Chikashvili, Elayne Clift, Alan Conway, Monique Daoud, Jenny Edelstein, Hannah Eisner, Mark Federman, Shoshana Sharabi Garber, Paul Glasser, Jillian Gould, Anita Graber, Mary Mevorah Hanoka, Rosy Harari, Esther Rudomin Hautzig, Zimra Israel, Anita Jacobson, Maria Kachkoff, Nina Kaplanides, Mollie Katzen, Amnun Kimyagarov, Solomon and Koula Kofinas, Marta Kovacs, Pippo Lattanzi, Joan Levy, Sue London, Rina Marcus, Diane Matza, Susan Meschel, Eudice Mesibov, Gilbert and Louise Metz, Rahel Musleah, Paulette Nehama, Chayele Palevsky, Chana Pollack, Rosaly Roffman, Michael Rosen, Anne Rosenzweig, Robert Rothstein, Vivienne Roumani-Denn, Elie Sabban, Tzippi Said, Houman Sarshar, Jackie Schectman, Talma Scheerson, David Schochet, Herb Schon, Zell Schulman, Deborah Schupack, Nancy Schwerner, Beth Shepard, Gail Shirazi, Irma and Marty Shore, Roz Snow, Agnes Sobel, Penina Meghnagi Solomon, Mervyn Sopher, Beverly Hanoka Spool, Rachel Suissa, Stanley Sultan, Laura Supino, Bruna Tedeschi, Fortuna Unger, Ellen Vaknine, Diana Cox Van Arsdale, Sarah Van Arsdale, Patricia Volk, Miriam Weinstein, and Stella Ymar.

Finally, my loving thanks go to Cassie Schwerner, who possesses more admirable qualities than I can adequately name or possibly deserve, among them keen intelligence, generosity of spirit, and boundless patience; she has been the best possible audience for my writing and cooking. All the meals I make are, in a very real sense, for her.

Introduction

There's an old joke that's told about a Martian who accidentally crashes his spaceship on the streets of New York. In search of a new set of tires for his craft, he happens to pass a bagel shop; noticing the bins of bagels in the window, the Martian goes in and inquires about purchasing some of those tires for his spaceship. "Those aren't tires, those are bagels," says the owner. "Here, try one."

The Martian takes a bite. "Man," he says, smacking his lips, "these would go great with cream cheese and lox!"

That time-tested combination might have been immediately obvious on Mars, perhaps (it's pleasant to think so), but it surely wouldn't have been in Casablanca, or Aleppo, or Calcutta, or in any of the other Jewish communities around the world where bagels were about as common as Martians. We might, for that matter, imagine an equally perplexed expression on the face of a Jew from Vilna offered up a plate of sizzling-hot *carciofi alla giudia*—for while this was a defining dish for Roman Jews, to a resident of the Pale the idea of "artichokes in the Jewish style" might well have seemed a contradiction in terms.

In Tunisia Jewish cooks have made couscous, in India curries, in Yemen flat breads, in New York cheesecake. So what, then, might legitimately be considered "Jewish food"? How would we even go about defining such a thing? If we were, for example, to restrict ourselves to foods made by all of the world's Jewish communities—the ones that our Roman and Vilner would both recognize as Jewish—the menu would be a very short one indeed, scarcely sufficient for a single meal. It would include those foods created to address religious needs common to Jews everywhere, among them the overnight Sabbath stew, prepared before Friday sundown to be eaten warm on Saturday, when work is prohibited (though the names for the stew, and the ingredients used in it, vary from place to place); charoset, the sweet paste that on Passover symbolizes the mortar used by Israelite slaves under Egyptian bondage (though the charoset of one country may well bear scant resemblance to that of its neighbor); and finally matzo, the bread of affliction (though not the many dishes made from the matzo).

Even here, in what we might call the foundational dishes of Jewish cookery, all but one are shared only in a broad sense, not in the specific details; surely a definition is too restrictive when it limits a cuisine to sheets of matzo. But neither should we head in the opposite direction, and declare Jewish food simply to be "food made by Jews." Though this would seem logical enough, and might once have made some sense, it is no longer applicable in a world where regional distinctions have blurred (so that in any metropolitan area one can choose from a multitude of ethnic cuisines, and the trendiest restaurants often feature the "fusion" of two or more), and when many Jews, even those who consider themselves observant, no longer keep kosher. Today, a list of foods made by Jews would include everything from cheeseburgers to jambalaya. Nor, in that regard, is the fact of a food being kosher sufficient in itself. After all, a tossed green salad is not a Jewish food merely because its components happen to conform to the dietary laws, and though it may have become a favorite buffet item at upscale Orthodox weddings, we would be hard-pressed to define sushi as Jewish.

Like all traditional foods, Jewish food is a product of history and geography; it is an expression of the area in which it has been made. In this case, the area happens to span not merely a particular country (as, for instance, with Italian or French food, which contain significant regional variations), or even much of a continent (as with Chinese food), but instead much of the world. To help in discussing such a broad geographical area, Jewish food is usually separated into two major categories: Ashkenazic and Sephardic.

Ashkenazic refers to those Jews who settled in France and Germany in the ninth and tenth centuries (*Ashkenaz* is the Hebrew name for Germany) and who, in flight from intensified persecution brought on by the Crusades and the bubonic plague, migrated eastward at the end of the medieval period into Eastern Europe and Russia. There, in those difficult conditions, the preponderance of Ashkenazic cuisine was wrought. The vegetables of the diet were those that could grow well in cold weather and poor soil—cabbages, potatoes, turnips, and the like—and could be stored to survive the long northern winter. With few available fresh herbs, the cooking leaned heavily on garlic for additional flavoring, with sugar, honey, and cinnamon for sweet dishes. As much of the region is land-locked, the fish were primarily freshwater species, such as carp and pike. Beef was a luxury item; chicken was far more plentiful, and not a bit of it was wasted, from the feet, used for thickening soup, to the fat that was, along with butter (for dairy meals), the chief frying agent. Of course, there were important differences within Ashkenazic cooking—the foods of Poland, for instance, tended to be sweeter, those of Lithuania more peppery—but overall, the foods were similar, as is to be expected from a relatively limited geographical area, and a terrain of such reluctant disposition.

Precisely the opposite is true of Sephardic food. The word *Sephardic* is taken from Sepharad, the biblical name for Spain, and specifically refers to Spanish Jewry. Over time, though, it has come to refer to all non-Ashkenazic Jews—some of whom descend from the Spanish Jews exiled in 1492, but many of whom do not, including those of the Mediterranean, the Balkans, North Africa, the Middle East, Central Asia, and India. There aren't many points of commonality to be found in the cooking of such a disparate geographic area; still, we can make some generalizations about Sephardic food, and particularly by contrasting it to the Ashkenazic. Thanks to a more agreeable climate, the cuisine features a far broader range of vegetables (eggplant, tomatoes, okra, artichokes, fennel, and countless more); rather than potatoes, the staple starch may be rice or couscous, augmented by legumes such as lentils or chickpeas; the frying agent is not chicken fat but oil, typically olive oil; often as not chicken is the luxury meat, with lamb or beef more common; and the essential flavorings include not just garlic, but a vast array of herbs and spices, including everything from cilantro and curry leaves to cumin, coriander, and cardamom.

From Moroccan mellah to Polish ghetto, Greek seaside to Hungarian countryside, Jewish cooks have worked with a remarkable diversity of ingredients and cooking styles. Since the days of the Babylonian exile the Jews have been a migratory people, uprooting themselves from established communities to seek out new ones, sometimes in pursuit of trade but more often in flight from economic hardship and religious persecution. Wherever they have wandered, from continent to continent, they have modified their cooking to accommodate the new ingredients, flavors, and even the traditional dishes of the adopted land. Oftentimes, of course, they had to adapt these dishes to conform to the Jewish dietary laws, by exchanging permitted cuts of meat or species of fish for forbidden ones, or by eliminating combinations of meat and dairy. This happened everywhere, but it was most common among the Jews of Central and Eastern Europe, where pork is a staple ingredient, lard is used for frying, and meat is often combined with dairy products. In Alsace, for instance, Jews replaced the slab bacon typically found in the local *choucroute garnie* with corned beef or pickled tongue, while in Russia borscht was made, in its meat varieties, with beef instead of pork, and was not garnished with sour cream. (That was saved, instead, for the dairy versions of the soup.)

Certain adaptations had to be made as well by the Jews living among Hindus in India, such as cooking meat dishes with oil instead of clarified butter, but in general these adaptations were less common there than in Christian Europe. They were even less so among the Jewish communities of North Africa and the Middle East, where the local Muslim population likewise eschews the consumption of pork, typically uses oil for frying, and rarely mixes meat and dairy in its cookery. Among these Sephardic Jews, it is by no means uncommon to find foods made in precisely the same manner as they are in the wider society—as with, say, hummus, which has long been popular in the Middle East, in Jewish and Arab communities alike. Hummus is thus simultaneously a Jewish and an Arab food, and in this it is but one of many. (A *New Yorker* cartoon from some years back shows a religious Jew sitting next to an Arab in Jerusalem, saying, "Why is it we never focus on the things that unite us, like felafel?")

So Jewish food cannot be reduced to a set of dietary laws, a particular cooking style, or a combination of favored ingredients. It cannot be defined by its internal similarities—for it varies too widely from place to place—nor by its differences from the non-Jewish food around it. It is at once something grander and, of necessity, less specific. Jewish food is that which has sustained the Jewish people for countless generations, wherever they happened to be. It is the loaves baked in community ovens, the stews kept warm overnight in the dying embers of the Sabbath fire. It is a honey-sweetened roast to greet the New Year, a lemony soup to break the fast after the Day of Atonement. It is a roast chicken on Friday night. It is the cookies and confections kept on hand to welcome friends who might drop in of an afternoon. It is all the dishes crafted to fashion—however briefly or incompletely—luxury from poverty; all the dishes whose names evoke memories of parents and grandparents, and dreams of those of whom one has heard only stories. It is the food that is still made in immigrant communities, held on to—like old photographs, letters, a tattered prayer book, the key to an ancestral home—to preserve a sense of connection to a place forever lost.

Food, after all, carries the past within it, is in fact a kind of repository of a community's history. Here, in its broad strokes, is the story of the Jews. *Wandering:* as, for instance, in the sweet-and-sour chicken dishes of the Baghdadi Jews who settled in Calcutta in the nineteenth century, in whose kitchens the Middle East made union with India. *Exile:* as in *albondigas*, the meatballs still made by Jews in Istanbul, that harken back to a golden age before the expulsion from Spain. *Poverty:* as in Russian latkes, made with buckwheat flour until the devastating crop failures of the mid-nineteenth century necessitated the widespread planting of potatoes. *Conquest:* as in the many Roman dishes made with raisins and pine nuts, a legacy of the former Arab dominion over Southern Europe. And of course, *Tradition:* in the recipes themselves, those enduring remnants of an earlier time.

Recipes, like any important cultural documents, are products of the communities out of which they have arisen, and have inevitably been shaped by the histories of those communities. And so in this book I have included numerous brief essays that locate the recipes within a broader historical and cultural context. There are three separate categories of essay. Those essays entitled "Ingredients" discuss how a particular foodstuff—meat, eggs, rice, olives, and so forth—has been put to use, often very differently, in the foods made by various Jewish communities. The essays entitled "Dishes" focus instead on a single important dish from the Jewish tradition—such as latkes, gefilte fish, and *albondigas*—tracing the dish's origins and how it has evolved over time. Finally, the essays entitled "Communities" examine in a more general way the histories and distinctive food styles of Jewish communities around the world, from Bombay to Baghdad.

Each essay is illustrative of the recipe or recipes that immediately follow it: the Rome essay, for instance, precedes the classic Roman dish of stewed salt cod; the chicken soup essay comes before several varieties from Eastern Europe, India, and Iraq; and the essay on matzo before recipes for matzo brei and the matzo meal pancakes called *chremslach.* Most of the recipes included in this book are traditional to one or more of the world's Jewish communities; generally I have provided the original name for the dish, along with an English-language description. In the case of dishes that have become famous, even iconic, in the United States (chopped liver, say, or cheesecake) I have given only the English name; the same is true with the occasional modern variation of a traditional dish.

My intention in this book is not simply to present food as a sweetly appealing segment of the Jewish "lifestyle," but rather to evoke its fullest, most challenging, and most deeply meaningful qualities: as object of sensory pleasure, medium of culinary artistry, and useful window into Jewish history and culture. As each community has a history, so too does each food—and knowing something about that history will inevitably make the food more interesting, and perhaps even more delicious.

In working on this book I have been privileged to meet scores of Jewish cooks—most of them immigrants or children of immigrants, from communities both abroad and here in the United States—who have been generous enough to share with me their family recipes. Some of the recipes are for dishes that have never before appeared in any cookbook; indeed, many of them had never even been written down. (Written recipes, after all, only become necessary when once-unitary cultures begin to fracture, when recipes are no longer passed down in the kitchen from one generation to the next.) So it wasn't at all unusual, in compiling these recipes, to run into the problem of exact measurement. Whether they happen to be Ashkenazic or Sephardic, many of these home cooks rely on what is known in Yiddish as the *sheet arayn* (pour in) method: that is, a method by which one simply keeps adding this or that ingredient until the dish looks or tastes right. (By which is meant how it has looked or tasted for the decades the cook has been preparing it.) I came across innumerable handwritten recipes that listed ingredients without quantities, or called for a handful or a "wineglass" of a particular ingredient. This last is a more common convention than you might suspect, or at least more common than I had anticipated; it is a perfectly useful standard, after all, in a family that possesses a single set of wineglasses. It's not that much use in a cookbook, though, and when I pressed them for more specificity, these home cooks proved to be exceedingly helpful. Many times, rather than simply guessing at the correct quantities, they would prepare the dishes again, in order to measure how much this particular hand or glass actually contains. Often they invited me into their homes, to cook along with them, so that I might see firsthand how these dishes are properly made.

Over the past several years I have encountered a world of Jewish food more vibrant, diverse, and exciting than I had even suspected. It is also far more endangered. Many of the people I've met come from communities that no longer exist, having been unable to withstand the twentieth century's combined pressures of assimilation, immigration, and annihilation. The once-great Jewish communities of Ioannina, Tangier, Baghdad, Warsaw, Samarkand, and so many others—that existed for hundreds or even thousands of years—are now, in Roman Vishniac's poignant descriptive, "vanished." In the twenty-first century the vast majority of the world's Jews live either in Israel or the United States: the Great Diaspora is, for all intents and purposes, ended.

The communities themselves are gone; their foods, however,

JEWISH FOOD

Appetizers, Salads, and Spreads

It was the Romans, those consummate gourmets, who introduced the idea of opening a meal with a selection of small dishes as a way of stimulating the appetite. The word *appetizer* is derived from the Latin *appete*, meaning "to desire, covet, or long for." An appetizer, then, is something that encourages desire—in this case, for the meal that will follow. It's a splendid practice, and one that was later adopted by, among others, the Jews of Eastern Europe, who, economic circumstances permitting, liked to begin meals with a cold appetizer, known in Yiddish as the *forshpayz*. Favorite appetizers included chopped liver, eggplant salad, and a variety of smoked or pickled fish, most commonly herring. In New York, the popularity of *forshpayzn* among Eastern European Jewish immigrants led to the creation of the institution known as the appetizing store, and over time the featured attractions of the appetizing store (herring, lox, cream cheese) evolved into the elements of Sunday brunch.

Among Sephardic Jews, a far broader complement of appetizers—called *mezze*, an Arabic word—begins the meal; they may even constitute the meal itself. *Mezze* include everything from olives and raw vegetables to cooked and uncooked vegetable salads, stuffed grape leaves, filled pastries (discussed in the savory pastries chapter), and spreads. These appetizers generally don't require much in the way of time or effort, so it's not at all difficult to prepare one or two as a prelude to dinner (especially as most can be made well beforehand). From garlicky hummus to a pomegranate-tart bulgur salad, from a sweet-and-sour celery salad to salty and spicy pickled turnips, these are richly flavored dishes, meant to be eaten in smallish portions—the better to tease the tongue and, in time-honored fashion, encourage the desire for what is to come.

INGREDIENTS: Olives

If one could choose a single agricultural product upon which to build a civilization, the olive would, at first glance, seem to be an unlikely candidate. The tree itself is gnomish, sprouting long, gnarled branches, in color a drab greenish gray. As for the fruit of the tree, its most distinguishing feature is how terrible it tastes. Pluck an olive from a tree and stick it in your mouth—or, on second thought, don't. The glucoside in it renders the fresh olive so bitter as to be virtually inedible.

The olive tree, however, provides us the most enduring lesson in how one should never be content with first glances. Given the proper climatic conditions, the tree is extremely hardy, with deep taproots that allow it to survive with little moisture, and to grow in meager ground or on the steep hillsides that rise from the Mediterranean Sea. Slow growing, an olive tree can live for centuries, and is almost indestructible: If an olive tree is burned to the ground, or cut down, its roots will send out shoots and several more will grow in its place. Cured for weeks or months in oil, salt, or brine—no one knows exactly how and when this process was first figured out—the olive becomes a tangy, meaty treat (though a taste that, like coffee, often needs to be "acquired"). Even more miraculous, the oil that can be pressed from the fruit turns out to be the most delicious, not to mention healthful, of any to be found anywhere on the planet.

As has been noted by Maggie Blyth Klein, co-owner of Oliveto restaurant in Oakland, California, and author of *The Feast of the Olive*, the olive has a history just about as long as that of Western civilization; indeed, it is difficult to imagine one without the other. Ancient Egypt holds the distinction of being the first importer of olive oil, from groves in Syria and the Western Maghreb. Egyptian mummies were preserved with, among other things, olive oil, and cured olives were left in the tombs of pharoahs to be consumed on the journey to the afterlife.

Greek mythology tells how Athena produced the first olive tree, and the olive branch became the most important symbol of ancient Greece; olive wreaths, for example, were placed on the heads of victorious athletes and soldiers. Olive oil was used in cookery, in lamps, and, in the absence of soap, for cleansing the skin. Laws were passed protecting the olive trees of Athens; anyone convicted of cutting one down was put to death. Those who harvested olives were compelled to swear an oath of chastity.

The Jews, of course, were a Mediterranean people as well, and like the Greeks they used olives and olive oil for everything from food to light (most vividly remembered in the story of the Maccabees and their miraculous oil) to religious ritual. The Bible is full of references to olives. In Exodus 27:20, for instance, God instructs Moses on Sinai to fill the lamps for the temple sanctuary with pure olive oil, and, two verses later, to use olive oil to anoint Aaron and his sons as priests. In Deuteronomy 8:8, olives and olive oil (with wheat, barley, figs, pomegranates, and honey) are among the blessings said to be found in the Promised Land. Beyond its practical uses, the olive tree also functioned as a symbol of hope and regeneration, specifically in Genesis 8:11, when Noah sends out a dove as a messenger to search for land, and it returns bearing in its beak an olive branch.

Though olives are an important food on all sides of the Mediterranean, there is a fascinating east-west split in their culinary use. On the western side of the olive divide—from Morocco and Tunisia up through Spain, France, and Italy—olives are included as part of many traditional dishes. On the eastern side, though—from Egypt and Libya into Greece, Turkey, and Syria—olives are commonly eaten as hors d'oeuvres or snacks, or used as garnishes, but are never used in cooking.

The Jewish foods of this region, as elsewhere, tend to be similar to their non-Jewish counterparts, and so the geographic divide holds true there as well. Perhaps the most extensive use of olives in Jewish cookery occurs in Morocco. Olives are a common ingredient in the stews known as tagines, after the conical earthenware pot in which they are prepared. The most famous of these tagines combines green olives with chicken—the olives' salty bitterness pairs perfectly with the stolidity of the chicken—often with chopped-up preserved lemons, one of the country's most unusual and interesting ingredients, and one that, like olives, has been produced by salt curing (see page 159). Green olives are also used in a variety of beef and lamb tagines and are roasted as a sauce for whole fish (see page 83), while black olives are partnered with oranges in one of the many salads that typically begin Shabbat dinners in the community (see page 7).

In Spain during the Middle Ages, lard was the most commonly used frying agent, except among Jews, who used olive oil, as pork fat was religiously forbidden. As a result, the use of olive oil for frying became, during Inquisition trials of suspected crypto-Jews, evidence of Jewish practice. In *A Drizzle of Honey*, David Gitlitz and Linda Kay Davidson quote Andrés Bernáldez, the chronicler of King Ferdinand and Queen Isabel, on this Jewish culinary tradition: "They cooked their meat in olive oil, which they used instead of salt-pork or other fat, so as to avoid pork. Olive oil with meat and other fried things leaves a very unpleasant odor, and so their houses and doorways stunk with the odor of that food. The Jews too gave off the same odor, on account of those foods, and because they were not baptized . . . "

Even in the eastern Mediterranean, in Turkey and Greece, where olives are not used in cooking, their oil has long been essential for frying, and even for deep-frying. Nowadays most cooks prefer to use other types of oil for deep frying, because these oils have a less pronounced flavor and a higher smoke point (the temperature at which a heated fat begins to smoke, rendering it unfit for use) than does olive oil. This preference has now spread to Turkey and Greece as well. Today, cooks there generally use sunflower oil, but this has been true only for the last generation or so. Before that, the Jews of those communities used olive oil for all of their deep-frying, including even sweet foods such as *loukomades*, the delicious honey-doused yeast fritters that are a staple for Greek Hanukkah celebrations.

Though it is rarely used anymore for deep frying, olive oil is still a perfect medium for most pan-frying, not least because it is a monounsaturated fat, which experiments have shown to reduce levels of low-density lipoproteins (LDL), the "bad" form of cholestoral. (Butter, margarine, and other forms of oil are not monounsaturated.) And when a raw oil is called for, in sauces and spreads and dressings, no oil can compare to a genuine extra-virgin olive oil. Only this has the deep green color, the lush texture, the fruity taste, the peppery aftertaste. Only olive oil—not corn, safflower, canola, or any other—has the complexity and variety of wine. When the psalmist wrote, in number 104, that God has given us "wine that maketh glad the heart of man/and oil to make his face to shine," can there be any doubt which oil he means?

SALADE D'ORANGES ET OLIVES NOIRES

MOROCCAN ORANGE AND BLACK OLIVE SALAD

Moroccan Jewish tradition is to present a variety of salads on every Sabbath table, usually served before the fish course. This is a classic Moroccan salad, which nicely blends salty, sweet, bitter, and spicy flavors. Make sure to use good marinated olives, not the canned kind.

SERVES 6

- 4 oranges
- 1 cup pitted black olives
- 2 tablespoons olive oil
- 1 tablespoon red wine vinegar
- 3 garlic cloves, finely chopped
- ½ teaspoon paprika
- ½ teaspoon salt
- Pinch of cayenne
- ¼ teaspoon sugar
- 2 tablespoons chopped fresh flat-leaf parsley

1. Peel the oranges. Cut them into sections and then cut the sections crosswise into thirds. Arrange the orange pieces with the olives in a salad bowl.
2. In a small bowl, whisk together the oil, vinegar, garlic, paprika, salt, cayenne, and sugar and pour the mixture over the oranges and olives. Stir to combine, then sprinkle with the parsley. Serve immediately.

SALADE DE CAROTTES CUITES

MOROCCAN CARROT SALAD

It's best to make this salad a few hours in advance, to let the flavors fully blend.

SERVES 4

- 2 pounds carrots, peeled
- 6 tablespoons olive oil
- 2 tablespoons lemon juice
- 3 or 4 garlic cloves, finely chopped
- 1 teaspoon ground cumin
- 1½ teaspoons paprika
- 1 teaspoon salt
- ¼ teaspoon cayenne
- 1 tablespoon chopped fresh flat-leaf parsley

1. Bring a large pot of salted water to a boil. Add the carrots and cook until tender. Drain and let cool slightly, then slice into rounds about ⅓ inch thick. Place in a salad bowl.
2. Whisk together the oil, lemon juice, garlic, cumin, paprika, salt, and cayenne and pour over the carrots. Toss to combine. Sprinkle with the parsley. Serve at room temperature.

DELJHAN

MOROCCAN EGGPLANT SALAD

Eggplant salad is typically one of the variety of cold salads that begin a traditional Moroccan Friday-night dinner. This version is a fixture on the menu of the Village Crown Moroccan restaurant in New York's East Village, long one of the most popular kosher restaurants in the city.

SERVES 6

FOR THE EGGPLANT

- 2 medium eggplants, each about 1¼ pounds
- Salt for sprinkling
- Olive oil for frying

- 1 red pepper, cut into small dice
- 2 garlic cloves, finely chopped
- 2 tablespoons white vinegar, or to taste
- 2 tablespoons lemon juice, or to taste
- ½ cup chopped fresh flat-leaf parsley
- Salt
- Freshly ground black pepper

1. For the eggplant: Trim and peel the eggplants and cut them into ½-inch cubes. Place the cubes in a large colander. Sprinkle generously with salt and let stand for 1 hour. Rinse and dry with paper towels.
2. In a large skillet, add oil to a depth of about ¼ inch and heat over medium heat. Add the eggplant cubes and fry, stirring often, until deeply golden and very soft, about 10 minutes. Remove with a slotted spoon and place on paper towels to drain. Let cool.
3. When the eggplant is cool, place it in a large serving bowl. Add the red pepper, garlic, vinegar, lemon juice, and parsley, and season with salt and pepper. Stir to combine. Taste and adjust for seasoning. Cover with plastic wrap and refrigerate until ready to serve.

COMMUNITIES: Spain

In the year 1492, as every American schoolchild has learned, Columbus sailed the ocean blue; this was also the year in which Columbus's patrons, King Ferdinand and Queen Isabella, issued an edict expelling all Jews from Spain. Before the year was out some 175,000 Spanish Jews had been cast into exile, bringing to an end a 1,500-year sojourn in Sepharad (the Hebrew word for Spain), during which time the Jews of Spain had created perhaps the most illustrious of all Jewish communities. Indeed, during the so-called Golden Age of Spanish Jewry, from the tenth through the twelfth centuries, the country's Jews came to think of Spain as a "second Jerusalem," and so the expulsion meant for them a kind of double exile, a fate especially bitter.

At the height of their glory, in the twelfth century, the Jews of Spain made up some 90 percent of the world's Jewish population. By 1700, however, after several centuries of assimilation in the West and destitution in the declining societies of North Africa and the Balkans (at a time when the Jews of Eastern Europe were undergoing a population explosion), they constituted only 50 percent, and by the beginning of the twentieth century the number had shrunk to less than 10 percent. Today, most of the world's Sephardic Jews—in the strict sense of the term, meaning Jews who can trace their ancestry back to Spain—live in either Israel or the United States.

Though legend has it that the first Jews arrived in Spain after the Babylonian exile in 586 B.C.E., a more likely scenario has Jewish merchants accompanying Roman soldiers there around the beginning of the Common Era. In the fifth century, Spain was conquered by the German tribes who had brought down the Roman Empire: the Suevi, Vandals, Alani, and most lastingly, the Visigoths. The years of Jewish life under Visigoth rule are obscure to us, but they were undoubtedly nasty and brutish, replete with famine, war, and religious persecution. The Visigoths, however, like the Romans before them, were shortly replaced by another conquering force. These were the Moors—

the Muslims of North Africa—who rode into Spain in the year 711, establishing an Arab presence that would last until (that historic year again) 1492, when their last stronghold of Granada finally fell to Christian armies.

Anti-Semitic stories in Spain have long been told of how the Jews of Toledo opened the gates of the city to the Muslim invaders, and while this is likely an exaggeration, it is easy to understand how, after centuries of oppression, they might have been enthusiastic about the prospect of a change in regime. As it turns out, this enthusiasm was not unfounded, for the succeeding centuries brought about a flowering in Jewish life in Spain that would earlier have been scarcely imaginable. The Muslim caliphs of the first Umayyad dynasty, centered in Córdoba, created a society of unprecedented religious tolerance, resulting in a rich synthesis of Muslim, Christian, and Jewish culture. It was a civilization marked by marble palaces, bazaars abundant with spices and jewels, public libraries, baths and fountains, hillsides newly planted with fig and almond trees. In cities such as Córdoba, Seville, Toledo, and Granada, Jews were at the center of Arab Spain's economic and cultural life. The multilingualism of the Jews made them invaluable in international commerce, and Jewish merchants traveled the world to obtain silk, timber, musk, spices; others served the caliphs as diplomats and ambassadors. After the harsh asceticism of the German tribes (who had, for instance, banned Roman baths as encouraging effeminacy), the sensuality and literacy of Arab culture must have been a tonic, and a new Jewish poetry began to be cultivated in the tiled courtyards and orange-shaded gardens of Spain: a rapturous, wine-drenched verse that celebrated the pleasures of religious scripture and romantic love alike. Jews were also key players in the age's advances in the sciences, from astronomy and medicine to cartography, which was at the time almost exclusively a Jewish occupation. (As Jane Gerber has noted in her book *The Jews of Spain*, the device used to determine a ship's position at sea, the quadrant, was known in Spain as the *quadrans Judaicus* after its Jewish inventor.) Jews were also well represented in the field of philosophy, most notably in the person of Moses ben Maimon, more commonly known as Maimonides, the author of *Guide for the Perplexed*, born in 1135 in Córdoba.

The Arabs introduced several important crops into Spain, as in the rest of their territories in Southern Europe, including lemons, bitter oranges, eggplants, almonds, artichokes, and rice, as well as spices such as saffron. The result was a revolution in the country's cuisine. In *La Cuisine Andalouse: Un Art de Vivre*, Lucie Bolens has translated into French three hundred Andalusian recipes from the eleventh through thirteenth centuries; the recipes reveal a pronounced North African influence, from the many different preparations for eggplant to the extensive use of couscous, semolina flour, and almond paste. Bolens includes five specifically Jewish recipes in her book, each of them extremely elaborate, involving many separate steps and lots of ingredients. In one of them, for instance, called Jewish Partridge, a partridge is stuffed in its cavity and under the skin with a mixture of almonds, pine nuts, eggs, oil, garum (a sauce that dates back to Roman times, made from fermented fish), coriander, cinnamon, pepper, and an aromatic herb called nard. The partridge is then placed in a heavy clay pot and stewed (over a copper pot filled with very red embers) in a sauce of oil, vinegar, mint, citron leaves, salt, and the pungent paste known as *murrí*. The partridge is served with a garnish of hard-boiled egg yolks and finished with a sprinkling of pepper, cinnamon, and sugar.

Another dish, Bolens notes, was prepared on Friday and left to cook overnight for the Sabbath. This dish begins with meatballs seasoned with cumin, rosewater, onion juice, and other flavorings and spices. The meatballs are placed in a clay pot between two layers of a sort of cinnamon-flavored omelet, and then covered with another omelet, which has been flavored with more cinnamon as well as pepper and rose- water. After long cooking over a low fire, the sealed pot is cracked open and the dish is presented with a garnish of mint, pistachios, and pine nuts.

Bolens calls this dish "*Recette juive de farce cachée*," literally Jewish Recipe of Hidden Stuffing; the name calls to mind the Sephardic overnight Sabbath stew known as *dafina* or *adafina*, from the Arabic word meaning buried or hidden. Generally the term is thought to refer to the pot being hidden in the smoldering embers, but here it seems at least as likely that the name indicates the meatballs hidden between two layers of egg. In any case, this is a dish that is no longer made anywhere, and in its lushness, and its very strangeness, it evokes for us the flavor of that glorious time, long passed.

For the Golden Age of Spain, like all golden ages, would not last long. In the twelfth century, the tolerant caliphs of Córdoba were overthrown by the Almohades, a fanatical Muslim tribe from North Africa. Facing the prospect of forced conversions, many Jews fled to the Christian territories in the north of the country. At the same time, Christian armies were pushing ever farther south, reconquering land lost to the Muslims centuries earlier. By the fourteenth century, a dangerous combination of religious intolerance and economic insecurity had begun to darken the future of the Jews in Spain. First came famine (the opening decade of the century was so strangely cold that it became known as the Little Ice Age), followed by flood, and then, for good measure, pestilence. The bubonic plague arrived in the port city of Barcelona in 1348, and within the year had ravaged the country: More deaths were recorded between August and November 1348 than for the previous twenty years combined. In the face of what must have seemed biblical-scale plagues, it was probably inevitable that scapegoats would be sought; before long popular sentiment began to turn against the Jews, who in their role as tax collectors and moneylenders were widely identified with the increasingly unpopular central government. Levels of anti-Semitism intensified as the century progressed, culminating in the pogroms of 1391, when the Jewish sections of several cities were attacked by mobs demanding that the Jews convert or die. They did so, it seems, in almost equal numbers: After a year of rioting, some 100,000 Jews had been killed, while another 100,000 converted to Christianity, and 100,000 more managed to survive by hiding or fleeing to safety.

Conversion was especially widespread among the upper classes of Jews, who had the most to lose, and by the fifteenth century the Spanish court was heavily populated with *conversos* and their descendants. Even King Ferdinand himself was the son of a *converso* mother—"a fact," notes Erna Paris in *The End of Days*, her history of the Jews of Spain, "which lends considerable psychological interest to the king's later sponsorship of the Inquisition."

The Spanish Inquisition—officially known as the Holy Inquisition against Depraved Heresy—was established in 1481 in the city of Castile, and subsequently spread throughout the Christian territories. The Inquisition was directed against *conversos,* former Jews, who were accused of religious heresy and political subversion through secret Jewish practice. To establish such practice, the Inquisition trials took testimony about the accused's alleged Jewish activities—many of them, as it happens, culinary in nature. One Inquisition list of Jewish food practices, quoted by David Gitlitz and Linda Kay Davidson in *A Drizzle of Honey: The Lives and Recipes of Spain's Secret Jews,* reads in part: " . . . cooking on the said Fridays such food as is required for the Saturdays and on the latter eating the meat thus cooked on Fridays as is the manner of the Jews; . . . cleansing or causing meat to be cleansed, cutting away from it all fat or grease and cutting away the nerve or sinew from the leg; . . . not eating pork, hare, rabbit, strangled birds, conger-eel, cuttle-fish, nor eels or other scaleless fish, as laid down in the Jewish law; and upon the death of parents . . . eating . . . such things as boiled eggs, olives, and other viands . . . "

On April 29, 1492, King Ferdinand and Queen Isabella signed the decree expelling all Jews from their kingdoms. The order gave the Jews four months to get their affairs in order, and barred them from taking out of the country any gold, silver, or precious metals. By the end of the summer 175,000 Spanish Jews had embarked on their difficult journeys into exile, during which they encountered every manner of hardship, including extortion, drowning, plague, and piracy.

The disparate paths taken by the various Jewish communities of Spain would forever shape the character of world Jewry. The Castilian Jews of the west of the country primarily traveled overland to Portugal, where they had been granted temporary asylum (in exchange for a hefty entrance fee—those who could not pay were sold into slavery), and from there by ship to Holland and its outposts in the New World: Brazil, the West Indies, and, eventually, America. (The earliest Jewish settlers in America, in the seventeenth century, were Sephardic.) The Jews of the south sailed across the Mediterranean into North Africa, while those of the north sailed to Italy and from there made their way farther east, to Turkey and throughout the Ottoman Empire. Asked about the wisdom of King Ferdinand's expulsion of the Jews, the Ottoman Sultan Beyazid II famously replied, "Can such a man be called wise—one who impoverishes his kingdom while enriching my own?"

It would be more than 400 hundred years before any Jews would again make their home in Spain. (Indeed, the Holy Office of the Inquisition was not officially abolished until 1834.) Still, the Sephardic Jews maintained a fierce connection to the homeland from which they had been exiled, singing its praises in ballads and poetry in the Spanish-Jewish language of Ladino. Many Sephardic families actually kept the keys to their ancestral home in Spain, which were passed down from generation to generation, preserving the dream of Spanish return with all the fervency of the Passover wish to be the next year in Jerusalem.

Jews finally began returning to Spain in the early decades of the twentieth century. The first great wave of émigrés came in the 1920s, from Turkey and the Balkans, following the dissolution of the Ottoman Empire. The next two decades brought a few thousand refugees from Germany and Eastern Europe; many more came in the 1950s and 1960s from Morocco and other Arab countries, at a time of heightened nationalism and anti-Jewish feeling. More recently, immigrants have been arriving from Latin America, especially Argentina, which is experiencing a period of economic crisis.

Today the Jews of Spain total about 20,000, although the exact figure is not known. The largest number are in Madrid and Barcelona, but there are thirteen officially recognized communities throughout the country. In the past few decades increasing efforts have been made to preserve a sense of Sephardic identity among the Jews of contemporary Spain, much of them focusing on traditional Jewish food. The Spanish Jewish organization called Red de Juderías de España, located in the beautiful Roman-era walled town of Girona (where the Jewish community took refuge in a stone tower during the pogroms of 1391), has sponsored workshops on traditional Spanish-Jewish cookery; the organization even issued a calendar for the year 2002 called "*Cocina Sephardí*" (Sephardic Cuisine), featuring photographs and recipes of several Sephardic dishes. The calendar is a symbol both of the remarkable tenacity of Spanish Jewry and, also, the problems attendant on any attempt to re-create a coherent Spanish-Jewish cuisine after so many centuries in exile.

Arriving as they did in overwhelming numbers, the Spanish Jews transformed the cuisine of many of the communities in which they took refuge, especially in northern Morocco, Turkey, and the Greek city of Salonika. But inevitably local influences filtered in as well, so that over time it became difficult to recall which dishes were of Spanish origin and which weren't, and even those from Spain had been altered to reflect the ingredients and cooking styles of the new homeland. In Turkey, for example, where many Jewish dishes still bear their Ladino names, the popular filled turnovers of the community are not known as *empanadas*, as they were in Spain, but rather *borekas*, from the Turkish pastries called *börek* (pages 205–206). Or, to take a different sort of example, the meatballs of the Turkish Jews are called *albondigas*, as in Spain, but in the Turkish version the meat is combined with chopped vegetables such as potato or celery (see pages 192–193); this is a custom of North Africa, Italy, Greece, and the Balkans, one not found in Spain.

The dramatic evolution of Sephardic cuisine after the Spanish expulsion can be seen very clearly in the "*Cocina Sephardí*" calendar. Some of the dishes included in it—such as *adafina* and *albondigas*—come from medieval Spain, but others are clearly of more recent provenance, and originate elsewhere. The *pastelitos de patata* (potato cakes), for example, feature an ingredient that didn't arrive in Spain until the middle of the sixteenth century, long after the Jews had been expelled. So too with the cooked salad called *ensalada cocha*, which includes the New World ingredients of tomatoes and peppers (see page 18). This applies as well to the grouper in green pepper sauce, and to the bitter-orange salad, which is spiced with paprika, made from ground red peppers.

In Spain today, Jewish food is Sephardic rather than Spanish. I once spent an evening in Barcelona with a group of women from Comunidad Israelita de Barcelona (popularly known as CIB), the largest synagogue in the city. Of the half-dozen women, only one had been born in Spain; the others were immigrants from France, Turkey, Lebanon, and Poland. For these women, the Jewish food that they made for holidays—it had become special-occasion fare—included dishes as various as the Sabbath stew *dafina*, the meat-and-bulgur dumplings called *kibbeh*, the bulgur salad tabbouleh, cheese-filled *borekas*, *pescado colorado* (fish in tomato sauce), *bimuelos*, and stuffed zucchini. Each of these dishes is Sephardic in the broad sense of the term (meaning not Ashkenazic), and some of them did originate in medieval Spain. But many others are of non-Spanish origin, and in any case, by now even the Spanish-era dishes have come to be popularly identified as North African, Balkan, or Middle Eastern rather than Spanish.

Still, in the end, the most remarkable thing is not that so few dishes have managed to find their way back to Spain, after so long away. Rather, it is that Jewish food of any kind is again being made there: that a Jewish community is being pieced together once more, little by little, from the thousand shatterings of its history.

ENSALADA COCHA

ROASTED PEPPER AND TOMATO SALAD

Versions of this salad are made throughout North Africa, as well as among the Jews of North African descent living in Spain, where it is known as ensalada cocha*—"cooked salad"—and is a common addition to the Sabbath table. (For a spicer version, add roasted and seeded hot peppers to taste.) This recipe comes from Ana Bensadón of Madrid, who has collected dozens of very old Sephardic recipes. Ana was born in Tangier and moved to Spain in 1963. Like many Jews from northern Morocco, she traces her family's roots back to medieval Spain. She has devoted her recent years to preserving and teaching Sephardic cookery.*

SERVES 8

2 green peppers
2 red peppers
4 pounds tomatoes
1/4 cup olive oil
4 garlic cloves, chopped
1 teaspoon paprika
1/2 teaspoon sugar
1 1/2 teaspoons salt
Freshly ground black pepper

1. Preheat the broiler.
2. Place the peppers on a foil-lined baking sheet and broil until blackened on all sides, turning as necessary. Place in a medium bowl and cover with plastic wrap until cool enough to handle. Peel away the blackened skin. Remove the seeds, core, and membranes and chop the peppers. Set aside.
3. Bring a pot of water to a boil. Place the tomatoes in the boiling water and blanch until the skin just begins to loosen, about 1 minute. Drain the tomatoes and rinse under cold water until cool enough to handle. Peel off the skin. Core the peeled tomatoes, cut them into halves, and squeeze out the seeds. Chop the tomato pulp.
4. Heat the olive oil in a large skillet over medium heat. Add the garlic and cook until golden. Add the tomatoes, paprika, sugar, salt, and pepper. Reduce the heat to medium-low and simmer, stirring occasionally, until most of the liquid has evaporated, about 25 minutes.
5. Add the roasted peppers and continue simmering, stirring occasionally, until all of the liquid has evaporated and the mixture has thickened to a jam-like consistency, 45 minutes to 1 hour. Remove from the heat and let cool. Serve at room temperature.

ROASTED BEET SALAD WITH APPLES AND HORSERADISH

One of the innumerable ways in which Ashkenazic Jews used beets was to make them into salads. This is one of my favorite beet salads: The sweetness of the beets and apples is nicely complemented by the bitterness of the horseradish and the sourness of the vinegar. I like orange-flavored vinegar because it seems to go especially well with beets, but if you can't find orange-flavored vinegar, any red wine or sherry vinegar will work fine.

SERVES 6

- 1¼ pounds small-to-medium beets, with ½-inch of stem
- 2 Granny Smith apples
- 1 tablespoon peeled and finely grated fresh horseradish root
- 2 tablespoons orange-flavored vinegar
- 4 teaspoons olive oil
- ½ teaspoon sugar
- Salt
- Freshly ground black pepper

1. Preheat the oven to 400 degrees. Wrap the beets in aluminum foil and place them in a roasting pan. Cook until the beets are fork-tender, 45 minutes to 1 hour. Unwrap and let cool slightly. When they are cool enough to handle, peel the beets and grate them on a box grater or in a food processor equipped with a shredding disk.
2. Peel and core the apples, and grate them on the box grater or in a food processor.
3. Place the beets, apples, and horseradish in a salad bowl. In a small bowl, whisk together the vinegar, oil, and sugar, and season with salt and pepper. Dress the salad and toss well. Cover and refrigerate for at least 1 hour so that the flavors can combine. Serve cold or at room temperature.

APYO

TURKISH SWEET-AND-SOUR CELERY SALAD

In this simple cooked salad from Turkey, the celery comes out tender and succulent, sort of sweet and woodsy all at once. Another version replaces the celery with sliced celery root.

SERVES 6

- 2 pounds celery, sliced 1/4 inch thick
- 2 carrots, peeled, halved lengthwise, and sliced 1/4 inch thick
- 1/4 cup olive oil
- Juice of 1 lemon
- 1 tablespoon sugar
- 1/2 teaspoon salt
- Freshly ground black pepper

1. Place all of the ingredients in a large saucepan and stir to combine. Cover and simmer over low heat, stirring occasionally, until the vegetables are soft, about 20 minutes. Taste and adjust the seasoning.
2. Let cool to room temperature, then transfer to a serving platter. Cover with plastic wrap and refrigerate for at least 2 hours or overnight. Serve cold or at room temperature.

KOBACHKOVYA IKRA

ZUCCHINI CAVIAR

The eggplant salad known as "eggplant caviar" is beloved by cooks throughout the Mediterranean, the Balkans, and the Middle East. It is possible, though, to make the "caviar" with other vegetables, as in this luscious and flavorful variety from the region of Moldavia in northern Romania. This recipe comes from Maria Kachkoff of Cliffside Park, New Jersey, who emigrated to the United States from Moldavia in 1975; she learned how to make the dish from her grandmother, Baella Roshkin, and mother, Klara Brodetsky.

SERVES 4 TO 6

- 3 tablespoons vegetable oil
- 1 onion, chopped
- 2 pounds zucchini, thinly sliced
- 1 carrot, peeled and grated
- Salt
- Freshly ground black pepper
- 1 tablespoon chopped fresh dill
- Crackers or bread for accompaniment

1. Heat the oil in a large skillet over medium-low heat. Add the onion and zucchini and cook, stirring often with a wooden spoon, until the onion is soft and translucent and the zucchini is lightly colored.
2. Add the carrot and season with salt and pepper. Reduce the heat to low and cook, stirring occasionally and breaking up the zucchini with the spoon, until the zucchini is very soft, about 45 minutes. (The consistency should be almost a puree, with some solid bits remaining for texture, as desired.) Stir in the chopped dill. Serve warm or at room temperature, with crackers or wedges of bread.

INGREDIENTS: Herring

You've heard, perhaps, the one about the Jew who asks his friend a riddle: What is green, hangs on the wall, and whistles? The answer, as it turns out, is a herring. "But a herring isn't green," protests his friend.

"*Nu*, paint it green."

"But a herring doesn't hang on a wall."

"So hang it on a wall."

"But a herring doesn't whistle!"

"I know," says the man. "I just put that in to make it hard."

Or the one about the herring that complains to a restaurant customer, "What's the matter you don't eat no more at Ratner's?" Or Woody Allen's parody of Hasidic tales, which turns on the question of whether a man's daughter most closely resembles a *matjes* or a Bismarck herring. Or any one of countless others—the point being that the herring, like the surly waiter or the arrogant beggar, has become, oddly enough, one of the defining motifs of Jewish humor.

It's an unexpected turn of events for the fish that has probably had, to quote Alan Davidson in *The Oxford Companion to Food*, the "most influence on the economic and political history of Europe." Indeed, the herring may well be rivaled only by the cod as the most important food fish in the history of the world. In large part this is because, in the days before refrigeration, both the herring and the cod could be easily cured, and thus eaten far from the point of capture. The earliest curing was simple air-drying, which worked better for cod (herring is too oily, and tends to spoil when hung up to dry), but once the process of smoking fish became widespread in the twelfth century, the herring assumed a place of primacy alongside the cod. Vast hauls of herring created riches for Danish, English, French, and Dutch traders (Amsterdam, it has been said, was built on herring bones); the national fishing fleets needed to catch all this herring required the building and deployment of huge naval forces to protect them, which in turn led to greater projection of seapower around the world. As the food historian Waverly Root noted, quoting an earlier French observer, herring is one of those products, like the coffee bean or the silkworm, that has determined the history of empires.

There are many types of cured herring, but several are most widely known. *Schmaltz* (meaning "fat" in German or Yiddish) herring are, as the name indicates, fatty herring, cured in a salt brine, with sometimes a touch of brown sugar added. *Matjes* herring are fish that have not yet reached reproductive age—in Dutch, *matjes* means "maidens"—small and tender, usually from Holland or Sweden, cured with brown sugar and salt (sometimes in a red sauce tinctured with sandalwood) to create a distinctive salty-sweet taste. A herring that has been heavily salted and smoked was traditionally called a *red herring,* a term, of course, that is well known in mystery novels, referring to a false clue. (This derives from an old English practice of dragging salted herrings across a fox trail to deceive the hounds.)

Both nourishing and long-lasting, herring was also the cheapest of all fish, and so a blessing to the impoverished Jewish masses. As late as 1929 the French food writer Edouard de Pomiane reported of the Jews of Poland, "It could be claimed that each Jew eats a herring a day." De Pomiane listed six recipes for herring in his book of Polish-Jewish cookery, among them a salad of chopped herring marinated with oil, vinegar, paprika, and raw onions; a brandade made by pounding herring and mixing it with oil and bread crumbs; a spread made from finely chopped herring mixed with mayonnaise and chopped green apple; and a casserole of herring layered with sliced potatoes and onions. This, of course, was but a fraction of the ways in which herring was prepared by the Jews of Eastern Europe. It was also, to name but a few, chopped and mixed with apples and hard-boiled eggs; sauced with sour cream; fried or grilled (a perfect preparation for an oily fish); and pickled with vinegar and sugar. Moreover, the herring roe was mixed with apple and onion and poured over the herring as a sauce, or mixed with a little oil and served on its own, much like the Greek tarama. Chopped herring was even used as a substitute for gefilte fish on the Sabbath.

In the United States herring became a staple of immigrant Jewish life, where it was sold from barrels for pennies apiece, usually wrapped in a page of Yiddish newsprint for easy transit to home or work. For decades the children and grandchildren of the immigrants largely rejected herring, because they saw it—not incorrectly—as a poor man's food, the product of a tenement past they were striving to overcome. Still, you can't keep a good fish down: According to Mark Russ Federman, proprietor of the venerable Russ & Daughters appetizing store on New York's Lower East Side (and a herring maven nonpareil), we are today witnessing a rebirth of the herring's popularity, as people are again coming to recognize the herring as a great food fish: flavorful, still relatively cheap, and (who knew?) very high in cholesterol-fighting omega-3 acids. These days, Russ & Daughters features herring in several different sauces, from the traditional cream and wine to lemon-ginger. More than carp, more than salmon, herring is *the* fish of the Jewish past, and, it turns out, maybe even the Jewish future. And that is no joke.

SELYODKA POD SHUBOY

RUSSIAN LAYERED HERRING AND VEGETABLE SALAD

The name of this dish literally means "herring in a winter coat," an evocative way of describing the heavy layering of vegetables that cover the herring. This recipe, given to me by Zell Schulman, author of the cookbook Passover Seders Made Simple, *comes from Zell's friend Nadezhda Zaretzky. Now living in Cincinnati, Ohio, Nadezhda Zaretzky was once a pediatrician in Odessa, Russia. She recalls how this dish was often served by Soviet Jews on Shabbat and after Yom Kippur, when Jewish rituals had to be practiced in secret.*

SERVES 12

- *Schmaltz* herring fillets, totaling about 12 ounces
- Milk for soaking
- 2 pounds russet potatoes, peeled, boiled until tender, and diced
- 12 ounces canned pickled beets, drained and diced
- 2 Granny Smith apples, grated
- 1 cup mayonnaise
- 2 carrots, peeled and grated
- 3 hard-boiled eggs, chopped
- 1 large onion, finely chopped
- 1½ to 2 cups chopped fresh flat-leaf parsley
- Slices of rye or pumpernickel bread for accompaniment

1. Place the herring in a large bowl and add milk to cover. Soak for 30 minutes in the refrigerator, then drain. Finely chop the herring and set aside.
2. In the center of a medium platter, arrange half of the potatoes into a circle about 8 inches in diameter. Top this with a layer of half the pickled beets and then a layer of half the apples. Spread a thin layer of mayonnaise over the apples. Add a layer of half the carrots, followed with a layer of half the eggs, a layer of half the onions, and finally all of the chopped herring.
3. Cover the herring with a layer of the remaining onions, followed by the remaining eggs, and then the remaining carrots. Spread a thin layer of mayonnaise over the carrots. Top this with a layer of the remaining apples, then the remaining pickled beets, and finally the remaining potatoes. Coat the entire salad with the remaining mayonnaise. Garnish the stacked salad with the parsley. Cover loosely with plastic wrap and refrigerate several hours or overnight. Slice into wedges and serve with slices of rye or pumpernickel bread.

WHITEFISH AND BAKED SALMON SALAD

This recipe comes from Mark Russ Federman, the proprietor of the legendary Russ & Daughters appetizing store on New York's Lower East Side. (Whitefish and baked salmon can be purchased at any good appetizing store, and at some seafood stores as well.) The salad, which takes only a few minutes to prepare, is perfect for a Sunday brunch, with bagels.

SERVES 8 TO 10

1 whitefish, 1½ to 2 pounds, filleted

½ pound baked salmon

½ cup mayonnaise

½ cup finely diced celery

¼ cup finely diced onion

Salt

Freshly ground black pepper

Crumble the fish gently by hand into a medium bowl, making sure to remove any small bones that may remain. Add the mayonnaise, celery, and onion and stir to combine. Season with salt and pepper. Serve cold or at room temperature.

CUCHUMBER

BOMBAY CUCUMBER AND TOMATO SALAD

This simple and refreshing uncooked salad is one of the many dishes of Bombay's Bene Israel community that use green mangoes as a souring agent. (Green mangoes can be purchased at many Indian markets.) The sourness of the mangoes is nicely balanced by the sweetness of the dates and the spiciness of the hot pepper.

SERVES 4

- 1 small cucumber, peeled and chopped
- 2 tomatoes, chopped
- ¼ cup peeled and finely chopped green mango
- 1 small onion, finely chopped
- 2 tablespoons chopped dates
- 2 tablespoons finely chopped cilantro
- 1 teaspoon minced, seeded, and deveined jalapeño pepper, or to taste
- ½ teaspoon salt
- Juice of ½ lime

Combine all of the ingredients in a medium salad bowl. Mix well and adjust for seasoning. Serve immediately, or refrigerate until ready to serve.

TABBOULEH

BULGUR SALAD WITH PARSLEY AND TOMATO

Tabbouleh is the best known of the Middle Eastern bulgur (cracked wheat) salads. I much prefer to use flat-leaf rather than curly parsley, for reasons of both flavor and texture. This is also an instance when you should break out the expensive extra-virgin olive oil.

SERVES 6

- 1 cup fine bulgur
- 2 tomatoes, chopped
- ½ large cucumber, peeled and finely diced
- 3 scallions, thinly sliced (both green and white parts)
- 1 cup finely chopped fresh flat-leaf parsley
- ¼ cup olive oil
- Juice of 1 or 2 lemons
- ½ teaspoon salt
- Freshly ground black pepper
- Oil-cured black olives for garnish

1. Place the bulgur in a medium bowl and cover with cold water. Let soak until tender, 20 to 30 minutes. Transfer to a sieve and squeeze out the excess water.
2. In a large serving bowl, combine the bulgur with the remaining ingredients and stir to combine. Refrigerate for at least 2 hours or overnight, stirring occasionally. Stir again just before serving. Place the olives around the side of the bowl. Serve at room temperature.

BAZARGAN

SYRIAN BULGUR SALAD WITH POMEGRANATE MOLASSES

This finely spiced bulgur salad, which deserves to be better known, is unique to the Jews of Syria. Most often tamarind concentrate is used for souring, but I prefer the fruitier and brighter-tasting pomegranate molasses. Pomegranate molasses can be purchased in Middle Eastern or Indian groceries.

SERVES 4 TO 6

- 1 cup fine bulgur
- ½ onion, finely diced (optional)
- ½ green or red pepper, finely diced
- 3 tablespoons pomegranate molasses
- 3 tablespoons tomato paste
- 2 tablespoons olive oil
- 1 tablespoon lemon juice
- 1 teaspoon ground cumin
- ¼ teaspoon cayenne
- ½ teaspoon salt
- ½ cup finely chopped walnuts

1. Place the bulgur in a large bowl and cover with cold water. Let soak until tender, 20 to 30 minutes. Transfer to a sieve and squeeze out the excess water.
2. In a large serving bowl, combine the bulgur with the remaining ingredients except the nuts and stir well. Let stand at room temperature for at least 2 hours, then taste and adjust for seasoning. Just before serving, add the walnuts and stir until they are incorporated. Serve at room temperature.

YAPRAK

STUFFED GRAPE LEAVES

*Stuffed grape leaves are enormously popular throughout Turkey, Greece, and the Middle East. When filled with ground beef or lamb, they are served hot; filled with rice, they are served cold and make a favorite Sabbath dish. (*Yaprak *is the Turkish word for leaf, which is also the derivation of the name* prakkes, *as stuffed cabbage is known in the Ukraine.) I've adapted this recipe from one made by Jenny Edelstein of Miami, who was born in Havana and came to the United States in 1963; like many of the Jews of Cuba, her family has Turkish roots. These stuffed grape leaves taste even better when eaten the day after they are made.*

MAKES ABOUT 32

8 ounces brine-packed grape leaves

FOR THE FILLING

1 cup long-grain white rice

2 tablespoons olive oil

3 onions, chopped

2 tablespoons chopped fresh mint

2 tablespoons chopped fresh flat-leaf parsley

Salt

Freshly ground black pepper

FOR THE COOKING LIQUID

½ cup olive oil

½ cup water

Juice of 2 lemons

Juice of 2 limes

1. Drain the grape leaves, rinse well, and pat dry.

2. For the filling: Place the rice in a bowl of cold water. Soak for 30 minutes. Drain.

3. Heat the oil in a large skillet over medium-low heat. Add the onions and cook, stirring often, until soft and lightly colored. Add the rice and cook, stirring often, for 5 minutes. Place in a medium bowl and combine with the mint and parsley. Season with salt and pepper. Set aside and let cool.

4. Place a grape leaf, shiny side down and with the stem end facing you, on a clean surface. Place about 2 teaspoons of the filling near the stem end. Fold this end up and over the filling, then pinch in the two sides toward the center and loosely roll up the leaf like a cigar, tucking in any wide parts of the leaf and loose ends. (Do not roll the leaf too tightly, because the rice expands somewhat during cooking.) Repeat until all of the filling has been used.

5. Line a Dutch oven or other large, heavy pot with the remaining loose grape leaves. Pack the stuffed grape leaves, seam sides down,

in one layer over the bottom of the pot, then place any remaining stuffed leaves in a second layer on top.

6. For the cooking liquid: In a medium bowl, whisk together the oil, water, lemon juice, and lime juice.

7. Pour the cooking liquid over the stuffed grape leaves. Cover and bring to a boil over medium-high heat. Lower the heat and simmer gently, covered, until the filling is fully cooked, about 45 minutes. Let the stuffed leaves cool in the pan, then transfer them to a large serving platter. Serve at room temperature.

TORSHI LIFT

PICKLED TURNIPS

Pickled vegetables, and especially pickled turnips, are a very common mezze*—appetizer—among the Jews of Syria and Egypt. I love them: They are salty, sour, spicy, and crunchy, and the sliced beet turns the turnips a lovely shade of pink.*

MAKES ABOUT 5 CUPS

1 small beet

2 pounds turnips

4 garlic cloves, sliced

Red pepper flakes to taste (optional)

3½ cups water

¼ cup white vinegar

3 tablespoons kosher salt

1. Peel the beet and cut it into slices. Place the slices at the bottom of a 2-quart glass jar (or divide between two 1-quart jars). Trim and peel the turnips and cut them in half, then slice them into ¼-inch-thick semicircles. Place them in the jar along with the garlic slices. If desired, sprinkle with red pepper flakes.
2. Combine the water, vinegar, and salt in a medium bowl and stir until the salt dissolves. Pour the mixture over the turnips. If necessary, add a bit more water to make sure the turnips are fully covered.
3. Seal the jar tightly and store it at room temperature in a cool, dark place for 3 days, then refrigerate until ready to serve. Store in the refrigerator for up to 3 months.

BABA GHANOUSH

EGGPLANT AND TAHINI SPREAD

In Arabic, baba ghanoush *literally means spoiled father (or, depending on the interpretation, "indulged father"), and given the silky luxuriousness of this spread, it's not hard to understand why. These are the measurements that I prefer, but you should really consider all of them "to taste." Once the eggplant has been cooked and processed, add the rest of the ingredients, a little at a time, until you find the blend that you like best.*

SERVES 6

- 2 medium eggplants, each about 1¼ pounds
- ¼ cup tahini (sesame paste)
- Juice of 1½ lemons
- 2 garlic cloves, finely chopped
- 1 teaspoon salt
- Pinch of cayenne
- 1 tablespoon chopped fresh flat-leaf parsley
- Wedges of pita bread for accompaniment

1. Preheat the broiler.
2. Prick the eggplants all over with a fork and broil them on a foil-lined baking sheet until their skins are charred and they are soft inside, 20 to 25 minutes, turning them once. Remove from the broiler and let cool.
3. When the eggplants are cool, cut them in half lengthwise and peel the skin away from the pulp. Discard the skin, stem, and seeds. Place the pulp in the bowl of a food processor and process until smooth.
4. Add the tahini, lemon juice, garlic, salt, and cayenne and process until well combined. Taste and adjust for seasoning. Spoon onto a large serving platter and sprinkle with the parsley. Serve at room temperature, with pita bread.

HUMMUS

CHICKPEA AND TAHINI SPREAD

The secret of this hummus's success is roasting the garlic, which gives the spread a unique mellowness and depth of flavor. For convenience's sake, you can use canned chickpeas, but the taste and texture won't be the same. As with my Baba Ghanoush *(page 33), these are the measurements that I prefer, but everyone likes their hummus slightly different. If you wish, add the seasonings a little at a time until you find the blend that you prefer.*

SERVES 10

- 1½ cups dried chickpeas (about 4½ cups cooked)
- 5 garlic cloves, peeled
- 2½ teaspoons salt
- 1 cup tahini (sesame paste)
- Juice of 4 lemons
- Olive oil for drizzling, plus 3 tablespoons
- Paprika for sprinkling
- Mixed olives and wedges of pita bread for accompaniment

1. Place the chickpeas in a large pot, cover with cold water by at least 2 inches, and soak overnight.
2. Drain the chickpea soaking water. Cover the chickpeas with fresh water and bring to a boil over high heat. Lower the heat and simmer until the peas are soft, about 30 minutes. Drain and let cool.
3. While the chickpeas are simmering, preheat the oven to 400 degrees.
4. Place the garlic cloves on a foil- or parchment-lined baking sheet and drizzle lightly with olive oil. Bake until golden brown, about 20 minutes. Remove from the oven, place in a small bowl, and allow to cool. When cool, sprinkle with 1 teaspoon of the salt, then with the back of a fork, mash into a paste.
5. Place the chickpeas, garlic paste, the remaining 1½ teaspoons salt, tahini, lemon juice, and the 3 tablespoons olive oil in the bowl of a food processor and process until smooth. Slowly add water (¾ cup or so) until the hummus reaches the desired consistency. Taste and adjust for seasoning. Spoon the hummus onto a large serving platter. Drizzle with olive oil, sprinkle with paprika, and serve with olives and pita bread.

CHOPPED LIVER

This recipe comes from Audrey Morgen Volk, the mother of Patty Volk, who is the author of the delightful memoir Stuffed: Adventures of a Restaurant Family. *Patty's family ran Morgen's, long a fixture of New York's garment center, as well as many other restaurants in the city. It is also a family of great culinary significance, Jewishly speaking: Patty's great-grandfather, Sussman Volk, a Romanian immigrant, introduced pastrami to the New World in the late 1880s in his delicatessen at 86½ Delancey Street on the Lower East Side. Amazingly enough, Sussman's older brother Albert was also the first shopkeeper to mix scallions into cream cheese.*

Though it's not included in the original recipe, I like to mix caramelized onions into the chopped liver. For a kosher version, score the liver, sprinkle it with salt, broil it to a light brown (about 3 minutes on each side) and then rinse it thoroughly under cold water to remove all blood.

Rendered chicken fat (or, more luxuriously, duck fat) can be purchased in stores, but it's easy enough to make at home. Just slowly cook the fat—which can be removed and stored in the freezer anytime you roast a chicken—in a little water for half an hour or so, until it melts. Store it in a jar in the refrigerator until ready to use.

SERVES 8 TO 10

- 3 tablespoons vegetable oil
- 3 onions, thinly sliced
- 1½ pounds fresh chicken livers, rinsed and trimmed
- 3 or 4 hard-boiled eggs
- 1 small onion, quartered
- 1 to 1½ teaspoons salt
- 2 to 3 tablespoons rendered chicken fat
- 2 tablespoons ice water
- Crackers or slices of rye bread for accompaniment

1. Heat the oil in a large skillet over medium-low heat. Add the onions and cook, stirring often, until they are a deep brown, at least 35 minutes. Set aside and let cool.
2. Bring a pot of water to a simmer. Add the chicken livers and cook until they lose all pinkness, about 5 minutes. Drain and let cool.
3. Place the livers, eggs, raw onion, and caramelized onions on a cutting board and chop to the desired consistency. Place in a large bowl. Add the chicken fat and salt and mix to combine. Stir in the ice water. Let stand at room temperature for at least 1 hour to let the flavors meld together. Serve at room temperature, with crackers or rye bread.

VEGETARIAN CHOPPED LIVER

Vegetarian chopped liver is obviously an oxymoron. Still, it isn't simply a nouveau rendering of a classic meat dish, like tofu hot dogs or some such thing; it has a significant lineage in its own right. As an appetizer for dairy meals, it was a staple in those two Jewish-American culinary institutions: the dairy restaurant and the Catskills hotel. (Combinations for vegetarian chopped liver appear, in fact, as the third and fourth recipes in Jennie Grossinger's legendary cookbook, The Art of Jewish Cooking, *one of which uses chopped sardines.) Although preparations vary somewhat, they generally involve chopped-up hard-boiled eggs, caramelized onions, string beans or peas, and walnuts. Does it taste like real chopped liver? Not exactly. Is it delicious? Absolutely.*

SERVES 6

- 3 tablespoons vegetable oil
- 3 large onions, sliced
- 3/4 pound green beans, trimmed
- 3 hard-boiled eggs
- 1/3 cup chopped walnuts
- 1 teaspoon salt
- Freshly ground black pepper
- Crackers or slices of rye bread for accompaniment

1. Heat the oil in a large skillet over medium-low heat. Add the onions and cook, stirring often, until they are a deep brown, at least 35 minutes. Set aside and let cool.
2. While the onions are cooking, bring a large pot of salted water to a boil. Add the beans and cook until tender, about 6 minutes. Drain and set aside.
3. Combine the onions and green beans with the remaining ingredients on a cutting board and chop to the desired consistency. Transfer to a large bowl. Let stand at room temperature for at least 1 hour to let the flavors meld together. Taste and adjust for seasoning. Serve at room temperature, with crackers or rye bread.

Soups

Soup is among the oldest of all foods. In biblical times, earthenware pots placed on clay stands were used to prepare soups made from vegetables and pulses and flavored with onion and garlic. Soup was called by the Hebrew word *marak*—a name that still identifies at least two traditional Jewish soups: The *marak* made by Yemenite Jews, which is flavored with the aromatic spice mixture called *hawaij*, and can include either beef or chicken; and (in slightly altered form) *marag*, the vibrantly colored chicken soup that was long a Saturday-night favorite among the Jews of Calcutta.

In that regard, special mention must be made of chicken soup, a dish that has come to be virtually synonymous with Jewish cooks. Its fame, of course, rests on the chicken soup of Eastern European Jews, but in fact chicken soup appears in the cooking of nearly every Jewish community, from the aforementioned Yemenite and Indian varieties to the Iraqi *shorba bi djaj*, made creamy with long-cooked rice.

Like chicken soup, the category of sour soup spans Ashkenazic and Sephardic cooking. The most famous of the sour soups is borscht, the Eastern European beet soup, made sour through the addition of vinegar or lemon juice, or, in earlier times, the beet brine called *rosl*. In the Sephardic world, perhaps the most well-known of the sour soups is the Middle Eastern lemony-sour red lentil soup called *shorba addes*. A good soup need not be sour, of course, or even savory; there are also delicious sweet soups, such as the chilled fruit soups of Central Europe, made from any of a number of fruits including cherries, apples, pears, peaches, and plums, additionally sweetened with sugar and ethereally flavored with some combination of lemon juice, vanilla, cinnamon, and wine.

Fruit soup is generally an appetizer, but almost all of these soups work equally well as appetizers or as meals in themselves. A bowl of soup with a loaf of bread and a glass of wine: There can scarcely be a combination more ancient, or more satisfying.

DISHES: Chicken Soup

The Yiddish proverb advises us, "When a poor man eats a chicken, either the man or the chicken is sick," but this state of affairs did not prevent chicken soup from becoming the single most defining dish of the Ashkenazic kitchen—a distinction that persists to this day. Among the Jews of Eastern Europe, chicken soup was known as *goldene yoich,* literally golden broth, which referred to the yellow fat globules that shimmered on the surface of the soup (the very same fat globules that today's health-conscious cook makes sure to strain away), but must also have reflected the soup's inordinate value in the culture. Chicken soup is, as Jewish-food historian Oded Schwartz has observed, "embedded deeply in the Jewish psyche." By itself or festooned with noodles, rice, matzo balls, or kreplach, chicken soup was a fixture at every important occasion of the Eastern European Jews, from Yom Kippur break fasts to Passover seders, Shabbat dinners to weddings, where it was ceremoniously served to the bride and groom to ensure a lifetime of good health.

This last, of course, speaks to chicken soup's legendary quality of being not just good, but good for you, especially when you are feeling under the weather: in the well-known phrase "Jewish penicillin." Talk of the health-giving properties of chicken soup dates back at least to the twelfth century, when Maimonides (among whose patients was the sultan of Egypt) recommended it for coughs and fevers. More recently—1978, to be exact—a study conducted at Mount Sinai Medical Center in Miami Beach (where else?) found that chicken soup proved more effective than simple hot or cold water in clearing congested nasal passages, thus providing an empirical basis for the accepted wisdom and giving countless generations of Jewish mothers license to do the I-told-you-so dance. No one, including the study's authors, knows the specific reason for the outcome, but it may be because chicken contains plentiful amounts of an amino acid called cystine, which is chemically similar to the drug acetylcysteine, used to treat bronchial infections. Probably as important, outside the laboratory environment, is that in the Jewish mind chicken soup has come to equal mother-love, and thus even a reheated can of it conjures up feelings of warmth and care, the most propitious atmosphere for any healing to begin. (The soup's association with healing has now made its way into the wider culture, as evidenced by the self-help bestseller *Chicken Soup for the Soul.*)

Chicken soup is popularly associated with Ashkenazic Jewry, but it is hardly a stranger to the Sephardic kitchen. The Jews of the Middle East, for instance, were ladling out chicken soup before Jews had even arrived in Eastern Europe. Among the most notable of the Middle Eastern soups is the Iranian chicken soup known as *gondi*, which features lots of little dumplings made from chickpea flour and ground chicken and flavored with a bit of turmeric and cardamom. Iraqi Jews prefer their chicken soup with rice, which is simmered so long that it softens and turns the broth thick and creamy (see page 45). Farther west, Jews eat their chicken broth blended with egg and lemon, in the ubiquitous soup known in Greece as *avgolemeno* and in Turkey as *sopa de huevo y limón*; in both places, the soup is commonly used to break the Yom Kippur fast. Across the Mediterranean, Italian Jews have long made a Passover chicken soup with rice that features chicken meatballs and immature eggs ("chicken three ways," it might be called on a trendy restaurant menu); another Passover chicken soup contains broken-up matzos. Among Yemenite Jews, chicken soup is flavored with the ethereal spice mixture *hawaij*, containing such aromatics as cumin, cardamom, and cloves (see page 360). This soup is called *marak*, from the Hebrew word for soup; it is not to be confused with Marag (page 44), the chicken soup that was among the most beloved soups of the Baghdadi Jewish community of Calcutta, where it was commonly served on Saturday nights.

Though Jews have, in a sense, stolen the show when it comes to public avowals of love for chicken soup, they are hardly alone in this; in various permutations chicken soup is served by everyone from the Danes to the Mexicans to the Chinese. Indeed, "the whole world loves chicken soup," as Mimi Sheraton stated it in the title of her 1995 cookbook. This notion might be put slightly differently: According to another Yiddish saying, when you're in love, the whole world seems Jewish; the same might well be said about when you are eating chicken soup.

GOLDENE YOICH

EASTERN EUROPEAN CHICKEN SOUP

There are at least a couple of secrets to a really good chicken soup. The first is not to salt the stock too early; the level of saltiness will increase as the soup cooks. Perhaps most important, do not boil the soup; rather, let it cook for a long time at a very gentle simmer, with barely any bubbles rising to the surface. This results in a clearer stock, softer meat, and a soup that is beautifully mild-tasting and sweet. Good chicken soup is slow food, and the most important ingredient is patience.

SERVES 10 TO 12

1 chicken, 3 to 4 pounds
12 cups cold water
4 parsnips, peeled
6 celery stalks with leaves
6 carrots, peeled
1 large onion, peeled and quartered
2 whole garlic cloves, peeled
3 sprigs fresh parsley
2 tablespoons vegetable oil
1 teaspoon salt, plus more to taste
Freshly ground black pepper
2 tablespoons chopped fresh dill

1. Place the chicken in a soup pot and add the water. (The water should cover the chicken by at least an inch; if not, add more as needed.) Bring to a boil, skimming off any foam that may develop on the surface.

2. Chop 2 parsnips, 3 celery stalks, and 3 carrots into 2-inch pieces. Add the chopped parsnips, celery, and carrots to the pot, along with the onion, garlic, parsley, and 1 teaspoon salt. Lower the heat and very gently simmer, partially covered, for 3 to 4 hours, until the soup is a deep golden color and is rich and tasty. Keep checking occasionally and skim off any foam.

3. Strain the soup into a large bowl. Discard the cooked vegetables. When the chicken has cooled slightly, shred the white meat into small pieces and reserve.

4. If you are serving the soup immediately, use a spoon to skim off some of the yellow fat globules on the surface of the strained soup. If you are serving the soup later, allow the soup to come to room temperature, then refrigerate for at least 3 hours or overnight. Lift off the congealed fat on the surface.

5. Return the soup to the pot and add the shredded chicken. Heat the oil in a medium skillet over medium-high heat. Slice the remaining 2 parsnips, 3 celery stalks (without leaves), and 3 carrots into ¼-inch pieces. Add them to the pan and cook, stirring occasionally, until slightly tender, about 5 minutes.

6. Add the vegetables to the soup. Taste and add salt and pepper as desired. Simmer, partially covered, for another hour. Just before serving, add the chopped dill. Serve hot.

MARAG

CALCUTTA CHICKEN SOUP

This vibrantly colored soup gets its name from the Hebrew word marak, *meaning soup. Says Mervyn Sopher of Shaker Heights, Ohio (who left India in 1948, when he was twenty-seven),* marag *is "a nice, friendly, warming soup." I add cauliflower to it, but this is not orthodox* marag *practice, and not part of Mervyn's recipe.*

SERVES 8

- 2 tablespoons vegetable oil
- 2 onions, chopped
- 2 or 3 garlic cloves, chopped
- ½ teaspoon peeled and minced fresh ginger
- ½ teaspoon turmeric
- 1 bay leaf
- 1 chicken, 3 to 4 pounds, cut into 8 pieces; or 4 split breasts, totaling about 3 pounds
- 1 small zucchini, quartered lengthwise and sliced
- 2 celery stalks with leaves, chopped
- 2 carrots, peeled and thinly sliced
- 1 cup diced cauliflower florets
- 1 russet potato, peeled and diced
- 2 tomatoes, chopped (optional)
- 2 teaspoons salt, plus more to taste
- Freshly ground black pepper
- 1 tablespoon chopped fresh cilantro
- Hot white rice, for serving

1. In a soup pot, heat the oil over medium heat. Add the onions and cook, stirring often, until just soft. Add the garlic, ginger, turmeric, bay leaf, and ½ cup of water and stir to combine. Cook, stirring often, until a thick sauce develops, about 5 minutes.
2. Add the chicken and water almost to cover. Cover the pot and bring to a boil over medium-high heat. Lower the heat and simmer for 20 minutes.
3. Add the vegetables, salt, pepper, and 5 more cups of water. Cover the pot and return the liquid to a boil. Lower the heat and continue to simmer, covered, until the vegetables are fully tender and the chicken is cooked through, about 20 minutes. (Skim off any foam that may develop on the surface.) Remove the chicken pieces, and when cool enough to handle, shred the meat, then return it to the pot, discarding the bones and skin. Remove the bay leaf. Stir in the cilantro. Serve hot, over white rice.

SHORBA BI DJAJ

IRAQI CREAMY CHICKEN SOUP WITH RICE

In Iraq, this thick, creamy soup was so popular that it was often called just shorba, *meaning soup. It was a favorite for cold winter mornings.*

SERVES 8

- ½ cup long-grain rice
- 2 tablespoons vegetable oil
- 1 onion, finely chopped
- 1½ pounds chicken wings, rinsed
- ½ teaspoon turmeric
- ½ teaspoon ground cardamom
- 2 teaspoons salt
- Freshly ground black pepper
- 10 cups water
- ½ cup red lentils, well washed

1. Wash the rice well. Place the rice in a large bowl of cold water and soak for 2 hours; drain and set aside.
2. In a soup pot, heat the oil over medium heat. Add the onion and cook, stirring often, until soft and translucent. Add the chicken wings, turmeric, cardamom, salt, pepper, and water. Cover and bring to a boil over medium-high heat.
3. Lower the heat and add the rice and lentils. Simmer gently until the rice has softened and the soup has become thick and creamy, about 2 hours. (Skim off any foam that may appear on the surface and stir occasionally to make sure that the rice does not stick to the bottom of the pot.)
4. When the soup is creamy, remove the chicken wings from the pot. When cool enough to handle, discard the skin and bones, shred the meat, and return it to the pot. Taste and adjust for seasoning. Serve hot.

KNEYDLACH

EASTERN EUROPEAN MATZO BALLS

These are the Golden Mean of matzo balls: not too heavy and not too light.

MAKES ABOUT 15 MATZO BALLS

6 eggs, lightly beaten

½ cup seltzer

3 tablespoons vegetable oil or rendered chicken fat

1½ teaspoons salt

Freshly ground black pepper

Pinch of freshly grated nutmeg (optional)

1½ cups matzo meal

1. In a medium bowl, whisk together the eggs, seltzer, oil or fat, salt, pepper, and (if using) the nutmeg. Slowly add the matzo meal, whisking continuously, until fully combined. Cover the bowl with plastic wrap and refrigerate for at least 4 hours or overnight.
2. Bring a large pot of salted water to a boil, then lower the heat to a simmer. With moistened hands, form the matzo dough into balls about 1½ inches in diameter. Gently drop the balls into the simmering water. Cover the pot and let cook until the matzo balls are cooked through, 30 to 40 minutes. Serve in bowls of hot chicken soup.

MATZOKNEPFLE

ALSATIAN MATZO BALLS WITH PARSLEY AND GINGER

Joan Levy is the proprieter of the bed-and-breakfast Joan's on Jones in Savannah, Georgia. Like thousands of other Jews, her great-great-grandparents, Benjamin H. and Sara Levy, emigrated to the American South from Alsace in the 1870s to avoid conscription into the German army. This is their recipe for matzo balls, prepared in the Alsatian style of using broken-up matzos rather than matzo meal; the matzo balls are also made distinctively Alsatian by the use of ginger, a German influence. I happened to be discussing this recipe once with Cathy Kahn of New Orleans, whose family also emigrated long ago from Alsace, and mentioned that these matzo balls contained ginger. She replied, "Of course they do. Don't all matzo balls have ginger?"

MAKES ABOUT 18 MATZO BALLS

- 3 matzos, broken into small pieces
- 2 tablespoons rendered chicken fat or vegetable oil
- 2 tablespoons finely chopped onion
- 3 eggs, lightly beaten
- 1½ teaspoons salt
- Freshly ground black pepper
- ¾ teaspoon powdered ginger
- 2 tablespoons finely chopped fresh flat-leaf parsley
- ¼ cup matzo meal

1. Place the matzo pieces in a bowl of cold water and soak until soft but not falling apart, about 2 minutes. Drain and set aside.
2. Heat the fat or oil in a large skillet over medium heat. Add the onion and cook, stirring often, until soft and lightly colored. Squeeze any excess water out of the matzo pieces and add them to the pan with the onion. Cook, stirring regularly, until dry. Remove the pan from the heat and let cool.
3. Place the matzo and onion mixture in a medium bowl. Add the eggs, salt, pepper, ginger, parsley, and matzo meal and mix until well combined. Cover with plastic wrap and refrigerate for at least 2 hours or overnight.
4. With moistened hands, pinch off pieces of the dough and form them into balls about 1½ inches in diameter. (They will expand during cooking.) Gently drop the balls into a large pot of simmering salted water or chicken soup. Tightly cover and simmer until the balls are cooked through, 30 to 40 minutes. Remove with a slotted spoon and serve in bowls of hot chicken soup.

KREPLACH

MEAT-FILLED PASTA FOR SOUP

According to Jewish-food historian John Cooper, the name kreplach *is derived from the medieval Latin terms* crispa, crespa, *and* crispus, *meaning pastry, from which also comes the French word* crepe. *A twelfth-century source from France tells us of a dish called* krepish, *which consisted of a piece of soft dough wrapped around a bird's stomach or intestine and then roasted. Later, as the Jews of Central and Eastern Europe began to speak Yiddish,* krepish *turned into kreplach. Throughout the Middle Ages, kreplach were variously filled with meat, cheese, or fruit and either baked or fried in oil; boiled kreplach, the preparation most common today, probably didn't begin to emerge until at least the seventeenth century.*

This is the classic meat kreplach that has adorned Eastern European Jewish chicken soup for generations. I like a bit of chopped fresh dill in the filling; it adds some flavor, and pairs well with the fresh dill that is the perfect finishing touch for a pot of homemade chicken soup.

MAKES 36 KREPLACH

FOR THE FILLING

¾ pound chuck roast or brisket

Salt

Freshly ground black pepper

2 tablespoons vegetable oil

1 onion, sliced

1 garlic clove, chopped

1 tablespoon chopped fresh dill

1 egg, lightly beaten

1. Make the filling: Season the meat with salt and pepper. Place the meat in a large pot and add water to cover. Bring to a boil over high heat. Lower the heat and simmer until the meat is tender, about 2½ hours. Remove to a plate and let cool. Reserve the cooking liquid.

2. While the meat is cooking, heat the oil in a medium skillet over medium heat. Add the onion and cook, stirring often, until soft and lightly colored. Add the garlic and cook for another minute. Remove from the heat.

3. Place the meat, onion, and garlic in the bowl of a food processor and pulse until coarsely ground. Transfer the ground-meat mixture in a medium bowl. Add the dill and egg and stir until the filling is moist and fully blended. (If necessary, add a spoonful or two of

the reserved cooking liquid to moisten the mixture slightly.) Cover and set aside.

4. Make the dough: Place the flour on a large wooden board or in a large mixing bowl. Make a well in the flour and add the beaten eggs and salt. Gradually work the flour into the eggs, using first a fork and then your hands, until fully combined. Place the dough on a lightly floured surface and knead until smooth, 5 to 10 minutes, adding flour as necessary to keep the dough from sticking. Cover the dough with a towel and let stand at room temperature for 30 minutes.

5. Make the kreplach: Roll the dough on a lightly floured surface ⅛ inch thick. With a sharp knife or pizza cutter, trim the dough to a 12-inch square, then cut the dough into 2-inch squares, using a ruler. (Gently press out each square a bit more thinly before filling.)

6. Have ready the eggwash. Place 1 teaspoon of the filling in the center of a dough square. Dab your finger in the eggwash and then around the inner edges of the dough. Fold the dough over to form a triangle. Pinch the moistened edges together and seal by pressing along the edges with a fork. Repeat with the remaining dough squares and filling.

7. Bring a large pot of salted water to a gentle boil. In batches of about 20, drop the kreplach into the pot and cook, stirring occasionally, until tender, about 20 minutes. Remove with a slotted spoon and drain. Store in a covered bowl until ready to serve. Add to bowls of hot chicken soup.

FOR THE DOUGH

2 cups unbleached all-purpose flour, plus additional for kneading and rolling

3 eggs, lightly beaten

½ teaspoon salt

FOR THE EGGWASH

1 beaten egg plus 1 teaspoon water for sealing kreplach

SWEET POTATO KREPLACH

Though the basic form of kreplach—beef-filled, served in chicken soup—is a sturdy and reassuring combination, there's no reason one can't also bring a bit of innovation to the repertoire. Probably my favorite variation is sweet potato kreplach, which is deliriously tasty partnered with hot Borscht (page 61). For a delicious alternative, try frying up the boiled kreplach with caramelized onions and then topping them with sour cream.

MAKES 36 KREPLACH

FOR THE FILLING

1 medium sweet potato (about 8 ounces), peeled and quartered

2 tablespoons olive oil

1 small onion, chopped

2 tablespoons butter or margarine

1 teaspoon ground coriander

Salt

Freshly ground black pepper

FOR THE DOUGH

2 cups unbleached all-purpose flour plus additional for kneading and rolling

3 eggs, beaten

½ teaspoon salt

FOR THE EGGWASH

1 beaten egg plus 1 teaspoon water for sealing kreplach

1. Make the filling: Bring a large pot of salted water to a boil. Add the sweet potato and cook until tender. Remove from the pot (keep the water for later) and let cool slightly. Place in a medium bowl and mash with a hand masher. Set aside.
2. Make the dough: Place the flour on a large wooden board or in a large mixing bowl. Make a well in the flour and add the beaten eggs and salt. Gradually work the flour into the liquid, using first a fork and then your hands, until fully combined. Place the dough on a floured surface and knead until smooth, 5 to 10 minutes. Cover with a towel and let stand at room temperature for 30 minutes.
3. While the dough is resting, heat the oil for the filling in a medium skillet over medium-low heat. Add the onion and cook, stirring often, until soft and lightly colored. Add the onion, the butter or margarine, coriander, salt, and pepper to the mashed sweet potato and mix well.
4. Make the kreplach: Roll the dough on a lightly floured surface to ⅛ inch thick. With a sharp knife or pizza cutter, trim the dough to a 12-inch square and then cut the dough into 2-inch squares, using a ruler. (Gently press out each square a bit more thinly before filling.)

5. Have ready the eggwash. Place 1 teaspoon of the sweet potato filling in the center of a dough square. With your finger dab edges of the dough with a bit of the eggwash. Fold the dough over to form a triangle. Pinch the moistened edges together and seal by pressing along the edges with the tines of a fork. Repeat with the remaining dough squares and filling.

6. Bring a large pot of salted water to a gentle boil. In batches of about 20, drop the kreplach into the pot. Cook, stirring occasionally, until tender, about 20 minutes. Remove with a slotted spoon and drain. Store in a covered bowl until ready to serve. Add to bowls of hot soup.

COMMUNITIES: Yemen

A pastrami sandwich and a pickle is one thing, but if you are looking for genuinely old-time Jewish food you'd be better advised to pass up the local deli and head instead to the nearest Yemenite kosher restaurant, because it is Yemenite cuisine, more than any other, that most closely resembles the Jewish food of biblical times.

Unfortunately, chances are strong that there isn't a Yemenite kosher restaurant in your neighborhood, and unless you happen to live in the New York area, probably not anywhere in your state. There are only about 10,000 Jews of Yemenite descent living in the United States, the vast majority of them in New York and New Jersey. Nearly all of the other 400,000 or so live in Israel. Yemenite Jews were among the first Jews to relocate to Palestine in the late nineteenth century, and in 1949 and 1950 "Operation Magic Carpet" airlifted virtually every Jew remaining in Yemen to Israel, thus bringing to an abrupt end one of the oldest indigenous Jewish communities in the world.

Yemen is located on the southwestern edge of the Arabian peninsula, bordered on the west by the Red Sea and the south by the Gulf of Aden, and just across the narrow strait of Bab el Mandeb from Ethiopia. No one can state with any certainty the beginning of the Jewish presence there, but local legends place it during the time of the Queen of Sheba, in the ninth century B.C.E. The archaeological record indicates a Jewish community in Yemen at least as far back as the late Hellenistic period, circa 200 B.C.E., when the region was at the center of a flourishing trade in perfumes and spices such as frankincense and myrrh. More Jews may have fled to Yemen after the destruction of the Second Temple in 70 C.E., and there was certainly a significant community there by the beginning of the sixth century, when the local Himyarite king, Yusef Asat Dhu Newwas—the Himyarites were an ancient tribe who ruled much of southwest Arabia—converted to Judaism and declared Yemen a Jewish kingdom. This remarkable state of affairs would last only briefly, however, until the year 525, when Yemen was conquered by Abyssinian Christians and Yusef was killed. (According to another Yemenite legend, Yusef rode his white horse into the sea rather than be captured by his enemies.)

Yemen's Islamic era began in the seventh century, and as was the case throughout the region, the Jews of the country thrived or suffered depending on the goodwill of the caliph in power at the time. Though Yemenite Jews were forced to endure difficult and often humiliating regulations, including restrictions on travel and the payment of special taxes, they were generally permitted to participate in the life of the society as a whole: Yemenite Jews, for example, played a critical role as intermediaries in the international trade that brought silk and spices from India to Europe, as the trade routes ran directly through the Yemeni city of Aden.

In large part because of the India trade, the merchant class of Jews lived in Aden, as well as in the capital city of Sanaa, but the majority of Yemenite Jews made their homes in hundreds of remote villages scattered around the country, providing essential crafts (blacksmithing, leather working, weaving, and the like) for what was predominantly an agricultural society. Because most Yemenite Jews lived in remote villages, they had little contact with the outside world, and so their culture remained almost as it had been during biblical times. This is perhaps most striking in Yemenite Hebrew. Before the creation of the state of Israel, Yemenites were the only community in the world who used Hebrew for communication, which linguistic scholars have proven is the only surviving descendant of the Babylonian dialect. As with the language, so too with the cuisine; as Professor Ephraim Isaac of Princeton University has noted, "The material and composition of Yemenite Jewish foods closely resemble those mentioned in the Hebrew Bible and the Mishnah."

The Yemenite cuisine is simple, even austere, with flavors coming not from fat or sugar (there is relatively little meat or dairy, and few sweets) but from abundant spicing. Bread is the staple, and though it may no longer be baked on hot rocks or inside clay ovens, most of the bread made today would be recognizeable to Yemenite Jews of thousands of years ago. Not surprisingly, given bread's importance to the cuisine, there are many varieties of it. Among the most popular is *jachnun* (also spelled *jahnun* and *jihnoon*, and in various other permutations), a sweet bread that is made by rolling out dough very thinly, brushing it with *samneh* (clarified butter) or margarine, then rolling it up into cylinders and cooking it overnight in a very low oven, at which point it comes out pleasingly brown and flaky. The round, flat, pita-like bread known as *Salouf* (page 305) is a staple of daily meals, often accompanied by *Z'houg* (page 36), the fiery-hot paste beloved by Yemenite Jews. *Z'houg* is also a central ingredient in the Yemenite relish called *hilbeh*, combined with tomato sauce and ground fenugreek seeds. *Z'houg* and *hilbeh* are standard accompaniments to meals, used much as Indian cuisine uses various chutneys. For cooking, however, the main flavoring comes from a yellow, vaguely curryish spice mixture called *Hawaij* (page 360). As with curry powder, the composition of *hawaij* will vary somewhat depending on who is making it, but it generally includes turmeric (which accounts for the color), black pepper, cumin, coriander, and cardamom.

Yemen is an ancient land, and some of the most important archaeological finds of Jewish history—Hebrew manuscripts carefully worked by community scribes—have been made there. Like those manuscripts, the Yemenite Jewish cuisine comes to us little changed by the intervening centuries, and so one approaches it with gratitude and a certain awe, as one does with all such artifacts, messengers bringing news from the distant past.

MARAK TEMANI

YEMENITE BEEF SOUP

Along with bread, soup is the staple of the Yemenite diet and is served as the centerpiece of the meal rather than the beginning of it. This soup (which is also made with chicken) is often served on weekdays, but it is especially common for Friday-night dinner. The soup can also be kept warm overnight and served for Saturday lunch, with the spicy chili paste Z'houg *(page 361) and slices of pita bread or* Salouf *(page 305). Says Tzippi Said, who has been the chef at Rectangles, the kosher Yemenite restaurant in New York's East Village ever since its opening in 1987, "My father would eat this soup for breakfast, lunch, and dinner, he loved it so much."*

SERVES 8 TO 10

2 beef marrow bones

2 onions, sliced

1 tablespoon chopped fresh cilantro

10 cups water

1 pound beef stew meat, cut into 1-inch cubes

2 teaspoons *Hawaij* (page 360)

2 teaspoons salt

Freshly ground black pepper

2 medium russet potatoes, peeled and cut into large chunks

2 carrots, peeled and cut into 1-inch pieces

1. Place the bones, onions, cilantro, and water in a soup pot. Bring to a boil over medium-high heat, then reduce the heat and simmer, covered, stirring occasionally, for 1 hour. Skim off any foam that may develop on the surface.
2. Add the beef cubes, *hawaij*, salt, and pepper and simmer, stirring occasionally, until the meat is nearly tender, about 1 hour. Skim off any foam that may develop on the surface.
3. Add the potatoes and carrots and continue cooking until the potatoes are soft and the meat is fully tender, about 30 minutes. Remove the bones before serving. Serve hot.

PSAROSOUPA

GREEK FISH SOUP

In the Greek seafaring town of Volos, this light soup was a common lunch dish in the summertime.

SERVES 8 TO 10

- 10 cups water
- 2 teaspoons salt
- 6 whole black peppercorns
- Juice of 1 lemon
- ¼ cup olive oil
- 1 large onion, quartered
- 2 medium red-skin potatoes, peeled
- ½ bunch fresh flat-leaf parsley
- 3 carrots, peeled
- 2 celery stalks, halved
- 1 whole fish, such as rockfish or red snapper, about 1½ pounds, cleaned and scaled

1. Place the water, salt, and peppercorns in a soup pot and bring to a boil. Add the lemon juice, olive oil, onion, potatoes, and parsley. Lower the heat and simmer for 15 minutes.
2. Add the carrots, celery, and the fish and bring to a boil. Lower the heat and simmer until the fish is cooked through and the vegetables are tender, about 20 minutes. Remove the fish, potatoes, celery, and carrots to a plate.
3. Strain the broth into a large bowl and return it to the pot. Taste and adjust for seasoning. Chop the vegetables into serving pieces and return them to the pot. Divide the fish into fillets and break them into serving pieces, discarding the head and bones. Return the fish pieces to the pot. Serve hot.

KARTOFFEL ZUP

POTATO SOUP

Potatoes were a fixture on the tables of East European Jews, and they were prepared in a myriad of ways. One very common preparation was to boil potatoes in a soup, often with grains such as barley and buckwheat, or with leeks and other root vegetables. Often the soup was enriched with milk or sour cream. This is a very good thick soup, full of lots of aromatic vegetables.

SERVES 8 TO 10

- 3 tablespoons butter
- 1 large onion, chopped
- 3 carrots, peeled and chopped
- 2 leeks (white and pale green parts only), well washed and chopped
- 3 celery stalks, chopped
- 1 parsnip, peeled and chopped
- 1 turnip, peeled and chopped
- Salt
- Freshly ground black pepper
- ¼ cup all-purpose flour
- 6 cups water
- 2 pounds red-skin potatoes, peeled and cut into small dice
- 1½ cups milk
- 3 tablespoons chopped fresh flat-leaf parsley

1. In a soup pot, melt the butter over medium heat. Add the onion, carrots, leeks, celery, parsnip, and turnip, and season with salt and pepper. Cook, stirring often, until the vegetables are soft and lightly colored. Add the flour and 1 cup of the water and continue cooking, stirring regularly, until the flour is dissolved and the mixture thickens.
2. Add the potatoes and the remaining 5 cups water and season with additional salt and pepper. Cover and bring to a boil. Lower the heat and simmer, stirring occasionally, until the potatoes are very soft, about 30 minutes.
3. Add the milk and stir until heated through, making sure not to let the soup boil. When the soup is hot, stir in the parsley. Taste and adjust for seasoning. Serve hot.

DISHES: Borscht

In Sholem Aleichem's 1906 story "Chava," Tevye the Milkman is engaged in a spirited debate with his third-eldest daughter, who has fallen in love with a gentile. She makes claims about universalism and the equality of all men; he counters with biblical quotations about how each group must seek its own kind. Finally Tevye's wife Golde calls out from the house, "Maybe you've done enough jabbering out there. The borscht has been sitting on the table for an hour and he's still out there singing Sabbath hymns."

"Another province heard from!" cries Tevye. "We are discussing important matters and she comes barging in with her borscht."

"My borscht," replies Golde firmly, "may be just as important as all those 'important matters' of yours."

Is there anyone out there who can tell her no? Amid poverty and oppression, not to mention family disputes untold, borscht was one of the handful of foods that sustained the Jews of Eastern Europe for centuries, and there are not many things, even "Sabbath hymns," that can be much more important than that.

So this we will stipulate, but then, what is borscht exactly? The answer is not so simple. Borscht, we might say, is a sweet-and-sour beet soup, but this definition, while technically accurate, scarcely reflects the far more complex reality. Some borschts are hot, while some are cold. Some borschts contain meat; others contain dairy. Some borschts taste more sour; others are more sweet. Some borschts are made with a thin stock; others are thickened. Some borschts include hard-boiled eggs or boiled potatoes; others, vegetables such as carrots or parsnips or mushrooms. Indeed, some borschts—the best-known variety is cabbage borscht (page 62)—don't even have beets at all.

So, given this definitional confusion, it might be best to start from first cases. As Alan Davidson points out in *The Oxford Companion to Food*, in gastronomy as in botany the origin of a species is likely the place where the largest number of varieties is recorded. For borscht, that place is the Ukraine. The soup's name, which can be found in Yiddish dictionaries (the plural is *borshtn*), derives from the Russian *borschtsh*, meaning cow parsnip, which tells us that the Ur-borscht was in fact parsnip soup. Beet borscht likely did not evolve until the mid-nineteenth century, which is when beets began to be widely planted in Eastern Europe and Russia.

The popularity of borscht in Eastern Europe, of course, was hardly limited to Jews. As with so many foods, borscht was a dish the Jews shared with their neighbors, yet as was also often true, they had to adapt it to conform to their dietary laws. Among the non-Jewish population of Eastern Europe, borscht was commonly made with a pork stock, and sometimes contained bits of pork sausage or chopped ham along with a topping of sour cream; the sausage and ham were omitted by Jewish cooks, and the soup made with a vegetable stock, or perhaps one enriched with beef, in which case no sour cream was added. What was retained were the essentials: the beets (most of the time, anyway) and the sweet-and-sour taste. The sweetness in the blend came from the beets, and the sourness from vinegar or, frequently, the classic Old World concoction known as *rosl*. *Rosl*—it is a Yiddish word derived from the Polish *rosól*, meaning brine—was made at home, often in preparation for Passover, by placing beets in a large, tightly sealed jar of water and letting them ferment in a warm place for a period of weeks. The sour, pickley brine that developed provided the foundation for borscht (when *rosl* was used, the soup was called *rosl borscht*) as well as a host of other dishes, including the tangy braised meat dish known as *roslfleysh*.

In Lithuania, borscht was, along with sauerkraut and pickles, one of the "sours" (*zoyers*) used to enliven an otherwise stodgy diet consisting mainly of potatoes, black bread, and gruel. Often a potato or a hard-boiled egg was placed directly into the soup. Or the soup might also be topped with a dollop of sour cream, which gave it greater richness and nutrition. Ukranian borscht, for its part, contained meat more often than borscht did in Lithuania. This borscht was heated for serving, for while *milkhedike* (dairy) borscht can be either hot or cold, meat borscht is invariably served hot. Ukranian borscht also sometimes contained tomatoes, unheard of in Lithuania and Poland, where the tomato was long considered not just poisonous—

a misconception widespread for centuries in Europe—but also *treyf* (unkosher), because it was thought to contain blood. The blood libel, as it were, led to a visceral distaste for the tomato among northern Jews. In his scholarly *The Yiddish Language in Northern Poland*, published in 1965, Marvin Herzog notes that several Polish-Jewish interviewees could still recall the fear and even fainting that accompanied their first tentative attempts to eat a tomato.

While Lithuanian Jews tended to emphasize the sour side of borscht's sweet-and-sour flavoring, in Poland the opposite was true. Polish-Jewish borscht, like other foods such as challah and gefilte fish, tended to be sweeter than it was elsewhere, though this predilection seems not to have arisen until the latter half of the nineteenth century, when a large number of Jewish-owned sugar beet refineries opened in Poland, aided by an extensive retail distribution network composed mostly of Jewish peddlers. Sugar became both cheap and accessible, and in Poland sweetness served as an aid to digestion in the way sourness did in Lithuania.

In the United States, Jewish immigration came from everywhere in Eastern Europe, and as a result no one variety of borscht predominates. What has predominated instead is the equation of borscht in the public mind with Jewish cuisine, a relationship nurtured by the 1930s-era appellation Borscht Belt, denoting the Jewish hotels, bungalow colonies, and *kuchaleyns* (an American Yiddish word referring to a boardinghouse with a shared kitchen) in New York's Catskill Mountains. Though borscht itself was but a small part of the legendarily plentiful mountain fare, which featured Old World specialties such as tsimmes, kreplach, kugel, and chopped liver, relentlessly tucked in to by patrons intent on getting their "money's worth" for their stay, by its very name it has become a staple of Jewish-American summer memory, of a piece with bungalows and *tummlers*.

In her 1949 book *An Alphabet for Gourmets* (specifically in the chapter "K Is for Kosher," another indication of the mid-century equation between borscht and Jewish cuisine), the great food writer M. F. K. Fisher wrote of borscht's variousness, "It can be hot, cold, thin, thick, rich, meager." So we have seen. She additionally noted, "I believe that it is one of the best soups in the world." There may be, ultimately, no more complete or more apt definition.

BORSCHT

SWEET-AND-SOUR BEET SOUP

There are innumerable varieties of borscht. This one, which is meant to be served hot, includes meat and potatoes and is a meal in itself.

SERVES 10

- 2 tablespoons vegetable oil
- 2 onions, chopped
- 2 to 2½ pounds flanken (short ribs)
- 10 cups water
- 2 teaspoons salt
- Freshly ground black pepper
- 2 pounds beets, peeled and cut into ½-inch dice
- 8 new potatoes, white- or red-skin, about 1½ pounds
- ¼ cup cider vinegar
- 3 tablespoons brown sugar
- 2 tablespoons chopped fresh dill

1. Heat the oil in a soup pot over medium heat. Add the onions and cook, stirring often, until soft and translucent.
2. Add the meat to the pot along with the water, salt, and pepper. Bring to a boil, skimming off any foam that develops on the surface. Lower the heat and simmer for 1 hour.
3. Add the beets and simmer for 1 hour more.
4. Add the potatoes, vinegar, and brown sugar, and continue simmering until the meat and potatoes are fully tender, about 30 minutes. Remove the meat and, when cool enough to handle, shred it. Discard the bones. Return the meat to the pot, taste the soup, and adjust for seasoning. Just before serving, stir in the chopped dill. Serve hot.

KROYT

CABBAGE BORSCHT

Like the borscht made from beets (see page 61), cabbage borscht has a sweet-and-sour flavor that comes from the addition of brown sugar and lemon juice. This particular version (which, because it uses tomatoes, probably originated in southern Russia) was a big hit among the residents of the Chaits bungalow colony in upstate New York, a summer getaway for generations of left-leaning Jews. Says Nancy Schwerner of Yellow Springs, Ohio, "Lots of women would sit around and discuss how their mothers made this soup. One of them (actually maybe more than one) said that her mother used ketchup, under the theory that all the spices were already in ketchup."

SERVES 8 TO 10

- 2 tablespoons vegetable oil
- 2 onions, chopped
- 2 to 2½ pounds flanken (short ribs)
- 9 cups water
- 1 medium green cabbage, about 2½ pounds, cored and cut into 1-inch chunks
- 2 bay leaves
- 28 ounces canned whole tomatoes, with juice
- 2 teaspoons salt
- Freshly ground black pepper
- 2 to 4 tablespoons fresh lemon juice, to taste
- 2 to 4 tablespoons brown sugar, to taste

1. Heat the oil in a soup pot over medium heat. Add the onions and cook, stirring often, until soft and translucent.
2. Add the meat to the pot along with the water, cabbage, bay leaves, tomatoes with their juice, salt, and pepper. (Break the tomatoes up with a spoon or your hands.) Bring to a boil, skimming off any foam that may develop on the surface. Lower the heat and simmer, covered, for 3 to 4 hours, until the meat is very tender.
3. Remove the meat and, when cool enough to handle, shred it. Discard the bones. Return the meat to the pot, and add the lemon juice and brown sugar, starting with the lesser amount, then adding more as needed of each to create the desired sweet-and-sour taste. Remove the bay leaves. Serve hot.

SHORBA ADDES

SOUR RED LENTIL SOUP

The word soup *in Arabic is* shorba. *Most of the time, though, lentil soup is referred to simply as* addes, *the word for lentils. Red lentils are generally used for soups, because they break down more readily than the brown ones. I make this soup all winter long. It's simple and quick (not to mention inexpensive), thick and hearty, with a zesty lilt to it.*

SERVES 4

1 cup red lentils

5½ cups water

⅓ cups flour

Juice of 2 lemons

1½ teaspoons salt

1 tablespoon olive oil

1 garlic clove, chopped

1 teaspoon ground coriander

Ground cumin and cayenne for sprinkling (optional)

1. Place the lentils and 3 cups of the water in a soup pot and bring to a boil. Lower the heat and simmer for 10 minutes.
2. In a medium bowl, mix the flour with ½ cup of the water to make a smooth paste. Gradually add the remaining 2 cups water, stirring constantly, then add the mixture to the lentils. Add the lemon juice and salt and cook over high heat until the soup comes to a boil. Reduce the heat to very low and simmer, partially covered, for 20 minutes, stirring occasionally with a wooden spoon to scrape the bottom of the pot.
3. Heat the oil in a small skillet over low heat. Add the garlic and cook until golden, about 1 minute. Add the coriander and cook another minute. Add to the soup, mix thoroughly, and then simmer for 5 minutes. Taste and adjust for seasoning. Serve hot. If desired, individual bowls of the soup can be sprinkled with ground cumin and cayenne.

RISHTA BI ADDES

SYRIAN BROWN LENTIL AND NOODLE SOUP

This dish can be made as a stew or, as in this version, as a soup. Rina Marcus of Austin, Texas, learned it from her mother, Julia Picciotto, who immigrated to New York from Aleppo, Syria, in 1921. Says Rina, "I think of this soup as Syrian comfort food. It's warming and filling and you won't be able to eat much else afterward." In the traditional preparation, the noodles come out very mushy. If you prefer that style, cook the noodles for 45 to 60 minutes, until they're the way you like them.

SERVES 4 TO 6

¾ cup brown lentils

1 tablespoon olive oil

7 cups water

4 ounces fettuccine or other medium-width noodles, broken in half

1½ teaspoons salt

Freshly ground black pepper

1. Place the lentils in a soup pot with the olive oil and water. Cover and bring to a boil. Lower the heat and simmer until the lentils are nearly tender, about 20 minutes.
2. Add the pasta or noodles, salt, and pepper, and cook until the lentils and noodles are fully tender, about 15 minutes. Serve hot.

MUSHROOM-BARLEY SOUP

On a cold winter's night, there's nothing quite so comforting as a bowl of hot mushroom-barley soup. It's a venerable Eastern European dish; indeed, until the mid-nineteenth century, when potatoes began to be widely planted, barley was one of the staple crops of the region. These days, dried mushrooms are a bit on the pricey side—in Eastern Europe, families used to dry their own mushrooms—but they add an unmistakable intensity of flavor.

SERVES 8 TO 10

- ½ ounce dried porcini mushrooms
- 1 cup boiling water
- 2 tablespoons olive oil
- 2 onions, chopped
- 3 carrots, peeled and diced
- 3 celery stalks, diced
- 1 pound fresh white or cremini mushrooms, thinly sliced
- 2 garlic cloves, chopped
- 10 cups water or chicken stock, or a combination of the two
- 1 cup (about 8 ounces) pearl barley
- 3 tablespoons chopped fresh dill
- 3 tablespoons chopped fresh flat-leaf parsley, plus additional for serving (optional)
- Salt
- Freshly ground black pepper
- Dash of sherry (optional)

1. Place the dried mushrooms in a small bowl and cover with the boiling water. Let steep for 30 minutes.
2. Heat the olive oil in a soup pot over medium heat. Add the onions, carrots, and celery and cook, stirring often, until the onions are soft and translucent. Add the fresh mushrooms and cook, stirring often, until they begin to brown. Add the garlic and cook for another minute.
3. Add the water or chicken stock, barley, dill, parsley, salt, and pepper. (The amount of salt needed will vary, depending on the amount and type of chicken stock used.) Remove the dried mushrooms from the small bowl and add them to the pot. Using a colander lined with cheesecloth or a paper coffee filter, strain the soaking liquid into a bowl and add it to the pot.
4. Cover the pot and bring to a boil, then reduce the heat and simmer, covered, for 2 hours. After one hour, begin tasting the soup and add salt and pepper as necessary. If desired, just before serving stir in a dash of sherry and some additional chopped parsley. Serve hot.

COMMUNITIES: Bombay

It sounds like a plot line from a nineteenth-century adventure novel: Shipwrecked, a small band of survivors struggle to build a new life for themselves in a jungle, entirely isolated from everything they have ever known. Centuries later their descendants, still carrying on the ancient handed-down ways, are discovered and returned once more to their people.

It's no novel, however. In essence, this is the story of one of the most remarkable of all Jewish communities, the Bene Israel, who have lived in India for more than two millennia. According to Bene Israel legend (and there is no historical documentation either to prove or disprove this), the community originated in the second century B.C.E., when a ship carrying Jews bound from Galilee foundered in the winds and rough seas off India's western coast. Most of the ship's passengers died, but fourteen of them—as the legend relates, seven men and seven women—managed to make it safely ashore, and there, in that unfamiliar land, set about rebuilding their community on the Konkan Coast of India.

For some nineteen centuries, the Bene Israel (literally, "children of Israel") lived entirely cut off from the rest of the world's Jews. Somehow they managed to maintain a Jewish life, though it was, needless to say, a sharply attenuated one. As the years passed, their knowledge of Judaism began little by little to erode, as succeeding generations no longer remembered the traditional practices or their religious significance. In time, their vestigial Jewish observances consisted only of Shabbat, circumcision, distinctions between "clean" and "unclean" food, a few holidays such as Passover (though they no longer connected it to the exodus from Egyptian slavery), and a single prayer, the *Shema*, which they recited whenever a prayer seemed appropriate.

The Bene Israel knew no Hebrew and spoke only Marathi, one of the languages of western India. They earned their living as farmers, soldiers in the local Hindu or Muslim armies and, primarily, as pressers of oil—sesame, peanut, and coconut. According to legend, many of the original shipwrecked passengers had learned the oil-pressing trade back in the olive groves of Galilee. Because the Bene Israel refrained from working on the Sabbath, they became known among the local people as the *Shanwar Teli*, or Saturday-Observing Oil Pressers.

There had long been another, more established Jewish community farther south, in the town of Cochin, and eventually rumors began to spread down the coast of a group of people in the remote villages of the Konkan who appeared, as unlikely as it might have seemed, to be Jews. The first outside Jewish contact with the Bene Israel was made by David Yechezkel Rahabi, the scion of one of the leading families of Cochini Jews. Shortly afterward members of the Cochin community started tutoring the Bene Israel in the ways of traditional Judaism. Through their ongoing contacts with the Cochini Jews (and ironically, with British Christian missionaries, who translated the Old Testament into Marathi and taught them Hebrew and English), the Bene Israel began to adopt a more orthodox form of Judaism as well as a more modern way of life. In the nineteenth century the majority of the Bene Israel community moved from their rural villages to the nearby city of Bombay. There they began to enter the civil service and professions and, through them, the Indian middle class.

Whether in the Konkan or in Bombay, Bene Israel food practices are fairly typical of western India, though with some important distinctions, mostly for the observance of *kashrut* and Jewish holidays. The Bene Israel, for instance, will not marinate lamb in yogurt, using lemon juice instead. However, like Hindus—but no other Jews outside of India—the Bene Israel do not mix fish and dairy. They also use coconut milk instead of oil for their cooking during Passover.

Beef dishes are rare in Bene Israel cuisine, owing in part to a longtime paucity of kosher slaughterers (unlike cows, chickens could be slaughtered at home) and, very likely, out of respect for the food taboos of the local Hindu community, for whom cows are sacred. Weekday dinners were simple meals of vegetables, rice, and lentils; the Bene Israel will eat only orange lentils, never red, because they say that red lentils were the pottage for which Esau sold his birthright. Meat was a luxury reserved for Shabbat and holidays, and consisted mainly of chicken and goat. (Among the Bene Israel outside of India, lamb has generally replaced goat in mutton dishes.) Fish, which is more readily available and may be served during the week, will usually appear on Shabbat tables as well, as it is thought to bring good luck.

The Bene Israel kitchen is distinguished by an abundant use of tomatoes and onions, especially in sauces. The cooking is not as spicy as that of the Cochini Jews to the south, though it does feature lots of dried red chilies, traditionally ground into a paste on stone mortars. Ginger and garlic are also ground into pastes, and show up in a wide range of savory dishes; other common spices include cumin, cinnamon, cardamom, cloves, turmeric, and black pepper, as well as fresh herbs such as cilantro and curry leaves, which grow abundantly along the western coast of India. Bene Israel dishes are wonderfully aromatic and surprisingly complex, a perfect balance of sweet, spicy, and sour flavors. Sweetness comes primarily from the unrefined sugar known as jaggery; the primary souring agents include lemon juice, unripe green mangoes, and the little purple-brown fruit called *kokam*. (Tamarind paste can be used in place of *kokam*, though it is more common to the south.)

Though desserts are not a main focus of the cuisine—meals will often end simply with fresh fruit, since most Indian desserts tend to be made with dairy foods. For festive occasions such as Rosh Hashanah there is the cardamom-flavored pudding called *kheer*, as well as a similar pudding (this one is cooled and cut into diamond shapes for serving) called *halwa*, unique to the Bene Israel. Coconut milk is also featured in savory dishes, such as a coconut curry flavored with curry leaves, cumin, garlic, cilantro, and green chilies; it is a staple dish during the summertime. Like everything else in the Bene Israel pantry, the coconut milk is made from scratch, by grating fresh coconut meat and pressing it with hot water—a procedure, of course, with which the Bene Israel have been familiar for some two thousand years.

Now, after all that time, most of the Bene Israel Jews have left the land that once gave them haven; of the 50,000 or so Bene Israel Jews in the world, only about 5,000 still live in India. The remainder have emigrated to Israel, with a handful living in the United States. So the cycle is completed: Two millennia after that legendary shipwreck, the "children of Israel" have at last found their way home.

NARLA CHI KADI

BOMBAY COCONUT AND GREEN MANGO SOUP

Among the Bene Israel Jews, this unusual but very delicious dish is served on holidays or other special occasions. It can be served by itself, as a soup, or served over rice as a side dish. Green mangoes are one of the chief souring agents of Bene Israel cookery, along with limes and the sour fruit known as kokam. *Green mangoes, curry leaves, and rice flour can be purchased in many Indian groceries. So can ginger and garlic paste, though you can use fresh instead.*

SERVES 6

- 2 tablespoons vegetable oil
- 3 to 4 whole dried red chili peppers
- 10 curry leaves
- ½ teaspoon cumin seeds
- ¼ teaspoon mustard seeds
- ½ teaspoon turmeric
- 1 teaspoon ginger paste or finely chopped ginger
- 1 teaspoon garlic paste or finely chopped garlic
- 1 (13-ounce) can unsweetened coconut milk
- 3 cups water
- 2 tablespoons rice flour
- 1 medium green mango, peeled and sliced into ½-inch cubes
- 1½ teaspoons salt
- ½ teaspoon sugar
- 1 tablespoon chopped fresh cilantro

1. Heat the oil in a soup pot over medium-high heat. Add the chilies, curry leaves, cumin seeds, mustard seeds, turmeric, ginger, and garlic and cook for 1 minute, stirring regularly.
2. In a medium bowl, combine the coconut milk, water, and rice flour and mix until smooth. Add the mixture to the pot and stir to combine. Add the green mango, salt, and sugar and stir to combine.
3. Cover the pot, raise the heat to high, and bring to a boil. Reduce the heat and simmer, stirring occasionally, until the mango is soft and the liquid has thickened slightly, about 20 minutes. With a slotted spoon, remove the chilies and curry leaves. Just before serving, stir in the cilantro. Serve hot.

GYÜMÖLCS LEVES

HUNGARIAN FRUIT SOUP

Chilled fruit soups have long been a summer staple in Central and Eastern Europe, among Jews and non-Jews alike. The fresh fruit is simmered in water until soft, and cheerily flavored with some combination of lemon juice, vanilla, cinnamon, sugar, and wine. If the meal does not include meat, then sour cream is mixed in just before serving. In Hungary, sour morello cherries are most often used for fruit soup, but other common ingredients include apples, pears, strawberries, and—as in this version, from Marta Kovacs of Hoboken, New Jersey, who emigrated from Budapest in 1993—peaches and plums. Use the ripest, most flavorful fruit you can find, and add sugar according to the sweetness of the fruit.

SERVES 10 TO 12

About 2 pounds peaches, pitted and chopped

About 1½ pounds plums, pitted and chopped

8 cups water

½ teaspoon salt

Juice and grated zest of 1 lemon

1 cinnamon stick

1 vanilla bean

About ½ cup sugar, to taste

½ cup sour cream

1. Put the fruit, water, and salt in a soup pot and bring to a boil. Add the lemon juice, lemon zest, cinnamon stick, vanilla bean, and ¼ cup of the sugar. Lower the heat and gently simmer for 15 minutes, stirring occasionally, until the fruit is very soft. Remove the cinnamon stick and vanilla bean.
2. Puree the soup with a hand blender, or in batches in a blender or food processor. Transfer to a bowl. Taste and add sugar as desired, then taste again and adjust for salt and lemon juice as necessary.
3. Refrigerate until cold, at least 5 hours or overnight. Just before serving, whisk in the sour cream.

Fish

In Numbers 11:5, the departing Israelites enumerate the foods they grieve to leave behind in their journey to the Promised Land: "We remember the fish, which we did eat in Egypt freely; the cucumbers, and the melons, and the leeks, and the onions, and the garlic."

In retrospect, it's fitting that fish is mentioned first, for unlike, say, cucumbers or melons, Jewish cuisine would be unthinkable without it. Like grains and vegetables, fish is considered *pareve*—neutral—and thus can be served as part of either a meat or dairy meal. Around the world it is a fixture at festive Jewish tables, from Passover seders to Shabbat dinners; indeed, the Talmud recommends that fish be eaten at all three Sabbath meals (as a Yiddish saying has it, "The Sabbath without fish is like a wedding without dancing"). How the fish is to be prepared for the Sabbath varies widely from community to community. Among the Bukharan Jews of Central Asia, for instance, Shabbat dinner traditionally begins with fried fish in a pungent garlic and cilantro sauce, followed by a selection of fresh and pickled vegetable salads. For Moroccan Jews, on the other hand, the salads are followed by the fish, which is often roasted with olives or red peppers. In Iraq, the Friday-night meal regularly featured the fish cakes called *arook bel samak.* Fish is topped with tomatoes and green peppers in Greece, with walnuts in Turkey, with garlic and chili peppers in Libya; it is sweet-and-sour in Italy, spicy in North Africa, curried in India.

These are some of the distinctive fish preparations in Sephardic communities. Among the Ashkenazim, it has been most common to serve fish cold. The most famous of these dishes, of course (though by no means the only one), is gefilte fish, the poached ground-fish balls that have long been an indispensable part of Sabbath and holiday meals. Traditionally gefilte fish has been served as an appetizer, and by this time it is difficult to imagine it any other way. But just about any of this chapter's other preparations (including a delicious Mexican variation of gefilte fish) can serve either as the first course of an elaborate meal or the main course of an everyday one. Flexible, nutritious, delicious, and simple to prepare—what more can the home cook desire? Now as then, let us remember the fish, and eat them freely.

INGREDIENTS: Fish

According to the Talmud, fish will be a centerpiece of the Meal of the Righteous that ushers in the Messianic age, and for a Jewish foodstuff there surely can't be any better endorsement than that. As it happens, fish has been a major part of the Jewish diet at least since Babylonian times—though less because of the Messiah than for the fact that it possesses certain qualities, gastronomic and symbolic alike, that makes it an especially appealing ingredient for Jewish cooks.

Perhaps most important, according to the kosher laws, fish are *pareve* (meaning neither milk nor meat), and so they are the only creatures that can be eaten, like vegetables or grains, at any meal. Further, unlike chicken or cows, fish do not require ritual slaughter to ensure proper drainage of blood. It would not be unusual to wonder why this is so, since fish obviously do have blood; but the prohibition against the consumption of blood in Leviticus 7:26–27 refers only to that of "birds and beasts." Fish blood is thus considered exempt.

That doesn't mean that any fish is permitted, however. A fish is deemed kosher only if it possesses fins and scales, after the injunction in Leviticus 11:9–10. This eliminates sea creatures such as octopus, eels, crustaceans, and mollusks, as well as numerous species of fish, among them shark, monkfish, catfish, and skate. Sturgeon and swordfish, which have embedded scales that are difficult to remove, are the subjects of ongoing rabbinic dispute; Orthodox rabbis state in no uncertain terms that these fish are forbidden, but the fish are permitted for consumption by most Reform and Conservative rabbis. Caviar is the roe of the sturgeon, and as such is equally acceptable or not, depending on one's own religious, or culinary, inclinations.

Beyond the flexibility it affords for kitchen use (at least compared to most other sources of protein), for Jews fish has also taken on some pretty significant symbolic weight. In Genesis 1:22, God blesses the fish and instructs them to "be fruitful and multiply," just as He does, a few verses on, with human beings. As a result, fish came to be seen by Jews as a symbol of fertility and abundance. In many Mediterranean communities (this has been noted by, among others, historian Miguel-Ángel Motis Dolader), it was traditional for a new Jewish bride to step three times over a tray of fish, while her family and friends wished her the same fertility as the fish; this ritual was called the "day of the fish." Fish also function as a symbol of sinlessness, for they were the only creatures not on Noah's Ark that did not perish in the Great Flood. Perhaps for this reason, Jews traditionally considered fish to be a protection against the *eynhore,* the "Evil Eye," although it may also be because fish live under water and are thus immune from any ill-intended looks. This belief was found, by the way, among Sephardic and Ashkenazic Jews alike: In the Middle East and North Africa, hand-shaped amulets called *chamsas* are often decorated with fish, while in Eastern Europe the Yiddish name Fishl came from the hope that the male child might be rendered safe from harm.

Fish is delicious cold as well as hot, and as a result it can be served on the Sabbath day, when work is prohibited. This practice has given rise to at least two well-known dishes, and another that rose to fame in an unexpected context. One of the dishes, jellied carp, was a delicacy beloved by Jews throughout France and Germany, especially in Alsace. Known as *carpe à la juive,* or carp in the Jewish style, the dish so scaled the heights of French haute cuisine that it earned four entries in *Larousse Gastronomique.* An even more common use of carp for the Sabbath was in Gefilte Fish (pages 88–89), originally a fish-based forcemeat sewn back into the skin of the fish (*gefilte* is the Yiddish word meaning stuffed) that over the years evolved into the poached fish balls with which we are familiar today.

Among the Jews of Spain and Portugal, fish fried in olive oil and served cold on the Sabbath was a favorite recipe, and one that they carried with them after their expulsion in the fifteenth century. In Great Britain, where fish was fried in lard not oil, the dish achieved a surprising renown, so much so that it came to be widely known, like the jellied carp farther east on the Continent, as "fried fish in the Jewish style." In the nineteenth century an Ashkenazic Jewish immi-

PLAKI

FISH IN TOMATO SAUCE

Variations of this simple and delicious fish preparation abound in the Sephardic world, from the Balkans to North Africa and the Middle East. It is a very common Friday-night dish.

SERVES 4

- 2 tablespoons olive oil
- 2 onions, chopped
- 1 (28-ounce) can crushed tomatoes
- Salt
- Freshly ground black pepper
- 1½ pounds fillet of firm, white-fleshed fish, such as cod, halibut, or red snapper
- ¼ cup chopped fresh flat-leaf parsley
- 2 or 3 garlic cloves, chopped
- Juice of 1 lemon

1. Preheat the oven to 350 degrees. In a large ovenproof skillet, heat the oil over medium heat. Add the onions and cook, stirring often, until soft and translucent. Add the tomatoes and season with salt and pepper. Cover and simmer for 10 minutes.
2. Rinse the fish and pat it dry; season with salt and pepper. Place the fish on the tomato sauce. Sprinkle the parsley, garlic, and lemon juice over the fish. Transfer the skillet to the oven and bake until the fish is cooked through, about 25 minutes. Serve hot.

PISHKADO REYNADO

TURKISH FISH WITH TOMATOES AND WALNUTS

In Turkey, anchovies are commonly used for this dish, but American tastes would likely substitute a milder-tasting fish. I've adapted this recipe from one in Sefarad Yemekleri *(Sephardic Food), a cookbook published by the Jewish community in Istanbul.*

SERVES 4

1 (28-ounce) can crushed tomatoes

½ cup chopped fresh flat-leaf parsley

2 slices white bread, crusts removed, soaked briefly in water and squeezed dry, then crumbled

½ cup walnuts, coarsely chopped

½ teaspoon salt

Freshly ground black pepper

Red pepper flakes (optional)

1½ pounds fillet of firm, white-fleshed fish, such as cod, halibut, or red snapper

1. Preheat the oven to 350 degrees. In a large bowl, stir together the tomatoes, parsley, bread, and walnuts. Season the mixture with salt, pepper, and (if using) red pepper flakes. Rinse the fish and pat it dry; season with salt and pepper.
2. Lightly oil a large (13 × 9 inch) baking dish. Place half of the tomato sauce over the bottom of the prepared dish. Lay the fish on the sauce, then cover the fish with the remaining sauce. Transfer the dish to the oven and bake until the fish is cooked through, 25 to 30 minutes. Transfer to a large serving platter. Serve hot.

COMMUNITIES: Northern Morocco

Like an archaeologist painstakingly mapping the contours of a ruined city, Alegria Bendelac spent ten years of her life creating a dictionary for a language that is no longer spoken. Dr. Bendelac, a petite, energetic woman who looks much younger than her years, was born and raised in Tangier, Morocco; her family was among the last few hundred Jews in a city where some 10,000 once resided. As André Aciman wrote about his own family living in Egypt, they were "at the very tail end of those whom history shrugs aside when it changes its mind." In 1963, Dr. Bendelac moved to the United States, where she eventually became a professor at Penn State University. Still, as the years passed she found that she was haunted by a language she knew only in bits and scraps, in memories of conversations overhead among older relatives. This was Jaquetia, which only a few generations earlier had been the daily language of the approximately 25,000 Jews of northern Morocco. It had begun to fall out of favor starting in the early 1900s, when Morocco was occupied by France and Spain, and French and Spanish became the languages of social status and eventually Jaquetia (pronounced HAH-kuh-DEE-uh) was regularly spoken almost only by old people. With the dispersion of the Jewish population following Morocco's independence in 1956, Jaquetia lost its natural base and was doomed to extinction.

Wanting to establish as comprehensive a historical record as possible before its last speakers had disappeared, Dr. Bendelac set to work, interviewing Moroccan immigrants dispersed across many countries, compiling lists of words and expressions. She spent a full decade on her project, which culminated in three volumes about Jaquetia, most impressively the 1,300-page *Diccionario del Judeo-espanol de los Sefardies del Norte de Marruecos.* It is the world's first Jaquetia dictionary, and probably the only one there will ever be.

Though Jaquetia was spoken only in Morocco—in fact, in little more than half a dozen cities there—its roots actually stretch across the Mediterranean, into Spain. Many thousands of Jews fleeing the Spanish terror of the fifteenth century ended up in Morocco, which was under Muslim rule and had a more lenient policy toward Jews. The Jewish exiles who settled in the southern and interior parts of the country generally assimilated, speaking Arabic and otherwise adopting the culture of those Jews who had been in Morocco since the fall of the Second Temple. Not so for the Jews who remained in the northernmost region of Morocco, just below the Straits of Gibraltar and to the west of the Rif mountains. Those Jews prided themselves on their Spanish heritage; they called themselves Los Nuestros, or Our People, and used the term *forasteros* (strangers) to refer to the Jews of the south and the interior.

These exiles had arrived in Morocco speaking Spanish, and this fifteenth-century Spanish was the language to which they clung. Over time, though, rarely used Spanish sounds, structures, and vocabulary began to be forgotten and disappear, to be replaced with elements from Hebrew and the local Arabic and Berber languages. Eventually the original language had evolved so dramatically that it became another language entirely, one that came to be known among its users as Jaquetia, perhaps from the Arabic verb *haka*, meaning to chat.

Though inevitably the Jews of northern Morocco would come to adopt many of the local customs, they maintained a more Mediterranean way of life than was found in the rest of the country. Whenever possible, their days included a *siesta*, the afternoon nap; they dined late, enjoyed the evening stroll called *el paseo*. Men socialized in *casinos* (men's clubs); women frequently set up chairs on sidewalks and patios and chatted with neighbors while peeling vegetables or mending clothes. Religious services contained psalms and poems of medieval Spanish origin.

Like so much of this culture, including Jaquetia itself, the cuisine of the Jews of northern Morocco was a blend of Spanish, Jewish, and Arabic traditions. One especially popular dish was *alboronía*, a stew of chicken and eggplant flavored with a bit of sugar and nutmeg, often served the evening before Yom Kippur. This was a variation of an ancient Spanish dish, one that had been brought to Spain by the Moorish invaders of the early Middle Ages. There was a lot of rice, as in Spain—often served with meat or fish in the Spanish style—but the cuisine included Arab couscous as well, though only a special sweet version (see pages 290–291), served only on festive occasions, not on a daily basis. Like Jews everywhere, they cooked an overnight Sabbath stew, which they called *adafina,* comprising beef, potatoes, sweet potatoes, chickpeas, and eggs. In general the cooking of the Jews of northern Morocco tended to use fewer spices than that of the southern Jews, who adopted more of the local Arab cooking styles. This difference is reflected in the *adafina,* which uses no cinnamon or nutmeg or turmeric, as elsewhere in the country, but only some caramelized sugar to add richness and color.

Lunch was the main meal of the day, and often featured soup (such as bean soup, or chicken soup with rice or pasta), salad, a meat dish, fruit, and dessert. Desserts were a particular specialty, featuring many types of pastries, such as *torrejas,* strips of filo dough rolled up and fried and then sprinkled with cinnamon and sugar. Alegria Bendelac remembers her mother serving as many as a dozen kinds of cakes on Purim, in almond, chocolate, orange, and other flavors. Among the most ornate was *bienmesabe* (literally, tastes good to me), a sponge cake filled with vanilla or lemon cream and decorated with glazed fruit and candied violets. A favorite sweet was jellied fruit called *letuario,* made variously from oranges, orange blossoms, peaches, quinces, apricots, even eggplants. It was a staple at weddings and other festive events, and was often kept around the house to offer to company, with tea or coffee in the afternoon, or after dinner with *rosoli,* a liqueur flavored with mint or mandarin orange. According to tradition, one had to always offer something sweet to anyone who came by to visit, with the spoken wish, "May you live in sweetness."

At one time some 10,000 Jews lived in Tangier; today that number is closer to 150. The long Jewish stay in northern Morocco is fast coming to an end. What will remain, finally, is memories: family stories, photographs, recipes, and now, at last, a dictionary of an almost forgotten language.

PESCADO EN COLORADO

MOROCCAN FISH IN TOMATO SAUCE WITH PEPPERS AND PAPRIKA

This recipe, given to me by Alegria Bendelac, was a very popular Sabbath dish among the Jews of northern Morocco, who also called it pescado cocho *(simply, cooked fish). How much spicing should one use?* "Al gusto," *they will reply—to taste.*

SERVES 4

2 tablespoons olive oil

1 green pepper, sliced

1 red pepper, sliced

10 to 12 garlic cloves, unpeeled but crushed

1 (28-ounce) can crushed tomatoes

1 tablespoon paprika

Red pepper flakes

Salt

Freshly ground black pepper

2 pounds swordfish or halibut steaks, each cut into 3 or 4 pieces

1. In a large skillet, heat the oil over medium heat. Add the peppers and garlic and cook until the peppers are soft, about 5 minutes. Add the tomatoes and season with paprika, red pepper flakes, salt, and pepper. Bring to a boil. Lower the heat and simmer for 5 minutes.
2. Rinse the fish and pat it dry. Season with salt and pepper. Add the fish to the pan in one layer. Cover the pan and simmer, spooning the sauce over the fish occasionally, until the fish is opaque and flakes easily, about 12 minutes. Taste the sauce and adjust for seasoning. Remove the garlic. Transfer the fish to a large serving platter and spoon the sauce over it. Serve hot.

POISSON AUX OLIVES

ROASTED FISH WITH OLIVES

This is one of my favorite fish dishes. The recipe was given to me by Stella Ymar of Rockville, Maryland, who left Casablanca in 1964. It was often served at Friday-night dinners there. Make sure to use good marinated green olives, not the canned kind.

SERVES 4

- 1 whole red snapper, about 2½ pounds, cleaned and scaled
- Salt
- Freshly ground black pepper
- 2 cups pitted green olives
- 3 tomatoes, chopped
- ¼ cup chopped fresh flat-leaf parsley
- 4 garlic cloves, chopped
- 1½ teaspoons paprika
- ½ cup olive oil
- 2 lemons, thinly sliced

1. Preheat the oven to 400 degrees. Rinse the fish and pat it dry. Season the outside and the cavity with salt and pepper.
2. In a medium bowl, mix together the olives, tomatoes, parsley, garlic, paprika, and oil, and season with salt and pepper.
3. Spoon the mixture into a roasting pan and place the fish on top of it. Arrange the lemon slices on top of the fish. Bake until the fish is cooked through, 35 to 40 minutes. Transfer the fish to a large serving platter and spoon the pan sauce over it. Serve hot.

PESCADO A LA GRECA

ROASTED FISH WITH TOMATO, ONION, AND LEMON

In the early decades of the twentieth century, many Jews of Salonikan descent settled in New Brunswick, New Jersey. In 1928 some of them formed Congregation Etz Ahaim, named after the oldest synagogue in Salonika, which at the time was the only Sephardic synagogue in New Jersey. By the 1960s many of the congregation's members had moved from New Brunswick to nearby Highland Park, and in 1963 the synagogue was relocated there. Today the congregation includes some 175 families, and though many of them are not Sephardic, Etz Ahaim continues to maintain its Sephardic traditions. In 1999 members of the synagogue published the excellent Sephardic cookbook Come, Es Bueno *(Eat, It's Good), from which this Salonikan recipe has been adapted.*

SERVES 4

- 5 tablespoons olive oil
- 2 onions, sliced
- 1 whole red snapper, about 2½ pounds, cleaned and scaled
- Salt
- Freshly ground black pepper
- Juice of 1 lemon
- 2 tablespoons finely chopped fresh flat-leaf parsley
- 1 lemon, thinly sliced
- 1 large tomato, cored and thinly sliced
- ¼ cup dry white wine

1. Preheat the oven to 400 degrees. Lightly oil a roasting pan.
2. In a medium skillet, heat 2 tablespoons of the oil over medium heat. Add the onions and cook, stirring often, until they are soft and lightly colored. Remove from the heat and set aside.
3. Rinse the fish and pat it dry. Season the outside and the cavity with salt and pepper. Place the fish in the roasting pan. Drizzle with the lemon juice and then sprinkle with the parsley. Cover with the onions, lemon slices, and tomato slices. Drizzle with the wine and the remaining 3 tablespoons of oil.
4. Bake until the fish is cooked through, 35 to 40 minutes. Transfer the fish and vegetables to a large serving platter. Serve hot.

DISHES: Gefilte Fish

Gefilte is a Yiddish word meaning stuffed; thus *gefilte fish* is stuffed fish, the name a vestigial remnant of the dish's medieval origins, when it was something very different from what we know today. Contemporary gefilte fish, of course, starts with a forcemeat made from ground-up freshwater fish mixed with matzo meal, eggs, chopped onion, and spices; the forcemeat is rolled into balls, poached in a fish stock, and served cold. In its earliest incarnation, though, the forcemeat was not rolled into balls, but rather stuffed back into the skin of the fish, at which point the fish was sewn up again and baked. This dish dates back to Germany in the Middle Ages. The earliest recipe for stuffed pike appears in a non-Jewish German manuscript circa 1350, and by the early fifteenth century a German rabbinic authority was discussing the *kashrut* implications of adding vinegar to fish hash on the Sabbath. Eventually the step of stuffing the fish was discarded, and the forcemeat itself became the focus of the dish, giving us the poached fish balls that over the centuries have become virtually synonymous with Ashkenazic cuisine.

Though pike was the original gefilte fish, by the seventeenth century carp was mostly used instead. Native to China, carp had been introduced into Europe in the fifteenth century, through Italy and Turkey, by traders working the silk routes. Two centuries later the fish had been carried eastward into Poland; the Jews there, who were excluded from most of the traditional European guilds, quickly seized on this new opportunity and began to breed carp in specially managed ponds. Thus plentiful and relatively inexpensive, carp became a fixture of the Sabbath meal, not just in gefilte fish but in other preparations as well, including most notably jellied carp—carp long-poached in water (sometimes with white wine) and then served cold in its own jelly.

As a rule, the Jews of Poland liked their food sweeter than Jews elsewhere, and this holds true for gefilte fish as well. By the middle of the nineteenth century, Polish gefilte fish was generally sweetened with sugar. David and Diane Roskies have speculated in *The Shtetl Book* that this variation may correlate with the rise of Hasidism in the region; the Hasidim tend to like their food sweet, associating sugar with the joy of religious celebration, though a more materialist explanation would point to the profusion of Jewish-owned sugar refineries in the surrounding area. In Lithuania, on the other hand, gefilte fish was heavily spiced with pepper and served with horseradish. In his 1965 doctoral dissertation *The Yiddish Language in Northern Poland: Its Geography and History*, based on interviews with Jews from pre-Holocaust Eastern Europe, Marvin Herzog presented what is now known as the "gefilte fish line." The line runs north to south, about 40 miles east of Warsaw; west of it, the preferred gefilte fish preparation was sweet, while to the east the fish was peppery.

It's not hard to understand why a recipe like gefilte fish would become such a mainstay among the Jews of Eastern Europe, poorer and often more strictly observant than their counterparts in the West. Fish is *pareve* and can thus be served as part of any kosher meal; further, as a cold dish, gefilte fish can be made in advance and then served on the Sabbath, and because it contains no bones that need to be picked out of the fish, it does not infringe on Sabbath regulations prohibiting work. Equally important, fish was relatively expensive and could be stretched by being combined with cheaper ingredients—certainly a major benefit for a Jewish housewife of limited means (and what's more, she could serve the poaching liquid as soup).

In the United States, gefilte fish has traditionally been made from carp mixed in equal parts with pike and whitefish; more carp will result in a somewhat deeper flavor, but turns the mixture a darker color. Sometimes the mixture was augmented with a fourth fish, buffalo fish (often known among Jewish immigrants as "buffel," from the Yiddish word meaning buffalo), which resembles carp and today can often be found in Chinese fish markets. In many American families, stories are told about how every year Bubbe used to keep a huge carp swimming around in the upstairs bathtub while the house was cleaned for Passover and the gefilte fish preparation could be begun. (As a bottom feeder, carp requires a long period in fresh water to remove its muddy taste.) These stories are amusing because of their very archaism, for today gefilte fish is rarely made at home, purchased, instead, in jars found in the appetizing cases of the local supermarket. This is a shame, because homemade gefilte fish can be feathery light and delicate in taste, two qualities not usually associated with the jarred variety. To make it so, the fish balls should be poached—at a very low simmer, and for not more than an hour or so—in a fish stock thriftily made with the heads, skin, and bones of the fish one is using. Refrigerate the fish balls overnight (like brisket, gefilte fish is best made the day before) and serve chilled, lightly coated in the jellied broth, with good horseradish on the side. Thus prepared, the gefilte fish will be beautifully glossy, soft, and very delicious, and you will have to be careful not to stuff yourself before the rest of the meal arrives.

GEFILTE FISH

POACHED FISH BALLS

This recipe, from Jackie Schectman of Boston, is a decidedly uptown version of gefilte fish, using, as it does, fresh herbs and white wine in the poaching liquid. This, however, seems not at all problematic to me, and not just because the white wine harks back to the original German jellied carp. Rather, it's because this is very good gefilte fish, not too far removed from the classic rendition. Have your fishmonger fillet and grind the fish for you, and reserve the heads, bones, and skin for the broth.

MAKES ABOUT 24 FISH BALLS

About 7 pounds whole fish (half carp and half white-fish and/or pike), flesh filleted and ground; head, skin, and bones reserved

FOR THE BROTH

1 onion, chopped

3 carrots, chopped

3 celery stalks, chopped

10 cups water

1 cup dry white wine

Several sprigs of thyme and fresh flat-leaf parsley

1 tablespoon salt

FOR THE FISH BALLS

2 onions, quartered

2 eggs, lightly beaten

½ cup matzo meal

½ cup cold water

Salt

1. Make the broth: Place the fish head, bones, and skin in a large pot. Add the onion, carrots, and celery and cover with the water. Cover the pot and bring to a boil, skimming off any foam that may develop on the surface. Add the wine, herbs, and salt. Lower the heat and simmer, uncovered, for 1 hour. Strain into a large bowl. Return the broth to the pot.
2. Make the fish balls: Place the ground fish in a large bowl. Place the onions in the bowl of a food processor and process until coarsely ground. Add to the ground fish.
3. Add the eggs, one at a time, mixing after each addition. Add the matzo meal, water, salt, and pepper and mix thoroughly. The mixture should be light and soft and just moist enough to hold its shape when pressed together. If necessary, add a bit more water or matzo meal.
4. Make the gefilte fish: Return the broth to a simmer and add the carrots. With moistened hands, form the fish mixture into oval-shaped balls about 3 inches in length and 2 inches in width. Drop them into the broth and cook at a low simmer, partially covered, for 1 hour. (Shake the pot occasionally so that the fish does not

stick to the bottom.) Turn off the heat and let the fish cool in the broth.

5. With a slotted spoon, remove the fish balls and carrots to a large, shallow serving bowl. Strain the broth into a large bowl. Ladle some of the broth over the fish and carrots, just enough to make a light glaze. Cover with plastic wrap and refrigerate overnight. Serve with freshly prepared horseradish.

Freshly ground black pepper

5 carrots, peeled and cut into 1-inch chunks

Horseradish for accompaniment (see page 367)

GEFILTE FISH A LA VERACRUZANA

MEXICAN FRIED FISH BALLS IN SPICY TOMATO SAUCE

In this unusual and very delicious main-course version of gefilte fish, the fish balls are lightly fried and then poached in tomato sauce. The dish was created by Raquel Gittler of Mexico City; her husband likes to call it "Gefilte Fish a la Raquelita."

SERVES 4 TO 6

FOR THE FISH BALLS

2 pounds skinless red snapper fillets

2 carrots, peeled and chopped

1 small onion, chopped

1 celery stalk, chopped

2 eggs, lightly beaten

Salt

Freshly ground black pepper

2 teaspoons sugar

¼ cup water

About ¼ cup matzo meal

Vegetable oil for frying

FOR THE SAUCE

2 tablespoons olive oil

1 onion, chopped

2 garlic cloves, chopped

2 red peppers, sliced

1 (28-ounce) can crushed tomatoes

¼ cup chopped fresh flat-leaf parsley

Salt

Freshly ground black pepper

½ teaspoon red pepper flakes

1. Make the gefilte fish: Rinse the fish, pat dry, and slice into 1-inch strips.
2. Place the fish, carrots, onion, and celery in the bowl of a food processor and process until a paste is formed. Transfer to a large mixing bowl. Add the eggs, salt, pepper, sugar, and water. Stir in enough matzo meal to make a soft mixture that will hold its shape when pressed together. Form the mixture into balls about 2 inches in diameter.
3. In a large skillet, add oil to a depth of about ½ inch and heat over medium heat. Fry the fish balls until they are lightly golden on all sides, turning as necessary. Remove with a slotted spoon and drain on paper towels.
4. Make the sauce: In a Dutch oven or other large, heavy pot, heat the olive oil over medium heat. Add the onion and cook, stirring often, until just soft. Add the garlic and the red peppers and cook, stirring occasionally, until the peppers are soft. Add the tomatoes and parsley and season with salt, pepper, and red pepper flakes. (Add a little water to thin the sauce, if desired.) Cover and bring to a boil. Lower the heat and simmer, stirring occasionally, for 10 minutes.
5. Add the fish balls to the sauce, cover, and simmer over low heat for 1 hour. Transfer the fish balls to a large serving platter and ladle the sauce over them. Serve warm or at room temperature.

PESCE ALL'EBRAICA

ITALIAN SWEET-AND-SOUR FISH WITH RAISINS AND PINE NUTS

The Italian cookbooks that have survived from the Middle Ages feature a vast collection of sweet-and-sour combinations, including some recipes in which the sourness of vinegar is balanced by the sweetness of ground prunes and dates. More often, though, vinegar was paired simply with sugar or with both sugar and raisins, as in this preparation, a modern version of an Italian medieval Jewish standard. (The use of raisins and pine nuts indicates its Sicilian, and before that Arab, origins.) In Italy, the fish called triglie *(red mullet) is generally used, but mullet is difficult to find in the United States. Red snapper makes an excellent alternative. Among Italian Jews, this dish is often served to break the Yom Kippur fast, and it's the one I use for that purpose.*

SERVES 4

½ cup pine nuts
½ cup raisins
⅓ cup red wine vinegar
5 tablespoons olive oil
2 tablespoons sugar
½ teaspoon salt
Freshly ground black pepper
1½ pounds red snapper fillets, with skin on
2 tablespoons chopped fresh flat-leaf parsley

1. In a small dry skillet, toast the pine nuts over low heat, stirring, until lightly golden. Place in a medium bowl. Add the raisins, vinegar, 4 tablespoons of the oil, and the sugar and stir to combine. Season with the salt and pepper. Set aside.
2. Rinse the fish and pat it dry. Season with salt and pepper. Heat the remaining 1 tablespoon oil in a large nonstick skillet over medium-high heat. Add the fish, flesh side down, and cook for 3 minutes. Turn the fish and add the sweet-and-sour mixture to the pan. Lower the heat, cover, and simmer until the fish is opaque and flakes easily, about 10 minutes. Transfer the fish to a large serving platter and pour the sauce over it, then sprinkle with the parsley. Serve hot.

MATZO MEAL FISH AND CHIPS

Among the most popular dishes in the nineteenth-century Anglo-Jewish community was batter-dipped fried fish, a legacy of the Jews who had been exiled from Spain in the fifteenth century. Owing to dietary restrictions, they fried the fish in oil rather than lard, which at the time was the common British frying agent. The invention of British fish and chips is generally attributed to a Jewish immigrant from Eastern Europe named Joseph Malin, who in 1860 set up a shop that served batter-dipped oil-fried fish alongside potato "chips," a street food sold by Irish immigrants. Thus an Ashkenazic Jewish immigrant combined a Sephardic Jewish immigrant food with an Irish immigrant food, and so created the British national dish.

In this variety of fish and chips, the fish is dipped in egg and matzo meal. (It comes out especially crunchy.) I've adapted the recipe from one given to me by Alan Conway, the longtime proprietor of the Upper Street Fish Shop in London. Originating in 1910 as a fish-and-chips stand owned by Conway's immigrant grandparents, Hershel and Hannah Kosky, the Upper Street Fish Shop was until its recent closing one of the premier fish-and-chips shops in London.

SERVES 4

2 pounds russet potatoes

Vegetable oil for deep frying

4 skinless cod fillets, each about 8 ounces

Salt

Freshly ground black pepper

2 eggs, lightly beaten, for dredging

Matzo meal for dredging

Malt vinegar or lemon wedges for accompaniment

1. Preheat the oven to 200 degrees. Peel the potatoes and cut them into chips about 3 inches long and ½ inch wide. Place them in a bowl of cold water while the oil is heating.
2. Pour at least 5 inches of the oil into a Dutch oven or other large, heavy pot and heat to 325 degrees on a deep-fry thermometer. Drain the potatoes and pat them dry. In batches, place the potatoes in the oil and cook until they are soft but not yet colored, about 3 minutes. Remove with a slotted spoon and drain on paper towels.
3. Raise the oil temperature to 375 degrees. Meanwhile, rinse the fish fillets and pat them dry. Slice in half crosswise and season with salt and pepper.

4. Place the eggs in a bowl and spread some matzo meal on a plate. In small batches, dredge the fish first in the egg and then in the matzo meal, shaking off any excess. Carefully place the pieces of fish in the oil and cook to a deep golden brown, about 8 minutes. Remove with a slotted spoon and drain on paper towels. Sprinkle with salt, transfer to a baking sheet, and keep warm in the preheated oven. Dredge and fry remaining fish in the same way.

5. In batches, return the potatoes to the hot oil and fry until golden brown and crispy, 4 to 5 minutes. Remove with a slotted spoon and drain on paper towels. Sprinkle with salt.

6. Transfer the fish and chips to a large serving platter. Serve hot, with malt vinegar or lemon wedges.

MASLI CHA KANJI

BOMBAY CURRIED FISH

Among the Bene Israel Jews of Bombay, the fish most often used for this wonderfully aromatic dish is pomfret, *known in the United States as pompano. Good pompano is not readily available in most places, so Dr. Zimra Israel, an immunologist who lives in New York City, replaces it with salmon. Curry leaves and tamarind concentrate can be purchased in many Indian groceries. This fish is especially good when served on top of* Jeera Bahat *(page 281).*

SERVES 4

- 2 pounds salmon fillet, skinned
- Salt
- 3 tablespoons olive oil
- 1 teaspoon cumin seeds
- 5 curry leaves
- 1 teaspoon garlic paste or finely chopped garlic
- ½ teaspoon turmeric
- 1½ teaspoons red chili paste
- 1 cup water
- 1 teaspoon tamarind concentrate
- 2 tablespoons chopped tomato
- 1 tablespoon brown sugar

1. Rinse the fish and pat it dry. Season lightly with salt and cut it into 2-inch cubes. Set aside.
2. In a large skillet, heat the oil over medium heat. Add the cumin seeds, curry leaves, garlic paste, turmeric, and red chili paste and cook, stirring regularly, for 3 minutes. Add the water, tamarind concentrate, tomato, brown sugar, and salt. Cover and bring to a boil. Lower the heat and simmer for 5 minutes.
3. Add the fish pieces to the pan. Cover and simmer until cooked through, about 10 minutes. Transfer the fish to a serving platter and pour the sauce over it. Serve hot.

COMMUNITIES: Rome

In Rome, of course, the Colosseum is the attraction that draws the tourists (and gets the starring roles in Hollywood movies), but directly next to it stands a monument that is fascinating in its own right: the Arch of Titus. Among the best preserved of all Roman ruins, this ornate marble structure features a huge plaque commemorating the military triumphs of the emperors Titus and Vespasian. If you look on the underside of the arch, though, you'll notice something unusual there: a bas-relief of a menorah. Look a little more closely and you'll see that the menorah is being borne aloft on the backs of Jewish slaves transported to Rome after the fall of Jerusalem in the year 70. It's just one of the many unexpected reminders around the city of the Jewish presence in Rome. Indeed, though Rome is firmly associated in the public mind with Catholicism, it is also the site of the oldest Jewish community in the Western world.

The first Jews likely arrived in Rome in the second century B.C.E., as envoys sent by Judah Maccabee to negotiate a treaty between Rome and Judea against their shared enemy of Seleucia. A Jewish community soon began to arise there, primarily composed of merchants from nearby Greece and Alexandria and, later, freed Judean slaves. As the Roman Republic gave way to the Empire, Julius Caesar established freedom of worship and exempted Jews from military service. Though later emperors proved to be not so favorably disposed toward the Jews—Tiberius, for example, briefly banned them from the city, and Hadrian outlawed circumcision—in general the Jewish community prospered, and in the year 212 Caracalla granted Jews full Roman citizenship. Exactly one century later, however, things took a decided turn for the worse, when Emperor Constantine decreed that Christianity would become the state religion, replacing the earlier forms of pagan worship. Thus began what would be, with brief periods of respite, fifteen centuries of institutionalized discrimination against the Jews of Rome. (In the eleventh century, to take just one example, Jews were forced to wear a conical hat designed to make them immediately recognizable and, in the thirteenth century—in an eerie prefiguring of the Nazi period—yellow identification badges.)

As with so many others, the Jewish community of Rome was ineradicably shaped by the Spanish Inquisition, in particular the expulsion edict of 1492. Sicily and southern Italy were under Spanish rule at the time, and with the expulsion the Jews of these areas fled northward. Like all immigrants, voluntary or involuntary, these Jews brought with them their favorite ingredients and recipes for preparing them. Thus were introduced to Rome eggplants and artichokes, as well as the use of raisins and pine nuts in sauces and sweets and the habit of deep frying fish and vegetables in oil, all of which have become central to the very notion of Roman Jewish cookery.

Jews were also arriving from Spain proper, and in smaller numbers from Germany, to escape the rising anti-Semitism there. The sudden and massive emigration of Jews into Italy created severe overcrowding and a deepening sense of crisis, and brought increased demands that Jews be isolated from the rest of the population. The first Jewish ghetto was instituted in Venice in 1516, on the site of what had once been a foundry. (The word is derived from the Venetian word for foundry, *getto.*) Forty years later Pope Paul IV decreed that all Jews living in the papal states would have to live in ghettoes, and so the Roman Jewish Ghetto was established on a low, marshy patch of land on the banks of the Tiber River. There lived the Jews of Rome for the next 300 years, behind high walls and five gates that shut each evening at sundown.

Though every Italian ghetto was wretched, Rome's, it is generally agreed, was the worst. Thousands of people were jammed into a scant seven acres regularly subject to flooding by the Tiber. The narrow, crooked streets were crowded by shabby stone houses, atop of which were jerry-built newer wood and metal structures. As the decades passed the houses rose ever higher and more precarious, up to six or seven stories, because there was nowhere for the expanding population to go but up. (During the time of the Ghetto, the Jewish community grew from 1,750 to perhaps 7,000.) Those who could worked as peddlers, rag sellers, secondhand dealers, and in the few other trades Jews were permitted to pursue. Desperately poor and without land of their own, the Jewish population was compelled to make their diet from whatever meager foodstuffs they could afford to buy. They ate lots of vegetables, thriftily using all of the parts (one well-known recipe was for braised spinach stems); chickpeas and broken bits of pasta that were put into soup; dried sausages made from odd cuts of beef; inexpensive varieties of fish such as cod and anchovies, and the roe from tuna and mullet. The cheapest and simplest preparation of all was frying, and the Jews of the Ghetto drew on this ancient method as the mainstay of their cookery. All through the Ghetto vendors known as *friggitori* operated large vats of hot oil, frying up in a thin batter bits of cod and vegetables that were too small, misshapen, or otherwise undesirable to be sold elsewhere.

The Ghetto was finally abolished in 1870, and Jews permitted to live throughout the city. Still, many continued to live in the Ghetto, and in 1904 this was where Rome's grandest synagogue was built. Tragically, the Ghetto was also the site of the Nazi raid of October 16, 1943, when its Jewish residents were seized and shipped to Auschwitz. Of the nearly 1,300 Jews taken by the Nazis that day, only 21 (20 men and 1 woman) ever came home. More than 10,000 Roman Jews went into exile or into hiding, in monasteries, farmhouses, city apartments, moving constantly from place to place. With the courageous assistance of many Italian anti-fascists, the vast majority of them managed to survive the Holocaust.

When the war was over, as the city's Jewish community (which today numbers about 15,000) began to reconstitute itself, the Ghetto became the focal point of community life. Though it is no longer primarily a Jewish neighborhood, the Ghetto features a number of shops selling Jewish-oriented crafts, books, and foods. Of the latter, by far the most venerable is the Pasticceria Il Boccione, on the Via Portico d'Ottavia. The bakery, which has been open for more than 200 years, offers a wide variety of treats, from macaroons and biscotti to the roasted pumpkin seeds called *bruscollini,* but it is especially known for two items: *pizza ebraica,* a dense, chewy pastry chock-filled with raisins, pine nuts, almonds, and candied fruit (see page 339); and a delectable, moist ricotta torte (served whole or in slices) flavored with either chocolate or sour cherries. Down the block is a very good kosher pizzeria, nearby is a kosher wine store, and two kosher restaurants have recently opened up, the first ones in the city for several decades.

The backbone of the restaurant's menus are modern renditions of those makeshift dishes ingeniously created out of want. Along with the classic stewed salt cod and deep-fried battered vegetables, for instance, there is also *concia*, thin slices of zucchini that are fried in oil and then marinated in vinegar, garlic, and fresh herbs. Those of a hardier disposition may prefer *indivia in salsa di alici*, which is bitter curly endive (also known as chicory) in a very pungent anchovy sauce, and perhaps the best example, at least culinarily, of the challenges of Ghetto life.

Meat, especially beef, was an extreme luxury in the Ghetto, served only on holidays, Sabbaths, or other celebratory occasions. Even then, the only beef that was available, due to cost and the laws of *kashrut*, was from the toughest cuts on the steer. Thus was born the Roman dish known as *straccato* (literally, overcooked), a beef roast stewed for hours with red wine and tomatoes, sort of the Italian version of an Ashkenazic brisket. When it's finished, the *straccato* also yields an aromatic liquid that can double as a sauce for the pasta course—a thrifty savings of both time and expense. (For meat meals, when grated cheese was not an option, Roman Jews would fry bread crumbs very quickly in oil and garlic until crisp and golden, a perfect topping for tomato sauce.) Another special Roman Jewish beef delicacy is tongue, braised whole and spiked with cloves, as is done elsewhere with ham.

These days some diners eschew beef dishes, owing to the mad cow scare in Italy (and especially so the Ghetto specialty of fried cow brains), but continue to feast on venerable Jewish foods such as pasta topped with vegetables and salty slices of mullet roe, sweet-and-sour fish with pine nuts and raisins (see page 91), and of course, the star of the show, *Carciofi alla Giudia:* fried artichokes in the Jewish style (pages 245–246). *Carciofi alla Giudia*, the very emblem of Ghetto life, has over the years become the most famous and beloved dish in all of Rome, served in restaurants everywhere. It is another example—happier, this one, than the Arch of Titus—of the ineradicable Jewish presence in the city.

BACCALÀ IN UMIDO ALLA ROMANA

ITALIAN SALT COD STEWED IN TOMATO SAUCE WITH RAISINS AND PINE NUTS

This is a family recipe given to me by Bruna Tedeschi, a distinguished member of the Roman Jewish community who often gives cooking classes at the offices of ADEI-WIZO (Associazione Donne Ebree d'Italia), the Italian Jewish women's organization. The preparation is made distinctly Roman by the addition of pine nuts and raisins to the sauce. As with many savory Roman Jewish dishes, cinnamon is added as a flavoring. Often the cod is served with roast potatoes on the side.

SERVES 6

- 2 pounds dried salt cod
- 2 tablespoons olive oil, plus more for frying
- 1 onion, sliced
- 1 (28-ounce) can chopped tomatoes
- 2 tablespoons chopped fresh basil
- ½ teaspoon ground cinnamon
- Salt
- Freshly ground black pepper
- Flour for dredging
- ½ cup raisins
- ¼ cup pine nuts

1. Soak the salt cod in cold water to cover for 36 to 48 hours, changing the water at least 3 times per day. Drain the cod, pat dry, and remove any bones. Cut the cod into 2-inch pieces and set aside.
2. Heat the 2 tablespoons oil in a large skillet over medium heat. Add the onion and cook, stirring often, until soft and lightly colored. Add the tomatoes, basil, and cinnamon, and season with salt and pepper. Simmer over low heat for 15 minutes.
3. Spread some flour on a plate and season it with salt and pepper. Dip the cod pieces in the flour on both sides to coat evenly, shaking off any excess.
4. In another large pan, add oil to a depth of about ¼ inch and heat over medium-high heat. In batches, add the cod pieces to the pan and fry until golden brown on both sides, about 3 minutes on each side. Remove with a slotted spoon and drain on paper towels.
5. Add the cod to the simmering tomato sauce, along with the raisins and pine nuts. Cover and simmer over medium-low heat until the cod is tender and cooked through, 15 to 20 minutes. (Add a bit of water if the sauce seems too thick.) Taste the sauce and adjust for seasoning. Transfer the fish to a large serving platter and pour the sauce over it. Serve hot.

HRAIMI

FISH IN SPICY GARLIC AND PEPPER SAUCE

Hraimi *is very popular among Jews of North African descent, but probably no more so than among those from Libya, where it was often served at holiday and Shabbat meals. This recipe comes from Vivienne Roumani-Denn, the executive director of the American Sephardi Federation in New York, who was born and raised in Benghazi, Libya, and came to the United States in 1962. For a spicier version, do not remove the veins of the chilies.*

SERVES 4

- 3 tablespoons olive oil
- 1½ cups water
- Juice of 1 lemon
- 2 tablespoons tomato paste
- ½ teaspoon salt
- 5 garlic cloves, finely chopped
- 1 teaspoon ground cumin
- 2 tablespoons minced, seeded, and deveined red or green chili pepper
- 1½ pounds white-fleshed fish fillets, such as sole or red snapper
- Lemon wedges for accompaniment

1. Heat the oil in a large skillet over low heat. In a small bowl, mix together ½ cup of the water, the lemon juice, tomato paste, salt, garlic, cumin, and chili pepper and add it to the pan. Simmer the mixture over low heat for 10 minutes.
2. Add the remaining 1 cup of water and stir to combine, then add the fish. Cover and bring to a boil. Reduce the heat to low and simmer until the fish is cooked through, about 10 minutes. Transfer the fish to a serving platter and pour the sauce over it. Serve hot with the lemon wedges.

PSARI STO FOURNO

GREEK FISH WITH TOMATOES AND GREEN PEPPER

This dish comes from the Greek town of Volos, which is on the eastern seacoast midway between Salonika and Athens. The recipe was given to me by Paulette Nehama of Bethesda, Maryland, who left Volos for the United States in 1958. (The recipe originates with Paulette's mother, Thalia Levy Mourtzoucos.) The Jewish community in Volos dates to the fifth century. Before the Holocaust, more than 1,000 Jews lived in Volos. Today there are fewer than 200, but the community is still intact, and the town's synagogue continues to function.

SERVES 4

- 1½ to 2 pounds cod or halibut fillets
- Salt
- Freshly ground black pepper
- Juice of ½ lemon
- ¼ cup olive oil
- ½ cup dry white wine
- 2 tomatoes, chopped
- 1 green pepper, chopped
- 3 scallions, white and pale green parts only, chopped
- 1 garlic clove, chopped (optional)
- 1 tablespoon chopped fresh flat-leaf parsley

1. Preheat the oven to 350 degrees. Lightly oil a baking dish.
2. Rinse the fish and pat it dry. Season the fish with salt and pepper, drizzle it with the lemon juice, and place it in the baking dish.
3. In a medium bowl, mix together the oil, wine, tomatoes, green pepper, scallions, and the garlic (if using). Season with salt and pepper. Pour the mixture over the fish. Sprinkle with the parsley.
4. Cover loosely with foil and bake for 20 minutes. Remove the foil and bake until the fish is cooked through, 5 to 10 minutes more. Transfer the fish to a large serving platter and spoon the vegetables and sauce over it. Serve warm or at room temperature.

PEIXE BAHIANA

BRAZILIAN FISH WITH TOMATOES, COCONUT MILK, AND CILANTRO

Rosy Harari, who now lives and works in New York City, was born in Egypt. Like thousands of Egypt's Jews, her family left Egypt after the Suez War of 1956, in which Israel sided with France and England against Egypt. Anti-Semitism, which had been on the rise in Egypt since Israel's 1948 defeat of the Arab armies, grew considerably worse, and many British, French, and Jewish families had their assets seized by the state. Others were simply expelled. Rosy Harari's family stayed briefly in France before emigrating to Brazil. There they discovered a popular dish of shrimp cooked in a rich sauce of tomatoes and coconut milk, flavored with fresh cilantro. Rosy's mother, Berthe Harari, adapted the recipe to conform to Jewish dietary laws.

SERVES 4

- 2 tablespoons olive oil
- 1 large onion, chopped
- 3 garlic cloves, chopped
- 1 (28-ounce) can crushed tomatoes
- Salt
- Freshly ground black pepper
- Red pepper flakes
- 1½ pounds skinless red snapper fillet, or other skinless firm, white-fleshed fish, cut into 1-inch cubes
- 1¼ cups unsweetened coconut milk
- ½ cup chopped fresh cilantro

1. In a large skillet, heat the oil over medium heat. Add the onion and cook, stirring often, until soft and translucent. Add the garlic and cook for 1 minute. Add the tomatoes and seasonings to taste. Cover and bring to a boil. Lower the heat and simmer for 30 minutes.
2. While the sauce cooks, rinse the fish and pat it dry. Season lightly with salt and pepper. Add the fish to the pan and cover gently with the tomato sauce, making sure not to break up the fish. (Add a bit more water if the sauce seems too thick.) Simmer for 10 minutes, or until the fish is nearly cooked through. Stir in the coconut milk and cilantro and simmer for 5 minutes. Transfer the fish to a large serving platter and pour the sauce over it. Serve hot.

Eggs and Dairy

In the beginning, at least, meat and milk were served together. In Genesis 18, we are informed that Abraham "took curd, and milk, and the calf which he had dressed, and set it before" his guests. Not until later, in Exodus and Deuteronomy, is there mention of any prohibition on the mixing of milk and meat—specifically, an injunction not to seethe a calf in its mother's milk, which was interpreted by later rabbis to be a general prohibition on the practice.

Since then, of course, the separation of meat and dairy products has become one of the genuinely defining aspects of Jewish food around the world and has led to the creation of a vast array of dishes based on the use of dairy products. These dishes may exclude that venerable luxury item, meat, but for the food of austerity and hardship one need turn elsewhere. Indeed, many of them are among the richest and most luscious of any made in the Jewish kitchen, involving, as they do, cheese, butter, sour cream, and eggs. (According to the kosher laws, eggs are neither meat nor milk, and they appear in a host of Jewish meat dishes; when they are among the featured ingredients in a dish, though—as, for instance, in the Sephardic *fritada* [see page 109] or the Alsatian onion tart [see page 116]—it is almost always as part of a dairy meal.)

It's well worth noting that all of the selections in this chapter are perfect for breakfast or brunch. The day has surely gotten off on the right foot when it starts with, say, lox and eggs and onions, cheese blintzes, or challah French toast. But as it happens, I first learned to love lox and eggs and onions at family dinners, and just about any of the other dishes here are likewise delicious at any meal, at any time of the day or night, whenever a bit of luxury seems called for.

INGREDIENTS: Eggs

At least as far as Jewish cooking is concerned, the time-honored conundrum has a ready answer: The egg came before the chicken. Unlike eggs, chickens are not mentioned in the Bible; although they were around Egypt at the time, those chickens seem to have been rather scrawny creatures, kept mainly for ceremonial purposes. Varieties of fowl were often to be found on the tables of Egyptians of all castes, but they included virtually every species *except* chicken, from goose, duck, and quail to pheasant, pigeon, and pelican.

Eggs, on the other hand, have always been exceedingly important to Jews, not just gastronomically but symbolically as well. Because of its round shape the egg has come to represent the cycle of life in many of the world's cultures, and in Jewish lore eggs can symbolize either life or death. Thus, raw (living) eggs have traditionally been eaten by newlywed women, to ensure fertility; cooked (dead) eggs are eaten after funerals and on the ninth day of the Hebrew month of Av, the date commemorating the destruction of the Second Temple. According to historian Miguel-Ángel Motis Dolader, during the Middle Ages many Sephardic Jews in Mediterranean communities ate only milk and eggs in the first week of mourning. On Passover, a roasted egg (*betzah*) is included among the foods on the Seder plate; the egg symbolizes not just the destroyed Temple in Jerusalem, but also the rebirth of the Jewish people after their Egyptian bondage. Here the egg invokes the idea of resurrection, much as the Easter egg does, and indeed in parts of Eastern Europe during the Middle Ages Jewish children were given colored eggs on Passover.

It's not hard to understand why eggs would be such an important foodstuff for Jewish peasants from Ternopol to Tunis: They are an efficient source of protein, and like milk, are regularly replenished for the farmer—for the cost, quite literally, of chicken feed. Also, according to the dictates of *kashrut*, the kosher dietary laws, eggs are *pareve*—neither meat nor dairy—and as a result can be included as part of any meal. (The egg, though, must be carefully checked before use, for if it contains even a single blood spot it has to be discarded.)

Why eggs are indispensable for cooking, Jewish or otherwise, is a somewhat more complicated matter. Essentially, it comes down to the fact that an egg is really two foods in one (it is, after all, the only food commonly separated into constituent parts before using). The yolk of an egg is less than half water, and almost one third of it is fat; an egg white, on the other hand, is nearly 90 percent water, the rest being almost entirely protein, with virtually no fat.

Because they have such different compositions, the two parts of the egg perform distinct but extremely useful functions in cooking. The yolk is the world's best emulsifier, perfect for keeping sauces from separating (or "breaking," in cooking parlance); yolks also add color, flavor, and texture to foods, such as with challah, where they help to give the bread its golden color and soft crumb, as well as the shiny glaze on the crust. As for the white of the egg, when it is beaten its proteins link together loosely around air bubbles. During baking these bubbles expand and then set, creating an interlocked network of tiny air pockets encased by hardened egg protein. In cakes, these air bubbles impart a decidedly light texture, a quality never more important than on Passover, when Jewish bakers, forbidden the use of yeast for leavening, rely on beaten egg whites to provide airiness for their sponge cakes (see pages 324–327).

When heated, the proteins in an egg—both the yolk and the white—also serve as a binding agent for the ingredients around them. This is why a bit of beaten egg is often dabbed along the edges of turnovers before they are sealed, and why eggs are also found in most kugels, to help them hold together during cooking. The same principle is at work with Potato Latkes (page 241), which may or may not contain flour or baking powder, but never fail to contain egg.

Combined with lemon, beaten eggs impart a thick, creamy texture to a popular Sephardic soup known as *sopa de huevo y limón* (called *avgolemono* by Greek Jews), often used to break the Yom Kippur fast. The two ingredients are also combined in an egg-and-lemon sauce, native to Greece and Turkey, that is poured over poached fish. Among

Sephardic Jews the long-cooked eggs known, from the Ladino, as *huevos haminados* (*beid hamine* in Arabic), are a staple ingredient of Sabbath stews and appear at virtually all community functions from seders to funerals (see page 110).

In Ashkenazic cooking, perhaps the most widespread use of eggs was in the aforementioned kugel, challah, and latkes, and in the egg noodles that were a staple of many households. Hard-boiled eggs were chopped up and mixed with beets or fried onions, and appeared in a variety of borscht made in Lithuania. In this regard, it should also be recalled that a tradition in medieval Germany was to give a child, on his first day of school, a hard-boiled egg with joyful religious inscriptions written on its shell. The egg is a reminder to us of the fullness of life, and its fragility.

SHAKSHUKA

TUNISIAN EGGS IN TOMATO SAUCE

In this traditional dish, tomato sauce is simmered with spices, forming a soft bed in which eggs are gently poached. With slices of warm pita bread, it's perfect for brunch. Just don't overcrowd the pan with too many eggs; to double the recipe, use two pans.

SERVES 2

4 large tomatoes

½ teaspoon paprika

½ teaspoon ground cumin

2 teaspoons finely chopped, seeded, and deveined jalapeño pepper, or to taste

Salt

1 tablespoon olive oil

4 eggs

1 tablespoon chopped fresh flat-leaf parsley

1. With a paring knife, core the tomatoes. Grate the tomatoes, using the coarse side of a box grater or a food processor equipped with a shredding disk. In a medium bowl, combine the grated tomatoes with the paprika, cumin, jalapeño pepper, and salt and mix well.
2. Heat the oil in a large, heavy skillet over medium-high heat. Add the tomato mixture and bring to a boil. Lower the heat and simmer gently for 5 minutes.
3. Carefully crack the eggs into the sauce and cook until they reach the desired consistency.
4. With a slotted spoon, transfer the eggs to a large serving plate and pour the sauce around them. Sprinkle with the parsley. Serve hot, with pita bread.

FRITADA DE TOMAT

TOMATO AND CHEESE FRITTATA

Fritada *is one of the mainstays of the Sephardic* desayuno, *the meal served on Saturday after morning services, but it is often made as a main dish for any type of dairy meal, including breakfast, lunch, and dinner. I've adapted this from a recipe in* Sefarad Yemekleri *(Sephardic Food), a cookbook published by the Jewish community of Istanbul.*

SERVES 8

- 8 eggs, lightly beaten
- 1¾ pounds tomatoes, seeded and chopped
- 4 slices country white bread, crusts removed, soaked briefly in water and squeezed dry, then crumbled
- ½ cup chopped fresh flat-leaf parsley
- 1 cup (about 8 ounces) firmly packed grated mild cheese, such as kashkaval or Muenster
- ½ cup (about 3 ounces) grated Parmesan cheese
- Salt
- Freshly ground black pepper

1. Preheat the oven to 375 degrees. Generously butter a 13- by 9-inch baking dish.
2. In a large bowl, mix together the eggs, tomatoes, bread, parsley, half of the mild cheese, and the Parmesan. Season with salt and pepper. Pour the mixture into the prepared baking dish and smooth the top. Sprinkle the remaining ½ cup cheese over the top.
3. Bake until the *fritada* has set and the top is golden brown, 25 to 30 minutes. Let cool slightly, then serve warm.

HUEVOS HAMINADOS

LONG-COOKED EGGS

The long-cooked eggs known from the Ladino as huevos haminados *are a genuinely distinctive feature of Sephardic cooking, one that seems to be found in no other cuisine. The eggs emerge from their long, slow cooking with creamy yolks and lovely brown-colored whites. (Onion skins and coffee grounds are often added to intensify the color, which make the inside of the pot look something like a compost pile.) In Jewish tradition, eggs can symbolize either life or death, and as such* huevos haminados *are eaten at nearly all of the important events of the Sephardic life cycle, from births to funerals, as well as on holidays including Passover, Yom Kippur, and Purim. They are also a fixture of the Sabbath breakfast.*

SERVES 6

Dry brown skins from 6 onions

2 tablespoons ground coffee

6 eggs, in their shells

1 teaspoon salt

3 tablespoons oil

1. Preheat the oven to 225 degrees.
2. Scatter the onion skins and coffee grounds over the bottom of a Dutch oven or other large, heavy pot with a tight-fitting cover. Add the eggs and cover with cold water by at least 2 inches. Season the water with the salt. Cover the pot and bring to a boil. Drizzle the oil over the surface of the water, to prevent evaporation. Cover the pot.
3. Place the tightly covered pot in the oven and bake for 8 to 12 hours. Serve the eggs warm or at room temperature.

DISHES: Lox

This is the strange truth of the modern American brunch: On any given Sunday morning, the majority of people who purchase "lox" to accompany their bagels and cream cheese are not, in fact, getting lox. They may ask for lox, and the product may even be labeled as lox, but what they are getting, instead, is smoked salmon. These days, sales of lox—salmon long cured in a salt brine—compared to those of smoked salmon are astonishingly low. Mark Russ Federman, the owner of Russ & Daughters, New York's premier appetizing store, estimates that lox accounts for only 15 to 20 percent of his salmon sales, which is actually a far higher number than it is in most retail outlets. This is attested to by the smokehouses that process and sell cured salmon to supermarkets and bagel stores everywhere. At Banner Smoked Fish of Coney Island, for instance, lox sales total only about 5 percent of those for smoked salmon. At Acme Smoked Fish in Williamsburg, Brooklyn, the largest smoked-fish house in the continental United States, the percentage is lower still; on average, Acme will sell some 25 to 30,000 pounds of smoked salmon a week, while sales of lox might not exceed 1,000 pounds.

The reason for this, quite simply, is changing American tastes. "It's not just lox," says Avi Attias, the owner of Banner Smoked Fish. "Everything that's salty is going down." The smoked-fish trade is rife with stories of customers who order a shipment of "lox" and then, having received it, send it back, complaining that it's too salty. This is why smokehouses will commonly double-check a lox order, making sure that the customer really means lox, rather than the milder-tasting smoked salmon. According to the saying that is widespread in the business, "You can't get lox without a note from your mother."

Lox and smoked salmon are both examples of what is known as cured fish. "Curing" a fish—like curing meat or cheese or any other foodstuff—means to treat it for the purposes of preservation. This can be done by any one of several methods (or a combination of methods), including pickling, smoking, and salting. In salt curing, the fish is packed in salt or, alternatively, submerged in a salty brine. The salt kills potentially harmful bacteria and also absorbs the moisture in which bacteria grow, resulting in a product that can be safely preserved for long periods of time without refrigeration. In smoke curing, the fish is subjected to several hours of wood smoke, which deposits certain tarry substances on the surface of the fish; like salting, the smoking process kills bacteria, while also creating an impermeable seal on the fish that reduces exposure to air, which can cause rancidity in fats. This is especially useful for fattier foods (bacon, for instance, or oily fish such as herring), but as a rule smoking is a less-efficient preservation technique and is usually performed in conjunction with another curing method.

Exactly when Jews first began to cure fish is not known, but the place of origin was likely medieval Germany, where the curing of fish had long been practiced. With the eastward migration of the late Middle Ages, the Jews carried their techniques for smoking and salting fish to Eastern Europe. There, as elsewhere around the world, Jews were prodigious fish-eaters, as fish is considered *pareve* and so can be eaten with either meat or dairy products. Smoked and salted fish were especially popular, because they were not cooked and thus, said the rabbis, permissable to eat even if prepared by non-Jews. (Salmon, by the way, was too expensive for most East European Jews; herring and carp were the staple fish.) The late nineteenth century brought the mass immigration from Eastern Europe, and Jews began to establish fish-smoking establishments in the West: in London (as, for example, the illustrious smokehouse H. Foreman & Son, founded in 1905 by a Russian Jewish immigrant and still operating in the East End), and especially in New York. The original New York smokers had been German, but by the end of World War I the business had become, for all intents and purposes, a Jewish one.

Herring continued to be an extremely popular food item among Jews in the New World (at least for another generation or two), but now it was supplemented by salmon, which in the United States was comparatively cheap and plentiful. In those days all salmon were caught in the wild, and then shipped from the place of capture by train. Refrigeration had not yet been invented, and so the salmon were packed in salt to preserve them during the long train ride. This heavily salted salmon—known in Yiddish as *lox*, from the German word for salmon, *Lachs*—remained pretty much the only game in town until the 1940s, when the advent of large-scale refrigeration rendered salting unnecessary, thus paving the way for the introduction of smoked salmon.

Lox is sometimes referred to as a variety of smoked salmon (as smoked salmon is sometimes known by the generic term "lox"), but this is a mistake, for no smoke is used to make lox. Instead, the salmon is immersed in a salt brine—just salt and water, nothing else—for anywhere from three to six months, after which the fish is removed and then briefly washed to remove any excess salt. This is the entire process. At no point is the salmon subjected to any smoking, any drying, or indeed any heating at all. (Mark Federman of Russ & Daughters likes to refer to lox as "Jewish sushi.")

In the old days, the lox came either from wild Pacific salmon or wild salmon caught in the waters off Nova Scotia or the nearby Gaspé Peninsula in Quebec. Today wild Atlantic salmon is virtually extinct, and Atlantic salmon comes instead from vast fish farms, most of them in Norway and Chile, with others in the Faeroe Islands, near Scotland. (Though Chile borders the Pacific Ocean, its salmon came originally from Norway, and so is considered Atlantic.) Farm-raised Atlantic salmon are richer and fattier than their wild counterparts, which makes sense, given their comparatively sedentary lifestyle (no swimming upstream to spawn, and so forth). Wild Pacific salmon, most of which come from Alaska, tend to have a stronger taste and a firmer texture, although paradoxically enough, they create a softer lox, for reasons that no one in the business can fully explain.

While the term "Nova" originally referred to lox, today it most often refers to smoked salmon, which is testament to the dramatic shifts that have taken place in the appetizing case. Nowadays, Nova refers not to a type of fish, but rather to a type of smoking, one that has been tailored to the tastes of New York consumers. Says Buzz

Billik, vice president of sales at Acme, "There are pockets in the Midwest and the West Coast that enjoy heavier smoke in the product, but this isn't a New York taste preference. Here they like it lightly salted, lightly smoked."

At Acme, the fourth generation of the founding family is now working in the company, and, as it happens, this is true at Russ & Daughters as well. The smoked-fish trade is going strong, and its New York outposts seem to be assured of at least another generation's span. Whether, at the end of that time, they will still be producing and selling lox is anybody's guess.

LOX AND EGGS AND ONIONS

When I was in high school, my mother announced that she was going back to work and would no longer make our family's dinner every night. Each of the five of us would now make dinner one night a week. My mother chose Monday night, when she would serve the gourmet dishes she had prepared the day before. In those days I tended to make dishes with ingredients like tempeh and miso, while my younger brother and sister leaned toward simple dishes like stir-fries and pasta. As for my father, he knew how to make only one dish: lox and eggs and onions. And so for some three years, until I left for college, I ate lox and eggs and onions every Tuesday night, and never grew tired of it.

SERVES 4

- 3 tablespoons vegetable oil
- 3 onions, halved and thinly sliced
- 8 eggs, well beaten
- Freshly ground black pepper
- ¼ pound lox, chopped
- Toasted rye bread or bagels for accompaniment

1. In a large nonstick skillet, heat the oil over medium-low heat. Add the onions and cook, stirring occasionally, until they are golden brown, about 30 minutes.
2. Pour the eggs over the onions. Season with pepper. Continue cooking over medium-low heat, stirring regularly and scraping the bottom of the pan with a rubber spatula, until the eggs have nearly set, about 7 minutes. Stir in the lox and cook until the eggs have reached the desired consistency. Serve hot, with slices of rye toast or bagels.

TARTE À L'OIGNON

ALSATIAN ONION TART

Onion tart is a favorite among Alsatian Jews, for whom kosher laws forbid the region's ham-and-cheese-filled quiche Lorraine. This wonderfully sweet and creamy tart—the recipe comes from Gilbert Metz of Jackson, Mississippi, who emigrated from Alsace after World War II—requires a bit of advance preparation (the crust can be made the day before), but it's not at all difficult to make, and is unfailingly delicious. I often make two at a time, because one never seems to be enough.

SERVES 6

FOR THE CRUST

1¾ cups unbleached all-purpose flour

12 tablespoons (1½ sticks) cold butter, in pieces

1 egg yolk, lightly beaten

1 teaspoon sugar

½ teaspoon salt

2 to 3 tablespoons milk

FOR THE FILLING

2 tablespoons butter

2 tablespoons olive oil

4 medium onions, 1 to 1¼ pounds, thinly sliced

2 teaspoons flour

2 eggs, lightly beaten

½ cup heavy cream

½ cup milk

1. Make the crust: Place the flour, butter, egg yolk, sugar, and salt in the bowl of a food processor. Pulse on and off several times until the ingredients start to blend. Slowly add the milk and process just until a dough ball is formed. Remove the dough and flatten it into a disk. Cover with plastic wrap and refrigerate for 1 hour.
2. On a lightly floured surface, roll the dough into an 11-inch circle. Lightly grease a 9-inch tart pan with a removable bottom and place the dough in the pan, pressing it into the bottom and sides. Trim any excess dough. Prick the bottom of the dough several times with a fork. Cover the dough with aluminum foil and refrigerate for at least 1 hour or overnight.
3. Preheat the oven to 350 degrees.
4. Place the foil-lined crust on a baking sheet. Weigh the dough down with dried beans or pie weights. Bake for 20 minutes. Remove the beans or weights and the foil and bake until the crust is lightly colored, about 10 minutes. Set aside.
5. Make the filling: While the crust is baking, heat the butter and oil in a large skillet over medium-low heat. Add the onions and cook, stirring often, until they are lightly caramelized, about 35 minutes.

Add the flour and cook for another 5 minutes. Remove to a medium bowl and let cool.

6. Raise the oven temperature to 475 degrees. In a large bowl, mix together the eggs, cream, milk, salt, pepper, and nutmeg. Add the onions and stir to combine. Pour the filling into the prebaked crust. Place the tart on the baking sheet and bake for 10 minutes. Lower the heat to 375 degrees and bake until the filling is thick and custardy and lightly browned on top, another 20 to 25 minutes. Remove the sides of the pan and serve hot.

½ teaspoon salt

¼ teaspoon freshly ground black pepper

¼ teaspoon freshly grated nutmeg

CHEESE BLINTZES

Blintzes are of Ukrainian origin, having evolved from the Russian pancakes known as blini. Interestingly, blini are a favorite in Russia during the week leading up to Lent, while blintzes have a long association with the Jewish springtime holiday of Shavuot. Dairy foods are traditionally served on Shavuot (calves, after all, are born in the spring), and blintzes are about as dairy a food as you can get, involving milk, butter, and cheese, not to mention the sour cream topping; moreover, two rolled-up blintzes side by side on a plate are said to resemble the stone tablets Moses brought down from Sinai.

Even with the decline of dairy restaurants, New York is probably still the world capital of blintzes, and for my money the city's best may be found at the Ukrainian restaurant Veselka, in the East Village. This, slightly adapted, is their recipe. For cherry blintzes, use the sour cherry filling on page 122. (The filling also makes a wonderful topping for these cheese blintzes.) For plain cheese blintzes, just dust them with confectioner's sugar and serve with applesauce and sour cream.

MAKES 10

FOR THE PANCAKES

1 cup unbleached all-purpose flour, sifted

1/4 cup sugar

1/4 teaspoon salt

3 eggs

1/2 teaspoon grated lemon zest

1/2 teaspoon vanilla

2 tablespoons Cognac

2 tablespoons butter, melted

1. Make the batter: Place the flour, sugar, and salt in a large mixing bowl. Add the eggs, one at a time, mixing until smooth. Mix in the lemon zest, vanilla, Cognac, and butter. Slowly add the milk and stir until the batter is the consistency of heavy cream. Cover the bowl with plastic wrap and refrigerate for at least 1 hour.
2. Make the filling: Combine all of the filling ingredients in a medium bowl and stir until smooth. Refrigerate for at least 1 hour.
3. Make the blintzes: Heat 1 tablespoon of butter in an 8-inch nonstick skillet over medium heat. Pour in a scant 1/4 cup batter, just enough to cover the bottom when you tilt and swirl the pan. When the pancake starts to look dry and the edges are lightly brown, run a spatula around the edges and gently flip it over. Cook the second

side for just a moment, then turn the pancake out onto wax paper. Continue making pancakes until all the batter has been used. Allow to cool to room temperature.

4. Preheat the oven to 200 degrees.

5. Set out a pancake with the more cooked side facing up on the work surface. Place 2 heaping tablespoons of the filling in the middle of the pancake. Spread the filling thinly over the entire pancake, leaving about a ½-inch border at the edge. Fold the pancake in about 1½ inches on the top and the bottom. Next, roll the pancake sideways, forming a cylinder about 5 inches long. Repeat the process with the remaining pancakes and filling.

6. Heat 1 tablespoon of butter in a large nonstick skillet over medium heat. Place 4 of the blintzes in the pan seam side down and cook until golden brown on both sides, about 2 minutes per side. Remove the blintzes from the pan and place on a baking sheet; place the sheet in the warm oven. Repeat the process with the remaining blintzes. Serve warm.

FOR THE FILLING

1½ pounds farmer's cheese

1 egg

2 tablespoons sugar

Juice and grated zest of 1 lemon

¼ teaspoon vanilla

Butter for frying

HUITLACOCHE BLINTZES

MEXICAN BAKED BLINTZES WITH VEGETABLES AND ROASTED POBLANOS

Talma Scheerson was born in Mexico City and now lives in Irvine, California. Her grandmother Sara taught her how to make these unusual, spicy, delicious blintzes. Sara was a Jewish immigrant from Lithuania; in the early 1930s she sold everything she had, and with the proceeds, bought a single diamond. She hid the diamond in her hair, then put a hat over it and boarded a ship bound for Mexico. From the port of Veracruz she made her way to Mexico City, which is where she lived for the rest of her life. Huitlacoche, *a fungus that forms on ears of corn and produces large, black kernels with a mushroomy sort of flavor, is very popular in Mexico. You can substitute fresh white mushrooms for the* huitlacoche.

MAKES 8

FOR THE PANCAKES

1 cup unbleached all-purpose flour

1½ cups milk

3 eggs, lightly beaten

FOR THE FILLING

4 poblano peppers

1 small red onion, chopped

1½ cups chopped white mushrooms

Salt

½ cup fresh, canned and drained, or thawed frozen corn kernels

½ cup (about 4 ounces) firmly packed grated mild white cheese, such as Monterey Jack or kashkaval

1. Make the batter: Place all of the batter ingredients in a medium bowl and whisk until smooth, or use a standing mixer at low speed. Cover the bowl with plastic wrap and refrigerate for at least 1 hour.
2. Make the filling: Roast the poblano peppers over the gas flame of a stove or under a broiler until the skin is blackened. Place them in a medium bowl and cover with plastic wrap. Let them sit for 10 minutes. Peel, remove the seeds and cores, and chop.
3. Heat 2 tablespoons of butter in a medium skillet over medium heat. Add the red onion and cook, stirring often, until soft and translucent. Add the mushrooms and poblanos, and season with salt. Cook for 3 minutes. Add the corn and cook for another 3 minutes. Remove to a plate.
4. Preheat the oven to 350 degrees. Lightly grease a 9-inch square baking dish.
5. Make the blintzes: Heat 1 tablespoon of butter in an 8-inch nonstick pan over medium-low heat. Pour about ¼ cup of batter into

the pan, just enough to cover the bottom when you tilt and swirl the pan. Cook for a minute or two, until the bottom is golden. Remove the pancake to a plate. Repeat the process to make 8 pancakes, adding butter to the pan if necessary.

6. Place a pancake with the cooked side facing up on the work surface. Place 3 tablespoons of filling in a rectangle shape about 4 inches long toward one side of the pancake, and sprinkle grated cheese over the filling. Fold the top and bottom of the pancake over the filling. Roll up to form a tight cylinder. Place the blintze seam side down in the prepared baking dish. Repeat with the remaining pancakes, filling, and cheese.

7. Brush the blintzes lightly with olive oil and bake until golden, about 25 minutes. Serve hot. If desired, top with sour cream and/or tomato sauce.

Butter for frying

Olive oil for brushing

Sour cream for topping (optional)

Tomato sauce for topping (optional)

VARENIKES

UKRAINIAN DUMPLINGS WITH SOUR CHERRY FILLING

Varenikes are delightful little dumplings from the Ukraine—sort of a first cousin of kreplach—that can be served as a first course, as a main course, or even for breakfast. They take a variety of sweet and savory fillings, including potato, cheese, and fruit. Probably the most popular and well-known one is made from sour cherries. (Fresh sour cherries, common in Northern and Eastern Europe, are very difficult to get in the United States, but canned may be used instead.) This recipe comes from Miriam Weinstein of Manchester, Massachusetts, who learned it from her cousins, Mischa and Sophia, of Kharkov, Ukraine. This happens to be an unusually rich and, therefore, delicious, varenik *dough. If you prefer, you can use low-fat sour cream. (By the way, you may have a bit of cherry filling left over—just enough for topping a bowl of vanilla ice cream.)*

MAKES ABOUT 32

FOR THE FILLING

- 3 cups canned pitted sour cherries, drained and chopped
- ½ cup sugar, or to taste
- 1 tablespoon lemon juice
- 1 tablespoon cornstarch dissolved in ¼ cup water

FOR THE DOUGH

- 2 tablespoons butter, melted and cooled
- 8 ounces sour cream
- 3 eggs
- ¼ teaspoon salt

1. Make the filling: Combine all of the filling ingredients in a medium saucepan. Cover and bring to a boil. Lower the heat, remove the cover, and simmer, stirring occasionally, until the mixture is thick and bubbly, about 10 minutes. Place in a medium bowl and let cool.
2. Make the dough: Place the butter, sour cream, eggs, and salt in a large mixing bowl or the bowl of a standing mixer and mix until well combined. Slowly add the flour and continue mixing until a soft dough is formed. Turn the dough out onto a lightly floured surface and knead just until the dough is smooth and uniform, about 3 minutes, adding flour as necessary to keep it from sticking. Cover the dough with a towel and let rest at room temperature for 30 minutes.
3. Make the *varenikes:* Bring a large pot of salted water to a boil. Divide the dough in half. On a lightly floured surface, roll out each of the dough halves to a thickness of about ¼ inch. With a 3-inch round

cookie cutter or the rim of a glass, cut out rounds. (With your fingers, gently press each dough round out a bit more thinly before filling it.)

4. Place about a teaspoon of the filling in the center of each round. Fold the dough over the filling, making a half-moon shape, and pinch the edges firmly together with the tines of a fork to seal the dough. (If you find that the *varenikes* are getting too soft during the filling process, put them on a baking sheet and place them in the refrigerator for a few minutes to firm up.)

5. In 2 batches, drop the *varenikes* into the boiling water and cook, stirring occasionally to prevent them from sticking, until tender, about 9 minutes. Remove with a slotted spoon. Serve hot, topped with sour cream or melted butter.

About 3½ cups unbleached all-purpose flour, sifted

Additional sour cream or melted butter for topping

RICE KNISHES

These unusual and very appealing knishes were once made every Shavuot by Fanny Constantine Pollack in the Ukrainian town of Galvanetskya. Today they are made by her son, Moshe Pollack. Originally Mrs. Pollack made the knishes with a homemade pastry dough, but in later years, living in Montreal, she switched over to frozen puff pastry.

MAKES 14

FOR THE FILLING

2 cups water

1 cup long-grain white rice

½ cup sweetened condensed milk

1 tablespoon butter

¼ teaspoon salt

1 sheet frozen puff pastry dough, fully thawed

1 egg beaten lightly with 1 tablespoon water for egg wash

1. Make the filling: Bring the water to a boil in a medium saucepan. Add the rice, condensed milk, butter, and salt. Cover the pan and reduce the heat to very low. Simmer until the liquid is absorbed and the rice is very soft, 25 to 30 minutes. Transfer to a bowl and let cool completely.
2. Prepare the dough: On a lightly floured surface, roll the puff pastry sheet into a rectangle 14 inches by 10 inches. With a sharp knife or pizza cutter, cut the dough in half lengthwise, creating two rectangles each 14 inches by 5 inches.
3. Preheat the oven to 400 degrees.
4. Make the knishes: Lightly grease a baking sheet or line it with parchment paper. Divide the filling in half, and spread it evenly along the dough. Roll up each dough half from one of its long sides into a long roll, pressing the seams and pinching the ends tight. Press down on top to flatten the rolls slightly. Place the rolls seam side down on the prepared baking sheet and brush the tops with the egg wash.
5. Bake until the dough is golden brown, 20 to 25 minutes. Use a serrated knife to cut the rolls into 2-inch slices. Serve warm or at room temperature.

DEEP-FRIED CHALLAH FRENCH TOAST

The French toast I carry in memory was made at a long-gone restaurant in Great Neck, Long Island, called Peter Pan. The Peter Pan French toast was made from challah, the crusts of which were removed and the bread sliced into thick triangular wedges before being—here is the master stroke—deep fried. My brother, Dan, is similarly haunted by the memory of Peter Pan French toast, and some years ago he and I set out to re-create it. After a good deal of experimentation, we finally found what we had so long sought: a French toast with the power to make the intervening years fall away. Deep fried to a chestnut brown, the outside is crunchy, sweet, and faintly nutty; the inside is a pale, creamy yellow with hints of cinnamon and vanilla. Try it with good maple syrup and sliced fresh fruit on the side.

SERVES 2 TO 4

- 1 medium loaf challah, about 1 pound
- 1 tablespoon sugar
- 1/4 teaspoon ground cinnamon
- 2 eggs
- 1 teaspoon vanilla
- 1/4 teaspoon salt
- 1 cup milk
- Vegetable oil for deep frying
- Confectioners' sugar for dusting

1. Cut the challah in half lengthwise. Cut each length in half crosswise, resulting in 4 equal quarters. Remove the crusts from each quarter, creating large triangular wedges.
2. Combine the sugar and cinnamon in a small bowl. In a large bowl, beat the eggs. Whisk in the cinnamon sugar until fully incorporated. Whisk in the vanilla, salt, and milk.
3. Pour at least 5 inches of oil into a large, heavy pot and heat to 375 degrees on a deep-fry thermometer. Preheat the oven to 200 degrees.
4. Place 2 challah wedges in the egg batter. Soak for 30 seconds, then turn both over and soak the other sides 30 seconds. Remove from the batter, shaking off any excess.
5. Carefully place the wedges in the hot oil. With tongs or a slotted spoon, turn the wedges every 30 seconds or so, until all sides are a deep brown, about 5 minutes.
6. With the tongs or a slotted spoon, remove the wedges from the oil and drain on paper towels. Place on a baking sheet and put in the oven. Repeat the process with the remaining 2 challah wedges. When ready to serve, dust the wedges with confectioners' sugar. Serve warm.

INGREDIENTS: Matzo

Hardship will often inhibit gastronomy, but it need not prevent it entirely. For evidence of this one doesn't have to consult the most extreme cases—say, for instance, the Prussian siege of Paris in 1870, when local chefs helped feed the city by cooking the animals of the zoo. (Parisian menus of that time featured courses such as "fillet of elephant with madeira sauce," "haunch of bear," and "galantine of peacock.") Instead, one can simply reflect on the innumerable Jewish cooks throughout the millennia, who each year manage to produce exquisite dishes made with matzo, certainly as much a food of hardship as any ever created by man.

Matzo, of course, is the flat, crisp, unleavened bread—really more cracker than bread—eaten by Jews at Passover to commemorate the flight of the Israelites from Egyptian bondage, when they could not wait for their bread to rise. Since then the consumption of leavened products has been forbidden to Jews during the seven days of Passover. This arises from an injunction in the Book of Exodus, one so important that it is stated two times in close proximity, first in 12:15 ("Seven days you shall eat unleavened bread") and then again, raising the bar slightly, in 12:19 ("Seven days shall there be no leavened products found in your homes"). Five grains in particular—wheat, barley, rye, oats, and spelt—were explicitly prohibited. In later years Ashkenazic rabbis added so-called lesser grains such as rice, corn, and buckwheat, as well as certain legumes, to the list of prohibited items. (Among Sephardim, whose cuisines are far more dependent on grains and legumes, these are generally considered acceptable.) Still, it is not the grains per se that are problematic, nor even the flour that can be made from them, but rather their capacity to ferment, which leads to leavening. Matzo is made with wheat flour, but it has been deemed religiously permissable because its production is carefully monitored to guard against the possibility of fermentation. In making matzo, no more than eighteen minutes can elapse between the moment that the water is first added to the flour and the moment that the finished matzos are pulled from the oven. In the case of *shmurah* matzo, the handmade matzo eaten by Orthodox Jews, the production has been overseen all the way back from the time, weeks or even months before, when the sheaves of wheat were first gathered in the field, to ensure that they have at no point come into contact with water.

Though itself a rather spartan ingredient, matzo is essential in the preparation of a host of splendid Passover creations, such as, for instance, matzo pie, a main-course dish beloved by Sephardim throughout what was once the Ottoman empire. Generally known as *mina de carne*, matzo pie is something like a meat lasagne, with softened sheets of matzo acting as the layered noodles; in a dairy variation, the *mina* is filled with spinach and feta cheese, a sort of Passover-friendly version of *spanakopita*.

Alternatively, the sheets of matzo can be broken up into small pieces and then briefly softened in water. From there they can be used in a number of ways, such as, to take a sweet example, by combining them with sugar and eggs and then forming the resulting batter into spoonful-sized fritters. The most famous of these are the Sephardic *bimuelos*, the name of which is derived from *bunuelo*, the Spanish word meaning fritter. Most of the year *bimuelos* are made from a yeast-leavened batter, and then deep fried and doused in a citrus-flavored sugar syrup. On Passover, though, such a batter is forbidden, and so the *bimuelos* are made instead from matzo. The matzo fritters called *pizzarelle*, a specialty of Italian Jews, are similar to *bimuelos*, but pine nuts and raisins are added to the batter, and the syrup is made from honey and flavored with cinnamon (see page 334).

Matzo can also be ground into a fine meal, at which point it becomes exceptionally flexible and can serve as a flour replacement in everything from blintzes to chocolate cake and even soufflé, where it combines with oil to make a kind of roux. Among Ashkenazic cooks, matzo meal often serves as a binder in certain kugels, while another very common use is in the little pancakes called *chremslach* (see pages 130–131). Still, as everyone knows, the most common use of all is in the matzo ball (see page 46), a bedrock constituent of Ashkenazic cooking and one of the most potent symbols of Jewish cuisine as a whole. ("Bedrock" happens to be an appropriate description of some of the matzo balls I have consumed.) Long into the twentieth century, matzo balls were known primarily by their Yiddish name, *kneydlekh*, the plural form of *kneydl*, derived from the German *Knödel*, meaning dumpling. The recipe is as ingenious as it is simple: Matzo meal and water make a dough, eggs bind and soften the dough, chicken fat (shmaltz of blessed memory) gives richness, salt and pepper add flavor. For heavier matzo balls, add a bit more meal and cook them for less time; more eggs, on the other hand, will create softer matzo balls.

Probably my own favorite way to use matzo, though, is in the dish of fried matzo known as matzo brei (see page 129). It's not clear just how that name came about, though it is likely Germanic in origin; in certain regions of Eastern Europe the dish was known as *gefrishte matzo*, or "freshened matzo." *Brei* rhymes with dry, which can be a problem when you're working with an ingredient like matzo, so, as with the pie and fritters, the matzo must first be moistened by a brief soaking in hot water. The softened matzo is broken up into small pieces and combined with beaten egg, and the mixture is then fried, ideally in butter, in a hot skillet.

Matzo brei is most often eaten for breakfast, served with jam or syrup or cinnamon sugar, but like many other breakfast specialties, from pancakes to omelettes, there's no need to restrict it to the morning hours alone. Matzo brei can also be made savory, and when it is, it's perfect anytime, a lesson that was proven daily by Anne Rosenzweig, one of New York's distinguished chefs, at her former Upper East Side restaurant the Lobster Club. (Her latest restaurant, Inside, is in Greenwich Village.) With a name like that, of course, the Lobster Club was hardly an outpost of kosher cooking, but it featured matzo brei on both the lunch and dinner menu—and not just during Passover, either, but all year round. Customers could get their matzo brei sweet, by request, but it was almost always served as a savory dish that varied with the season. In the winter, for instance, matzo brei can be served with wild mushrooms; in the spring, with leeks and onions; come summer, with fresh dill and smoked salmon. Thus is splendor wrought from the bread of affliction.

MATZO BREI (FRIED MATZO) WITH ASPARAGUS AND CARAMELIZED ONIONS

In Anne Rosenzweig's matzo brei, the matzo is soft and chewy, but ever so slightly crisp and browned around the edges; it provides a perfect backdrop for the vernal freshness of the asparagus. And caramelized onions add sweet flavor while helping to keep everything moist. This is an innovative matzo brei, to be sure, but it is, at the same time, comfortingly familiar. "People say, 'I grew up eating matzo brei, my mother and grandmother always made it, and it tasted like cardboard,'" Anne says. "I tell them, 'Well, you haven't tasted this *matzo brei.'"*

SERVES 6

- 4 tablespoons (½ stick) butter
- 2 onions, chopped
- 18 asparagus spears, cut into 2-inch pieces
- 12 eggs
- 6 matzos
- Salt
- Freshly ground black pepper

1. Heat 2 tablespoons of the butter in a large skillet over medium-low heat. Add the onions and cook, stirring often, until they are lightly caramelized, about 30 minutes. Remove to a plate.
2. Bring a large pot of salted water to a boil. Add the asparagus and cook until just tender, about 3 minutes. Place briefly in a bowl of ice water to stop the cooking; drain.
3. Place the eggs in a large bowl and beat well. Fill another large bowl with warm water, add the matzos, and soak for 1 minute. Drain well, break into pieces (of about 2 inches), and combine with the beaten eggs. Add the asparagus and onions and stir to combine well. Season with salt and pepper.
4. Place the remaining 2 tablespoons of butter in a large nonstick skillet over medium heat. When the butter begins to sizzle, stir in the matzo-egg mixture. Cook until the matzo is browned and the eggs have set. (For the scrambled version, stir the matzo brei occasionally while it cooks; for the pancake version, let the matzo brei cook undisturbed until browned on the bottom, then flip it and cook the other side until browned.) Serve hot.

COTTAGE CHEESE CHREMSLACH (MATZO MEAL PANCAKES) WITH STRAWBERRY COMPOTE

The Italian name for the thin pasta vermicelli is derived from the Latin term for worm, vermis. *According to Jewish-food historian John Cooper, during the Middle Ages Jewish merchants and rabbinic families brought an ancestor of vermicelli, called* grimseli, *from Italy to Germany. This pasta appears to have been thin strips of dough baked in an oven, then doused with honey. As Jews migrated into Eastern Europe and began speaking Yiddish, the dish evolved, both in its name—which became* chremslach*—and in its preparation, which ceased to mean thin strips of dough and instead referred to fritters or pancakes. Among the Jews of Eastern Europe,* chremslach*—formed into balls or pancakes, baked, fried, or deep fried, but always made with matzo meal—were a staple of Passover season.* Chremslach *could be savory, but most often were sweet, sprinkled with sugar and filled or topped with fresh fruit. In her 1871* Jewish Cookery Book, *Mrs. Esther Levy gave a recipe for "grimslechs" that called for chopped raisins and almonds, apples, currants, brown sugar, nutmeg, cinnamon, fat (half a pound!), lemon rind, and soaked matzos. This almost unimaginably lighter version is made by Selma Cherkas of Worcester, Massachusetts, to whom it had been passed down from family members who emigrated from Riga, Latvia. Top the* chremslach *with applesauce or this simple but lovely strawberry compote.*

SERVES 4 TO 6

FOR THE COMPOTE

3 cups coarsely chopped strawberries (fresh or thawed frozen)

⅓ cup water

1 tablespoon Cointreau or other liqueur (optional)

¼ cup sugar, or to taste

1. Make the compote: Combine the strawberries, water, liqueur (if using), and sugar in a medium saucepan and bring to a boil. Lower the heat and simmer, stirring occasionally, until thickened slightly, about 10 minutes. Set aside and keep warm.
2. Make the batter: Lightly beat the eggs in a large bowl. Add the remaining pancake ingredients and whisk until a uniform batter forms.

3. Preheat the oven to 200 degrees.

4. Make the *chremslach*: Butter a large nonstick skillet or griddle over medium heat. Pour ¼ cup of the batter into the hot skillet or onto the griddle, making a pancake about 4 inches in diameter. Fry until golden brown on both sides. Place on a baking sheet and put the baking sheet in the oven.

5. Repeat until all of the batter has been used, re-buttering the fry surface as necessary to keep the pancakes from sticking. Serve hot, drizzled with the warm strawberry compote.

FOR THE PANCAKES

8 eggs

2 cups cottage cheese

2 cups matzo meal

½ teaspoon salt

2 tablespoons sugar

½ teaspoon ground cinnamon

1½ cups whole milk

Butter for frying

BABANATZA

SWEETENED CORNMEAL SQUARES WITH CHEESE

Traditionally, babanatza *is a Greek sweetened semolina and raisin pudding, poured into a dish and then baked until set. On Passover, crumbled matzos are used in place of the semolina. In Diana Matza's family, though, the* babanatza *was less sweet and made with cornmeal and grated cheese, much like Romanian* Mamaliga *(page 294). Matza is a professor of English at Utica College and the editor of the anthology* Sephardic-American Voices: Two Hundred Years of a Literary Legacy. *Her father's family emigrated to America from the Greek city of Ioannina, and her mother's from Spain by way of the Macedonian city of Bitola, known at the time by the Turkish name of Monastir. This version of* babanatza, *warm and cheesy, is especially good for breakfast.*

SERVES 6 TO 8

8 cups water

2 teaspoons salt

2½ cups yellow cornmeal

¼ cup sugar, or more to taste

1 cup (about 8 ounces) crumbled feta cheese

½ cup (about 4 ounces) firmly packed grated kashkaval (or other mild white cheese such as Gouda or Meunster)

1. Bring the water and salt to a boil in a large saucepan. Slowly pour the cornmeal into the boiling water, whisking vigorously to prevent lumps from forming. Lower the heat and simmer for 30 to 40 minutes, stirring often with a wooden spoon, until the mixture is very thick. Use a spatter guard or a loosely covered lid when not stirring. Add more water if the cornmeal becomes thick too quickly.
2. Preheat the oven to 350 degrees. Butter a 13- by 9-inch baking dish.
3. Add the sugar and feta cheese to the cornmeal and stir to combine. Pour the mixture into the prepared baking dish and sprinkle the grated cheese on top. Bake until the top becomes crisp and lightly browned, about 40 minutes. Let cool until set, at least 20 minutes. (The longer you wait, the more solid the *babanatza* will be.) Cut into squares. Serve warm.

Poultry

Yiddish literature is full of stories of Jewish housewives who bring questionable chickens to the local rabbi—according to the kosher laws, a chicken cannot be eaten if it has blemishes on any internal organs—and anxiously await the rabbi's ruling about whether or not the bird is acceptable. In Eastern Europe a chicken was an exceedingly valuable commodity, for a multitude of reasons, not least of them its role as the centerpiece of most Sabbath and holiday meals. This was a tradition that survived the immigration to America. As the famed Catskills hotel-keeper Jennie Grossinger wrote in *The Art of Jewish Cooking*, "Everyone knows that the classic Friday night meal of Jewish families throughout the world consists of chicken soup, followed by boiled or roast chicken. To serve anything else might almost border on the sacrilegious in the minds of many who have had no other Friday night dinner during their lifetimes."

As Jennie Grossinger indicates, the love of chicken is one that is shared by Jewish communities everywhere, Ashkenazic and Sephardic alike. Chicken is a relatively bland-tasting food, and provides a welcoming base for a variety of rich and flavorful sauces of the sort often found in Sephardic cooking. (This is in marked contrast with Eastern Europe, where chicken was prepared far more austerely, usually just roasted or boiled, and served without much garnish.) In Morocco, for instance, a famous dish pairs chicken with green olives and preserved lemons; the olives are rich and fatty, and the lemons sour and salty, and the combination would not work nearly so well with a meat that provided more of its own distinctive flavor. Chicken is also the centerpiece of *tabeet*, the most splendid dish made by

Iraqi Jews, which consists of a chicken long cooked with rice, and lavishly flavored with an array of fragrant spices. In *chitarnee*, one of the special dishes made by the Baghdadi Jews of Calcutta, the chicken stews in a luxuriantly glossy sweet-and-sour onion sauce.

Roast chicken is a centerpiece of Jewish cooking everywhere around the world, prepared in innumerable styles; it is, to mention just a few especially delectable examples, accompanied with mushrooms in Hungary, with peppers and olives in Italy, and with dried fruit and nuts in Morocco. Each of these dishes, like most of the others in this chapter, was originally intended for the Sabbath or some other festive occasion, but they need not be reserved only for then. A well-made chicken dinner, of the sort beloved by Jews everywhere, is reason alone to be festive.

INGREDIENTS: Chicken

Though a chicken cooking in a Jewish pot now seems about as natural and inevitable as the sun rising in the morning sky (and about as frequent), it might not necessarily have been so. The Bible never mentions chicken, and the dietary laws therein regulating its consumption are ambiguous at best. Unlike the other three categories of animal—fish, mammals, and invertebrates—the Bible cites no characteristics that distinguish kosher from nonkosher birds. Instead, it simply lists twenty-four nonkosher species (among them eagles, vultures, and hawks), the implication being that all other species are to be considered kosher. While this approach sufficed during biblical times, in later centuries the particular species mentioned in the Bible could no longer be definitely identified, and so a number of eminent rabbis attempted to elucidate the features that make any species of bird acceptable or unacceptable for consumption. As has been discussed by Rabbi Ari Zivotofsky in a fascinating article entitled "Is Turkey Kosher?," the first stipulation was that a bird could not be a *dores*, or predatory species. The precise definition of such a species, however, was the subject of impassioned debate: No less authorities than Rashi and Rambam believed that the category should include any bird that holds down its prey with its claws and breaks off pieces to eat. This interpretation was rejected by other rabbis, notes Rabbi Zivotofsky pointedly, "because it would seem to include chickens." Instead, these rabbis asserted that a predator is a bird that ingests its prey while it is still alive. Chickens, though, eat live worms—and have been known to hold them down with their claws—and so the rabbis hastened to add that this does not present a problem, as worms are not to be considered true "animals." Thus were we granted chicken soup and chopped liver.

Although there were chickens in Egypt, they were kept primarily for ceremonial purposes; the preferred poultry of the time included geese, duck, dove, and quail. The Romans, on the other hand, were great lovers of chicken, raising them for fattening on special farms, and it seems likely that this is the period that Jews first began eating chicken. Interestingly enough, the taste for chicken did not survive the fall of the Roman Empire, among Jews or non-Jews. Chickens were not eaten in Europe throughout the Dark Ages; not until the Crusades and the subsequent rise of European cuisine in the twelfth century would chicken again be widely consumed.

Among Jews it was only in the late medieval period, with the migration to Eastern Europe, that chickens would achieve a position of centrality in the cuisine. In Central Europe, geese had been the poultry of choice, but in Eastern Europe it was far more common for rural Jewish families to keep chickens. Chickens were very cheap and easy to raise; unlike geese, they could be kept year round, and, unlike larger animals, they could be slaughtered according to the kosher laws without the necessity of a ritual slaughterer. Indeed, for the Jews of Eastern Europe the chicken came to be rivaled only by the potato as the most important foodstuff, and as such, none of it went to waste. To paraphrase an American Southern expression about (*lehavdil*) pigs, Eastern European Jews used every part of the chicken but the squawk. The chicken's fat, or shmaltz, became the chief frying agent; the skin was rendered into the delicious cracklings known as *gribenes*; the head and feet went into the soup pot to thicken and enrich the broth; the liver, of course, was chopped, while the giblets were fried; the neck served as a casing to be stuffed; and chicken eggs, useful in countless ways in the kitchen, provided another major source of protein. Moreover, the chicken's feathers were plucked and put into pillows and bedding; and even the droppings were collected and scattered for fertilizer.

In the Sephardic world chicken was generally not a staple; in many places it was the most expensive form of protein, and reserved for special occasions such as the Sabbath, weddings, and holidays including Rosh Hashanah and Yom Kippur. Chicken has long been associated with Yom Kippur, among Sephardim and Ashkenazim alike, in part because of the venerable atonement ritual of *kapparot* (*kapores* in Yiddish). *Kapparot* is performed by swinging a live chicken around one's head three times while reciting prayers requesting that the chicken be sacrificed in one's stead, the idea being to symbolically transfer one's own sins to the chicken. As for the now sin-laden chicken, it is slaughtered and either it or its monetary equivalent is donated to the poor. (Presumably sins—unlike, say, salmonella—cannot be transmitted from the chicken to the eater.)

Because there were often lots of chickens around as a result of *kapparot,* and because it is an easily digested food, it has been chicken with which many Jews throughout the world have traditionally begun the Yom Kippur fast. It is chicken with which they have, as often as not, welcomed in the New Year, and each week, the Sabbath. Prepared in one form or another, it has also been chicken served at the Jewish sickbed. From chopped liver to roast chicken and chicken soup, it is almost impossible to imagine Jewish cuisine, indeed Jewish life, without it. A Yiddish proverb tells us, "Better a chicken in the hand than an eagle in the sky." The eagle we know isn't kosher; as for the chicken, well, let us just be grateful that everything worked out.

ROAST CHICKEN WITH CARROTS AND POTATOES

Here is a classic roast chicken, of the sort that has been a standard Friday-night repast for generations. There may be nothing quite as satisfying.

SERVES 4

- 1 chicken, 3 to 4 pounds
- Salt
- Freshly ground black pepper
- 1 lemon, halved
- 10 thyme sprigs
- 1 tablespoon vegetable oil
- 1 pound carrots, peeled and cut into 1-inch slices
- 6 medium red-skin potatoes, cut into 1-inch chunks
- 2 onions, peeled and quartered

1. Preheat the oven to 450 degrees. Rinse the chicken and pat it dry. Generously season the cavity with salt and pepper. Add a lemon half and the thyme sprigs to the cavity. Rub the skin of the chicken with 1 teaspoon of the oil and then drizzle the juice from the remaining lemon half over it. Season with salt and pepper.
2. Place the chicken on a rack in a large roasting pan. Arrange the carrots, potatoes, and onions in the pan. Drizzle the vegetables with the remaining 2 teaspoons of oil and season them with salt and pepper. Pour 1 cup of water into the pan.
3. Roast the chicken and vegetables for 30 minutes, then lower the heat to 350 degrees and continue cooking until the vegetables are soft, the chicken is well browned, and the chicken juices run clear when poked with a knife, another 1 to 1¼ hours. (Check occasionally and add water to the pan as necessary; there should always be about ¼ inch of water in the pan.)
4. When the chicken has finished cooking, remove it to a carving board and let it rest for 10 minutes. Arrange the cooked vegetables on a large serving platter. Remove the thyme and lemon half from the cavity, then carve the chicken and transfer it to the platter. Serve warm.

POLLO ARROSTO CON PEPERONI E OLIVE

ITALIAN ROAST CHICKEN WITH PEPPERS AND OLIVES

For a long time chicken was more expensive than beef in Italy, and as a result it was not much used in Italian Jewish cooking (with the exception of fried chicken, which was a Hanukkah staple). In the last century, however, chicken has become much more plentiful and inexpensive, and now it is quite common for Friday-night dinners and for Rosh Hashanah celebrations. This is a good, simple Italian roast chicken. I like to rub the chicken with a teaspoon or so of olive oil to enhance browning, but this isn't called for in the original recipe, and you can do it or not as you choose.

SERVES 4

4 green or red peppers (or a mixture)

1 chicken, 3 to 4 pounds

Juice of ½ lemon

1 teaspoon olive oil (optional)

Salt

Freshly ground black pepper

1½ cups mixed pitted black and green olives

1. Preheat the broiler. Place the peppers on a foil-lined baking sheet and broil until blackened on all sides, turning as necessary. Place in a medium bowl and cover with plastic wrap until cool enough to handle. Peel away the blackened skin. Remove the seeds and cores and slice the peppers into thick strips. Set aside.

2. Preheat the oven to 350 degrees. Rinse the chicken and pat it dry. Rub the chicken all over with the lemon juice and, if desired, the olive oil. Season it inside and out with salt and pepper. Place the chicken in a large roasting pan. Pour 1 cup of water into the pan.

3. Roast the chicken until the skin is golden brown, about 1½ hours (turn it once for even browning). Add the roasted pepper strips and olives to the pan and cook for 15 minutes, until the chicken is a deep golden brown and its juices run clear when poked with a knife.

4. When the chicken has finished cooking, remove it to a carving board and let it rest for 10 minutes. Carve the chicken, then transfer it to a serving platter and arrange the peppers and olives around it. Serve warm.

DJAJ TANZIA

MOROCCAN ROAST CHICKEN WITH DRIED FRUITS AND NUTS

This splendid chicken dish, in which the fruit cooks down into a magnificent marmalade, is from Rachel Suissa of Hollywood, Florida, who grew up in Casablanca. In her family this dish was commonly served on Rosh Hashanah, Passover, and other festive events. Not at all difficult to make, it is perfect whenever you're looking for something a bit grander than a simple roast chicken.

SERVES 4

- 6 tablespoons plus 1 teaspoon olive oil
- 2 pounds onions, thinly sliced
- 1 cup pitted prunes, halved
- 1 cup dried apricots, halved
- 1 cup dried figs, halved
- 1 cup shelled walnut pieces
- Salt
- Freshly ground black pepper
- 2 tablespoons sugar
- 1 teaspoon ground cinnamon
- 1 chicken, 3 to 4 pounds
- ½ teaspoon turmeric
- Salt
- Freshly ground black pepper
- ½ cup blanched almonds for sprinkling

1. Heat the 6 tablespoons of oil in a large skillet over medium heat. Add the onions and cook, stirring often, until lightly caramelized, about 30 minutes. Transfer to a large bowl.
2. Add the next 8 ingredients to the bowl. Stir until fully combined.
3. Preheat the oven to 350 degrees. Rub the chicken with the remaining teaspoon of oil, then rub it with the turmeric. Season it inside and out with salt and pepper. Place the chicken in a large roasting pan. Spoon the fruit-nut mixture around the chicken, adding some of it to the cavity. Add 2 cups of water to the pan.
4. Roast the chicken for 1½ to 1¾ hours, turn it once for even browning, until the skin is well browned and the chicken juices run clear when the chicken is poked with a knife. After 1 hour, check the pan to make sure it still has liquid in it. If not, add water as necessary.
5. While the chicken is cooking, toast the almonds in a dry medium skillet over medium-low heat, stirring regularly, until lightly colored, about 5 minutes. Set aside.
6. When the chicken is fully cooked, remove it to a carving board and let it rest for 10 minutes. Remove the fruit-nut stuffing from the cavity and place it on a large serving platter, along with the rest of the fruit-nut mixture. Carve the chicken and transfer it to the serving platter. Sprinkle with the toasted almonds. Serve warm.

TÖLTÖTT CSIRKE

HUNGARIAN ROAST CHICKEN WITH MUSHROOM STUFFING

This recipe was given to me by Agnes Sobel, the manager of the dining room of the First Hungarian Literary Society, who emigrated to the United States from Hungary in 1956. Founded in 1889, the society is located on New York's Upper East Side, in a now-posh neighborhood that was once a German and Hungarian enclave known as Yorkville. The mushroom stuffing, spicy and earthy, makes the chicken incredibly flavorful.

SERVES 4

- 2 tablespoons plus 1 teaspoon vegetable oil
- 1 large onion, chopped
- 2 cups chopped white or cremini mushrooms
- 3 cups diced (small) crustless Italian bread or challah
- 1 egg, beaten
- 1 teaspoon paprika
- Salt
- Freshly ground black pepper
- 1 chicken, 3 to 4 pounds

1. Preheat the oven to 450 degrees. Heat the 2 tablespoons oil in a medium skillet over medium heat. Add the onion and cook, stirring often, until soft and translucent. Add the mushrooms and cook until soft. Place in a bowl and let cool. Add the bread, egg, ½ teaspoon of paprika, salt and pepper, and stir well to combine.
2. Rinse the chicken and pat it dry. Season the cavity of the chicken with salt and pepper. With your fingers or a butter knife, gently pull the skin of the chicken away from the meat. Insert the mushroom mixture under the skin of the chicken breasts, thighs, and legs. Place any remaining stuffing in the cavity. Rub the skin of the chicken with the remaining 1 teaspoon oil, then lightly season all sides of the chicken with salt and pepper and the remaining ½ teaspoon paprika.
3. Pour 1 cup of water into a roasting pan. Place the chicken on a rack in the pan. Roast the chicken for 30 minutes. Lower the heat to 350 degrees and continue cooking for another 1 to 1¼ hours, until the chicken is well browned and its juices run clear when poked with a knife. Check occasionally to make sure that there is still water in the pan. Add more as necessary.
4. Transfer the chicken to a carving board and let it rest for 10 minutes. Remove the stuffing from the cavity to a serving platter. Carve the chicken, keeping the stuffing under the skin of the individual pieces. Transfer the chicken to the serving platter. Serve warm.

COMMUNITIES: Baghdad

The life of the oldest continuous Jewish community in all the world has come now to an end, and has done so in the saddest possible way: in silence, and without marker. In Baghdad, no museums honor the glories of Babylonian Jewish culture; no monuments stand in memory of the Jews who lived there, or those who fled in terror; no schools cultivate the talents of future generations. Indeed, virtually no Jews remain at all, in a city where, within the past century, Jews constituted roughly 20 percent of the entire population.

The Iraqi Jewish community can trace its origins as far back as the year 586 B.C.E., when, after the destruction of the First Temple, King Nebuchadnezzar of Babylon conquered Jerusalem and deported most its inhabitants to his kingdom. ("By the rivers of Babylon," says Psalm 137, "where we sat down and wept / when we remembered Zion . . . ") In 525 B.C.E., Nebuchadnezzar was defeated by Cyrus, the king of Persia, who possessed a more tolerant attitude toward his Jewish subjects and invited them to return to Jerusalem and build a new Temple there. Many of the Babylonian exiles returned to Jerusalem, but many others decided to remain in Babylonia (now Iraq), where a large and stable Jewish community existed until our own time.

In Babylon, the Jewish community grew into the leading center of Jewish scholarship, producing, among other works, the Babylonian Talmud. In later centuries the community established world-renowned educational institutions, including the academies of Sura and Pumbedita, led by the *gaonim*, the "genius rabbis," who answered Jewish religious questions posed to them from all over the world. The community was largely self-governing, ruled by the exilarchs, who had broad powers of taxation and even imprisonment.

Arab rule over Iraq came to an end in the thirteenth century, and over the next 700 years the land was dominated by a series of invaders, from the Mongols to the Persians and, finally, the Turks, who ruled from 1638 to 1917. As was true in that other great Jewish commercial center, Salonika, the Jews of Baghdad thrived under Ottoman rule, becoming centrally involved in the country's commercial life. Jewish merchants traded with their contacts, often fellow Jews, throughout Europe and the Far East. Baghdad's Jews traded in a wide range of goods, notably textiles, silk, precious stones, metal, porcelain, and various foods and liquors. As in Salonika, the city's markets were run primarily by Jews and were closed for business on Saturdays.

The year 1908 brought the rebellion of the so-called Young Turks in Istanbul, who installed equal rights and freedom of religion, further improving the lot of the Iraqi Jews (several of whom were elected as Iraqi delegates to the Turkish parliament). Progress accelerated in 1917, when the Ottoman Empire collapsed and the country was placed under the British Mandate. By this time the number of Jews of Baghdad had grown to perhaps 120,000, and this period, between the world wars, was a kind of golden age for the Iraqi Jewish community. As David Kazzaz writes in *Mother of the Pound,* his history and memoir of the Jews of Iraq, "In my memories of the 1920s in the city of my birth, it is always springtime."

Most of the houses in the city were made of brick, one or two stories high, surrounding a central courtyard. When the weather grew warm, the air carried the scent of roses and orange blossoms from backyard gardens. Sabbath afternoons meant a leisurely stroll over the pontoon bridge that had been built across the Tigris River. In the summer, when it was very hot, families would haul cots up to the flat, tiled roofs of the houses and sleep under the stars.

Mothers and fathers were called not by their first names, but rather as *um* (mother of) or *abu* (father of) the name of the firstborn son. For centuries the men of the community had worn Middle Eastern robes, and over their dresses women had covered themselves from head to toe in black silk *abayas,* sometimes with a black veil. By the early decades of the twentieth century the robes had been replaced by Western suits, and women shed the *abaya,* except when going to the marketplace or to Muslim neighborhoods. They spoke Arabic or French or English when conducting business with the outside world, but to each other they also spoke Arabi mal Yehud (Judeo-Arabic), a language spoken only by the Jews of Iraq, consisting of a mixture of Arabic and Hebrew, as well as scattered words from Aramaic, Persian,

Turkish, French, and English. As with so many of the world's traditional Jewish languages, Judeo-Arabic is today spoken mostly by the elderly.

Like language, cuisine is a repository of a community's history, often in the vestigial foodways of foreign invaders long since repelled. Some of this can be seen in Iraqi Jewish cuisine as well, such as in the Persian-inspired combination of fruit and meat (one popular dish is meatballs in apricot sauce; see page 194). Traces of the Ottoman Empire also appear, for instance, in the use of filo in sweet and savory pastries, but in general the cooking was less influenced by Turkey than that of other Jewish communities closer to the center of the Ottoman Empire.

In Iraq, as in much of the Sephardic world, the main meal of the day was lunch, and none was as splendid as the Sabbath lunch. This was especially true during the cold months, when Saturday lunch invariably meant the exquisitely spiced chicken-and-rice dish known as Tabeet (pages 148–149). The dish began, of course, with the chicken, which was usually purchased live during the week and kept in a cage until Friday, when it was taken to the local *shokhet* to be slaughtered in accordance with the kosher laws. Back home, the chicken was stuffed with long-grain rice and finely chopped gizzards flavored with a distinctive spice mixture that was used only for this dish. The proportion of the spices in the mixture varied from family to family, but it always contained seven aromatic spices: cardamom, cloves, cinnamon, nutmeg, ginger, allspice, and dried rose petals.

Once the chicken was stuffed, it was placed on a bed of similarly spiced rice in a heavy pot and left to simmer on the stove overnight. Usually eggs were placed on the lid of the pot and they cooked along with the *tabeet*, so that by the next morning they had become the creamy, long-cooked eggs so beloved in Sephardic communities, served for breakfast after synagogue services with a variety of cold vegetable salads, fried eggplant, and a pickled mango condiment called *umba*.

The main meal on Thursday was *Kitchree*, a stew of rice and red lentils topped with yogurt (page 287); this was a lighter dairy meal, in preparation for the Shabbat meal the following day. The Friday-evening meal usually featured fish, the most popular variety of which was *shabbut*, a species of carp not found in the West. Sometimes the fish was cooked in a sweet-and-sour sauce (the sweet-and-sour combination was very popular among Iraqi Jews, probably a legacy of the Persian conquerors) with tomatoes, onions, and peppers; or the fish might be ground into patties, called *arook bel samak*. Beloved by Jew and Muslim alike was the fish preparation called *masgouf*, in which *shabbut* freshly caught by the river's boatmen were skewered on stakes and grilled whole over a smoky wood fire (when the embers burned down the fish were placed directly on them), and then served with chopped tomatoes and pickled mango. The *masgouf* could be prepared in one's backyard, or, more festively, in a family picnic by the river. It could also be purchased in one of the many outdoor cafés that operated along the shore; *masgouf* was the only dish that the Jews of Baghdad ate from non-Jewish kitchens.

Another favorite delicacy was the little meat-filled dumplings called *kooba*, which bear a strong resemblance to the Syrian *kibbeh*, though the shell is made not from bulgur, as in Syria, but rather from softened rice or rice flour. The *kooba* were usually simmered in a vegetable sauce, most often made from beets or okra. The filling, usually, was ground lamb; lamb in general was very common, both during the week and for holidays such as Rosh Hashanah. It was traditional for a family to purchase the lamb several weeks before the holiday and raise it themselves. After the slaughtering by the *shokhet*, the family kept only a part of the lamb and gave the rest to charity.

For Hanukkah there were fried semolina turnovers called *Sambousak bel Tawa* (pages 208–209), filled with ground chickpeas, while the Iraqi Passover table featured a unique *charoset* made from the date syrup called *halek*. In the springtime fresh dates would be collected and left in the sun to dry. Later, the syrup that exuded from them would be boiled until it became thick. Chopped walnuts were added to the syrup to make *charoset*—a version that is not produced anywhere else—and the remaining *halek* would be jarred and used throughout the year as a sweetener in place of honey or sugar.

Passover, of course, is the holiday commemorating the Jewish exodus from Egypt; the exodus from Iraq is a far more recent one, and ironically dates to Purim of 1950, the day that the Iraqi government announced the law of the Taskeet, or "renunciation." The Taskeet allowed Jews to leave the country, as long as they renounced their Iraqi citizenship and agreed to leave their money and possessions behind. Despite these harsh conditions, by the end of the year nearly all of Iraq's Jews—some 125,000—had emigrated to Israel in an airlift known as Operation Ezra and Nehemiah.

Today, only a handful of Jews remain in Iraq. According to a 2000 report by Mitchell Bard of the American-Israeli Cooperative Enterprise, the most recent Jewish wedding took place in 1980. The last rabbi of Baghdad died in 1996, and none of the remaining Jews is capable of performing services. David Kazzaz is now a retired psychologist living in Denver. He does not believe that a significant Jewish presence will ever reappear in Iraq. "It is possible that some Jews might go back for business reasons," he says, "but it is unlikely that there will be a stable, thriving community there again."

All that remains, then, is memories. Monique Daoud, who in 1972 was one of the last Jews to leave Iraq, likes to recall her family's home, with its fine marble floors, the gardens out back full of eucalyptus and pomegranates and sweet lemons. Mostly, though, she remembers how she knew everyone in the community, how closely knit their lives were. "We were all together," she says, "grandparents, aunts, uncles, friends we had known for years." Asked if she would choose to return to Iraq with the change in regime there, Monique responds, "I've always thought about that, but I don't think so. If it were the Iraq of the first few years of my life, that would be nice, but I don't think that will ever happen. Still, I hope I can go back and see it again. I always tell my kids, 'One day, when it is safe, I would like to take you back and show you where I lived.'"

TABEET

IRAQI CHICKEN WITH RICE

This exquisitely spiced dish may well be the most splendid in all of Iraqi Jewish cuisine. It is the dish that, in cold weather, all Iraqi Jewish families ate for Saturday lunch. On Fridays the dish would be prepared in a large pot placed over a charcoal or wood fire, where it would cook all night long over the dying embers, with the heat kept in by towels and blankets carefully wrapped around the top. Every Iraqi Jewish family prepared their own tabeet*-spice mixture; the proportions varied somewhat, but the mixture always included the spices listed below.*

SERVES 6

FOR THE STUFFING

¼ cup basmati or other long-grain rice, washed and soaked in boiling water for 1 hour

3 tablespoons olive oil

1 large tomato, chopped

Giblets from 1 chicken, finely chopped

1 small onion, finely chopped

Salt

Freshly ground black pepper

¼ teaspoon turmeric

¼ teaspoon ground cinnamon

Pinch of ground cloves

Pinch of ground cardamom

Pinch of freshly grated nutmeg

Pinch of powdered ginger

1. Make the stuffing: Drain the soaking ¼ cup rice and place in a medium bowl along with all of the remaining stuffing ingredients. Stir well to combine.

2. Rinse the chicken and pat it dry. Fill the cavity of the chicken with the stuffing, then secure the opening with wooden toothpicks.

3. Prick the chicken all over with a fork. Place it in a Dutch oven or other large, heavy pot over low heat. Cook for about 15 minutes, turning as necessary, until golden all over. Remove the chicken from the pot and add the onion. Raise the heat to medium and cook, stirring often, until soft and translucent.

4. Return the chicken to the pot and add the 4 cups water. Cover the pot and bring to a boil. Lower the heat and simmer, covered, for 30 minutes. Remove the chicken from the pot to a large plate.

5. Preheat the oven to 400 degrees. Add the tomato paste, salt, pepper, and the spices to the pot and stir until fully combined. Stir in the rice. Cover and bring to a boil. Lower the heat and gently simmer until all of the water has been absorbed, about 20 minutes. Drizzle the oil on top of the rice and then return the chicken to the pot, pressing it down into the rice.

6. Cover the pot and place it in the oven. Bake for 30 minutes. Lower the heat to 250 degrees and bake for 2 hours.

7. To serve, transfer the chicken to a carving board. With a large spoon, scrape the rice from the bottom of the pot to a large serving platter, turning it over so that the crusty part is on top. Carve the chicken and arrange the meat and stuffing on the platter. Serve warm.

1 chicken, about 4 pounds

1 onion, finely chopped

4 cups water

2½ tablespoons tomato paste

2 teaspoons salt

¼ teaspoon freshly ground black pepper

¼ teaspoon turmeric

¼ teaspoon ground cloves

¼ teaspoon freshly grated nutmeg

¼ teaspoon powdered ginger

½ teaspoon ground cardamom

½ teaspoon ground cinnamon

2 cups basmati or other long-grain rice, well washed

¼ cup olive oil

KOMBDI CHA KANJI

BOMBAY CURRIED CHICKEN

Curried chicken is representative of much of the Bene Israel cooking style, in that it uses lots of onions and tomatoes and spices, including ginger, garlic, turmeric, bay leaves, cinnamon, cloves, and cardamom, as well as fresh cilantro. It was often the centerpiece of Friday-evening and holiday meals. This curry should be served on top of rice, such as Jeera Bahat *(page 281). Tamarind concentrate and the spice mixture called garam masala can be purchased in Indian and specialty shops.*

SERVES 4

¼ cup olive oil

4 onions, chopped

1 teaspoon red chili paste

1 tablespoon ginger paste or peeled and minced fresh ginger

1 tablespoon garlic paste or minced fresh garlic

½ teaspoon turmeric

1 tablespoon garam masala

2 teaspoons tamarind concentrate

1 teaspoon salt

1 (15-ounce) can chopped tomatoes

4 bay leaves

1 cup water

1 chicken, 3 to 4 pounds, cut into 8 pieces; or 4 split breasts, totaling about 3 pounds

1 tablespoon chopped fresh cilantro

1. Heat the oil in a large skillet over medium-high heat. Add the onion and cook, stirring often, until lightly colored. Add the chili paste, ginger, garlic, turmeric, and garam masala and cook for about 2 minutes, stirring regularly. Add the tamarind concentrate, salt, tomatoes, bay leaves, and water and stir to combine. Cover the pot and bring to a boil.

2. Rinse the chicken pieces and pat them dry. Add them to the pot. Lower the heat, cover, and simmer until the chicken is cooked through, about 40 minutes. Remove the bay leaves. Transfer the chicken to a large serving platter and pour the sauce over it. Sprinkle with the cilantro. Serve hot, with rice.

KOTOPOULO LEMONATO

GREEK LEMON CHICKEN

In Greece, this simple, flavorful dish was very common for Friday nights. This particular preparation comes from the town of Volos. Sometimes cut-up potatoes are added as well.

SERVES 4

- 1 chicken, 3 to 4 pounds, cut into 8 pieces; or 4 split breasts, totaling about 3 pounds
- Salt
- Freshly ground black pepper
- 3 tablespoons olive oil
- Juice of 2 lemons
- 1 tablespoon dried oregano
- 1¼ cups water
- 4 carrots, peeled and sliced into ½-inch rounds
- 2 tablespoons chopped fresh flat-leaf parsley

1. Rinse the chicken pieces and pat them dry. Season with salt and pepper.
2. Heat the oil in a large skillet over medium-high heat. Add the chicken and cook until browned on all sides.
3. Add the lemon juice, oregano, and water and season with salt and pepper. Cover and bring to a boil. Lower the heat and simmer, covered, for 20 minutes. Add the carrots and cook until they are soft and the chicken is cooked through, about another 15 minutes.
4. Transfer the chicken and carrots to a large serving platter and pour some of the cooking liquid over them. Sprinkle with the parsley. Serve hot.

COMMUNITIES: Calcutta

If you are ever in Calcutta and find yourself with a sudden hankering for baklava, the place to go is Nahoum and Sons. Located in the city's New Market since 1902, the bakery features a wide range of pastries both savory and sweet, including many, like baklava, of Middle Eastern origin. More than the city's several ornate but almost empty synagogues, Nahoum's is the most tangible remnant of the Jewish community that once flourished in Calcutta.

At its high point, in the early decades of the twentieth century, the Calcutta Jewish community totaled some 6,000—not an insignificant number, to be sure, though scarcely a drop in a city of more than four million people. Still, for many years the community was able to maintain synagogues, schools, charities, and a newspaper. All that came to an end in the 1930s and 1940s, when, nervous about the growing strength of the Indian independence movement and the rise in ethnic tensions, the Jews of Calcutta began to leave in large numbers. Today only a handful of Jews remain in the city.

Then as now, the Jews of Calcutta were known as the "Baghdadi" Jews, although they actually descend from several Middle Eastern countries, and the community's patriarch, one Shalom Obadiah Ha-Cohen, emigrated to Calcutta not from Iraq but from Aleppo, Syria. Drawn by the success of several large British trading houses in the city, Ha-Cohen arrived in Calcutta in 1798 and set up shop as a trader in silks, cloth, diamonds, and indigo. Eventually word spread back to the Middle East about the money to be made in Calcutta, and in the second decade of the nineteenth century, Jewish immigrants began to arrive in the city from Syria, Persia, and Yemen. The 1820s and 1830s brought a wave of Jewish émigrés from Iraq, and by the middle of the nineteenth century Iraqi (or "Baghdadi") Jews had become the majority of the community.

Developing a vast network of contacts among their co-religionists throughout Europe, the Middle East, and Asia, the Baghdadi merchants traded in just about everything that was worth anything, from diamonds, ivory, silk, and coral to spices, coffee, and, perhaps most lucratively, opium. As Nathan Katz notes in his book *Who Are the Jews of India?*, "Opium was the source of many Jewish fortunes. . . . Jewish merchants bought chests of opium at government auction and shipped them to members of their extended family in Penang, Singapore, Hong Kong, or Shanghai. They traded the opium to Chinese merchants in exchange for tea, which they sold for gold in England." This version of the triangle trade ended only in the early twentieth century, when, after two wars over the issue, China finally managed to ban the traffic in opium. By that time the families who had made their fortunes in black tar had moved on to more stable ventures in real estate and cotton manufacture.

Not all the Jews of Calcutta were traders, though. Many, like Nahoum Israel Mordecai of Nahoum and Sons, were confectioners, or grocers, or the owners of small businesses; others went into professions or the civil service. Still, compared to the two other major Jewish communities in India, in Bombay and Cochin, the Jews of Calcutta were far more prosperous. Moreover, both of those communities had been in India for many centuries, whereas the Baghdadi Jews were relative newcomers, and did not as readily assimilate to the native culture. Arabic was their primary language until at least the end of the nineteenth century, at which point it was slowly eclipsed by English. Similarly, the clothing worn by members of the Baghdadi community was mostly of Middle Eastern style until, again, the twentieth century, when British dress became the vogue. The Baghdadi Jews identified themselves at once with their ancestors in the Middle East and with the British rulers of India, and they occupied a shifting, sometimes uncomfortable position between the British elite at the top of the social ladder and the native Indian masses at the bottom. They were holders, in a certain sense, of multiple passports: a status made evident in their unwieldy official designation as "Arabian Jews of the British Raj."

For some 150 years—until the community was decimated by emigration in the 1930s and 1940s—the Baghdadi Jews preserved a surprisingly unitary Middle Eastern culture in the midst of India's second most populous city. Happily enough, though, the gates around the house did not extend as far as the kitchen. There, in the realm of cuisine, the most interesting and productive interaction took place between the traditions of their erstwhile homeland and those of their newly adopted one. Sweet-and-sour dishes became infused with curry flavorings; the vast array of Middle Eastern dumplings and turnovers grew aromatic with the addition of ginger and turmeric; Middle Eastern stews were served alongside Indian rice *pilaus*, accompanied by fenugreek relish or mango chutney; desserts could be baklava or coconut cookies, or creamy puddings in which the milk of a coconut replaced that of a cow. In the kitchens of Calcutta's Jews, the Middle East made union with India, resulting in something entirely new.

There may be no more significant example of this than the unassuming little dumplings known as *kooba*. They are a long-time Friday-night specialty in Iraq (among Syrian Jews, with whom they are also extremely popular, they are called *kibbeh*, while in Egypt the name is *kobeba*), where they are filled with ground beef or lamb. In Calcutta, though, a beef- or lamb-filled *kooba* was very rare; they were almost always made with chicken. The reason for this is not, as might be expected, because the Baghdadi Jews had adopted the local taboos against eating beef. Rather, it is because Calcutta, with its relatively small Jewish community, had no *shokhet* (ritual slaughterer) who could slaughter cows (though one occasionally came in from Bombay before holidays). As a result, relatively little beef appears in the Baghdadi cuisine, while there is an abundance of chicken and fish. Sometimes chicken simply replaced beef in traditional dishes, as was the case not just with *kooba* but also with the Sabbath stew known in Calcutta, as in much of the Middle East, as *hamin*. The Calcutta version uses not beef but chicken, which is long-cooked with rice and sometimes eggs, and flavored in an aromatic—and distinctively Indian—fashion. Some Middle Eastern *hamins* may include such spices as ginger, cinnamon, or saffron, but this is surely the only *hamin* in the world also to feature cardamom and cloves.

Roast chicken was common, too, often stuffed, called *hashwa*. This is another traditional Middle Eastern preparation, although here, too, the ground beef has disappeared from the stuffing and the flavor set has undergone a metamorphosis, from cinnamon and allspice to cardamom and cloves. Another favorite chicken dish was *Gazar Meetha* (page 158), a sweet-and-sour stew made with chicken and shredded carrots; *koobas* were often added to this dish as well. Of all the chicken dishes in the Baghdadi Jewish repertoire, however, the best known and most fondly remembered is *Chitarnee* (page 157), chicken stewed in a luxuriantly glossy onion sauce. Like so many others, the essential dish is of Middle Eastern origin—with the sweet-and-sour flavoring common in Iraqi cookery—but the stay in India brought the addition of spices such as turmeric, cardamom, and coriander, which provide an ethereal counterpoint to the foundation of lemon juice and sugar.

From the Middle East, too, came stuffed vegetables, a fixture of Sephardic cookery. Most often they were eggplant, tomatoes, or onions, though small cucumbers were also used, filled with a flavorful mixture of ground chicken and rice. From India came the vegetable stews called *bhajis*, using whatever vegetable was available in the local market, from eggplant to okra and cauliflower. Also distinctively Indian were the various curry dishes, modified slightly to conform to Jewish dietary laws. Sesame or peanut oil would be used, for instance, instead of *ghee*, the Indian clarified butter, and, when the curries included chicken or lamb, coconut milk replaced yogurt and cream. Curries were accompanied always by *pilau*, long-grain white rice made beautifully yellow with saffron or turmeric, and flavored with sweet spices of cardamom, cinnamon, and cloves. *Pilau* was an everyday dish, but for holidays, weddings and other festive occasions there was a special celebratory version called *Pilau Kismish Badam* (page 280), made with raisins and toasted almonds. And no celebration was complete without *Aloo Makala* (page 235), the deep-fried whole potatoes that are a hallmark of Baghdadi Jewish cuisine, and the dish that will still be made by the community's descendants after the others have been forgotten.

Like so many other Jewish communities around the world, Calcutta's Jewish community could not survive the combined assaults of the modern age. Nervous about the upsurge of nationalist sentiment there, in the 1930s Calcutta's Jews began emigrating in large numbers to Great Britain (the nation with which they had long identified), Australia, South Africa, Canada, and the United States; thousands more departed for Israel after its creation in 1948. No one knows exactly how many Jews remain in the city; Rahel Musleah, who was born in Calcutta and returned there in 1997, estimates that there are about fifty. Those who are left, reported the sociologist Daniel Elazar of the Jerusalem Center for Public Affairs, "are mostly minor clerks or unemployed." Elazar wrote that back in 1986, and the situation is surely worse today. Two of the city's five synagogues still manage to maintain daily *minyanim*, but do so by paying the participants to attend. Almost all of the remaining Jews in Calcutta are elderly. Barring a miraculous event, in another generation or two the community will no longer be large or vigorous enough to function. All that will remain, then, will be a few startling remnants of an earlier time: synagogues and school buildings shuttered or converted to other uses, and baklava sold in the central market.

CHITARNEE

CALCUTTA SWEET-AND-SOUR CHICKEN IN ONION SAUCE

Aromatic, glossy, its flavors in perfect balance, chitarnee *is one of the jewels of Calcutta Jewish cuisine. This recipe comes from Rahel Musleah of Great Neck, New York, whose family emigrated to the United States when she was six. Hers was a distinguished Calcutta family: Her father, Rabbi Ezekiel Musleah, was the author of the highly regarded history* On the Banks of the Ganga, *while her cousin, Mavis Hyman, wrote the books* Indian-Jewish Cooking *and* Jews of the Raj. *Ms. Musleah is herself an author and educator who lectures widely on Indian Jewry.*

SERVES 4

- 1 chicken, 3 to 4 pounds, cut into 8 pieces; or 4 split breasts, totaling about 3 pounds
- Salt
- Freshly ground black pepper
- 2 tablespoons vegetable oil
- 2 pounds onions, sliced
- 2 or 3 garlic cloves, chopped
- 1 teaspoon peeled and minced fresh ginger
- 1½ teaspoons ground cumin
- 1½ teaspoons ground coriander
- 3 cardamom pods
- 1 teaspoon turmeric
- ½ teaspoon chili powder, or to taste
- 1 (15-ounce) can whole tomatoes, drained
- 2 tablespoons lemon juice
- 1 to 2 teaspoons sugar

1. Rinse the chicken pieces and pat them dry. Season them with salt and pepper.
2. In a large skillet, heat the oil over medium-high heat. Add the chicken and cook until browned on all sides. Remove to a plate.
3. Lower the heat to medium. Add the onions to the pan and cook, stirring often, until soft and translucent. Add the garlic, ginger, cumin, coriander, cardamom pods, turmeric, and chili powder and cook for 5 minutes. Add enough water just to cover the onions. Cover the pan and continue cooking until the water is almost gone but the mixture remains loose, 20 to 25 minutes.
4. Add the tomatoes and another ½ teaspoon salt and stir to combine, breaking up the tomatoes with a wooden spoon. Return the chicken to the pan, cover, and simmer until the chicken is cooked through, about 35 minutes. When the chicken is cooked, remove the pieces to a large serving platter and cover with aluminum foil to keep warm.
5. Raise the heat slightly and cook the sauce, uncovered, until the liquid is absorbed and the sauce becomes thick and shiny, about 15 minutes. Stir in the lemon juice and sugar and cook for another minute. Taste and adjust for seasoning. Remove the cardamom pods. Pour the sauce over the chicken. Serve hot.

GAZAR MEETHA

CALCUTTA SWEET-AND-SOUR CHICKEN WITH CARROTS

Like much of the cookery of the Baghdadi Jews of Calcutta, this dish uses the procedure known as hammiss, *which refers to cooking onions with spices and a little bit of water to develop a thick, aromatic sauce. This dish can be served over white rice, or with a* pilau *like the one on page 280.*

SERVES 4

¼ cup vegetable oil

1½ pounds carrots, peeled and grated

Salt

Freshly ground black pepper

2 onions, chopped

2 garlic cloves, chopped

½ teaspoon turmeric

1 teaspoon peeled and minced fresh ginger

1 cinnamon stick

4 cloves

5 cardamom pods

1 bay leaf

1½ cups water

1 chicken, 3 to 4 pounds, cut into 8 pieces; or 4 split breasts, totaling about 3 pounds

Juice of 1 lemon

1 to 2 teaspoons sugar (optional)

1. In a large skillet, heat 2 tablespoons of the oil over medium heat. Add the carrots and season with salt and pepper. Cook until soft, about 3 minutes. Remove to a plate.
2. Add the remaining 2 tablespoons of oil to the pan. Add the onions and cook, stirring often, until soft and translucent. Add the garlic, turmeric, ginger, cinnamon stick, cloves, cardamom pods, bay leaf, and ½ cup of the water and stir to combine. Cook, stirring regularly, until a thick sauce forms, about 5 minutes.
3. Rinse the chicken pieces and pat them dry. Season them with salt and pepper. Add the chicken to the pan and cook until golden on all sides. Add the remaining 1 cup water. Cover the pan and bring to a boil. Lower the heat and simmer, covered, until the chicken is nearly tender, about 25 minutes.
4. Add the grated carrots and lemon juice to the pan, and simmer, uncovered, for 15 minutes, or until the chicken is cooked through. Remove the bay leaf. Taste the sauce and add the sugar, if desired. Transfer the chicken and sauce to a large serving platter. Serve hot, with rice.

POULET AUX OLIVES ET CITRONS CONFITS

MOROCCAN CHICKEN WITH GREEN OLIVES AND PRESERVED LEMONS

Moroccan Jews often break the Yom Kippur fast with this dish. The preserved lemon rind brightens a headily aromatic sauce, providing cheerful upper notes against the olives' deeper, more somber tones. Preserved lemons are available in many Middle Eastern and specialty shops, or by mail order from the New York spice emporium Kalustyan's, at (212) 685-3451 or www.kalustyan.com.

SERVES 4

- 1 preserved lemon, halved or quartered
- 1 chicken, 3 to 4 pounds, cut into 8 pieces; or 4 split breasts, totaling about 3 pounds
- 3 tablespoons olive oil
- 1 onion, sliced
- 2 garlic cloves, chopped
- ½ teaspoon peeled and minced fresh ginger
- ½ teaspoon turmeric
- 1½ cups chicken stock
- 1 cup green olives, pitted and halved
- 1 tablespoon chopped fresh cilantro for garnish

1. Rinse the lemon well and pat it dry. Discard the pulp and slice the rind into matchstick-sized strips. Set aside.
2. Rinse the chicken pieces and pat them dry. Season them with salt and pepper.
3. Heat the oil in a large skillet over medium-high heat. Add the chicken and brown well on all sides. Remove and drain on paper towels.
4. Lower the heat to medium. Add the onion and cook, stirring often, until soft and translucent. Add the garlic, ginger, and turmeric and cook, stirring regularly, for 2 minutes.
5. Add the chicken stock and scrape up any brown chicken bits on the bottom of the pan with a wooden spoon. Add the olives and the sliced lemon rind and return the chicken to the pan. Bring to a boil. Lower the heat and simmer, covered, occasionally spooning the sauce over the chicken, until the chicken is cooked through, about 35 minutes. Taste the sauce and adjust for seasoning. Remove the chicken to a large serving platter. Spoon the sauce on top and garnish with the cilantro. Serve hot.

INGREDIENTS: Pomegranates

Pomegranates are sometimes known as Chinese apples, and at first glance, a pomegranate does look something like an apple—just a bit larger, but round and with a faintly yellow, roseate blush to the skin. Look a little more closely, though, and you notice that its skin is dull and leathery, without an apple's clear shine, and the fruit is softer, gnarled and misshapen. But cut it open, and the pomegranate will reveal its hidden treasure: hundreds of glistening red seeds packed tightly into pale membranes, like rubies in a bed of cotton.

The *tapuach*—the fruit of Eden's tree of knowledge—has for many centuries been depicted as an apple, but some scholars now believe that the real forbidden fruit was more likely intended to be a pomegranate. Though this in itself seems unlikely (most of the historical clues do point to the apple), no other fruit may be quite so resonant with meaning to the Jewish people as is the pomegranate. Native to northern Persia, the pomegranate is one of the world's oldest cultivated fruits, having been first domesticated around 4000 B.C.E.; carbonized pomegranates have been found in a tomb in Jericho dating to the Bronze Age. The Egyptians began importing pomegranates from the Holy Land around 1150 B.C.E., and the pomegranate was a favorite treat of the Hebrews living in Egypt, who pressed refreshing juice from its seeds, and sometimes made a spiced wine from it. Wandering in the desert, the Hebrews yearned for the pomegranates and other fruits they had left behind in Egypt, challenging Moses to explain why he had led them to "a place of no seed, or of figs, or of vines, or of pomegranates." Moses was concerned enough about this backsliding that he sent spies out into Canaan to reconnoiter the territory, then reported back to his people (recorded in Deuteronomy 8:8) that God was leading them into a prosperous land, "a land of wheat and barley, of vines, of fig trees and pomegranates, a land of olive trees and honey."

King Solomon is said to have maintained a grove of pomegranate trees (surely a sign of wisdom), and the pillars of his temple in Jerusalem were festooned with hundreds of brass pomegranates. Images of pomegranates were woven onto the hem of priestly robes—between bells of pure gold, says the book of Exodus—and on the faces of coins (namely, the silver shekel of Jerusalem, in circulation during the second century B.C.E.). Pomegranates are referred to again and again in the Bible, including no fewer than six times in the greatest love poem of all, the Song of Songs; one of the Song's lovers, for instance, praises the other, "The curve of your cheek [is] a pomegranate in the thicket of your hair," and then again shortly after, "Your branches are an orchard of pomegranate trees heavy with fruit."

Throughout the Bible the pomegranate is a symbol of lushness, abundance, joy. In Joel 1:12, to take one example, the prophet laments that the pomegranate tree has withered, because joy has withered among the sons of men. Over time the pomegranate came to represent in the Jewish mind fertility itself, this obviously owing to the copiousness of its seeds. (According to Kabbalistic lore, a pomegranate contains 613 seeds, precisely the number of *mitzvot* Jews are commanded by God to obey; empirical observations do not bear out this assertion.) As a symbol of abundance and fertility, it's not surprising that the pomegranate has long been part of Jewish rituals to welcome the New Year. Sephardic Jews eat a slice of pomegranate during the Rosh Hashanah feast, reciting the prayer: "May it be Your Will, O Creator, that our year be rich and replete with blessings as the pomegranate is rich and replete with seeds." On the second night of Rosh Hashanah, it is customary to eat at least one "new" fruit, one that you have not eaten over the past year. Among Ashkenazic and Sephardic families alike, that fruit is often a pomegranate.

Pomegranates also play a role in another Jewish New Year celebration, Tu Bishvat, the New Year of the Trees. At the Tu Bishvat seder, which falls six weeks after Hanukkah, the custom is to eat fruit and nuts associated with land of Israel, particularly from among the seven promised by Moses to the Israelites as they wandered brokenheartedly through the desert. Just the thought of pomegranates was a comfort to Jews then; so imagine the pleasure we might get from pomegranates now, when we actually have them to hold and cut open, and revel in the treasure before us.

CHICKEN IN POMEGRANATE SAUCE WITH WALNUTS AND FIGS

Culinarily, the best way of using pomegranates may be with pomegranate molasses, a fixture in the cookery of Jews from Syria, Iran, and Iraq. A thick, brown syrup, pomegranate molasses has a tangily sour taste with a slight undertone of sweetness. It's used to flavor the sweet-and-sour dishes prominent in the cuisine of the region, in much the same way as tamarind concentrate; to my taste, though, pomegranate molasses is more pleasing, fruitier and less powerfully acerbic.

Perhaps the most well known of the dishes using pomegranate molasses is in the Iranian pomegranate and walnut sauce called fesenjan. *It is most commonly made with duck, though it can also be made with chicken, quail, or even meatballs. In my adaptation of* fesenjan, *I've added fresh figs (like pomegranates, one of the seven fruits celebrated in Tu Bishvat), whose lush sweetness helps to balance the astringency of the pomegranate molasses. If you can't find fresh figs, you can used dried instead. Pomegranate molasses can be purchased at most Middle Eastern groceries.*

SERVES 4

- 1 chicken, 3 to 4 pounds, cut into 8 pieces; or 4 split breasts, totaling about 3 pounds
- Salt
- Freshly ground black pepper
- 2 tablespoons olive oil
- 1 onion, chopped
- 1 cup finely chopped walnuts
- 2 cups chicken stock
- 12 fresh figs, quartered
- 1/3 cup pomegranate molasses
- 2 tablespoons honey

1. Rinse the chicken pieces and pat them dry. Season them with salt and pepper.
2. Heat the oil in a large skillet over medium-high heat. Add the chicken and cook until browned on all sides. Remove and drain on paper towels.
3. Lower the heat to medium, then add the onion to the pan and cook, stirring often, until soft and translucent. Lower the heat to medium-low and add the walnuts. Cook, stirring regularly, until they have just begun to change color, about 3 minutes.
4. Add the chicken stock, figs, pomegranate molasses, and honey and mix well. Cover and bring to a boil. Lower the heat and simmer, covered, for 10 minutes, stirring occasionally.
5. Return the chicken to the pan and simmer, uncovered, until cooked through, about 35 minutes. Transfer the chicken to a large serving platter and pour the sauce over it. Serve hot.

CHAKHOKHBILI

GEORGIAN STEWED CHICKEN IN TOMATO SAUCE WITH FRESH HERBS

Jews have been living in Georgia for the better part of three millennia. In 1998, Georgian President Eduard Shevardnadze presided over festivities commemorating the twenty-sixth centennial of the Georgian Jewish community. Georgia became independent only in 1991; independence led to reduced barriers on immigration, and the Jewish community in Georgia—facing an increase in anti-Semitic violence amid political instability in the region—made use of the opportunity. From a high of some 43,000 Jews living in Georgia in 1970, today there are perhaps 10,000, the majority having emigrated to Israel and, to a lesser extent, the United States.

This recipe comes from Lea Chikashvili of Rego Park, New York, a renowned cook in the local Georgian Jewish community. To my mind, it is among the most delicious of all chicken dishes.

SERVES 4

- 1 chicken, 3 to 4 pounds, cut into 8 pieces; or 4 split breasts, totaling about 3 pounds
- Salt
- Freshly ground black pepper
- 3 tablespoons olive oil
- ½ each red, yellow, and green pepper, sliced
- 2 celery stalks, chopped
- 1 carrot, peeled and chopped
- 2 red onions, sliced
- 6 garlic cloves, finely chopped
- 5 tomatoes, chopped
- 2 tablespoons tomato paste
- ½ cup water
- ½ teaspoon paprika
- ¼ teaspoon red pepper flakes
- 1 tablespoon chopped fresh mint
- 2 tablespoons each fresh flat-leaf parsley, fresh cilantro, and fresh dill, chopped

1. Rinse the chicken pieces and pat them dry. Season them with salt and pepper.
2. In a large pot or Dutch oven, heat the oil over medium-high heat. Add the chicken and cook until browned on all sides.
3. Add the peppers, celery, carrot, onions, garlic, tomatoes, tomato paste, water, paprika, and red pepper flakes, and season with salt and pepper. Stir to combine. Simmer, covered, until the chicken is cooked through, about 35 minutes. Remove from the heat, then add the herbs and stir them through the stew. Serve hot.

CSIRKE PAPRIKÁS

HUNGARIAN CHICKEN PAPRIKASH

In Hungary, the Yom Kippur fast was traditionally broken with a glass of schnapps, followed by coffee and cake. Later came the main meal: chicken paprikash. In the old days, the chicken and onions would be cooked in chicken fat; today, vegetable oil is mostly used instead. Unlike other versions of chicken paprikash, the Jewish variety uses no sour cream. I love this dish served over egg noodles, to soak up the flavorful sauce.

SERVES 4

1 chicken, 3 to 4 pounds, cut into 8 pieces; or 4 split breasts, totaling about 3 pounds

Salt

Freshly ground black pepper

2 tablespoons vegetable oil or rendered chicken fat

2 onions, chopped

1 large tomato, chopped

1 green pepper, chopped

1 tablespoon tomato paste

3/4 cup chicken stock

2 teaspoons paprika

1/4 teaspoon red pepper flakes

1. Rinse the chicken pieces and pat them dry. Season them with salt and pepper.

2. Heat the oil or chicken fat in a large skillet over medium-high heat. Add the chicken and cook until well browned on all sides. Remove and drain on paper towels.

3. Lower the heat to medium. Add the onions, tomato, and green pepper to the pan and cook, stirring often, until the onions are soft and lightly colored. Add the tomato paste, chicken stock, paprika, red pepper flakes, and salt and pepper to taste and stir to combine. Return the chicken to the pan.

4. Cover and bring to a boil. Lower the heat and simmer, covered, occasionally ladling the sauce over the chicken, until it is cooked through, about 35 minutes. Taste the sauce and adjust for seasoning. Transfer the chicken to a large serving platter and pour the sauce over it. Serve hot, with egg noodles.

PETTI DI POLLO ALLE ERBE

ITALIAN CHICKEN BREASTS WITH FRESH HERBS

In Italy, the dish known as petti di pollo alla giudia *(chicken breasts in the Jewish style) consists of chicken breasts that have been simply dredged in beaten egg and bread crumbs and fried in olive oil. My friend Laura Supino of Rome alters the recipe slightly, by adding a flavorful mixture of fresh herbs to the crumbs, sometimes dispensing with the egg entirely. Like roast chicken with peppers and olives (see page 140), this dish is often served on Friday nights in Jewish homes in Italy.*

SERVES 4

- 2 whole boneless skinless chicken breasts, divided into 4 halves
- Salt
- Freshly ground black pepper
- ¼ cup olive oil for frying
- 2 eggs
- ¾ cup bread crumbs for dredging
- ⅓ cup mixed finely chopped fresh herbs, such as sage, rosemary, thyme, and oregano, for dredging

1. Rinse the chicken breasts and pat them dry. Place them between two pieces of wax paper and pound them to a uniform thickness of about ⅓ inch. Season with salt and pepper.
2. Heat the oil in a large skillet over medium-low heat.
3. Place the eggs in a bowl and beat lightly to combine. Combine the bread crumbs with the herbs and spread the mixture on a plate.
4. Dredge the chicken first in the beaten eggs, then in the herbed crumb mixture, shaking off any excess. Carefully place the chicken in the pan.
5. Cook until the bottom is golden brown and crispy, about 5 minutes. Turn the pieces and continue cooking until the bottom is golden brown and crispy and the chicken is cooked through, about another 5 minutes. Transfer to a large serving platter. Serve hot.

POLPETTINE DI TACCHINO

ITALIAN TURKEY MEATBALLS IN BROTH

Laura Supino, an architect and consultant to Rome's Museo Ebraico, likes to say, "Two Jewish cooks, three opinions." This is her family's recipe for turkey meatballs, but there are many others. Some cooks put the chopped vegetables directly in the meatballs. Others do not fry the meatballs, and rather than serving them on their own, put them in chicken soup. Sometimes the meatballs are referred to not as polpettine *but as* boccetti, *"small balls" (as with the Italian game of* bocce*). Still, however the meatballs are made, or whatever they are called, in Italy they are often served at Rosh Hashanah, as well as in the meal that breaks the Yom Kippur fast.*

SERVES 4

1 pound ground turkey

3/4 cup fresh bread crumbs (crusts removed)

1 egg, lightly beaten

3 garlic cloves, finely chopped

1½ tablespoons mixed chopped fresh sage, rosemary, marjoram, and thyme

Salt

Freshly ground black pepper

2 tablespoons olive oil

1 onion, chopped

4 carrots, peeled and diced

4 celery stalks, diced

Water or chicken stock as needed

1. In a large bowl, mix together the ground turkey, bread crumbs, beaten egg, garlic, and herbs. Season the mixture with salt and pepper. Form into balls about 1 inch in diameter.
2. Heat the oil in a large skillet over medium-high heat. Fry the meatballs until lightly browned on all sides. Drain on paper towels.
3. Lower the heat to medium and add the onion, carrots, and celery to the pan, adding more olive oil, if needed, and cook, stirring often, until the onion is soft and translucent.
4. Return the meatballs to the pan and add water or chicken stock nearly to cover. Cover the pan and bring to a boil. Uncover, lower the heat, and simmer until the meatballs are cooked through, about 15 minutes. Taste the broth and adjust for seasoning. Serve the meatballs in bowls with the vegetables and some of the broth.

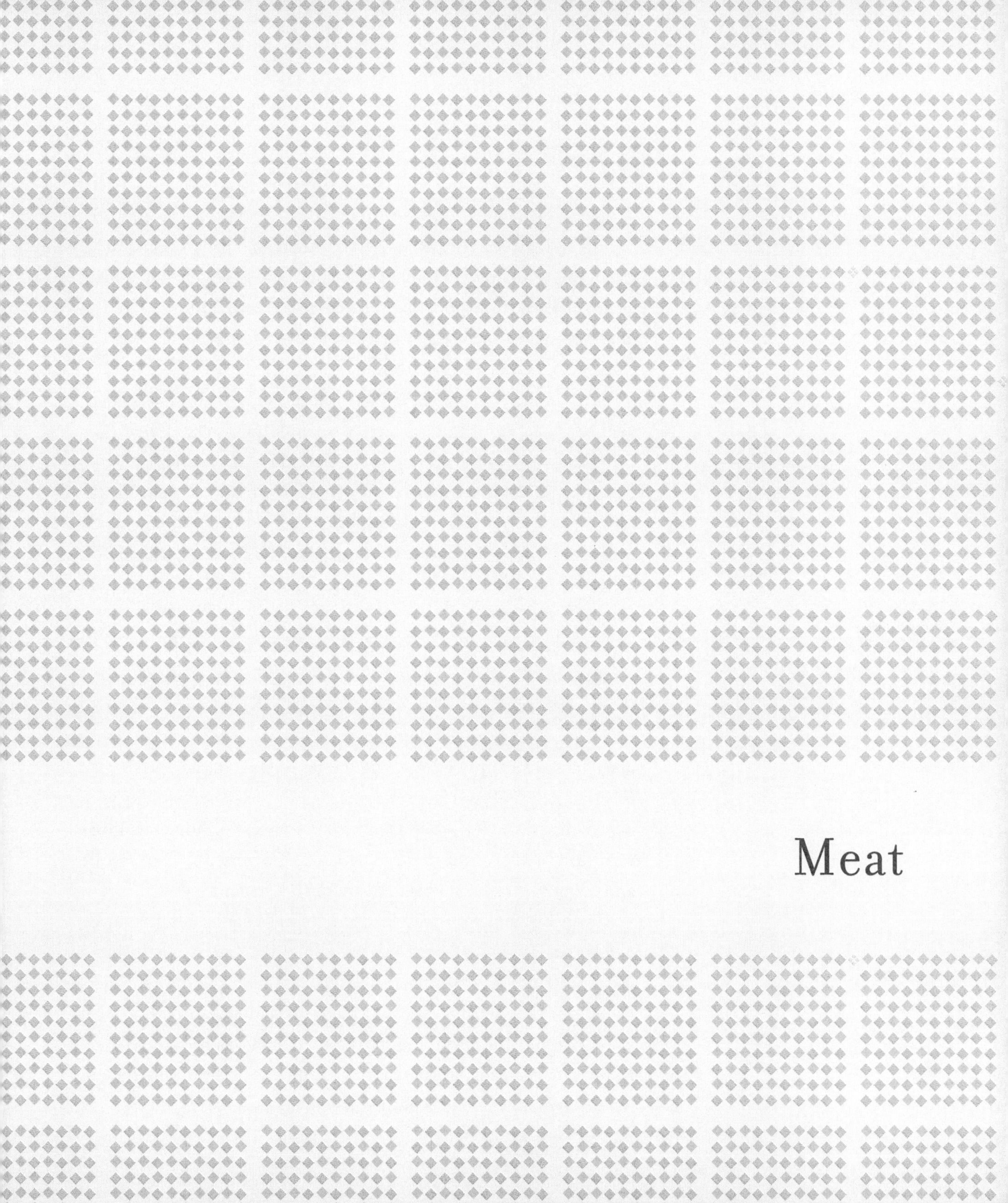

Meat

A passage near the end of Genesis 32 describes a fight between the patriarch Jacob and an angel; though Jacob ultimately emerges victorious, the angel strikes a blow against a vein in Jacob's thigh, leaving him with a limp. This, the chapter tells us, has led to the Jewish tradition of not eating the thigh vein, that is, the sciatic nerve.

The sciatic nerve is found in the hindquarters of animals, which, as it happens, is also the source of the tenderest cuts of meat; the meat that was permitted to Jews tended to be much tougher. (It is possible to remove the sciatic nerve, but this is an exceedingly painstaking process.) Furthermore, once an animal has been slaughtered, the kosher laws require that the meat be soaked and salted within 72 hours, less time than is necessary for it to be fully aged and tenderized.

The combination of these two dictates meant that Jews had to rely on other means to produce tender meat. So they often turned to the slow, moist cooking of braises and stews, the perfect technique for tenderizing otherwise tough cuts. What resulted were some of the most prized—and delicious—dishes in the entire Jewish repertoire. From an Ashkenazic pot roast or flanken to a Sephardic lamb stew, they are the very essence of home cooking: food done simply and in large batches (the better to feed family and friends), and delicious time after time, year after year.

This is, to be sure, slow food; the dishes all require long cooking, and some are ideally begun the day before serving. There is much to recommend this approach, though. It is about as low-stress as cooking gets—almost all of your time is spent doing something else while the pot simmers—and, in the end, about as rewarding. The meat that went into the pot may have been one of the humbler cuts, but that which emerges is nothing short of glorious.

DISHES: Pot Roast

Success in cooking, as in so much of life, lies in large part in knowing the relevant rules of thumb, those handy little apothegms that give one a general feel for the subject at hand. In cooking with beef, the most important rule of thumb is this: The closer to the head or hoof the meat is, the tougher it will be.

The tenderest beef of all comes from the short loin, a narrow section in the middle of the steer's back, which gets very little exercise and thus never toughens. The short loin gives us both the New York strip and the tenderloin, commonly known as filet mignon; when the two cuts are served on their common bone, you have a porterhouse. As it happens, the porterhouse is not a kosher cut of meat, and neither is its immediate neighbor, the sirloin steak. These cuts come from the steer's hindquarters, which contains the sciatic nerve, consumption of which is prohibited by the kosher laws.

Why God chose to withhold from the Jews the choicest meat on the steer is a question probably best left to the philosophers. What this dictate has meant, however, is that Jews who keep kosher must make do with beef taken from the front and lower portions of the animal. As our rule of thumb reminds us, these are the tougher, muscley parts, and tend to contain lots of connective tissue as well. As a result they must be tenderized, best done through slow, moist cooking. This is the technique known as braising, in which a piece of meat is long-cooked in a relatively small amount of liquid in a tightly sealed pot. Each of these elements is an essential part of the equation: The heat must be moist, so that it can melt the collagen found in the connective tissue (the dissolved collagen imparts great flavor and body to the cooking liquid), and it must be slow—at a simmer, not a boil, for boiling will cause the meat to toughen. The cooking can be done either on the stovetop or in the oven, as long as the heat is moderate and the pot is tightly sealed (a piece of aluminum foil placed under the lid helps), so that the liquid does not escape as steam.

In a proper braise, the meat is first browned, by searing it in a small amount of hot oil before the liquid is added. Conventional wisdom has it that this serves to "seal in the juices" of the meat, helping it to stay moist, but as the eminent food writer Harold McGee pointed out in *The Curious Cook*, this is a piece of culinary mythology, based on a theory propounded by the nineteenth-century German chemist Justus von Liebig who, as McGee notes, "never bothered to test his theory by experiment." In fact, a seared piece of meat will tend to lose slightly *more* moisture than one cooked straight through at a low temperature. The purpose of searing, rather, is to intensify flavor. Caramelizing the surface of the meat, as happens with a good sear, produces hundreds of new flavor compounds, thanks to what is known as the "browning reaction" (also known as the Maillard reaction, after the French scientist who spent eight years studying it).

The liquid in which the meat cooks can be as simple as plain water, although additional flavor can be provided by the use of other liquids—stock, wine, tomato sauce, or even coffee—to augment or replace the water. The cooking liquid (which, when reduced, will become sauce for the meat) can be further flavored with garlic, aromatic vegetables such as onions and carrots, and, for a sweet-and-sour taste, vinegar and brown sugar. Among the Jews of Eastern Europe, the dish that resulted was called *gedempte fleysh*, Yiddish for stewed meat. In America, the dish is called pot roast, something of a misnomer, actually, as the meat is braised rather than roasted.

Most often the meat used in pot roasts is brisket, a flat, boneless, flavorful cut taken from the breast of the steer. (Briskets can be purchased whole, but these generally run ten to fifteen pounds, so you'll likely want a cut brisket. First-cut brisket is leaner and more expensive; the second cut is fattier, and thus more flavorful.) Brisket is so popular for making pot roasts, in fact, that sometimes people confuse the terms, or use them interchangeably, but the two aren't the same: Brisket refers to a cut of meat; pot roast to a cooking technique. Or, to put it another way, we might say that a brisket is always a pot roast, but a pot roast is not always a brisket. Indeed, though I find brisket unsurpassed for braising, an excellent pot roast can perfectly well be obtained using a different cut of meat. In the

Jewish tradition, which, again, prohibits meat from the back of the animal, such as the bottom round, a cut often used for pot roasts, this is usually chuck roast, taken from the shoulder of the steer. Like brisket, chuck roast is a flat cut, usually boneless, and, when cooked correctly, very flavorful.

No matter which cut you use, though, it's always best to cook the pot roast the day before and let it sit overnight in the refrigerator, which deepens the flavor. The next day, slice the meat when it's cold, making sure to slice it against the grain, or else it will be stringy. Overnight refrigeration is also useful because it solidifies the fat on top of the cooking liquid, allowing it to be easily removed. Return the sliced meat to the now de-fatted liquid, and slowly reheat. The meat that results will be tasty, richly sauced, and amazingly tender, crumbling at the first pressure from a fork. It's enough to make you believe, if only for the time it takes to finish dinner, that you understand what God had intended after all.

SWEET-AND-SOUR POT ROAST

Sweet-and-sour dishes have been a staple of the Ashkenazic culinary repertoire since the Middle Ages. In Central Europe, among the most common of the Jewish sweet-and-sour dishes was esig fleysh, *sweet-and-sour beef, flavored with lemon juice or vinegar, red wine, brown sugar, and ginger. They are much the same flavorings used in this modern version of* esig fleysh, *made by Beth Shepard of Gill, Massachusetts. Beth learned it from her mother, Beatrice Simms, who had learned it from her mother, Rebecca Rosenthal, an immigrant from the Ukraine. I have made this pot roast for many dinner parties and other gatherings, and it has always drawn raves.*

SERVES 6 TO 8

FOR THE SAUCE

1 large onion, coarsely chopped
2 garlic cloves
½ cup red wine vinegar
¼ cup lightly packed brown sugar
½ cup canned crushed tomatoes
¼ teaspoon red pepper flakes
½ teaspoon dried oregano
½ teaspoon dried thyme
½ teaspoon salt
¼ teaspoon freshly ground black pepper
½ cup cold coffee

1 chuck roast or brisket, about 4 pounds
Salt
Freshly ground black pepper
2 tablespoons vegetable oil
8 to 10 gingersnaps, crushed

1. Preheat the oven to 350 degrees.
2. Combine all the sauce ingredients in the bowl of a food processor. Pulse until the mixture is well chopped, but not pureed. Set aside.
3. Season the meat generously with salt and pepper. Heat the oil in a Dutch oven or other large, heavy pot over medium-high heat. Add the meat and brown well on both sides. If necessary, remove the meat and pour off any excess fat from the pot. Pour the sauce over the meat in the pot and bring to a boil.
4. Cover the pot with a tight-fitting lid and place it in the oven. Braise until the meat is not quite fork-tender, about 2½ hours. Remove from the oven and let cool. Cover the pot and refrigerate for several hours or overnight.
5. Remove the meat from the pot to a cutting board and skim off any solidified fat on the surface of the sauce. Slice the meat thinly against the grain.
6. Add the crushed gingersnaps to the sauce in the pot and stir until well combined. Return the sliced meat to the pot and cook on the stovetop over low heat until the meat is fully tender, about another hour. Transfer the meat to a large serving platter and ladle the sauce over it. Serve hot.

ONION-SMOTHERED BRISKET WITH ALLSPICE

This recipe comes from David Schochet of Shelburne Falls, Massachusetts. He inherited it from his grandmother, Henrietta Kravitz Hertz, an excellent cook, who in her adult years ran a boardinghouse in the Catskills. The dish is attractively simple, relying for the most part on the moisture from the caramelized onions, the lush sweetness of which melds perfectly with the spicy, clove-like flavor of whole allspice berries. This preparation is also wonderful for people on low-sodium diets, because it needs almost no salt and, indeed, would be perfectly fine without any at all.

SERVES 8

- 3 tablespoons vegetable oil
- 8 onions, thinly sliced
- 1 brisket, 4 to 5 pounds
- Salt
- Freshly ground black pepper
- 8 allspice berries
- 3 tablespoons water or beef stock
- 4 carrots, peeled and sliced ½ inch thick
- 3 tablespoons dry white wine

1. Preheat the oven to 350 degrees.
2. Heat the oil in a Dutch oven or other large, heavy pot over medium-low heat. Add the onions and cook, stirring occasionally, until caramelized, at least 35 minutes. Remove to a plate.
3. Season the meat with salt and pepper. Add it to the pot along with the allspice berries. Raise the heat to medium-high and brown the brisket on both sides. Return the onions to the pot. Add the water or beef stock. Cover the pot with a tight-fitting lid and place it in the oven. Braise until the meat is not quite fork-tender, about 2½ hours. Let cool. Cover the pot and refrigerate for several hours or overnight.
4. Remove the meat from the pot to a cutting board, and skim off any solidified fat on the surface of the cooking liquid. Slice the meat thinly against the grain. Return the meat to the pot, add the carrots and white wine, and simmer on the stovetop over low heat until the meat and vegetables are fork-tender, about 1 hour. Taste and add salt, if necessary. Transfer the meat to a large serving platter and ladle the sauce over it. Serve hot.

FLOYMEN TSIMMES

HONEY-SWEETENED BRISKET WITH VEGETABLES AND PRUNES

Tsimmes *originated in Germany, where there is a long history of cooking meat with fruit and vegetables in long-simmered stews. The word comes from the Middle High German* zuomose, *which referred to a dish served alongside the main course; often this was in the form of a compote—that is, a stewed puree—made with vegetables, herbs, and dried fruit. Over time the Yiddish word assumed another connotation, "a big fuss"—as in the phrase, "Don't make such a* tsimmes *out of it"—a reference to the peeling and chopping required to make a* tsimmes. *Still, the returns are well worth the effort. Sweetened with honey,* tsimmes *is a venerable Rosh Hashanah dish; there's no more delicious way to start off the New Year. This recipe, slightly adapted, comes from Esther Rudomin Hautzig of New York, who learned it from her mother, Raya. Esther is the author of several acclaimed novels for young readers, including The* Endless Steppe, A Gift for Mama, *and* A Picture of Grandmother, *the latter two set in her childhood home of Vilna. (Esther finishes the dish in the oven; I prefer to do it on the stovetop.)*

SERVES 8 TO 10

1 brisket, 4 to 5 pounds
½ teaspoon paprika
Salt
Freshly ground black pepper
Flour for dredging
3 tablespoons vegetable oil
4 onions, sliced
About 3 cups beef stock
3 pounds small white-skinned potatoes, halved

1. Preheat the oven to 350 degrees.
2. Season the meat with the paprika and salt and pepper.
3. Spread some flour in a roasting pan. Dredge the brisket in the flour, shaking off the excess. Set aside.
4. Heat the oil in a Dutch oven or other large, heavy pot over medium heat. Add the onions and cook, stirring often, until soft and lightly colored. Remove to a plate.
5. Raise the heat to medium-high. Add the meat and cook until well browned on both sides.
6. Return the onions to the pot. Add the beef stock. Cover the pot with a heavy, tight-fitting lid and place it in the oven. Braise until the

meat is not quite fork-tender, about 2½ hours, basting the meat several times with the cooking liquid. Remove the pot from the oven. Scrape the onions off the meat back into the liquid. Let cool to room temperature. Cover the pot and refrigerate for several hours or overnight.

7. Remove the meat from the pot and skim off any solidified fat on the surface of the sauce. Slice the meat thinly against the grain. Return the sliced meat to the pot. Add the potatoes, carrots, prunes, and honey. Cover and cook on the stovetop over low heat, stirring occasionally, until the meat and vegetables are fully tender, about another hour. Transfer to a large serving platter. Serve hot.

1½ pounds carrots, peeled and cut into 2-inch chunks

1½ cups pitted prunes

⅓ cup honey

BRISKET WITH CARAMELIZED ONIONS AND COCA-COLA

Trust me: This dish tastes a lot better than it sounds. Louise Metz of Jackson, Mississippi, adapted the recipe from an old Louisiana Cajun cookbook and regularly serves it as the centerpiece for Passover and other holiday meals. The use of Coca-Cola here is not as strange as it might at first seem, for the sugar in it helps to brown the meat, and the combination of the cola (there isn't actually that much), the meat juices, and the liquid from the caramelized onions creates a coffee-colored sauce that is rich and luscious. Your guests will never guess the secret ingredient.

SERVES 8

3 tablespoons olive oil

5 onions, sliced

1 brisket, 4 to 5 pounds

Salt

Freshly ground black pepper

1 teaspoon paprika

1 cup Coca-Cola

1. Preheat the oven to 350 degrees.
2. Heat the oil in a Dutch oven or other large, heavy pot over medium-low heat. Add the onions and cook, stirring occasionally, until lightly caramelized, 30 to 35 minutes. Remove to a plate.
3. Season the brisket with salt and pepper. Add it to the pot. Raise the heat to medium-high and brown well on both sides. Sprinkle the meat with the paprika, and pour the Coca-Cola over the top. Return the onions to the pot, strewing them over the meat.
4. Cover the pot with a heavy, tight-fitting lid and place the pot in the oven. Braise until the meat is not quite fork-tender, about 2½ hours, basting the meat several times with the cooking liquid. Remove the pot from the oven. Scrape the onions off the meat back into the liquid. Let cool, then cover the pot and refrigerate for several hours or overnight.
5. Remove the meat from the pot to a cutting board and skim off any solidified fat on the surface of the sauce. Slice the meat thinly against the grain. Return the sliced meat to the pot and simmer on the stovetop over low heat until the meat is fully tender, about 1 hour. If desired, add a bit of water or beef stock to thin the sauce. Transfer the meat and sauce to a large serving platter. Serve hot.

FLANKEN

BRAISED SHORT RIBS

Flanken *is a Yiddish word meaning flanks—the sides of an animal between the hip and the ribs. Culinarily speaking, it refers to short ribs, strips of beef cut across the rib bones so that each piece contains chunks of beef along with several sliced (short) ribs. Short ribs are sold as individual chunks of beef, but flanken-style short ribs are always long strips with several bones. Like brisket, flanken is capable of wonderful flavor and tenderness, but this must be drawn out through long, slow cooking in liquid. The meat is served with a little bit of the broth and with horseradish (see page 367) on the side. Egg noodles are perfect for soaking up the flavorful broth.*

SERVES 4

- 4 pounds flanken or short ribs
- Salt
- Freshly ground black pepper
- Paprika
- Flour for dredging
- 3 tablespoons vegetable oil
- 6 cups water
- 1 small onion, chopped
- 1 large carrot, peeled and chopped
- 1 large parsnip, peeled and chopped
- 1 celery stalk, chopped
- 2 garlic cloves, chopped
- 1 bay leaf

1. Preheat the oven to 350 degrees.
2. Season the meat generously with salt, pepper, and paprika. Dredge it in flour, shaking off any excess. Heat the oil in a large, heavy pot over medium-high heat. Add the meat, in batches to prevent crowding, and brown well on all sides. Remove to a plate.
3. Pour off the fat in the pot. Add the remaining ingredients plus more salt and pepper to taste. Return the meat to the pot. (You may have to cut it into smaller pieces to fit.) Bring to a boil, skimming off any foam that develops on the surface.
4. Cover the pot with a tight-fitting lid. Place it in the oven and braise until the meat is fork-tender, about 2 hours. If time allows, remove the pot from the oven, let cool, then refrigerate for several hours or overnight.
5. Remove the meat and take off any solidified fat on the surface of the broth. Heat the broth slightly, so that it thins, and strain it into a bowl. Remove the meat from the bones and chop it into bite-sized chunks. Discard the bones and return the meat to the pot. Return the strained cooking liquid to the pot, bring to a boil, and simmer until the meat is reheated. Transfer the meat to a large serving platter and pour some of the broth over it. Serve hot, accompanied by horseradish.

DISHES: Sabbath Stew

Jewish ritual, the great theologian Abraham Joshua Heschel noted in his book *The Sabbath*, might be characterized as "the architecture of time." Most of the Jewish observances, from prayers to festivals to the Jubilee year, depend on a certain hour, a certain day, a certain season. We remember the day Moses stood on Sinai, we mark the day our names are inscribed in the Book of Life, and our greatest hope is for the End of Days: the end of time itself.

The Sabbath, wrote Heschel, is when we "turn from the results of creation to the mystery of creation; from the world of creation to the creation of the world." We do this by setting aside, if only temporarily, our worldly cares, and traditionally this has meant abstinence from all work—more specifically, work that involves the creation or transformation of an object. In the Mishna, the rabbis enumerated thirty-nine classes of forbidden labors, among them plowing, sewing, writing, dyeing, and transporting goods. Also included is lighting a fire, for this is considered (unlike, say, opening a book) an act of creation. On the other hand, Talmudic commentary informs us that it is a *mitzvah* to eat warm food on the Sabbath. This would seem, at first glance, an insoluble problem—warm food, no fire—but it is not, thanks to the rabbinic allowance that a source of heat can be maintained throughout the Sabbath, as long as it was lit before the Sabbath, and not adjusted during it. And so we were provided the Sabbath stew, an ingenious one-pot main dish that is prepared before sundown on Friday and then simmered at a very low heat overnight so that it can be eaten warm on the Sabbath day.

In older times, the stewpots were tightly sealed with a flour-and-water paste, then placed in the oven of the community bakehouse on Friday afternoon, where they remained until they were picked up by their owners after Saturday services. (Because the pots were so tightly sealed, they could even be placed in ovens containing non-kosher food.) The modern world, though, has wrought the breakdown of communal institutions almost everywhere, and today's Sabbath stews are prepared not in central bakehouses but in private homes, either in an electric cookpot, on the stove at the lowest possible flame (aided by a thin aluminum plate, known as a *blech,* that serves to disperse heat), or in the oven at a very low setting. The ingredients that go into the stew vary somewhat from place to place, but the preparation of this dish, like the observance of the Sabbath it serves, is a ritual that binds Jewish communities everywhere.

In the Sephardic world, the Sabbath stew is most often called *dafina* or *adafina* (see page 182), from an Arabic word meaning hidden or buried, a result of the pot having originally been buried in fireplace embers. Sometimes the stew is known as *hamin,* from the Hebrew *kham,* meaning hot. (In Morocco the stew may also be called *skhena,* from an Arabic word meaning hot.) By whatever name it may be called, a Sephardic Sabbath stew usually comprises meat—such as brisket, beef shin, or lamb shoulder, all tough cuts amenable to the long, slow cooking of the Sabbath pot—chickpeas, and potatoes or sweet potatoes, and is abundantly flavored with spices, including cayenne, nutmeg, cumin, and saffron. Sometimes pitted dates might be thrown into the pot as well; they dissolve during the long cooking, sweetening the broth. And always there are eggs still in their shells, which emerge the next day with brown-colored whites and creamy yolks. These long-cooked eggs are most often known as *huevos haminados,* a Ladino term that originated with the Jews who arrived in North Africa having fled Spain after the 1492 edict of expulsion.

Among Ashkenazim, the Sabbath stew goes by only one name—*cholent*—though the origin of this name is clouded, and the debates on this topic have been, befitting the dish itself, long and heated. One explanation, colorful though surely mistaken, posits *cholent* as a modified portmanteau word, from the Yiddish *shul end* (describing when the dish was eaten, at the close of synagogue services). Another finds the word's origins in the French words *chaud* (hot) and *lent* (slow). I have always admired the elegance of this proposition, but sadly enough, in linguistics, unlike physics, the elegant solution is not always the correct one. Today, most linguists concur with the hypothesis put forward by Max Weinreich in his magisterial *History of the*

Yiddish Language, which traces *cholent*'s etymology to the Latin verb *calere,* meaning to be warm and, specifically, to its present participle, *calentem,* meaning that which is warm. (However, Dr. Weinreich did praise the French-based notion as "coming close to the truth," since *chaud* has its roots in the same Latin verb.)

Most *cholents* are pretty similar, comprising meat, beans (generally white beans, which darken considerably during cooking, although sometimes kidney beans are used instead), potatoes, and barley. Ashkenazic *cholents* do not as a rule include hard-boiled eggs and use few seasonings other than salt, pepper, and garlic. The meat is mostly a tough, fatty cut such as short ribs, brisket, or chuck roast, but some communities have their own versions. A Hungarian *cholent,* for instance, uses whole beef tongue, and an Alsatian one goose.

The Sephardic *dafina* is traditionally separated into different dishes before serving, while *cholent* is served as one dish, with the ingredients combined. Either style, though, provides that same wondrous moment, when the lid is first removed, revealing the pot's long-held mystery—tender meat and soft, plump beans submerged in a bubbling, richly fragrant broth, offering up the depth of flavor that can only come from slow, patient cooking: warm, delicious, humble, filling. We sit and eat, and praise the world for the gifts it has given us.

SOLET

HUNGARIAN SABBATH STEW

Either brisket or chuck roast works fine here. In Hungary, a whole beef tongue is also often used.

SERVES 8

- 1 pound (about 2½ cups) dried pinto beans
- 2 to 3 pounds brisket or chuck roast, cut into pieces
- 2 tablespoons vegetable oil
- 1 large onion, chopped
- 3 garlic cloves, chopped
- 1 large marrow bone (optional)
- ⅔ cup pearl barley
- 1 green pepper, cored and quartered
- 1 tomato, cored and quartered
- 2 teaspoons paprika
- 1 to 2 teaspoons salt
- Freshly ground black pepper

1. Place the beans in a large pot and cover with at least 2 inches of water. Let soak overnight, drain, and set aside.
2. Heat the oil in a Dutch oven or other large, heavy pot over medium-high heat. Add the meat and cook until it is browned on all sides. Remove the meat, lower the heat to medium, add the onion, and cook, stirring often, until soft and translucent. Add the garlic and cook for another minute. Return the meat to the pot and add the marrow bone (if using), beans, barley, green pepper, and tomato. Sprinkle each layer with a bit of salt and pepper and paprika.
3. Add water to cover. Cover the pot and bring to a boil. Lower the heat and simmer for 30 minutes, skimming off any foam that develops on the surface.
4. While the meat cooks, preheat the oven to 225 degrees.
5. Cover the pot tightly. To make the seal even tighter, place a piece of aluminum foil under the lid. Place the pot in the oven and cook overnight, 12 to 20 hours. (Or place the pot in a preheated 350-degree oven until the meat is fully tender, about 2 hours.) Serve hot.

DAFINA

MOROCCAN SABBATH STEW

Among the Jews of Morocco, the Sabbath stew was most often called dafina *or* adafina. *The Jaquetia-speaking Jews of Northern Morocco replaced the aromatic spices with 3 tablespoons of caramelized sugar. In Tangier, fried onion or an intestine stuffed with ground beef was sometimes added. A spicier version of Moroccan Sabbath stew, called* orissa, *uses hot chilies. Traditionally, the various elements of the* dafina*—chickpeas and liquid, eggs, potatoes, and meat—are served on separate platters.*

SERVES 6

- 1 cup dried chickpeas
- 2 pounds brisket or chuck roast, cut into 4 pieces
- Pinch of saffron or ½ teaspoon turmeric
- ½ teaspoon ground cinnamon
- 1 teaspoon paprika
- 2 teaspoons salt
- Freshly ground black pepper
- 4 medium red-skin potatoes, about 1½ pounds, peeled
- 3 medium sweet potatoes, 2 to 2½ pounds, peeled
- 6 pitted dried dates
- ¼ cup olive oil
- 6 eggs, in their shells (optional)

1. Place the chickpeas in a large pot and cover with at least 2 inches of water. Let soak overnight, drain, and set aside.
2. Place the chickpeas in the bottom of a Dutch oven or other large, heavy pot. Place the meat on top of the chickpeas and cover with water. Cover the pot and bring to a boil. Lower the heat and simmer for 30 minutes, skimming off any foam that develops on the surface. Add the saffron or turmeric, cinnamon, paprika, and salt and pepper and simmer for another 30 minutes.
3. Add the potatoes, sweet potatoes, dates, and additional water almost to cover, making sure to leave at least 1 inch of headroom from the top of the pot. Drizzle the oil over the liquid. If you are cooking the stew overnight, arrange the eggs (if using) around the top.
4. Preheat the oven to 225 degrees.
5. Cover the pot tightly. To make the seal even tighter, place a piece of aluminum foil under the lid. Place the pot in the oven and bake overnight, 12 to 20 hours. (Or place the pot in a preheated 350-degree oven until the meat is fully tender, about 2 hours.) Serve hot.

LUBIYA BEL CAMOUN

TUNISIAN BEEF STEW WITH WHITE BEANS AND CUMIN

In 1948, some 100,000 Jews lived in Tunisia. Then came a period of mass emigration, mostly to Israel and France (at the time the colonial power), and today fewer than 2,000 Jews still live in Tunisia. This is a very popular dish among Tunisian Jews. Lots of cumin, paprika, and garlic make the sauce rich and flavorful, and the beans come out soft and lovely.

SERVES 6

- 1 pound (about 2¼ cups) dried navy or other white beans
- 2 pounds chuck roast, cut into 1½-inch cubes
- Salt
- Freshly ground black pepper
- ½ cup olive oil
- 5 garlic cloves, chopped
- 2 tablespoons ground cumin
- 1 tablespoon paprika
- 2 tablespoons tomato paste
- 6 cups water

1. Place the beans in a large pot and cover with at least 2 inches of water. Let soak overnight, drain, and set aside.
2. Season the meat generously with salt and pepper. Heat 2 tablespoons of the oil in a Dutch oven or other large, heavy pot over medium-high heat. Add the meat, in batches if necessary, and cook until well browned on all sides.
3. Add the remaining oil, the beans, garlic, cumin, paprika, and tomato paste and stir to combine. Add the water and bring to a boil, skimming off any foam that develops on the surface. Lower the heat and simmer, covered, until the meat and beans are fully tender, about 1½ hours. Taste and add salt as needed. Transfer the meat and beans to a large serving platter and spoon some of the cooking liquid over them. Serve hot.

KHORESHT BEH VA ALOU

IRANIAN BEEF STEW WITH QUINCES AND PRUNES

In Iran, a khoresht *refers to a stew containing meat (usually beef, but chicken or duck can also be used) and either fruit or vegetables that is served with its sauce. Quinces are indigenous to Iran and are featured in many dishes, both sweet and savory. This is a great thick, hearty stew, with a pleasing touch of sweetness from the fruit. It can be served with the crusty rice called* Chelou *(page 279) or plain white rice.*

SERVES 4

- 2 tablespoons vegetable oil
- 1½ pounds chuck roast, cut into 1-inch cubes
- 1 onion, chopped
- Salt
- Freshly ground black pepper
- 2 cups water
- Juice of 1 lemon
- ¼ cup dried split peas
- 2 quinces
- 1 cup pitted prunes, halved

1. Heat the oil in a Dutch oven or other large, heavy pot over medium heat. Season the beef generously with salt and pepper. Add it to the pot, in batches if necessary to avoid overcrowding, and cook until it is well browned on all sides. Remove to a plate. Add the onion and cook, stirring often, until soft and translucent.
2. Return the meat to the pot. Add the water, lemon juice, split peas, and salt and pepper. Bring to a boil, skimming off any foam that develops on the surface. Lower the heat and simmer, covered, until the meat is nearly tender, about 1¼ hours.
3. Peel and core the quinces and chop them into ½-inch dice. Add the quinces and prunes to the pot and simmer until the meat and fruit are fully tender, about 25 minutes. Transfer the meat and fruit to a large serving platter and pour the sauce over it. Serve hot.

INGRIYI

IRAQI SWEET-AND-SOUR MEAT WITH EGGPLANT AND PEPPERS

This was a festive dish among the Jews of Iraq. In her book Indian-Jewish Cooking, *Mavis Hyman gives a recipe of the Baghdadi Jews of Calcutta for a dish called* ingree, *which is essentially the same as this one except that it uses chicken instead of meat. Like the version from Iraq, it was a favorite for holidays and Friday-night dinners.*

SERVES 6

- 1/4 cup olive or vegetable oil
- 1 onion, chopped
- 1½ pounds beef or lamb stew meat, cut into 1-inch cubes
- Salt
- Freshly ground black pepper
- 1 large eggplant, about 1½ pounds, cut into ½-inch slices
- 2 tomatoes, thinly sliced
- 1 red pepper, thinly sliced
- 1 green pepper, thinly sliced
- 1 cup tomato juice
- ½ cup fresh lemon juice (about 4 lemons)
- 3 tablespoons sugar

1. Heat 2 tablespoons of the oil in a Dutch oven or other large pot over medium heat. Add the onion and cook, stirring often, until soft and translucent. Remove to a plate.
2. Season the meat with salt and pepper. Add the meat to the pot, raise the heat to medium-high, and continue cooking until the meat is well browned on all sides.
3. Return the onion to the pot. Add enough water to cover the meat and onion. Bring to a boil, skimming off any foam that develops on the surface. Lower the heat and simmer, covered, for 1 hour. Drain and set aside.
4. While the meat is cooking, heat the remaining 2 tablespoons of oil in a large skillet over medium-high heat. In batches, add the eggplant and cook until lightly browned on both sides. Add a bit more oil if necessary. Drain on paper towels.
5. Preheat the oven to 350 degrees.
6. Arrange the eggplant in a large baking dish. Cover with a layer of meat and onion and top with the tomatoes and peppers. Season with salt and pepper.
7. In a small bowl, combine the tomato juice, lemon juice, and sugar. Taste and adjust the flavoring as desired. Pour the mixture over the layered meat and vegetables. Loosely cover with foil and cook for 1 to 1½ hours, until the meat is very tender. Transfer to a large serving platter. Serve hot.

MSOKI

TUNISIAN LAMB STEW WITH MIXED VEGETABLES AND FRESH HERBS

This is the Tunisian Passover specialty, a genuine celebration of spring's abundance. It is delicious, very festive, and rather elaborate, although the only real effort comes beforehand, from assembling and then cutting up the many different vegetables. The recipe comes from Elie Sabban of Chevy Chase, Maryland, who grew up in Sfax—a seaport on the eastern coast of Tunisia and the country's second-largest city after Tunis—and immigrated to the United States in 1962.

SERVES 10

3 pounds boneless lamb shoulder, well trimmed, cut into 1-inch cubes

Salt

Freshly ground black pepper

½ cup olive oil

2 onions, chopped

2 leeks (white and pale green parts only), well washed and chopped

8 garlic cloves, chopped

2 pounds fresh spinach, well washed and chopped

1 pound fresh or frozen peas

1 fennel bulb, cored and cut into ¼-inch slices

4 carrots, peeled and sliced into ½-inch rounds

4 fresh or canned artichoke hearts, quartered

3 turnips, peeled and diced

1 small green cabbage, about 1½ pounds, cored and chopped

4 celery stalks, cut into ½-inch pieces

1 zucchini, halved lengthwise and cut into ½-inch pieces

1 cinnamon stick

½ teaspoon freshly grated nutmeg

1 teaspoon ground allspice

2 teaspoons salt

Freshly ground black pepper

3 medium russet potatoes, peeled and cut into ¼-inch dice

½ cup chopped fresh cilantro

½ cup chopped fresh flat-leaf parsley

½ cup chopped fresh dill

10 mint leaves, chopped

4 matzos, broken into small pieces, for serving

1. Season the meat generously with salt and pepper. In a large pot, heat ¼ cup of the oil over medium-high heat. Add the meat in batches and cook until browned on all sides. Remove to a plate.

2. Add the onions and leeks and cook, stirring often, until soft and translucent. Add the garlic and cook for another minute.

3. Return the meat to the pot. Add the remaining ingredients except for the potatoes and herbs, plus the remaining ¼ cup of oil, and stir to combine. Add water just to cover. Cover the pot and bring to a boil. Lower the heat and simmer for 1½ hours.

4. Add the potatoes and the herbs and continue simmering for about another 30 minutes, until the potatoes are soft and the meat is very tender. Taste and adjust for seasoning. Ladle hot into bowls and top with pieces of matzo.

AGNEAU AUX AMANDES ET PRUNEAUX

MOROCCAN LAMB WITH ALMONDS AND PRUNES

In Morocco, tagine *refers both to a stew and to the earthenware pot with a conical lid in which the stew is cooked. There are many kinds of* tagines; *the majority are made with lamb, though others use chicken or fish, or are vegetarian. The* tagines *may also include such Moroccan staples as olives, preserved lemon, artichokes, fennel, and fava beans, and commonly include nuts and dried fruit.*

SERVES 6

- 2 tablespoons olive oil
- 1 onion, chopped
- 2 garlic cloves, chopped
- 1 boneless lamb shoulder, about 2½ pounds, well trimmed, cut into 1½-inch cubes
- Salt
- Freshly ground black pepper
- ½ teaspoon turmeric or a pinch of crushed saffron threads
- ½ teaspoon powdered ginger
- ½ teaspoon ground cinnamon
- 1 tablespoon honey
- 2 cups water
- 1¼ cups pitted prunes, halved
- ¾ cup blanched whole almonds

1. Heat the oil in a large, heavy pot or Dutch oven over medium heat. Add the onion and cook, stirring often, until soft and translucent. Add the garlic and cook, stirring, for 1 minute. Remove the onion and garlic to a plate.
2. Season the lamb well with salt and pepper. Raise the heat to medium-high. In batches, add the lamb to the pot and cook until well browned on all sides. Add the turmeric or saffron, ginger, cinnamon, and salt to taste and cook, stirring, for 1 minute.
3. Return the onion and garlic to the pot, and add the honey and water. Cover and bring to a boil. Lower the heat and simmer until the meat is tender, about 1½ hours. Add the prunes and simmer for 5 minutes.
4. In a medium dry skillet, cook the almonds, stirring regularly, over low heat until lightly toasted, about 5 minutes. Remove from the heat.
5. Transfer the meat and prunes to a large serving platter and ladle some of the cooking liquid over them. Sprinkle with the toasted almonds. Serve hot.

DISHES: Albondigas

It may not be possible to read the future in tea leaves or coffee grounds, but it is possible to read the past in meatballs. Certain ones, anyway—like the delicious Turkish Jewish meatballs called *albondigas.*

I had long heard about *albondigas*, but I had never tasted one until a Turkish friend sent me a copy of *Sefarad Yemekleri* (Sephardic Food), a cookbook published in 1990 by members of Istanbul's Jewish community to raise money for a senior-citizens' home there. *Sefarad Yemekleri* is a fascinating compilation of traditional Turkish Jewish recipes, among them such favorites as *almodrote de berengena* (eggplant gratin), *apyo* (sweet-and-sour celery), and the sweetened rice-flour pudding, *sutlach.* Of the 141 recipes included in the book, 7 are for *albondigas*, which says something about their importance to the community. *Albondigas* are perhaps the most beloved of all Turkish Jewish foods, served on the Sabbath, on holidays, at weddings, or, for that matter, on almost any other festive occasion. So it has been for a very long time. Says Klara Perahya, a writer for the Istanbul Jewish weekly newspaper *Shalom*, "When I make *albondigas*, they are the same as my grandmother's *albondigas* from seventy years ago. A lot of things have changed, but *albondigas* never did."

Correctly prepared, *albondigas* come out of the frying pan crisp outside and remarkably light inside, almost fluffy. The surprising softness of the interior results from the ground meat having been mixed not just with starch, as in most other meatballs, but also with some form of cooked vegetable. (These meatballs are, in fact, mostly vegetable.) It is not unusual for *albondigas* to contain potato, spinach, celery, or eggplant, but the most famous and popular variety is certainly the *albondigas de prasa:* leek meatballs.

As it happens, adding chopped vegetables to meatballs seems to be one of the distinctive features of Jewish cuisine. It is commonplace in Jewish communities in Turkey, Italy, the Balkans, and parts of North

Africa, but unknown outside them. I asked Nicholas Stavroulakis, the leading authority on Greek Jewish food, about this. "I can't say that we are the only people to do this," he told me, "but we certainly do, and mixing vegetables and meat together to form meatballs is certainly neither Turkish nor Greek nor Bulgarian."

Why this is so has never definitively been answered, but it likely has to do with the very popularity of the meatball among Jewish cooks. For them, the generally tenderer cuts of meat in the back of the animal are outlawed by the dictates of *kashrut.* As a result, Jews had to adopt various methods of tenderizing the tougher meat from the forequarters. This resulted in the celebrated Jewish affinity for long-stewed pot roasts. But many times whole cuts were unavailable, and all the cook could obtain were scraps, flavorful but very tough, that required chopping or grinding to be made palatable. Still, even this humble meat was relatively expensive for those in the lower reaches of society, and so thrifty cooks naturally sought to stretch the meat by combining it with cheaper, more plentiful ingredients. Meatballs were a perfect medium, as bread crumbs, cooked rice, or mashed potato could be easily incorporated into them. In this way, meatballs are like that other classic forcemeat, gefilte fish; and like gefilte fish, meatballs could, if necessary, be made ahead of time and served cold on the Sabbath, when cooking was prohibited. So the meatball proved a special boon to Jewish cooks, who over time found that adding finely chopped vegetables to the meatballs not only further stretched the meat but also gave variety to a dish that might otherwise have become too familiar. In Turkey, the result was *albondigas.*

And that, finally, brings us to the name itself. The word *albondigas* is not Turkish, which immediately raises questions about why a dish that has been made in Turkey for several hundred years does not have a Turkish name. Turkish meatballs (which can include chopped onions, but not the wide variety of cooked vegetables in *albondigas*) are called *kofte,* from the Persian verb meaning to pound, also the root of the Greek *keftedes.* The word *albondigas* probably comes from the Arabic *al bundaq,* meaning round, although it might be a corrupted form of *albidaca,* meaning chopped meat. As John Cooper noted in *Eat and Be Satisfied: A Social History of Jewish Food*, the Arabs of the early medieval period, like the Jews of a slightly later one, would often make use of the toughest pieces of meat by chopping them up and turning them into meatballs. Both the name and the practice, then, would indicate that these meatballs had their origin in the Middle East and migrated west with the Moorish conquests, until they arrived in Spain and became known as *albondigas*.

Albondigas were extremely popular with the Jewish community in Spain, so much so that during Inquisition trials the preparation of *albondigas*, like the Sabbath stew *dafina*, was presented by prosecutors as evidence of secret Jewish practice. Of course the vast majority of Spain's Jews were never subject to these trials, because they had long since fled, bringing the recipes for their beloved *albondigas* with them wherever they went, including to Turkey, where meatballs are still called *albondigas*, half a millennium after the Spanish exile, by the Jewish community there.

So the full import of these meatballs now begins to come clear. Meatballs represent, in a real sense, the momentary capacity of the poor to become rich: to overcome the strictures of poverty and turn the rudest of fare into something delicious. In the meat, painstakingly tenderized by chopping and pounding in home kitchens, we see the struggle to craft pleasing sustenance from seemingly forbidding ingredients; in the vegetables we see the challenge to an otherwise wearying routine. Indeed, in the very name itself—*albondigas*—we can detect broad swaths of European history, from the Arab conquests of the west to the exile of the Spanish Jews. In the present-day use of the name, too, we see the noble efforts of the Jews of Turkey to maintain their historical connection, over long centuries, to the homeland they so fervently loved and from which they fled in terror. Seemingly one of the lowliest of foods, this meatball turns out to be among the most magnificent.

ALBONDIGAS DE PRASA KON MUEZ

LEEK MEATBALLS WITH WALNUTS

I've adapted this recipe from one in Sefarad Yemekleri, *a cookbook published by the Jewish community of Istanbul. Make sure that you have squeezed out all of the excess water in the potatoes and leeks, or else the* albondigas *will not have the proper consistency.*

SERVES 6 TO 8

- 2 pounds medium leeks
- 1 large russet potato (about 12 ounces), peeled and quartered
- 3/4 pound ground beef or lamb
- 3 tablespoons coarsely chopped walnuts
- 3 eggs
- Salt
- Freshly ground black pepper
- Vegetable oil for frying
- Flour or matzo meal for dredging
- Lemon wedges for drizzling

1. Trim the leeks, reserving only the white and pale green parts. Cut them into ½-inch pieces and soak in a large bowl of cold water, making sure to remove any dirt that may be clinging to them.
2. Bring a large pot of salted water to a boil. Add the leeks and the potato and cook until soft. Drain well and let cool. Carefully squeeze out all the excess water from the leeks and mash the potato.
3. Place the leeks and mashed potato in a large bowl. Add the meat, walnuts, and 1 of the eggs and season with a generous amount of salt and pepper. Stir to combine. Place the mixture in the bowl of a food processor and pulse until it just comes together in a soft paste. Roll the paste into balls about 1 inch in diameter. (You should have about 48 meatballs.)
4. Preheat the oven to 200 degrees. In a large skillet, add oil to a depth of about ½ inch and heat over medium-high heat.
5. Beat the remaining 2 eggs in a bowl and spread some flour on a plate. Roll the meatballs in the flour, shaking off any excess, and then in the eggs. Place the meatballs gently in the hot oil. Do this in batches, so as not to reduce the oil temperature too much.
6. Cook the meatballs until they are golden brown all over and cooked through, about 10 minutes, turning as necessary. Drain them on paper towels, then place them on a plate and put the plate in the oven. When all the meatballs are cooked, transfer them to a large serving platter. Drizzle with the lemon juice. Serve hot.

BOULETTES AUX POIS ET CÉLERI

MOROCCAN MEATBALLS WITH PEAS AND CELERY

This is a gorgeously colored dish, with the crispily browned meatballs simmering in a sauce of bright-green peas and celery. It comes from Stella Ymar of Rockville, Maryland, who left Casablanca in 1964.

SERVES 6

FOR THE MEATBALLS

2 pounds ground beef

¼ cup bread crumbs, fresh or dried

½ teaspoon salt

Freshly ground black pepper

¼ teaspoon freshly grated nutmeg

1 small onion, finely chopped

2 tablespoons chopped fresh flat-leaf parsley

2 eggs, lightly beaten

3 tablespoons olive oil

FOR THE SAUCE

1 large onion, chopped

4 celery stalks, diced

1 box (10 ounces) frozen peas

Juice of ½ lemon

1 cup water

Pinch of saffron

Salt

Freshly ground black pepper

1. Make the meatballs: Place all of the meatball ingredients in a large bowl and stir until completely combined. With moistened hands, roll the mixture into balls about 1¼ inches in diameter. (You should have about 40 meatballs.)
2. Heat the oil in a large skillet over medium-high heat. In batches, add the meatballs and cook until browned. Drain on paper towels.
3. Make the sauce: Lower the heat to medium, then add the onion to the pan. (If desired, drain excess oil from the pan.) Cook, stirring often, until the onion is soft and lightly colored. Add the celery, peas, lemon juice, water, and saffron, and season with salt and pepper. Cover the pot and bring to a boil. Lower the heat and simmer, covered, for 5 minutes.
4. Add the meatballs and simmer, covered, for 15 minutes. Transfer to a large serving platter. Serve hot.

KOFTA MESHEMSHIYA

IRAQI MEATBALLS IN APRICOT SAUCE

The Jews of Iraq had a taste for sweet-and-sour flavorings, as well as for dishes that combined meat and fruit. Both are likely a legacy of the Persians, who occupied the country at various times during the sixteenth and seventeenth centuries, and both can be found in this vibrantly colored, lushly flavored dish.

SERVES 4

FOR THE MEATBALLS

1½ pounds ground beef or lamb

1 small onion, finely chopped

¼ cup chopped fresh flat-leaf parsley

¼ teaspoon ground cloves

½ teaspoon turmeric

Juice of 1 lemon

½ teaspoon salt

Freshly ground black pepper

FOR THE SAUCE

3 tablespoons olive oil

1 onion, chopped

1 cup tomato juice

¾ cup water

Juice of 2 lemons

2 teaspoons sugar

1 cup dried apricots, chopped

½ cup raisins

Salt

Freshly ground black pepper

1. Make the meatballs: Place all of the meatball ingredients in a large bowl and mix until fully combined. With moistened hands, form the mixture into balls about 1½ inches in diameter. (You should have about 24 meatballs.)

2. Make the sauce: Heat the oil in a large skillet over medium heat. Add the onion and cook, stirring often, until soft and translucent. Add the meatballs to the pan and cook, turning as necessary, until browned on all sides.

3. Add the remaining ingredients and stir to combine. Cover and bring to a boil. Lower the heat and simmer, stirring occasionally, until the meatballs are fully cooked through, about 30 minutes. Taste and adjust for seasoning. Transfer the meatballs to a large serving platter and pour the sauce over them. Serve hot.

ZIS UN ZOYER KNEYDLACH

EASTERN EUROPEAN SWEET-AND-SOUR MEATBALLS

Originally an Eastern European dish, sweet-and-sour meatballs came to the United States with the mass Jewish immigration of the late nineteenth and early twentieth centuries. In the postwar years they were often "modernized" by the addition of such unlikely ingredients as canned chili sauce and grape jelly. This recipe contains no such adornments. It is from Mrs. Chayele Palevsky, who learned it from her mother, Malke Porus, in her childhood home near Vilna, in Lithuania. Chayele Palevsky, one of the heroic partisans of the Vilna ghetto, now lives in the Bronx.

SERVES 4

FOR THE MEATBALLS

1½ pounds ground beef

1 small onion, grated

1 egg, lightly beaten

3 tablespoons matzo meal

Salt

Freshly ground black pepper

FOR THE SAUCE

2 cups canned chopped tomatoes

1 cup water

1 onion, thinly sliced

1 carrot, peeled and grated

2 apples, peeled and grated

2 tablespoons honey or sugar

Juice of ½ lemon

Salt

1 tablespoon cornstarch

⅓ cup water

1. Make the meatballs: Combine all of the meatball ingredients in a large bowl and stir until fully combined. With moistened hands, form the mixture into balls about 1 inch in diameter. (You should have about 36 meatballs.)
2. Make the sauce: In a large saucepan, combine the tomatoes, water, onion, carrot, apples, honey or sugar, and lemon juice, and season with salt. Cover and bring to a boil. Lower the heat and simmer, stirring occasionally, for 10 minutes.
3. Place the meatballs in the sauce. Cover and simmer over very low heat, stirring occasionally to prevent the meatballs from sticking, for 1 hour.
4. Dissolve the cornstarch in the water and stir the mixture into the sauce. Continue simmering, stirring, until the sauce has thickened slightly. Taste and adjust for seasoning. Transfer the meatballs to a large serving platter and pour the sauce over them. Serve hot.

Meat

KEFTIKES DE ESPINAKA

SPINACH MEAT PATTIES

Spinach meat patties are a specialty of Salonika, where they are among the most popular of all keftikes. *This recipe comes from Beverly Hanoka Spool of Highland Park, New Jersey, whose father, Isaac, immigrated to the United States from Salonika, and whose mother, Mary, is also from a family of Salonikan descent. Mary Hanoka would always serve* keftikes de espinaka *for Rosh Hashanah.*

SERVES 4

2 pounds fresh spinach
1 pound ground beef
½ cup matzo meal
2 eggs, lightly beaten
Salt
Freshly ground black pepper
¼ teaspoon freshly grated nutmeg (optional)
Vegetable oil for frying

1. Preheat the oven to 200 degrees.
2. Wash the spinach thoroughly. Place the still-wet spinach in a large saucepan over medium heat and cook until just wilted, about 3 minutes, turning often. Do this in batches, if necessary. Place in a bowl and let cool. Squeeze to remove water, then chop very finely.
3. Place the spinach, meat, matzo meal, and eggs in a large bowl and stir to combine. Season with salt and pepper, and (if using) nutmeg. Roll the mixture into firm, golfball-sized balls, then press them gently between your hands to form patties, each about 3 inches in diameter. (You should have about 16 patties.)
4. In a large skillet, add oil to a depth of about ¼ inch and heat it over medium-high heat. Add the meat patties in batches, frying them until they are well browned on both sides, about 4 minutes per side. Drain the patties on paper towels, place them on a baking sheet, and put the sheet in the oven. Repeat until all of the patties have been fried. Serve hot.

KEFTIKES DE PATATA

POTATO MEAT PATTIES

The classic combination of meat and potatoes is found in a number of Sephardic dishes, but perhaps it is never quite so homey and comforting as when the two are combined into meat patties. This Salonikan recipe for potato-meat patties—crisp on the outside, soft on the inside—comes from Mary Mevorah Hanoka, who is of Salonikan descent and now, like many other Salonikan Jews, lives in Highland Park, New Jersey.

SERVES 4

- 2½ pounds russet potatoes, peeled and quartered
- 1 pound ground beef
- 3 garlic cloves, finely chopped
- 2 tablespoons matzo meal
- 2 eggs, lightly beaten
- Salt
- Freshly ground black pepper
- Vegetable oil for frying

1. Bring a large pot of salted water to a boil. Add the potatoes and cook until tender. Drain and let cool.
2. Preheat the oven to 200 degrees.
3. Place the potatoes in a large bowl and mash to a slightly chunky consistency. Add the meat, garlic, matzo meal, and eggs and mix until thoroughly combined. Season with salt and pepper. With moistened hands, roll the mixture into firm, golfball-sized balls, then press them gently between your hands to form patties about 3 inches in diameter. (You should have about 16 patties.)
4. In a large skillet, add oil to a depth of about ¼ inch and heat over medium-high heat. Add the meat patties in batches, frying them until they are well browned on both sides, about 4 minutes per side. Drain the patties on paper towels, place them on a baking sheet, and put the sheet in the oven. Repeat until all of the patties have been fried. Serve hot.

Savory Pastries

In medieval Spain, the little turnovers called *empanadas* were beloved by the Jewish community; *empanadas* contained a wide variety of fillings, including vegetables, cheese, fish, and meats, among the latter at least one version, a Sabbath favorite, made from long-stewed sheep's heads. That particular delicacy has not stood the test of time, but the Jewish love for savory pastries in general endures, among the descendants of the Spanish exiles as well as the Jews of many other communities around the world.

In Turkey, the Jews who had arrived from Spain discovered the local turnovers called *börek;* they Ladinized the word to *borekas,* the name by which, half a millennium later, the turnovers are still known by Turkish Jews. In much of the Middle East, the most popular turnovers are called *sambousak,* made with a semolina dough. *Sambousak* are most often filled with cheese or meat, although Jews of Iraqi descent prepare a special chickpea-filled variety for Purim. *Kibbeh,* a different sort of savory pastry—dumpling rather than turnover—is a particular specialty of Syrian Jews. Encased in a bulgur dough, *kibbeh* (see pages 213–214) are most often filled with ground meat, but they can take a host of fillings, and can be made in a remarkable variety of shapes and sizes, as befits the dish's importance to the cuisine.

A rather different variety of *kibbeh,* called *Kibbeh fel Saniyeh* (page 227), is prepared not as little dumplings but instead as a large meat and bulgur pie. There, too—savory pies—we find a multitude of traditional Jewish dishes, prominent among them the Moroccan *Pastilla* (pages 225–226), which features delicately spiced chicken or some other type of poultry encased in layers of flaky filo dough; and Pastel de Espinaka (page 224), the double-crusted spinach pie that has long been among the most beloved dishes of the Jewish community of Salonika.

These pies are decidedly hearty and are meant to be served as a main course; on the other hand, the little pastries that begin this chapter can be served either as an appetizer or main course, or even, in the case of the knishes, as a side dish. Thus they are admirably versatile as well as very delicious, which is surely reason enough to account for their enduring appeal.

DISHES: Borekas

Some food concepts make so much sense, are so fundamentally *right*, that they are represented in almost all of the world's cuisines. Of this there may be no more shining example than the little filled pastry that is known by a thousand names, but for our purposes might simply be described as the turnover.

The basic idea is as simple as it is ingenious: Roll out a piece of dough into a square or round, fill it with a bit of something delicious, and then fold (or "turn") the dough over the filling, pressing it closed to create a triangle or half-moon shape. From here, the filled turnover can be finished by almost any form of concentrated heat that the kitchen provides: baking, boiling, steaming, or frying. The advantages offered by this preparation are manifold: As anyone who has ever eaten a knish on the run already knows, dough wrapping makes a dish handily self-contained, so it can be eaten just about anywhere. Moreover, the use of dough—which can be made from just flour, water, and oil, allows the thrifty home cook to stretch expensive, and therefore generally scarce, protein into a filling meal. So it's not at all surprising that the turnover family boasts a multitude of international cousins, among them the British pasty, Russian piroshki, Italian calzone, Indian samosa, and Chinese wonton, as well as many others residing in equally far-flung regions.

Nor have Jewish cooks, east or west, been immune to the charms of the turnover. With turnovers, as with most dishes, Jews have adapted the indigenous cookery to their own uses, and so over the centuries Jewish kitchens have turned out piroshki, calzones, and samosas, to name but a few. Still, of all turnovers, none has been more important or beloved to Jewish cooks than the *boreka* (the variant spellings of which include *bureka*, *boureka*, and *burreca*), the Sephardic version of the class of Turkish pastries known collectively as *börek*.

Though the variations in *börek* are almost limitless, the term generally refers to very thin sheets of pastry (called *yufka*) that are layered and then filled with either a savory or sweet filling before being baked or fried. Probably no other dish, including the famed pilaf, has been as central to the development of Turkish cuisine as has *börek*. The name *börek* seems to have been derived from a dumpling-like dish known as *bugra*, named for the Bugra Khan, ruler of East Turkmenestan, while the practice of *börek*-making descends from various ancient types of folded bread in the region. Some form of what we would recognize as *börek* may have been prepared as early as the eleventh century. In any case, according to Ayla Algar in *Classical Turkish Cooking*, by the middle of the fifteenth century, *börek* was an integral part of Ottoman cuisine. (Algar quotes a seventeenth-century traveler who reported that Istanbul contained no fewer than 4,000 *börek* shops—four times the number of bakeries then in the city.)

By the end of the fifteenth century, Jews had begun to arrive in Turkey in large numbers, in the wake of the 1492 decree of expulsion. *Börek* reminded them of the filled *empanadas* they had known back in Spain, and they adopted it for their own, Ladinizing the Turkish name into *boreka*. *Borekas* were likewise adopted by Jews living in other regions conquered by the Ottoman Empire, notably in the Balkans and in Greece, where they are called *bourekakia*, while across the Mediterranean, in Italy, they are known as *burriche*.

Like the Turkish *börek*, Sephardic *borekas* can be made with a variety of fillings, savory and sweet alike. Most often, though, they are filled with a mixture of sharp and mild cheeses and a vegetable, generally either potato, eggplant, or spinach; among the cheeses commonly used are feta, Parmesan, Gouda, kashkaval (popular in the Balkans), and farmer's cheese. A rather different *boreka* made by Turkish Jews is the *boreka de handrajo*, featuring a ratatouille-like filling made from grated eggplant, tomatoes, and squash, inside a dough enriched with cheese and yogurt.

Though today *yufka* has given way to far simpler pastry dough (or store-bought puff pastry), *borekas* still require a bit of time and care to prepare, and as a result home cooks tend to reserve them for holi-

BOREKAS DE PATATA KON KEZO

TURNOVERS WITH POTATO AND CHEESE FILLING

Temple Moses in Miami Beach has a large Cuban American membership, many of them from families of Turkish descent. This is the recipe, slightly adapted, for the borekas *that some of the women of the synagogue serve at community activities such as concerts, fairs, and bar mitzvahs. Their recipe calls for pinching off bits of dough and rolling out the rounds individually, which is the traditional method. I find it much easier to roll out the dough as a whole and then cut out 4-inch rounds. However you do it, I urge you to try making them; your efforts will be amply rewarded.*

MAKES ABOUT 24

FOR THE DOUGH

½ cup vegetable oil

8 tablespoons (1 stick) butter, melted

½ cup water

3½ to 4 cups unbleached all-purpose flour

1 teaspoon salt

FOR THE FILLING

1 large russet potato (about 10 ounces), peeled and quartered

2 tablespoons butter

¾ cup (about 6 ounces) firmly packed grated Gouda cheese

¼ cup grated Parmesan cheese, plus more for sprinkling

1 egg, lightly beaten

1. Make the dough: Place the oil, butter, and water in the bowl of a standing electric mixer and beat to combine.
2. Sift together 4 cups of flour and the salt and gradually add it to the liquid ingredients, beating to combine. Add enough flour to create a soft, oily dough that holds together and pulls away cleanly from the sides of the bowl. Divide the dough in half and form it into two disks. Cover each disk with plastic wrap and refrigerate for 45 minutes.
3. Make the filling: Bring a pot of salted water to a boil. Add the potato and cook until soft. Drain, place in a medium bowl, and mash with a hand masher. Stir in the butter and let cool. When cool, add the remaining filling ingredients and mix well to combine.
4. Preheat the oven to 350 degrees. Grease 2 large baking sheets or line them with parchment paper.
5. Make the *borekas:* On a lightly floured surface, roll out each of the dough disks to a thickness of about ⅛ inch. With a cookie cutter or the edge of a wide glass, cut out rounds 4 inches in diameter. With your fingers, press out each round a bit more thinly before filling it.

(continued)

Salt

Freshly ground black pepper

1 egg beaten with 1 tablespoon water for egg wash

6. Place about 2 teaspoons of the filling in the center of a round. Fold the dough over the filling, making a half-moon shape, and pinch the edges firmly together with the tines of a fork to seal the dough. Repeat with the remaining dough rounds and filling.
7. Place the *borekas* 1 inch apart on the prepared baking sheets and brush them lightly with the egg wash. Sprinkle with grated Parmesan. Bake until golden, about 30 minutes. Serve warm or at room temperature.

SAMBOUSAK

SEMOLINA TURNOVERS WITH CHEESE FILLING

Cheese sambousak *are among the most popular of the savory pastries of the Jews of the Middle East and the Baghdadi Jews of Calcutta.*

MAKES ABOUT 26

FOR THE DOUGH

2 cups unbleached all-purpose flour

1 cup fine semolina or farina

½ teaspoon salt

½ pound (2 sticks) butter, softened

½ cup hot water

FOR THE FILLING

1 pound Muenster or kashkaval cheese, grated

2 eggs, lightly beaten

1 teaspoon salt

Freshly ground black pepper

1 egg beaten with 1 tablespoon water for egg wash

About 2 tablespoons sesame seeds for topping

1. Make the dough: Sift together the flour, semolina or farina, and salt. Place the butter in the bowl of a standing electric mixer and beat at medium speed until creamy. Slowly add the dry ingredients and beat until fully combined. Add the water and beat to create a uniform dough. Turn the dough out onto a lightly floured surface and knead briefly, just to make a soft, smooth dough. Cover with a towel and set aside while making the filling.
2. Make the filling: Place the cheese in a large mixing bowl. Add the eggs, salt, and pepper and stir until fully combined.
3. Preheat the oven to 350 degrees. Grease 2 baking sheets or line them with parchment paper.
4. Make the *sambousak:* On a lightly floured surface, roll out the dough to a thickness of ⅛ inch. With a cookie cutter or the edge of a wide glass, cut out rounds 4 inches in diameter. With your fingers, gently press out each round a bit more thinly before filling it.
5. Place about 2 teaspoons of the filling in the center of a round. Fold the dough over the filling, making a half-moon shape, and pinch the edges firmly together. Seal by crimping the edge or pressing it with the tines of a fork. Repeat with the remaining dough rounds and filling.
6. Place the *sambousak* on the prepared baking sheets and brush them lightly with the egg wash. Sprinkle them with the sesame seeds. Bake until golden brown, about 20 minutes. Serve warm or at room temperature.

SAMBOUSAK BEL TAWA

IRAQI SAMBOUSAK WITH CHICKPEA FILLING

These chickpea-filled sambousak*—ground chicken is sometimes added as well—were a Purim mainstay of the Jews of Iraq. (Esther, it is said, ate only pulses and seeds while in King Ahasuerus's court, so that she wouldn't have to violate the laws of* kashrut*.)* Tawa *means pan in Arabic, a reference to the* sambousak *being fried rather than baked.*

MAKES ABOUT 24

FOR THE FILLING

2/3 cup dried chickpeas

2 tablespoons vegetable oil

1 onion, chopped

1/2 teaspoon turmeric

3/4 teaspoon ground cumin

Salt

Freshly ground black pepper

FOR THE DOUGH

2 1/2 cups unbleached all-purpose flour

1 cup fine semolina or farina

1/2 teaspoon salt

3/4 cup vegetable oil

1/2 cup water or chicken broth

1 egg beaten with 1 teaspoon water for egg wash

Vegetable oil for frying

1. Make the filling: Place the chickpeas in a large pot, cover with at least 2 inches of water, and let soak overnight.

2. Drain the chickpea soaking water and cover the chickpeas with fresh water. Cover the pot and bring to a boil. Lower the heat and simmer until soft, about 30 minutes. Drain and let cool. When cool, place in the bowl of a food processor and process until finely ground.

3. Heat the oil in a large skillet over medium heat. Add the onion and cook, stirring often, until soft and lightly colored. Add the chickpeas, turmeric, cumin, and salt and pepper and cook, stirring often, for 5 minutes. Set aside and let cool.

4. Make the dough: Sift together the flour, semolina or farina, and salt. Place the oil and water in the bowl of a standing electric mixer. Slowly add the dry ingredients and beat at medium speed to form a soft, slightly oily dough that pulls away from the sides of the bowl. If the dough seems a bit dry, add a little more water. Turn the dough out onto a lightly floured surface and knead for 1 minute, just to make a smooth, firm dough. Cover with a towel and let stand at room temperature for 30 minutes.

5. Make the *sambousak:* On a lightly floured surface, roll out the dough to a thickness of ⅛ inch. With a cookie cutter or the rim of a wide glass, cut out rounds 4 inches in diameter. With your fingers, gently press out each round a bit more thinly before filling it.

6. Place about 2 teaspoons of the filling in the center of a round. Lightly brush the edges of the round with the egg wash. Fold the dough over the filling, making a half-moon shape, and pinch the edges firmly together. Seal by crimping the edge or pressing it with the tines of a fork. Repeat with the remaining dough rounds and filling.

7. Preheat the oven to 200 degrees. In a large skillet, add oil to a depth of about ½ inch and heat over medium-high heat until the oil is very hot but not smoking. Add the *sambousak* in batches and fry until golden brown on both sides, about 4 minutes per side. Remove with a slotted spoon and drain on paper towels. Transfer to a baking sheet and place the sheet in the oven until ready to serve. Serve warm.

DISHES: Kibbeh

"The future is the worst thing about the present," said Gustave Flaubert, which may seem a bit extreme, until you consider the case of *kibbeh.* For those of you unfortunate enough not to be acquainted with them, *kibbeh* are exquisite little dumplings made of a thin bulgur shell filled with spiced meat. They are one of the glories of the Syrian kitchen; they are also, as much as the ozone layer or the Montreal Expos, gravely endangered by the modern world.

It's not that *kibbeh,* unlike the Expos, are facing any immediate threat of extinction. There may well be as many *kibbeh* produced each day as ever before. The problem, rather, is that *kibbeh* are relatively time-consuming to make, what with all that shell shaping and meat stuffing, and when free time has itself come to seem an endangered species, fewer and fewer people are willing to invest the amount necessary to make them at home. Instead, they buy their *kibbeh* in the frozen-foods case of their local Middle Eastern grocery. Store-bought *kibbeh,* though, bears about as much relationship to the homemade variety as, say, a fast-food Hot Apple Pie does to a hot apple pie.

As with pies, the best way to learn how to make *kibbeh* is to ask your grandmother. If, like me, your grandmother didn't know from *kibbeh,* then your next best bet is to find someone else's willing grandmother, and ideally one of Syrian descent. For my part, I did this one better, and learned how to make *kibbeh* at the elbow of a great-grandmother. (Born in Aleppo, she is a well-known figure in the Syrian Jewish community of Brooklyn, but prefers, for modesty's sake, to remain anonymous.) It was from her that I learned the art of *kibbeh:* how to fashion a shell that is pleasingly thin and delicate, but will not break when filled and cooked.

In the traditional method of preparation, the shell is formed by pressing one's moistened forefinger into a little ball of the bulgur dough—really a soft, moist paste—and then carefully smoothing the dough around the finger to create a torpedo shape. As was the case with the deep-fried potatoes called *aloo makala* among Calcuttan Jews, at one time Syrian women were judged by their ability to make proper *kibbeh*, and those possessing long forefingers (known as the "*kibbeh* finger") considered themselves especially fortunate. Still, modern ways have influenced even the traditionalists, and these days most home *kibbeh* makers mechanically extrude the dough with a standing electric mixer fitted with an attachment for making sausage. (On this issue I line up with the minority of the minority, but for reasons of practicality rather than belief: While the machine does create perfectly shaped hollow cylinders, I find these shells difficult to work with, and as a result I prefer to make *kibbeh* by the traditional method.)

I have been speaking of *kibbeh* as if it were a single item, but in fact there is an astonishing variety. The variations touch on every aspect of the production, from the shape, to the composition of the shell and filling, to the manner of cooking. The word *kibbeh* is Arabic for dome, but the dumplings actually come in a number of shapes, from round to flattened to cylindrical. Once shaped, they may be cooked by deep frying, baking, or simmering in soups or sauces. *Kibbeh hamda*, for instance, are simmered in a sauce made sour by lemon juice (*hamud* means sour in Arabic), additionally flavored with garlic and mint. The especially large balls called *kibbeh yachniyeh* are a great favorite in chicken soup, though smaller ones may be added instead. The smaller balls are also a regular addition to the vegetable stews that are a mainstay of Syrian cooking. The shell may or may not include finely ground beef along with the bulgur (and the bulgur may be replaced by ground rice), while in the filling the traditional beef or lamb is sometimes replaced with ground chicken or turkey by modern cooks looking to reduce their consumption of red meat. One variety, known as *kibbeh samak*, is filled with ground fish, while others are stuffed with mushrooms, potatoes, or eggplant. The uncooked *kibbeh nayeh* are stuffed with lentils. They can even be sweet: To celebrate Rosh Hashanah, especially small balls are stuffed with chopped walnuts, sugar, and cinnamon, much like the Ashkenazic rugelach.

Kibbeh, in fact, need not be dumplings at all, as in the case of the popular dish *Kibbeh fel Saniyeh* (page 227). Literally meaning kibbeh on a tray, this is like a large double-crusted pie, with a layer of meat filling sandwiched between two layers of a bulgur-and-meat dough. Here, too, variations abound: The dough may be enriched with tomato paste and is often spiced with cumin, although cinnamon and allspice may be used instead; the meat filling is commonly studded with chopped walnuts and/or pine nuts and is itself often flavored with cinnamon and allspice, or may be made sour by the addition of tamarind concentrate.

Though less elegant than traditional *kibbeh*, *kibbeh fel saniyeh* is also far less time-consuming to prepare. As a result, it is in the ascendance in modern home kitchens, even those equipped with standing electric mixers with sausage attachments. Still, I have no quibble with *kibbeh fel saniyeh*; it is unquestionably delicious, and has a nice homey feel to it. That is, at least until that day—still a long ways off, one fervently hopes—when it is made by machines, in huge batches, and then wrapped up for delivery to the grocer's freezer.

KIBBEH NAMASHIYEH

SYRIAN MEAT-FILLED BULGUR DUMPLINGS

Catastrophe visited the Syrian Jewish community in 1869, due not to political persecution but rather to the opening of the Suez Canal in Egypt. Where once goods had been borne overland through the desert, now they were shipped by sea. The result was a precipitous economic decline, and in subsequent decades many of Syria's 50,000 Jews immigrated—some to Cairo, others to Manchester, England, or to the United States. The immigration to the United States intensified in the early 1920s, with the breakup of the Ottoman Empire, which had ruled Syria for four centuries. Today, more than 30,000 Jews of Syrian descent live in Brooklyn. This excellent recipe comes from there.

MAKES ABOUT 24

FOR THE DOUGH

2 cups fine bulgur (cracked wheat)

½ cup unbleached all-purpose flour

2 tablespoons matzo meal

2 tablespoons tomato paste

¼ teaspoon red pepper flakes (optional)

½ teaspoon ground cumin (optional)

½ teaspoon salt

FOR THE FILLING

1 tablespoon olive oil

1 small onion, chopped

½ pound ground beef or lamb

2 tablespoons pine nuts

(continued)

1. Make the dough: Place the bulgur in a large bowl of cold water and let soak for 10 minutes. Rinse thoroughly and drain, squeezing out any excess water. Place the bulgur in a large bowl. Mix in the flour, matzo meal, and tomato paste, then season with the red pepper flakes and cumin (if using), and salt and stir to combine. You should have a soft, smooth paste that holds together when rolled into a ball. If the dough is too dry or wet, add a few tablespoons of water or flour to create the proper consistency. Cover the bowl with plastic wrap and refrigerate for 30 minutes.

2. Make the filling: Heat the oil in a medium skillet over medium heat. Add the onion and cook, stirring often, until soft and translucent. Add the meat and cook, stirring and breaking it up with a wooden spoon, until browned. Stir in the pine nuts and season with allspice, and salt and pepper. Place in a medium bowl and let cool.

3. Make the *kibbeh:* Set out a bowl of cold water. Moisten your hands, then tear off a piece of dough about the size of a golf ball. Roll it into a ball. Holding the ball with one hand, slowly press your other

¼ teaspoon ground allspice

Salt

Freshly ground black pepper

Vegetable oil for deep frying

Tahini (sesame seed paste) and lemon wedges for accompaniment

forefinger into the ball. Gently smooth the dough around the finger. Rotating your finger slightly, shape the ball into a long cylinder with thin walls. Carefully remove your finger, leaving a hollow shell.

4. Add a teaspoon or two of filling to the shell, so that it is about three-quarters full. Moisten the open end, then pinch it closed. The filled pastry should resemble a torpedo. Place on a large tray. Repeat with the remaining dough and filling, making sure to keep your hands moistened at all times.

5. Preheat the oven to 200 degrees.

6. Heat about 2 inches of oil in a Dutch oven or other large, heavy pot to 375 degrees. Add the *kibbeh* in batches and fry to a deep brown, about 3 minutes. Remove with a slotted spoon and drain on paper towels. Transfer to a baking sheet and place the sheet in the oven until ready to serve. Serve hot, accompanied with tahini and lemon wedges.

LAHAMAGINE

SMALL MEAT PIZZAS

These little meat-topped pizzas are a very popular snack in the Middle East, and nowhere more so than in Syria. The use of allspice and cinnamon to flavor the meat is typically Syrian; sour tamarind concentrate or pomegranate molasses may be added as well. It's been my experience that lahamagine, *like Italian pizza, is great cold the next day, for lunch or breakfast.*

MAKES 16

FOR THE DOUGH

1 package (about 2½ teaspoons) active dry yeast

½ teaspoon sugar

1 cup warm water

3½ to 4 cups unbleached all-purpose flour

2 teaspoons salt

¼ cup vegetable oil

FOR THE TOPPING

3 tablespoons olive oil

1 pound ground beef or lamb

3 onions, finely chopped

1 red pepper, finely chopped

¼ cup pine nuts

½ teaspoon ground cumin

½ teaspoon ground allspice

(continued)

1. Make the dough: In a small bowl, dissolve the yeast and sugar in the warm water and let stand until the mixture begins to bubble, about 5 minutes.
2. In the bowl of a standing electric mixer, combine 2 cups of the flour with the salt, oil, and the yeast mixture and beat at low speed to combine. Gradually add the rest of the flour until the dough is firm, holds together well, and cleans the sides of the bowl.
3. Turn the dough out onto a lightly floured board and knead until it is smooth and elastic, about 10 minutes, adding flour as necessary to keep the dough from sticking. Place the dough in a large, lightly oiled bowl and turn once to coat. Cover with a towel and let rise until doubled in size, about 2 hours.
4. Make the topping: Heat the oil in a large skillet over medium heat. Add the meat and onions and cook, stirring often and breaking the meat up with a wooden spoon, until the onions are soft and translucent. Add the red pepper and pine nuts and cook, stirring often, for 5 minutes. Add the spices and tomato paste, stir to combine, and cook for 2 minutes. Remove from the heat and let cool.
5. Preheat the oven to 475 degrees.

¼ teaspoon ground cinnamon

1 tablespoon tomato paste

Salt

Freshly ground black pepper

Cornmeal for sprinkling

6. Make the *lahamagine:* Sprinkle several baking sheets with cornmeal. Punch down the dough and cut it into 16 equal pieces. On a lightly floured surface, roll each piece into a round about ⅛ inch thick and about 5 inches in diameter (it doesn't have to be exact). Place the rounds on the prepared baking sheets. Spread about 2½ tablespoons of the topping evenly over each round, leaving an edge of about ½ inch.

7. Bake until the bottoms of the rounds are crisp and the edges are golden brown, about 12 minutes. Serve hot.

POTATO KNISHES

The knish has become the most well-known filled pastry of the Eastern European Jews and is certainly among the most various, with fillings that include potato, cabbage, kasha, and many others. (The Jewish American Cook Book, *published in 1946, includes twenty-four types of knish, among them apple, banana, beet, molasses, and raisin and jelly.) Miriam Weinstein, author of the splendid history* Yiddish: A Nation of Words, *learned how to make knishes from her grandmother Millie (née Mirke), an immigrant from Odessa. Unlike the pillowy knishes that have become standard in the United States, Millie's knishes were made like strudel: rolled up and then cut into pieces. (If you prefer slightly larger knishes, cut them into 3-inch slices instead of 2-inch ones.) Try them as an accompaniment to roast chicken; they're scrumptious.*

MAKES ABOUT 14

FOR THE FILLING

2 pounds russet potatoes, peeled and quartered

¼ cup milk (optional)

2 tablespoons vegetable oil

2 onions, chopped

¾ cup finely chopped mushrooms

1 teaspoon salt

Freshly ground black pepper

FOR THE DOUGH

2 eggs

3 tablespoons vegetable oil

½ cup water

(continued)

1. Make the filling: Bring a pot of salted water to a boil. Add the potatoes and cook until tender. Drain and place in a large bowl. Add the milk (if using) and mash until smooth. Set aside.
2. Heat the oil in a large skillet over medium heat. Add the onions and cook, stirring often, until soft and lightly colored. Add the mushrooms, salt, and a generous amount of pepper and cook, stirring often, until the mushrooms are soft and well browned. Let cool slightly. Add to the potatoes and stir to combine. Set aside.
3. Make the dough: Place the eggs, oil, water, and salt in a large bowl and stir to combine. Add the flour gradually, stirring first with a spoon and then working the mixture with your hands, until it is fully combined. Turn the dough out onto a lightly floured surface and knead just until smooth, adding flour as necessary to keep the dough from sticking. Form the dough into a ball. Cover with a towel and let rest for 30 minutes.

½ teaspoon salt

3 cups unbleached all-purpose flour

1 egg beaten lightly with 1 tablespoon water for egg wash

4. Preheat the oven to 400 degrees. Lightly grease a baking sheet or line it with parchment paper.

5. Make the knishes: On a lightly floured surface, roll the dough out into a rectangle 14 by 10 inches. Cut the dough in half lengthwise, creating 2 rectangles each 14 inches by 5 inches. Divide the filling in half, and spread it evenly along the dough, leaving about ½ inch along each long edge. Roll each dough half from one of its long sides into a long roll, pressing the seams together and pinching the ends tight. Press down on the top to flatten the rolls slightly. Place the rolls, seam side down, on the prepared baking sheet and brush the tops with the egg wash.

6. Bake until the dough is golden brown, 20 to 25 minutes. Use a serrated knife to cut the rolls into 2-inch slices. Serve warm or at room temperature.

COMMUNITIES: Salonika

There was once a great city, a cosmopolitan center of commerce and culture. Its port long welcomed immigrants fleeing terror and want; its dense, bustling streets presented a kaleidoscopic variety of native dress, and hummed with the sound of the world's languages. Built on the twin pillars of tolerance and trade, the city was a beacon of pluralism, whose daily existence gave the lie to the modern siren songs of nationalism and ethnic hatred.

This great city is not New York but Salonika, "the Pearl of the Mediterranean." Located on Greece's northeast coast, along the Aegean Sea, Salonika (today officially known by the Greek name Thessaloniki) was once one of the most Jewish cities in the world. Though its population comprised a multitude of religions and ethnicities—Greek, Turkish, Armenian, Bulgarian, Serb, and countless others—Jews were by far the largest single group in the city. Indeed, by the sixteenth century Jews actually constituted a majority of the population, although this percentage would later decline somewhat. According to the census of 1900 (a high-water mark of sorts for the city, before the tragedies that were shortly to arrive), of Salonika's 173,000 residents some 80,000 were Jewish, 60,000 Muslim, and 30,000 Christian. The Jewish population in Salonika, in fact, was more than ten times the number of Greece's second-largest Jewish center, Athens.

Jews had lived in Salonika since the second century before the Common Era, but a significant community did not exist until the Byzantine period, when several hundred Jews lived there. The first European immigrants to Salonika were Hungarians who arrived in 1376; a larger number of Bavarian Jews settled in 1470, founding the small Ashkenazi community. The Jewish population of the city grew enormously in the fifteenth and sixteenth centuries, with the arrival of some 20,000 refugees from Spain, Portugal, Italy, Sicily, and North Africa, fleeing the ever-expanding reach of the Spanish terror. This sudden influx would ineradicably shape the identity of the Salonikan

Jewish community, which over time became a kind of Sephardic enclave on the Greek mainland.

As was true in many Mediterranean and Asian centers, the Jews of Salonika were largely involved in international trade, much of it in silk, cotton, and grain; a sizable number were craftsmen, who became well known in the region for their skill in weaving, dyeing, and the manufacture of jewelry, while still others worked as fishermen, in tobacco production, and the mining of gold and silver. (The Salonikan port—the city's economic lifeblood—was run almost entirely by Jews, and like most of the city's businesses was closed on Saturdays in observance of the Jewish Sabbath.) Commerce and all of the other daily activities of the Jewish community were conducted in Ladino, the language of Spanish Jewry, although by the early twentieth century French had become the primary language of some of the wealthier families, who had been educated in the schools of the Alliance Israélite Universelle. Hebrew, of course, was reserved for religious activities, which flourished in Salonika. The city had thirty-two synagogues, whose names reflected the origins of their congregants: the Aragonese synagogue, the Castille, Catalan, Majorca, Lisbon, and so forth. Salonika was a center for the study of Torah and Kabbalah (the seventeenth-century false messiah Sabbatai Zvi found fertile ground for his ideas among the Jews of Salonika, and a sect of his followers survived there until the twentieth century), as well as secular subjects including medicine and the natural sciences. As Vilna was long known as "the Jerusalem of Lithuania," Salonika was known, even more expansively, as "the Jerusalem of the Balkans."

All through the heyday of the Jewish community in Salonika, from the sixteenth through the beginning of the twentieth century, the city was part of the Ottoman Empire, and the Jewish cuisine that developed in Salonika mixed Turkish and native Greek influences, with many of the dishes descended from the earlier stay in Spain. Meatballs, for instance, were sometimes formed simply from beef—mixed with egg and bread before rolling and frying, and often simmered in tomato sauce—but more often the meat was extended, and lightened, with vegetables that included spinach, leeks, and potatoes. The result was very similar to the Sephardic meatballs made in Turkey and known, from the Ladino, as *albondigas;* among the Jews in the rest of

Greece, these meatballs were called *keftedes.* In Salonika, however, they were called neither *albondigas* nor *keftedes* but instead *keftikes,* not quite Greek and not quite Turkish—a fitting testament to the city's singular nature.

As the city was a thriving seaport, fish was a staple, served countless ways: grilled and roasted and fried, in an egg-and-lemon sauce, with greengage plums, drizzled with vinegar and chopped walnuts. A whole carp was traditional for Rosh Hashanah, with the head (or *rosh*) reserved for the father of the house.

A favorite food for Sabbath eve—and just about every time else, for that matter—was a stew of white beans (variously called *avas,* or *avicas,* or *fijones*), to which meat was often added. On Saturday nights, it was common practice to prepare rice with tomatoes and then serve this with the leftover beans from the night before. On Saturday mornings, the Salonikan table (like that of other Greek Jews) was arrayed with bread, cheese, olives, cucumbers, tomato, and, always, the long-cooked eggs known as *huevos haminados.*

Among the cooked desserts of Salonika, a special favorite was *sutlach,* a creamy sweet pudding made from rice flour, simmered on the stove until thick and then sometimes baked to create a brown, wrinkled skin on top. Traditionally *sutlach* was made in a tin-lined copper pan called a *kazan,* which in Salonika was known instead as a *kazandibi.* In the Middle East *sutlach* is often flavored with rose or orange-flower water, but in Salonika, as in Turkey, ground cinnamon was used instead. Many families maintained the charming tradition of sprinkling the cinnamon atop each individual bowl in the name or initials of the person who would receive it.

Often dessert consisted simply of fresh fruit, widely available from the trees planted all over the city, which included orange, peach, apricot, cherry, plum, and fig. The fruit was also turned into a variety of preserves and candies, known as *dulces,* among them *dulce de cayesi,* in which dried apricots are boiled with sugar and water until thick, then turned out onto a board to cool before being cut into diamond shapes. A very old Salonikan sweet, now virtually forgotten, is *alkashou,* a Passover confection made from mixing ground walnuts, broken-up matzos, sugar, and honey with orange rinds that have been soaked in water for up to three days. These sweets were kept on hand for visitors who happened to stop by in the afternoons or on Shabbat, served on the *tavla de dulces* (tray of sweets), the traditional dish that is something of an emblem of Sephardic hospitality. In Salonika, though, guests were not served thick coffee with their *dulces*, as elsewhere in the Sephardic world, but rather a tall glass of water.

By the outset of the twentieth century, the Ottoman Empire was widely derided as "the sick man of Europe," and in 1912, after a long civil war, the Greek army took control of Salonika. As has been noted by the historian Nicholas Stavroulakis, the Greeks were "faced with a city whose inner life was manifestly Jewish, if not Spanish," and the new government undertook a long campaign to Hellenize the city, including instituting a Sunday Sabbath. In 1917, a fire swept through Salonika, destroying most of the city's Jewish quarter. More than 53,000 Jews were left homeless, which sparked the first of the Jewish emigrations out of Salonika, mostly to the United States, France, and South America. The emigrations intensified beginning in 1922, when Greece and Turkey undertook a massive population exchange, resettling some 100,000 ethnic Greeks from Turkish lands back to Salonika, in an effort by the Greek government to dilute the Jewish character of the city. Emigration, especially to Palestine, further increased in the 1930s in the wake of several anti-Semitic riots, including one that burned an entire Jewish neighborhood to the ground. The ultimate catastrophe, however, had not yet arrived.

On April 9, 1941, German armies entered the city, and by the next year the terrible and familiar machinery had been started up: racial designations, ghettoes, curfews, forced labor. In March of 1943 the first deportations to Poland began, and the next two years were the darkest in the two millennia of the community's history. Of the 56,000 Jews still living in Salonika in 1941, 54,000 of them perished in the Holocaust, most of them exterminated in the Auschwitz and Birkenau death camps.

The devastation to Salonika was almost unthinkably large, and the community has never recovered. Today about 1,200 Jews live in Salonika, in a population that has grown to more than 1,200,000. Where Jews were once the largest religious group in the city—and at one time an absolute majority—today they number scarcely one in a thousand. In a city that once sustained nearly three dozen synagogues, today only two remain, Monastiriota and Yad Lezikiron, and only the former holds daily services. The community now supports but a single rabbi, Rabbi Itshak Dayan, Moroccan born and Israeli bred, and had none at all until he arrived in 1994. "At the time," Rabbi Dayan told me, "there was no infrastructure of Judaism here whatsoever. So, let us say, we didn't start from zero. We started from minus fifty."

Today the Jews of Salonika are, as in centuries past, engaged in all manner of occupations—except, the rabbi is quick to point out, politics: "Because we are such a minority, we can't constitute a Jewish lobby." Greek is now the first language, and (as is the case just about everywhere in Europe) English has become the second. Some of the older members of the community—Holocaust survivors—still speak Ladino, as do a few of the younger members. For these congregants the synagogue sponsors a biweekly Ladino conversation group, much as many Ashkenazic synagogues do with Yiddish, but Ladino is no longer a language of daily conversation, and its long-term future in Salonika appears no brighter than that of Yiddish in the United States.

Many of the traditional Jewish foods of Salonika are still prepared in the community, but their future seems tied to the continued existence of the Jewish community as a whole. Unlike many other Greek cities and towns—notably Ioannina, the former capital of Romaniote Greek Jewry—the Salonikan Jewish community is numerous enough to sustain itself, though at but a shadow of its former glory, and only by maintaining the valiant efforts that have recently been made. Asked about the future of the Jews in Salonika, Rabbi Dayan gives a brief laugh. "It is difficult," is all he will say, "to know the answer to that question."

PASTEL DE ESPINAKA

SALONIKAN SPINACH PIE

Perhaps the most beloved of all the Salonikan delicacies were the double-crusted pies known, as in Spain, as pasteles. *They were always savory rather than sweet, most often filled either with meat or, as here, with a combination of cheese and spinach.* Pastel de espinaka *is much like* spanakopita, *except that it uses pastry dough rather than filo. It is one of my favorite dishes.*

SERVES 8

FOR THE FILLING

2 pounds fresh spinach

1 cup (about 8 ounces) cottage cheese

1 cup (about 6 ounces) crumbled feta cheese

½ cup grated Parmesan cheese

3 eggs, lightly beaten

1 small onion, finely chopped

Salt

Freshly ground black pepper

FOR THE CRUSTS

2½ cups unbleached all-purpose flour

½ cup vegetable oil

½ cup warm water

1 teaspoon salt

1 egg beaten with 1 tablespoon water for egg wash

1. Make the filling: Wash the spinach well and remove the stems. Place the still-wet spinach in a large saucepan over medium heat and cook until just wilted, about 3 minutes, turning often. Do this in batches, if necessary. Place in a bowl and let cool.
2. Make the crusts: Sift together the flour and salt. Place the oil, water, and salt in the bowl of a standing electric mixer and stir to combine. Slowly add the flour to form a dough that holds together and pulls away from the sides of the bowl. Turn the dough out onto a lightly floured surface and knead until smooth, about 3 minutes. Divide the dough in half and form 2 rectangles. Cover with a towel and let rest at room temperature for 20 minutes.
3. Squeeze out the water from the cooled spinach and finely chop. Place the spinach and the remaining filling ingredients in a large bowl and stir until blended.
4. Make the *pastel:* Preheat the oven to 350 degrees. Grease a 13- by 9-inch baking dish. On a lightly floured surface, roll out one of the dough halves to a rectangle about 14 by 10 inches. Place it in the prepared dish, letting it extend slightly up the sides. Spoon the filling into the dish and smooth the top. Roll out the second piece of dough to 14 by 10 inches and cover the filling with it, trimming the excess. Lightly brush the top crust with the egg wash.
5. Bake until the top crust is golden, about 45 minutes. Let cool slightly before serving.

PASTILLA

MOROCCAN CHICKEN PIE

*Pastilla (also known as bastilla and basteya) is one of the grandest of Moroccan creations. It is an elaborate deep-dish pie filled with aromatic layers of shredded chicken or squab—*pastilla *is often referred to as a "pigeon pie"—eggs, and chopped almonds in a flaky pastry crust gaily decorated with powdered sugar and cinnamon.* Pastilla *is served for special occasions among Moroccan Jews, just as it is among Moroccan Muslims; the difference in the preparation is that Jews use olive oil in place of butter. Sprinkling sugar and cinnamon on savory dishes is a practice that dates back to the medieval period.*

SERVES 8

FOR THE FILLING

2 cups blanched almonds

¼ cup sugar

1 chicken, about 3 pounds

¼ cup olive oil

3 large onions, chopped

6 eggs, well beaten

1 cup chicken stock

½ cup chopped fresh parsley or cilantro

½ teaspoon turmeric

½ teaspoon powdered ginger

Salt

Freshly ground black pepper

FOR THE CRUST

18 sheets of filo dough

Olive oil for brushing

1. Preheat the oven to 300 degrees.
2. Make the filling: Place the almonds on an ungreased baking sheet and bake until golden, stirring them occasionally, about 15 minutes. Let cool, then place them in the bowl of a food processor with the sugar and process until the nuts are finely chopped but not fully ground. Set aside.
3. Place the chicken in a large pot of boiling salted water. Cover, lower the heat, and simmer for 1 hour. Drain and let cool. When the chicken is cool enough to handle, remove the meat, discarding the skin and bones, and shred it. Place in a large bowl.
4. While the chicken is cooking, heat the oil in a large skillet over medium heat. Add the onions and cook, stirring often, until soft and lightly colored. Set aside, then add them to the chicken in the bowl.
5. Place the beaten eggs in a large saucepan. Add the chicken stock and the parsley or cilantro. Cook over low heat, stirring regularly, until the eggs become dry and crumbly, 10 to 12 minutes. Drain in a colander to remove any excess liquid, then add to the filling mixture.

(continued)

Confectioners' sugar for sprinkling

Ground cinnamon for sprinkling

6. Add the almond-sugar mixture, turmeric, ginger, and salt and pepper and stir until the filling mixture is fully combined. Set aside.

7. Preheat the oven to 350 degrees. Brush the bottom and sides of an 11-inch round baking dish with olive oil. Set out a stack of sheets of filo dough. (Keep the filo dough under a damp towel while working to prevent it from drying out.)

8. Place a sheet of filo dough in the prepared dish, letting the excess drape over the side. Brush the filo sheet with oil. Continue layering and brushing with 7 more sheets of filo, overlapping them to fully cover the pan.

9. Place half of the filling mixture in the baking dish. Cover the filling with another 4 sheets of filo, oiling each one, with the excess draped over the sides. Place the remaining half of the filling mixture in the dish. Cover with another 4 sheets of filo, oiling each one.

10. Fold the draped edges of the filo dough into the center of the dish to cover. Place another 2 sheets over the top of the pie, folding them under the pie to seal it. Brush the top with oil.

11. Bake until golden brown, 20 to 25 minutes. Invert the *pastilla* onto a large serving platter. Sprinkle lightly with confectioners' sugar. Sprinkle the top of the pie with crisscrossing lines of cinnamon. Serve warm.

KIBBEH FEL SANIYEH

LAYERED MEAT AND BULGUR PIE

This is the easy version of the Syrian meat-filled bulgur dumplings (see page 213): a layer of spiced meat is spread between two layers of bulgur dough. Sometimes pine nuts or pomegranate seeds are also added to the meat.

SERVES 8

FOR THE DOUGH

2½ cups fine bulgur (cracked wheat)

2 teaspoons salt

¼ teaspoon cayenne

1 tablespoon ground cumin

3 tablespoons tomato paste

½ pound ground beef

FOR THE FILLING

2 tablespoons olive oil

1 large onion, chopped

1½ pounds ground beef

½ cup coarsely chopped walnuts

1 teaspoon ground allspice

1 teaspoon ground cinnamon

Salt

Freshly ground black pepper

2 to 3 tablespoons olive oil for brushing

1. Make the dough: Place the bulgur in a large bowl of cold water and let soak for 10 minutes. Rinse thoroughly and drain, squeezing out any excess water. Place the bulgur in a large bowl. Add the salt, cayenne, cumin, tomato paste, and beef and knead with your hands until the mixture is fully combined. Set aside while preparing the filling.
2. Make the filling: Heat the oil in a large skillet over medium heat. Add the onion and cook, stirring often, until soft and translucent. Add the beef and cook, stirring often and breaking it up with a wooden spoon, until nearly browned. Add the walnuts, allspice, cinnamon, and salt and pepper and continue cooking until the meat is fully browned. Set aside and let cool.
3. Preheat the oven to 350 degrees. Lightly grease a 13- by 9-inch baking dish.
4. Make the pie: Spread half of the dough in the prepared baking dish, pressing it down gently with your fingers. Spread the filling over the dough, smoothing the top. Carefully spread the remaining dough on top of the filling, pressing it down gently with your fingers.
5. Cut the pie into squares or diamond shapes. Brush the top lightly with the oil. Bake until the top is golden brown and crispy, about 40 minutes. Remove from the oven and let stand for 10 minutes. Serve warm.

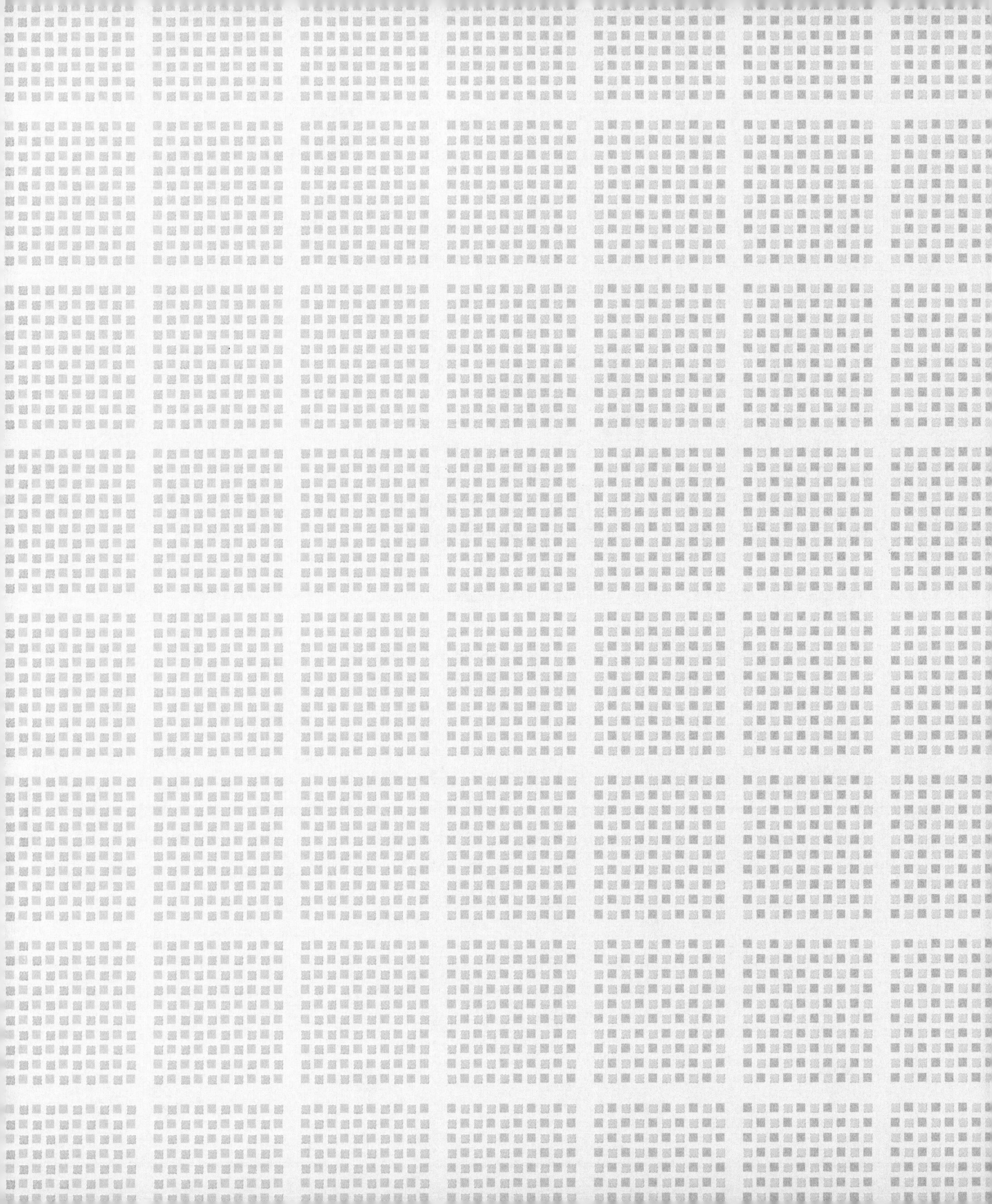

Vegetables

The vegetables that played a major role in the Ashkenazic diet—potatoes, cabbages, turnips, onions, and the like—were ones that could be stored through the long northern winter, and in their stoicism and pallor seem to carry the chill of winter inside them. (The most striking exception to this is the beet, which imparted its vibrant garnet color to a host of dishes.) Cabbages could be stuffed and stewed, or shredded and simmered in soups; turnips could be roasted; onions could be fried. But for sheer ingeniousness of preparation no vegetable compared to the potato. Among the Jews of Eastern Europe, potatoes were mashed, boiled, creamed, baked in puddings, roasted in stews, kneaded in doughs, simmered in soups, ground up and turned into dumplings, and, of course, grated and fried in ceremonial oil.

Potatoes were hardly unknown in the Sephardic world. They were, for instance, stuffed with meat in the traditional Libyan Jewish dish *torshi,* and baked with spinach in a gratin called *sfongo* that is a favorite of Turkish Jews. For the Sephardim, though, potatoes were just one vegetable among many; from North Africa to India, Sephardic cooking was blessed with a cornucopia of vegetables—spinach, artichokes, green beans, okra, cauliflower, peas, peppers, fennel, and eggplant, to name but a few. The vegetables were cooked in a myriad of ways: baked with cheese in gratins, simmered with herbs and spices in tomato sauce, deep fried until crispy, long-roasted until meltingly tender. They might be paired with meat or chicken in occasion dishes. Vegetable dishes were the backbone of everyday cooking.

So too can these be. Lots of the dishes in this chapter—the gingered mashed turnips and potatoes, for instance, or the red cabbage with apples—are perfect as side dishes for a meat or chicken course, but many can also provide the centerpiece of the meal itself. A lush and creamy eggplant gratin, a spicy stew of spinach and chickpeas, long-roasted mixed vegetables topped with chunks of feta cheese: these are dishes worthy of building a meal around any, or every, day of the week.

INGREDIENTS: Potatoes

The potato's origins give scant indication that it would come to play such an important role in Jewish life. Indigenous to the Andes Mountains of South America, the potato was first domesticated in Peru about 3000 B.C.E. and was being cultivated by the Incas some two millennia later. It was entirely unknown to Europeans until the 1530s, when a band of Spanish conquistadors first made their way into the Andean highlands. The potato they discovered there, however, bore scarce resemblance to the one we know today. The custom among the indigenous peoples was to eat their biggest and best potatoes and replant their least appetizing ones. This makes sense intuitively, but the unfortunate result was that their potatoes were growing ever smaller and less tasty. By the time of the Spanish conquests, the potato was not much larger than a peanut. When the potato eventually reached Europe, having been shipped back there on Spanish boats, the food cognoscenti of the time took one look at the small, dark, gnarled tuber and pronounced it a relative of the truffle. They called it *tartuffo* (after the Latin for truffle, *taratufli*), from which was eventually derived the German *Kartoffel* and the Yiddish *kartofl*.

Like many other newly encountered foods of the time, the potato was at first widely believed to be poisonous. In 1596 the Swiss botanist Caspar Bauhin named the potato *Solanum tuberosum*, classifying it as a member of the family Solanaceae—the Borgias of the plant world—whose members include not just the eggplant and tomato but also belladonna, tobacco, and deadly nightshade. Bauhin contended that consumption of the potato caused leprosy, and, what's more, aroused sexual desire (an accusation that led to it being known colloquially as "Eve's apple" and "earth's testicle"). Thus did the potato come to represent both sex and death: Eros and Thanatos in one package. Needless to say, this rather inhibited public demand, and in most areas potatoes were not widely planted until local crop failures had left no practicable alternatives.

By the middle of the nineteenth century the potato had become a staple food of peasants across the continent. Still, perhaps nowhere other than in Ireland—where dependence on the potato led to tragedy when a potato blight arrived in the mid-1840s, was the potato as central to daily life as it was to the Jewish peasantry of Eastern Europe and Russia. Until 1840 the staple crops of that region were grains such as buckwheat and barley, but when those crops failed the potato proved to be a wildly successful replacement. It was easy to grow (requiring for tools only a spade), ripened in only two months (as opposed to ten months for grains), yielded more than six times as many tons per acre as wheat or oats, and was richer in carbohydrates as well as vitamin C and essential minerals.

Throughout Eastern Europe, Jewish peasants ate potatoes two or even three times a day. (This monotonous state of affairs is humorously recounted in the well-known Yiddish folksong, "*Bulbes,*" the lyrics of which run, "Sunday—potatoes, Monday—potatoes, Tuesday and Wednesday—potatoes," and so forth; on Shabbos, "for a change," the singer gets to eat potato kugel.) Most often potatoes were eaten in a basic state, either plainly boiled or baked in their skins, but necessity has always been the mother of culinary invention, and over time a number of more interesting preparations evolved. In his memoir of pre-Shoah Jewish life in Lithuania, *Profiles of a Lost World,* Hirsz Abramowicz recalls that for Jewish peasants "the potato was like manna, lending itself to various modes of preparation." Extremely popular were the potato cakes called *bondes,* made by shredding potatoes and combining them with a little rye or buckwheat flour before baking. Most of the time *bondes* were eaten cold with milk and sour soup, though among more prosperous families they were sometimes eaten warm with sour cream or butter. In one especially luxurious version of *bondes,* called "gypsies," the cakes were covered with poppy seeds (the name refers to the cakes' dark color), and sometimes slathered with sour cream or butter before being placed in the oven again.

According to Abramowicz, the "king" of potato dishes was *teygekhts,* in which grated potato was combined with flour, chopped onions, and butter and then baked in a pan in the oven. This batter was also used to make small dumplings, eaten with dairy soups. In the winter the batter was made into large dumplings, often filled with oats, chopped onions, and goose or chicken fat, and then cooked for several hours in oat porridge. These were known as *kneydlekh*, meaning simply dumplings, though Abramowicz recalls that they were sometimes referred to, jokingly, as "bombs."

Throughout Eastern Europe, Jewish housewives baked potato bread, with a dough made from mashed potatoes mixed with flour, yeast, egg, and oil. Grated potatoes and chopped onions were also combined with yeast, flour, salt, and water to make a potato pudding called *bulbavnik*, later Anglicized in the United States to "potatonik." (Jewish baker George Greenstein has recalled that in the late 1950s, as the Space Race commenced, he and his colleagues at the bakery began calling it "Spudnik.") In the United States, as in Eastern Europe, the potato played the central role in two defining Jewish foods, one of them everyday and one holiday in nature. By this I mean, of course, the knish and the latke. Both have been, and continue to be, made with numerous other ingredients—from kasha and cabbage in the former to, in the latter, all manner of vegetable—but there can be no doubt that here, as in so many traditional Jewish foods, the potato reigns supreme.

So let us, then, consider the potato. Initially feared, scorned, and despised, it has managed not just to endure but to triumph. Named after the truffle, it has proven itself infinitely more valuable.

ALOO MAKALA

CALCUTTA DEEP-FRIED POTATOES

Aloo makala—*whole potatoes that are peeled and then deep fried—is the most celebrated and beloved dish in the repertoire of Calcutta Jewish cookery. It was served on Friday nights, at weddings, and for all other celebratory occasions. As was similarly true, for instance, of the Georgian chicken stew known as* Chakhokhbili *(page 163), at one time women in the Calcutta Jewish community were judged by their ability to make a proper* aloo makala. *Unlike, say, French fries, the potatoes in* aloo makala *do not cook quickly in hot oil, but rather simmer for a long time in the oil. The result is a potato that is white and creamy on the inside, but encased in a remarkably crisp, golden-brown crust. Indeed, when* aloo makala *is made correctly, the outside is so crisp that it causes the potato to "jump" on the plate when pierced by a fork, which has led to the dish being nicknamed "jumping potatoes."*

SERVES 6 AS A SIDE DISH

4 pounds small russet potatoes (or larger ones, cut in half), peeled

About 2 quarts peanut or vegetable oil for deep frying

1. Bring a large pot of salted water to a boil. Add the potatoes and boil for 5 minutes. Drain and let cool.
2. Pierce the potatoes with a fork all over. Place them in a heavy, wide-bottomed pot and add oil to cover. Heat the oil over medium-high heat, then cook (do not stir) until tiny bubbles appear on the potatoes, about 15 minutes. Reduce the heat to medium-low and let the potatoes continue to cook, stirring occasionally, until they are medium-gold, about 2 hours. (At this point, the heat can be turned off and the potatoes can remain in the oil until ready to serve, up to 3 hours.)
3. Just before serving, turn the heat to medium-high and fry the potatoes until they are very crisp and golden brown, about 15 minutes. Use a slotted spoon to remove the potatoes and drain them on paper towels. Serve hot.

TORSHI

LIBYAN MASHED POTATOES AND SQUASH

When Italy occupied Libya in 1911, some 20,000 Jews were living there. According to statistics compiled by the World Jewish Congress, by the beginning of World War II Jews accounted for a quarter of the population of Tripoli and maintained forty-four synagogues in the city. As a result of the Italian occupation, the cuisine of the Jews of Libya is a mixture of North African and Italian influences, featuring both couscous and pasta. (A favorite Sunday-night dinner among Libyan Jews was spaghetti with tomato sauce.) Potatoes and squash are two of Libya's major crops, and caraway seeds are a common flavoring in the cooking. All of these ingredients are represented in this recipe from Penina Meghnagi Solomon of Burbank, California.

SERVES 4 AS A SIDE DISH

- 1 butternut squash, about 2 pounds, peeled, seeded, and cut into 1-inch cubes
- 2 medium russet potatoes, peeled and cut into 1-inch cubes
- 1 teaspoon salt
- ½ teaspoon cayenne
- 1 teaspoon ground caraway seeds
- 2 tablespoons olive oil
- 1 tablespoon lemon juice
- 2 garlic cloves, finely chopped

1. Bring a large pot of salted water to a boil. Add the cubed squash and potatoes and cook until tender, about 20 minutes. Drain, retaining some of the cooking water.
2. Place the squash and potatoes in a large bowl and mash with a potato masher, keeping a slightly chunky texture. Add the remaining ingredients and stir to combine. If desired, add a little of the cooking water for a thinner consistency. Serve hot.

NAVETS ALSACIENS

ALSATIAN GINGERED MASHED TURNIPS AND POTATOES

Turnips grow quickly and well even in the poorest soil, and as such were long one of the critically important root vegetables of the Jewish peasantry in Eastern and Central Europe. When first peeled, turnips give off a spicy, almost horseradishy aroma, but as they cook they develop a complex sweet and spicy flavor and a silken texture. In this preparation, the turnips are sautéed with a bit of sugar to create a sweet glaze before they are boiled.

SERVES 6 AS A SIDE DISH

- 4 to 5 tablespoons butter or olive oil
- 1 onion, chopped
- 2 pounds turnips, peeled and cut into 1-inch chunks
- 6 tablespoons sugar
- 1 pound medium red-skin potatoes, peeled and quartered
- 1 teaspoon powdered ginger
- Salt
- Freshly ground black pepper

1. Heat 2 tablespoons of the butter or oil in a large saucepan or Dutch oven over medium heat. Add the onion and cook, stirring occasionally, until soft and translucent. Add the turnips and 2 tablespoons of the sugar and continue cooking, stirring occasionally, until the turnips are lightly browned, about 15 minutes.
2. Add the potatoes, ginger, salt and pepper, and the remaining 4 tablespoons sugar. Add water just to cover. Cover the pan and bring to a boil. Uncover and cook until the vegetables are fully tender, about 20 minutes. Drain.
3. Place the vegetables in a large bowl with the remaining butter or oil. With a potato masher, mash to the desired consistency. Taste and adjust for seasoning. Serve hot.

DISHES: Latkes

According to the *Oxford English Dictionary*, the first published reference to latkes in the United States dates to 1927, specifically to the phrase "luscious potato *latkes*—pancakes made of grated, raw potatoes," from an article in H. L. Mencken's popular monthly *The American Mercury*. The *OED* goes on to note several subsequent citations, mostly from cookbooks, but among them an aside from the great 1964 comic novel *To an Early Grave*: "I make a few latkes, I paint the kitchen chairs." Though surely of limited etymological use, the citation is delightful nonetheless, if only for the fact of the *Oxford English Dictionary* quoting Wallace Markfield.

In any case, by the third decade of the twentieth century, when *The American Mercury* first announced them to the general public, latkes were already commonplace in Yiddish literature—as in, for example, Sholem Aleichem's 1900 story "*Khanike Gelt*" (Hanukkah Money), which begins: "Can you guess, children, which is the best of all holidays? Hanukkah, of course. You don't go to school for eight days in a row, you eat latkes every day . . . " The reason for the time lag, of course, is that *latke* is Yiddish, and like most immigrant parlance took a while to find its way into the pages of English. The Yiddish word derives from the Russian *oladka*, the diminutive of *oladya*, defined as "a flat cake of unleavened wheat dough." (Alternatively, it may come from the Belarusian *aladka*, a word with a similar meaning.) The etymological sources agree that the word seems to have descended, unexpectedly enough, from the Middle Greek *eladion*, an oil cake (the *American Heritage Dictionary* prefers to define it as a "little oily thing"), derived from the Greek *elaion*, meaning olive oil.

The distance from the Yiddish *latke* to the Greek *elaion* is about as vast as Diaspora itself, but the relationship is interesting because the first latkes were little cakes made from curd cheese and fried in butter or olive oil. (Eating cheese on Hanukkah is said to refer to the Apocryphal story of Judith, who fed salty cheesecakes to the Syrian general Holofornes to make him thirsty, and then plied him with wine until he was so inebriated she could chop off his head with a sword; this symbolic connection, though, was not made until many centuries after the first cheese latkes.) As Jews began to migrate eastward into Eastern Europe, butter and oil grew increasingly precious and expensive, and poultry fat became the chief frying agent; this made the use of cheese off limits, and so by the Middle Ages latkes were most often made not from dairy ingredients, but rather with a simple batter made from buckwheat flour (recall the original Russian meaning of "a flat cake made from unleavened wheat flour").

As for the potato, it was certainly not finding its way into any latkes at that time, because potatoes were unknown in Europe until the late sixteenth century, when they were shipped back from the New World by Spanish conquistadors. Further complicating matters, potatoes were rumored to be a carrier of typhoid and leprosy and were not widely planted in Europe until disastrous harvests of the staple grains left farmers no alternatives. This happened in stages throughout the continent, culminating in Russia in the 1840s. It is only at this time, the mid-nineteenth century, that we first start to see references to latkes being made from potatoes.

Sometimes the latkes were made with potato flour, after the earlier buckwheat version, but more often they were made in a new way, by grating the potatoes and frying them in rendered chicken fat, or, more luxuriously, goose fat. Geese, which were fattened in summer and fall and slaughtered when the weather turned cold, were especially plentiful just before Hanukkah season, and so it is no surprise that latkes fried in goose fat would become a trademark of this holiday celebrating fried foods. Often the latkes were served with the roasted goose, which would be a worthy feast for most anyone, but for impoverished *shtetl* peasants must have seemed a glimpse of Paradise.

Even without a crackling roast goose alongside, potato latkes are about the most satisfying food imaginable—hot, crispily browned, slightly salty, shimmering with a patina of oil. Though their pedigree is shorter than we might have suspected, by this time potato latkes have become the very embodiment of Jewish American holiday food, and the subject of impassioned debate about the best way to make them. The intensity of these arguments recalls those about the making of matzo balls, the other Jewish American holiday food nonpareil, but while I tend to be a middle-of-the-roader on the matzo ball question, when it comes to potato latkes I am a Maccabee-like partisan. The latke must be thin rather than thick (if the fryable surface area is too small the latke will never attain the necessary crispness) and must use starchy russet potatoes (not the waxy red-skinned variety). If at all possible, the potato should be hand grated; only hand grating can create the chunky texture that defines the genuine potato latke.

Finally, there is the question of oil. The secret to flavorful, crispy, not-greasy latkes is proper oil temperature, so make sure that your oil is very hot (though not smoking) before adding the latkes, and don't crowd the pan, as that will cause the oil temperature to fall. The heat of the oil causes browning in the natural sugars with which it comes into contact, resulting in intense flavor. And if the oil is hot enough, steam will be produced inside the food, which pushes outward from the center and prevents the oil from being absorbed. Though immersed in liquid, the latke remains crisp. It is a culinary miracle worthy of celebration, at Hanukkah time or any other.

POTATO LATKES

This is the latke recipe that I make every year for Hanukkah; it seems perfect to me. It comes from Anita Jacobson, an instructor at the Institute for Culinary Education in New York, who learned it from her mother, Minnie Smoler.

MAKES ABOUT 14

- 2 pounds russet potatoes
- Salt
- 1 onion
- 2 eggs, lightly beaten
- 2 tablespoons unbleached all-purpose flour
- Freshly ground black pepper
- Vegetable oil for frying
- Applesauce and sour cream for topping

1. Preheat the oven to 200 degrees.
2. Peel the potatoes and grate them. (This can be done in a food processor, but the texture is better if done by hand.) Place the grated potatoes in a colander with a plate beneath it. Sprinkle salt on the potatoes, then cover them with a layer of paper towels. Place a heavy object, such as a heavy bowl or can, on top. Allow the potatoes to drain for 10 minutes.
3. While the potatoes are draining, peel and grate the onion.
4. Pat the potatoes dry with paper towels. In a large bowl, combine the potatoes, onion, eggs, and flour and season generously with salt and pepper. Mix well.
5. In a large, heavy skillet, add oil to a depth of about ¼ inch and heat over medium-high heat until very hot but not smoking. Drop ¼ cup of the potato mixture into the hot oil, flattening with a spatula. Fry the latkes until deep brown and crisp on both sides.
6. Drain the latkes on paper towels, patting them with the towels on both sides. Transfer in a single layer to a baking sheet and keep warm in the oven until all of them have been made. Serve hot, with applesauce and sour cream.

LATKES DE PATATA

MEXICAN POTATO PANCAKES WITH CARROTS AND CORN

This is the classic Hanukkah dish as made by Talma Scheerson's family in Mexico City. Says Talma, "They're a hit every time—often there are none left to bring to the table, because everyone comes into the kitchen to try 'just one.'" I love them: They're a vibrant orange-yellow and taste like a cross between potato latkes and corn fritters.

MAKES ABOUT 15

2 pounds russet potatoes

Salt for sprinkling plus 1 teaspoon

1 red onion

1 carrot

½ cup canned or thawed frozen corn kernels

3 eggs, lightly beaten

½ cup matzo meal

Freshly ground black pepper

Vegetable oil for frying

Applesauce and sour cream for topping

1. Preheat the oven to 200 degrees.
2. Peel the potatoes and grate them by hand or in a food processor. Place the grated potatoes in a colander with a plate beneath it. Sprinkle salt on the potatoes, then cover them with a layer of paper towels. Place a heavy object, such as a heavy bowl or can, on top. Allow the potatoes to drain for 10 minutes.
3. While the potatoes are draining, peel and grate the onion and carrot.
4. Pat the potatoes dry with paper towels. In a large bowl, combine the potatoes, onion, carrot, corn, eggs, and matzo meal and season generously with salt and pepper. Mix well.
5. In a large, heavy skillet, add oil to a depth of ¼ inch and heat over medium-high heat until very hot but not smoking. Drop a heaping ¼ cup of the potato mixture into the hot oil, flattening it with a spatula. Fry the latkes until deep brown on both sides.
6. Drain the latkes on paper towels, patting them with the towels on both sides. Transfer in a single layer to a baking sheet and keep warm in the oven until all of them have been made. Serve hot, with applesauce and sour cream.

BEET LATKES WITH GOAT CHEESE

I make these latkes at least once every year during Hanukkah. I love goat cheese as a topping, because its salty creaminess goes astonishingly well with beets, and never more so than when the beets are piping hot from the frying pan, causing the goat cheese to melt lusciously into them.

MAKES ABOUT 16

- 2 pounds raw beets, peeled
- 1 small onion
- 2 teaspoons finely chopped fresh tarragon (optional)
- Grated zest of ½ orange
- ¾ cup unbleached all-purpose flour
- 2 eggs, lightly beaten
- ½ teaspoon salt
- Freshly ground black pepper
- Vegetable oil for frying
- 3 ounces goat cheese for topping

1. Grate the beets and the onion in a food processor equipped with a shredding disk or by hand with a box grater. In a large bowl, mix the beets and onion with the tarragon (if using), orange zest, flour, and eggs and stir until fully combined. Season with the salt and pepper.
2. Preheat the oven to 200 degrees.
3. In a large, heavy skillet, add oil to a depth of ¼ inch and heat over medium-high heat until very hot but not smoking. Drop a firmly packed ¼ cup of the beet mixture into the hot oil, flattening it with a spatula. Fry the latkes until the bottoms are browned and crisp, about 7 minutes, then turn and repeat on the other side. (The second side will not need to cook as long.)
4. Drain the latkes on paper towels. Transfer them in a single layer to a baking sheet and keep them warm in the oven until all of them have been made. Serve hot, topping each with a small slice of goat cheese before serving.

BAMIA

OKRA IN TOMATO SAUCE

Okra is a staple of the Sephardic world, from North Africa to the Middle East and India. (In Libya, for instance, okra was considered a food of mourning, and was traditionally eaten, with onions and tomato sauce, before Tisha B'av.) In this simple preparation from Edith Arditti de Benveniste of Buenos Aires, the okra is sautéed, stewed, baked, and then broiled, turning out crispily brown and delicious.

SERVES 4 AS A SIDE DISH

2 tablespoons olive oil

3 garlic cloves, chopped

1½ pounds okra, preferably small, tops trimmed

1 (28-ounce) can whole tomatoes, with juice

1 teaspoon sugar

Salt

Freshly ground black pepper

1. Preheat the oven to 375 degrees.
2. In a large skillet, heat the oil over medium heat. Add the garlic and cook for 1 minute. Add the okra and cook, stirring occasionally, for another 5 minutes. Add the tomatoes with their juice and sugar and season with salt and pepper. Cover and bring to a boil. Lower the heat and simmer, uncovered, breaking up the tomatoes with a wooden spoon, until the okra is tender, 5 to 8 minutes.
3. Pour the okra and sauce into a roasting pan and bake for 20 minutes.
4. Preheat the broiler. Broil the okra in the roasting pan, checking often, until the top of the okra browns, 3 to 4 minutes. Serve hot.

CARCIOFI ALLA GIUDIA

ITALIAN FRIED ARTICHOKES

Meaning artichokes in the Jewish style, carciofi alla giudia *is the most celebrated and well known of all Italian Jewish dishes. It was born during the time of the Rome Ghetto, when food was scarce and frying was the cheapest and easiest of food preparations.* Carciofi alla giudia *is still featured in the restaurants of the Jewish ghetto, such as Al Pompiere and La Taverna del Ghetto, but its popularity has spread and, today, it is offered in restaurants all over Rome. The preparation is nothing short of spectacular, the artichoke arriving on the plate opened up as beautiful as a chrysanthemum, its outer leaves brown and crispy, soft and flavorful at the heart. Italians have varieties of artichoke that are different from the ones in the United States, so we have to make do the best we can: Use the smallest artichokes you can get (though not baby artichokes, which are too small to produce the desired flower shape), with stems that are long and tender.*

SERVES 4

- 2 lemons, halved
- 4 small-to-medium artichokes
- Olive or vegetable oil (or a combination of the two) for frying
- Salt

1. Fill a large bowl with cold water and add the juice of one of the lemons.
2. Trim the stem of one of the artichokes to about 1½ inches in length. With a sharp paring knife, cut away the hard green exterior of the stem, leaving the soft whitish part below. Snap off several layers of tough, dark-green leaves, until only the interior pale-green leaves remain. Cut away the hard green bottom edges of the removed leaves, exposing the white flesh below.
3. With a serrated knife, cut off about 1 inch from the top of the artichoke. Rub the exposed parts of the artichoke with the other lemon to prevent discoloration. Carefully open the artichoke and with a sharp spoon or melon baller remove the thistly purple choke. Drop the artichoke into the bowl of acidulated water. Repeat with the remaining 3 artichokes.

(continued)

4. In a Dutch oven or other large, heavy pot, add oil to a depth of about 2 inches and heat over medium-high heat until very hot but not smoking. While the oil is heating, remove the artichokes from the water and pat them dry with paper towels. Gently press the artichokes down on a plate or other clean surface so that they open and flatten, taking care not to break them.

5. When the oil is hot, carefully place the artichokes in the oil and fry them, turning as necessary with tongs, until they are crispily browned, 15 to 20 minutes. Just before removing, hold the artichokes by their stems and press down gently so that they open to resemble a flower in bloom. Drain on paper towels and sprinkle with salt. Serve warm.

COMMUNITIES: Ioannina

The streets of New York's Lower East Side seem layered into strata, like bedrock. Most of the conversations at street level are carried on in Chinese and Spanish, but up above, the dilapidated storefronts still feature proprietors with names like Himmelstein and Goldfarb, and here and there are signs in Hebrew advertising religious items and burial monuments. On Broome, off Allen, the narrow street is caverned by tenements on both sides—except for one building, cloaked in an unassuming gray stone, half the height of the buildings surrounding it. Up close, one can make out Hebrew lettering above the doorway, and an emblem of lions curled around a pair of stone tablets. This is Kehila Kedosha Janina, built in 1927, and the only functioning Greek synagogue in the city.

Inside, the central hall is small, ringed by wooden benches installed by the original congregrants. At the time, the synagogue had some 400 members, who had been meeting for more than two decades in stores and private homes before they finally raised enough money to erect their own synagogue. Today, says the synagogue's Secretary, Solomon Kofinas (a member since 1955), Saturday services usually draw 25 to 30 attendees. "Most of the time we have a minyan," he says, "but not always. We're open on Saturdays and holidays. We used to be open on Friday nights, but the old-timers don't want to come out at nighttime, so we don't open then anymore."

The members of the synagogue are descended from residents of the Greek town of Ioannina (pronounced YAH-nee-nah), the capital of the so-called Romaniot Jews, a community that traces its origins back to Roman times. (The word *Romaniot* is a Hellenized Latin term for Greece, or "second Rome.") No one knows exactly when the first Jews arrived in Greece—legend has it that they were escaping a slave ship from Jerusalem bound for Rome—but many Jewish refugees from the Maccabeean wars settled in Greece in the second century B.C.E., and by the early decades of the Common Era significant Jewish communities had already developed in Athens, Corinth, and other

Greek cities. The Jewish population in Greece grew dramatically in the early Middle Ages, thanks to an influx of Central European Jews, while later centuries brought thousands of Sephardic Jews fleeing Spain during the time of the expulsion. In the face of assimilation and immigration, the Jews of only a few towns managed to maintain their ancient Romaniot traditions (among them a unique Greek-Jewish dialect), perhaps most prominently the Jews of Ioannina.

Ioannina is a small city lying in the center-west of the country, inland from the Ionian Sea—all of which factors contributed to the simplicity, even austerity, of its cuisine: less diverse than that of larger cities, less spicy than that of the south of the country (where Arab influence was greater), with less seafood than that of cities along the coast. As late as the twentieth century, food preparation was decidedly rustic; most homes didn't have ovens (much cooking was done on a wood fire), and so the ingredients for the evening's meal would often be put into a large pot and sent to the community bakehouse, to be picked up later for dinner. Only on special occasions did a meal have more than one course. Usually dinner consisted of soup or a single type of vegetable—commonly eggplant, zucchini, green beans, or fava beans—cooked simply, often in tomato sauce with lemon juice or fresh herbs, and accompanied by plain white bread. Other times, the vegetables were combined with white beans in a stew called *Fasoulia* (page 263).

"You had meat once a week," says Koula, Mr. Kofinas's wife, adding, "if you were lucky." Most of the time the meat was little more than marrow bones, used to flavor the traditional Friday-night dish *fasoula*, a white bean stew with tomato sauce into which a cinnamon stick was sometimes added for flavor. Beef was also to be found in the Sabbath stew known, as in much of the Sephardic world, as *hamin*. This, however, was an especially frugal version of the dish, cooked only with onion and *pligouri*, a form of cracked wheat similar to bulgur. A mainstay of the Sabbath table was also the long-cooked eggs, *Huevos Haminados* (page 110). Indeed, the custom of eating *huevos haminados*, according to Nicholas Stavroulakis in his *Cookbook of the Jews of Greece*, "is as ubiquitous among Greek Jews as gefilte fish, a particular abomination to the Sephardim, is among Ashkenazic Jews." Lamb was reserved for celebratory occasions such as Passover, when it was traditional to serve roast leg of lamb, strongly flavored with garlic both inside and out, or a lamb stew. Chickens were used mostly for their eggs, but on occasion one was roasted or boiled to make chicken stock, often for the popular egg-and-lemon soup called *avgolemono*.

Though today *avgolemono* is generally associated with Greece, it's actually Turkish in origin, which speaks to the overwhelming influence that Turkey has exerted on the food of Ioannina and the rest of the country. The Ottoman Empire, after all, controlled Greece for 400 years, into the early years of the twentieth century. Culinarily, the single most important contribution was probably filo dough, which has since become a staple of Greek cookery (as in the world-famous baklava, another dish of Turkish origin); filo dough is also integral to the class of pastries known collectively as *börek*, in which a filling—usually savory but sometimes sweet—is wrapped up in filo or other dough. In one especially delicious variety of *börek*, called *Galaktoboureko* (pages 336-337), a sweetened semolina custard is baked inside layers of filo and then doused with a cinnamon-flavored sugar syrup. Similar to *galaktoboureko*, but baked in a flat pan and sprinkled with powdered sugar, is *bougatsa*, a breakfast favorite often accompanied by thick Turkish coffee—though Solomon Kofinas notes with a smile, "The old guys get offended if you call it that. So we say 'Greek coffee.'"

Mr. Kofinas has been back to Ioannina several times since the war, but of course everything is different now. The former capital of Romaniot Jewry no longer sustains a recognizable Jewish presence. Eighty percent of Ioannina's Jewish population—some 1,600 souls—perished in the Holocaust, and today perhaps 50 Jews still reside in Ioannina, fewer than the number who belong to Kehila Kedosha Janina. Currently, leaders of the congregation are engaged in efforts to the raise the existing walls around Ioannina's Jewish cemetery, to protect the dead from vandals.

FASOULAKIA

GREEN BEANS IN TOMATO SAUCE WITH FRESH HERBS

Green beans stewed in tomato sauce is a common dish in Sephardic cooking. In Greece, it is called fasoulakia. *In Ioannina, the green beans were cooked at a boil, because a high flame was necessary to keep the fire underneath the pot from going out, but you can cook them at a simmer. The style was also to cook the beans for about 45 minutes, until they were extremely soft. I have adapted the recipe to the contemporary taste for crisper vegetables.*

SERVES 6 AS A SIDE DISH

3 to 4 tablespoons olive oil

2 onions, chopped

2 garlic cloves, finely chopped

2 pounds green beans, trimmed

1 (15-ounce) can crushed tomatoes

1 tablespoon chopped fresh flat-leaf parsley

1 tablespoon chopped fresh oregano or 1 teaspoon dried

Salt

Freshly ground black pepper

1. In a Dutch oven or other large saucepan, heat 2 tablespoons of the oil over medium heat. Add the onions and cook, stirring often, until soft and translucent. Add the garlic and cook for a minute longer.
2. Add the beans, tomatoes, and herbs, and season with salt and pepper. Drizzle the remaining olive oil over the top. Add water just to cover. Cover the pot and bring to a boil. Lower the heat and simmer, uncovered, for 15 to 20 minutes, or until the beans are cooked to the desired tenderness. Serve hot.

ÉPINARDS AUX POIS CHICHES

SPINACH AND CHICKPEAS

Chickpeas are one of the very best sources of cheap protein, and as such they're a staple of peasant cooking the world over. So it's not at all surprising that the chickpea was an important part of the Jewish diet for many centuries, especially in Mediterranean and North African countries. The dish of spinach and chickpeas is very common in Sephardic communities; this particular version comes from Egypt. It's great served over rice.

SERVES 6

- 1½ cups dried chickpeas
- 3 tablespoons olive oil
- 1 onion, chopped
- Red pepper flakes (optional)
- 2 teaspoons paprika
- 2 teaspoons ground cumin
- 1 teaspoon turmeric
- 2 garlic cloves, chopped
- 1 (15-ounce) can whole tomatoes, with juice
- 1 (15-ounce) can tomato sauce
- 2 teaspoons sugar
- Salt
- Freshly ground black pepper
- 1¼ pounds fresh spinach, washed, stemmed, and coarsely chopped

1. Place the chickpeas in a large pot and cover with at least 2 inches of water. Let soak overnight. Drain and set aside.
2. Heat the oil in a Dutch oven or other large pot over medium heat. Add the onion, red pepper flakes (if using), paprika, cumin, and turmeric and cook, stirring often, until the onion is soft and translucent. Add the garlic and cook for another minute. Add the chickpeas and cook for 3 minutes.
3. Add the tomatoes with their juice, tomato sauce, and sugar and season with salt and pepper, breaking up the tomatoes with a wooden spoon. Bring to a boil. Reduce the heat to low and simmer, covered, stirring occasionally, until the chickpeas are soft, about 1 hour. If the sauce becomes too thick, add a little water.
4. Place the spinach on top of the chickpeas. Cover the pot and let the spinach steam until wilted, 5 to 10 minutes. Stir everything together to combine. Taste and adjust for seasoning. Serve hot.

SFONGO

SPINACH AND POTATO GRATIN

Among the Turkish Jewish community, the vegetable gratin known as sfongo *is very common at dairy meals and during Passover. This particular preparation is quite beautiful—golden domes amid a green field. The cookbook* Sefarad Yemekleri, *from which I've adapted this recipe, recommends that the gratin be served with yogurt, but that seems to me an overload of dairy. I prefer a simple green or tomato salad on the side.*

SERVES 6

- 4 to 5 russet potatoes, about 3 pounds total, peeled and quartered
- ½ cup milk
- 1 cup (about 8 ounces) firmly packed grated kashkaval or other mild white cheese
- ½ cup (about 3 ounces) grated Parmesan cheese
- 4 eggs, lightly beaten
- 1½ teaspoons salt
- Freshly ground black pepper
- 2 pounds fresh spinach

1. Bring a large pot of salted water to a boil. Add the potatoes and cook until tender. Drain and place in a large bowl. Add the milk and mash until smooth. Let cool slightly.
2. In a small bowl, combine the grated white cheese with the grated Parmesan cheese. Add 1 cup of the cheese mixture and the eggs to the potatoes and stir until well combined. Season with salt and pepper.
3. Wash the spinach well and remove the stems. In batches, place the still-wet spinach in a large saucepan over medium heat and cook turning often, until just wilted, about 3 minutes. Remove from the heat and finely chop. Place the spinach in a medium bowl, add half of the potato-cheese mixture, and stir to combine.
4. Preheat the oven to 375 degrees. Butter a 13- by 9-inch baking dish.
5. Place the spinach and potato-cheese mixture in the prepared baking dish, smoothing it evenly. Make 6 round 3-inch holes in the mixture about 1 inch apart. Fill the holes with the remaining half of the potato-cheese mixture, forming rounded domes at the top of each one. Sprinkle with the remaining cheese.
6. Bake until golden brown on top, about 40 minutes. Let cool slightly. Serve warm.

FINOCCHI COLLA BESCIAMELA

ITALIAN FENNEL GRATIN

These days, the artichoke is the vegetable most associated in the popular mind with Italian Jewish cooking, but eggplant and fennel can make a stronger claim to this distinction, as for centuries Jews were virtually the only Italians to eat them. As Edda Servi Machlin notes in her cookbook-cum-memoir The Classic Cuisine of the Italian Jews, *"It's hard to believe . . . that eggplant and* finocchio *(fennel), the quintessence of Italian cooking, were originally used only by Jews." She goes on to quote the nineteenth-century food writer Pellegrino Artusi: "Forty years ago one could hardly see eggplant and fennel on the Florentine market; they were considered vile foods of the Jews, the latter offering evidence here, as in more important issues, of having, better than Christians, a flair for discovering good things."*

In this preparation from restaurateur Pippo Lattanzi (the owner of three popular Roman Jewish restaurants in New York), fennel slices are layered and baked in a béchamel sauce, something like a white lasagna. The sauce is luscious and custardy, a rich counterpoint to the fennel's sweetness, and the bread crumbs sprinkled on top add a nice crunch. Try it with a simple green salad and a good loaf of crusty bread.

SERVES 4 TO 6

8 fennel bulbs, stalks and fronds removed

FOR THE SAUCE

4 tablespoons (1/2 stick) butter

1/4 cup unbleached all-purpose flour

2 cups milk, heated until hot

Salt

(continued)

1. Preheat the oven to 400 degrees. Butter a 9-inch square baking dish.
2. Bring a large pot of salted water to a boil. Cut away the hard inner core of each fennel bulb and remove the bulb's thick outer layer. Cut the bulbs lengthwise into 1/4-inch slices and boil until tender, about 15 minutes.
3. Make the sauce: Melt the butter in a medium saucepan over low heat. Add the flour and cook over low heat, stirring, until the mixture is light brown, about 5 minutes. Add the hot milk all at once

Freshly ground black pepper

1 cup grated Parmesan cheese

4 tablespoons (½ stick) butter, melted

¼ cup dried bread crumbs

and cook, stirring, for another 5 minutes, until slightly thickened. Season with salt and pepper and set aside.

4. When the fennel is tender, drain and arrange half of the slices in the prepared baking dish. Drizzle with half of the melted butter, then top with half of the Parmesan cheese and half of the sauce. Make another layer of fennel and cover in the same way. Finish the top with the bread crumbs.

5. Bake until the top is golden brown, about 30 minutes. Let cool slightly. Serve warm.

ALMODROTE DE BERENGENA

EGGPLANT GRATIN

Of the many eggplant dishes in Turkish Jewish cookery, this one—a delightfully light, creamy casserole, almost like a baked pudding—may be the most beloved. As with so much of the cuisine, its roots lie in medieval Spain, where a dish of mashed eggplant mixed with cheese and bread crumbs was a favorite for the desayuno *meal after Saturday-morning services. A similar dish, called* almodrote de kalavasa, *is made with grated zucchini.*

I've adapted this recipe from one in Sefarad Yemekleri, *a cookbook published by the Jewish community of Istanbul.*

SERVES 6

3 medium eggplants, about 1¼ pounds each

4 slices white bread, crusts removed, briefly soaked in cold water and squeezed dry, then crumbled

2 eggs, lightly beaten

¼ cup vegetable or olive oil

¾ cup well-crumbled feta cheese

1 cup firmly packed grated kashkaval, Gouda, or other mild cheese

Salt

Freshly ground black pepper

1. Preheat the broiler. Place the eggplants on a baking sheet and prick them several times with a fork. Broil the eggplants, turning them once, until soft, about 25 minutes. Remove them to a colander and let cool.

2. When the eggplants are cool, press down on them with your hand to remove as much juice as possible. Chop off the stems and strip away the skin from the pulp, discarding the stems, skin, and seeds. Place the eggplant pulp in a large bowl and mash it well with a fork.

3. Add the soaked bread, eggs, 3 tablespoons of the oil, the feta cheese, and ¾ cup of the mild cheese to the eggplant and stir to combine. Season with salt and pepper.

4. Preheat the oven to 350 degrees. Lightly grease a 10-inch round baking dish.

5. Spoon the mixture into the prepared baking dish, smoothing the top. Sprinkle the remaining ¼ cup mild cheese over the top. Drizzle with the remaining tablespoon oil. Bake until set and golden brown on top, 35 to 40 minutes. Let cool slightly. Serve warm.

VATANA CAULIFLOWER BHAJI

BOMBAY CURRIED CAULIFLOWER AND PEAS

This flavorful dish comes from the Bene Israel community of Bombay. Curry leaves can be purchased in Indian groceries.

SERVES 6 AS A SIDE DISH

3 tablespoons vegetable oil

1 onion, chopped

1 teaspoon mustard seeds

6 curry leaves

½ teaspoon cumin seeds

2 teaspoons minced jalapeño pepper (seeded and deveined)

½ teaspoon turmeric

2 tomatoes, chopped

1 medium cauliflower, about 2½ pounds, cored and cut into 1-inch chunks

1½ teaspoons salt

1 cup water

1 cup frozen peas

1 tablespoon chopped fresh cilantro

1. In a large skillet, heat the oil over medium heat. Add the onion and cook, stirring often, until soft and lightly colored. Add the mustard seeds, curry leaves, cumin seeds, jalapeño pepper, and turmeric and cook, stirring regularly, for another 2 minutes.

2. Add the tomatoes, cauliflower, salt, and water. Cover and bring to a boil. Lower the heat and simmer, stirring occasionally, until the cauliflower is just tender, about 13 minutes. Add the peas and cook until they are heated through, another 2 minutes or so. Just before serving, stir in the cilantro. Serve hot.

INGREDIENTS: Cabbage

Among vegetables, there is perhaps none quite so humble as the cabbage. Pale, stolid, self-enclosed, surviving under the most difficult conditions, the cabbage is a reflection of the peasants who for centuries cultivated it. Lewis Carroll seemed cognizant of this in *Through the Looking-Glass*, when he counterposed cabbages with kings—not just because of the nice alliteration but because a cabbage seems about as distant from royalty as the mind can conceive.

Indeed, writers have long used the cabbage as a kind of trope of unsophistication. In *Pudd'nhead Wilson*, for example, Mark Twain remarked that a cauliflower is "a cabbage with a college education," while Flannery O'Connor described the mother in her short story "A Good Man Is Hard to Find" as having a face "as broad and innocent as a cabbage," a description meant to limn, in a single stroke, the character's essential simplicity.

So it's a bit of a shock to discover that the lowly cabbage is actually the product of a long and noble lineage. Cabbage was prized by the ancient Egyptians and the Greeks, who went so far as to surmise that it first sprang from the sweat of Zeus, most powerful of all the gods. The Romans esteemed cabbage so highly, in part for what they believed were its many medicinal uses (Cato the Elder claimed that cabbage's medicinal value "surpasses [that of] all other vegetables," from providing a poultice for wounds to restoring hearing in the deaf), that at one time it was only affordable for the most well-to-do of the society.

The variety of cabbage so beloved by the ancients was headless, more closely resembling kale or loose forms of lettuce. According to food anthropologist Margaret Visser, cabbage of the sort we recognize today (the name, by the way, comes from the French *caboche*, meaning big head) was probably first cultivated by monastic gardeners during the Middle Ages. Cabbage turned out to be a perfect foodstuff for northern Europe: It is an excellent source of calcium as well as vitamins A and C (difficult to get in a cold, sunless climate) and is especially hardy, able to survive even after the first frost. It's not surprising, then, that cabbage was quickly seized upon by, among others, the Jewish peasantry. In Eastern Europe, Jews were dining on cabbages when potatoes were still small gnarled tubers being grown by the Incas of Peru.

In the fall, cabbages were shredded, salted, sprinkled with caraway seeds, and then placed in large barrels, where over time they became pickled and could last through the winter; this work was often done by several families together, accompanied by singing. Shredded cabbage was fried to fill kreplach, simmered and mixed with noodles, steamed with chopped apples, and sometimes even eaten raw. It was also often added to soups, such as cabbage borscht, which like beet borscht has a sweet-and-sour flavor that comes from the addition of brown sugar and lemon juice. In Germany, cabbage soup was traditionally eaten on Hoshana Rabbah, the seventh day of Sukkot, thanks to a bit of poetic allusion: the German *Kohl mit Wasser*, cabbage and water, refers to the Hebrew phrase *kol mevaser* ("a voice proclaiming") recited on that day.

Still, when it comes to Jews and cabbage, one dish—stuffed cabbage—reigns supreme; perhaps no other dish has been prepared under as many different names. (As the Aleuts are said to have numerous words for snow, so do the Jews have numerous words for stuffed cabbage.) In Poland and northern Russia stuffed cabbage was known, among several other variations, as *holoptshes*, *holishkes*, and *geluptzes*, all of these being derivations of the Russian word *goluptzi*, meaning, curiously enough, little pigeon. In the Ukraine the dish was generally known as *prakkes*, a name derived from the Turkish word for leaf, *yaprak*.

Stuffed vegetables—notable among them eggplant, tomatoes, peppers, and zucchini—are something of a specialty of Jewish cooking, both Ashkenazic and Sephardic. In these preparations, the vegetables are generally hollowed out and then stuffed whole; cabbage, however, is a leafy vegetable, and so stuffing it requires a rather different sort of method. In making stuffed cabbage, individual leaves are filled and then rolled up. Since the filling usually comprises ground beef mixed with other ingredients, this was, for an impoverished peasantry, a clever method of stretching expensive meat.

Cabbage has been a source of sustenance for the Jewish people for centuries, but as it happens, it wasn't until 1973 that its true power was finally revealed. In 1960, Mel Brooks and Carl Reiner disclosed the existence of a 2000 Year Old Man ("medically certified"), a Jew who, remarkably, had been alive since the time of Christ; twelve years later, they recorded another album of conversations with this medical marvel. At one point the interviewer, curious about how his subject has managed to survive for so long, asks him what foods he eats. Replies the now 2013 Year Old Man, "Only cool mountain water, ten degrees below room temperature."

"And that's all you eat?" asks the incredulous interviewer.

"Just that."

"That's all you eat, all day?"

"That . . . and a stuffed cabbage."

PRAKKES

SWEET-AND-SOUR STUFFED CABBAGE

This recipe was handed down to Elayne Clift of Saxtons River, Vermont, from her mother and grandmother, who came to the United States, says Elayne, "from somewhere near Odessa." Odessa is in the Ukraine, which is why her family called the dish prakkes. *This version is somewhat unusual—and, to my taste, especially wonderful—because of the addition of mushrooms. I put the mushrooms and onions in the stuffing instead of the sauce, where it was in the original recipe, but you can do it however you prefer.*

SERVES 6

1 large green cabbage, about 3½ pounds

FOR THE STUFFING

2 tablespoons vegetable oil

1 large onion, chopped

1½ cups chopped mushrooms

2 pounds ground beef

Salt

Freshly ground black pepper

FOR THE SAUCE

2 cups tomato puree

½ cup lightly packed brown sugar

½ cup red wine vinegar

½ cup water

Salt

Freshly ground black pepper

1. Bring a large pot of salted water to a boil. Place the cabbage in the pot and cook just until the outer layer of leaves are pliable and can be removed without breaking, about 2 minutes. Remove the leaves and put them in a large bowl of cold water. Continue cooking the cabbage until the next outer layer of leaves are pliable. Repeat until 18 cabbage leaves have been removed and reserve the rest of the cabbage for lining the cooking pot.
2. Pat the leaves dry. With a sharp paring knife held parallel to the cabbage leaf, trim the tough center rib of each leaf. Set the leaves aside.
3. Make the stuffing: Heat the oil in a large skillet over medium heat. Add the onion and mushrooms and cook, stirring often, until the onions are soft and lightly colored and the mushrooms are well browned. Remove to a medium bowl.
4. In the same skillet, cook the ground meat until well browned, stirring often and breaking the meat up with a wooden spoon. Add it to the mushroom-onion mixture, season with salt and pepper, and stir to combine. Set aside and let cool.
5. Line the bottom of a Dutch oven or other large, heavy pot with the leftover cabbage leaves.

6. Place about ¼ cup of the meat stuffing in the center of a cabbage leaf. Fold in both sides of the leaf to trap the stuffing, then roll the leaf up to form a cylinder. Place the stuffed leaf in the pot, seam side down. Repeat with the remaining 17 leaves.
7. Make the sauce: In a medium bowl, combine the tomato puree, brown sugar, vinegar, and water, and season with salt and pepper, and stir to combine. Taste and adjust for seasoning. Pour the mixture over the stuffed cabbage.
8. Cover the pot and bring to a boil. Lower the heat and simmer, covered, until the cabbage is very tender, at least 1½ hours. Transfer the cabbage to a large serving platter and spoon some of the sauce over it. Serve warm.

PÄROLT VOROSKÄPOSZTA

HUNGARIAN RED CABBAGE WITH APPLES

Braised red cabbage with apples is a classic Central European combination. Tangy and not overly sweet (for more of a sweet-and-sour flavor, add a tablespoon or two of sugar), it is a perfect side dish for meat or poultry. This recipe, from Susan Meschel of Chicago, was made by her grandmother Gisella Kollman. Born in 1873 in the Hungarian town of Udvard, Mrs. Kollman worked as a teacher and also raised eight children before perishing in the Budapest ghetto during the Holocaust. "As she was a professional teacher," recalls Susan of her grandmother, "she did a lot of things to make the holidays pedagogically meaningful." Among them was to serve this dish on Passover, as a symbol of the Red Sea. Another lovely Passover tradition—still carried on in her family—was to fill a washtub with water and beet juice before the seder. The tub was placed at the door of the dining room; at the start of the seder the children had to jump across the washtub, to symbolize how on Passover we are all personally crossing the Red Sea.

SERVES 8 AS A SIDE DISH

- 2 tablespoons vegetable oil
- 1 large red cabbage, about 3 pounds, cored and shredded
- 2 Granny Smith apples, cored and grated
- ½ cup water
- Juice of 1 lemon
- 2 bay leaves
- Pinch of caraway seeds
- Salt
- Freshly ground black pepper

1. Heat the oil in a Dutch oven or other large, heavy pot over medium heat. Add the cabbage and cook, stirring occasionally, until just wilted, about 3 minutes.
2. Add the remaining ingredients and stir to combine. Cover and bring to a boil. Lower the heat and simmer, stirring occasionally, until the cabbage is very soft, about 30 minutes. Taste and adjust for seasoning. Serve hot.

FASOULIA

GREEK WHITE BEAN AND VEGETABLE STEW

Rosaly Roffman, who grew up in the Bronx, is now professor of English at Indiana University of Pennsylvania. Her grandmother Rosina came from Ioannina. A shrewd and strong-minded woman, Rosina was renowned for her expertise at reading coffee grounds and was also a superb cook of Greek specialties. Among them was fasoulia, *a splendid thick-sauced stew of white beans and vegetables. This dish was traditionally served on Friday nights in Ioannina. Served with chunks of good bread, to soak up the sauce, it's a meal on its own.*

SERVES 6

- 1 pound (about 2¼ cups) dried Great Northern beans
- 6 tablespoons olive oil
- 2 onions, thinly sliced
- 4 carrots, peeled and diced
- 2 celery stalks with leaves, diced
- 2 garlic cloves, finely chopped
- 1 bay leaf
- ½ cup chopped fresh flat-leaf parsley
- ½ teaspoon dried thyme or oregano
- 3 tomatoes, chopped
- 2 teaspoons honey
- 2 cups water
- Salt
- Freshly ground black pepper
- 2½ teaspoons red wine vinegar

1. Place the beans in a Dutch oven or other large pot and cover with at least 2 inches of water. Let soak overnight. Drain and set aside.
2. Return the beans to the pot and cover with water. Cover the pot and bring to a boil. Lower the heat and gently simmer until the beans are nearly soft, 30 to 45 minutes. Drain and set aside.
3. Heat 4 tablespoons of the oil in the pot over medium heat. Add the onions, carrots, celery, garlic, and the bay leaf and cook, stirring often, until the vegetables are soft. Add the beans, ¼ cup of the parsley, the thyme or oregano, tomatoes, honey, water, and salt and pepper, and stir to combine. Cover and simmer over low heat, stirring occasionally, until the beans are very soft but still hold their shape and a rich sauce has developed, 45 minutes to 1 hour.
4. Remove the bay leaf. Stir in the remaining ¼ cup parsley, the remaining 2 tablespoons oil, and the vinegar. Taste and adjust for seasoning. Serve hot.

BRIAMI

GREEK LONG-COOKED MIXED VEGETABLES

This dish was known in Greece as briami *or, alternatively,* tourlou *(which is Turkish rather than Greek in derivation). This is a wonderful summer lunch dish, which can be served warm or cold, by itself, or over rice or pasta.*

SERVES 8

- 1 medium eggplant, about 1¼ pounds, cut into ¾-inch dice
- 2 or 3 zucchini, sliced into ¼-inch rounds
- 1 large tomato, chopped
- 1 onion, sliced
- 1 large russet potato, halved lengthwise and thinly sliced
- 2 carrots, peeled and sliced into ⅓-inch rounds
- 1 green pepper, coarsely chopped
- 1 red or yellow pepper, coarsely chopped
- 1 cup green beans, trimmed
- 2 garlic cloves, sliced (optional)
- ½ cup olive oil, plus more for drizzling
- 1 tablespoon dried oregano
- 1 tablespoon dried thyme
- Salt
- Freshly ground black pepper
- 1 cup tomato juice or water
- Crumbled feta cheese for sprinkling

1. Preheat the oven to 325 degrees.
2. In a large bowl, combine the eggplant, zucchini, tomato, onion, potato, carrots, green and red or yellow peppers, green beans, garlic (if using), olive oil, oregano, and thyme, and season with salt and pepper. Stir until the mixture is fully combined.
3. Lightly grease a large roasting pan. Scrape the vegetable mixture into the prepared pan, smoothing it evenly. Pour the tomato juice or water over the mixture and drizzle with a little more olive oil. Cover with aluminum foil.
4. Bake the vegetables, covered, for 30 minutes. Remove the foil and stir the vegetables with a large spoon. If they seem dry, add a bit more tomato juice or water. Cook, uncovered, for another 1 to 1¼ hours, stirring every 30 minutes or so and checking to make sure that there is some liquid at the bottom of the pan, until the vegetables are very brown and soft. Just before serving, sprinkle crumbled feta cheese on top. Serve warm or cold.

VEGETARIAN TSIMMES

SWEETENED FRUIT AND VEGETABLE STEW

When it's made with meat, tsimmes *is a main course (see pages 174–175); without, it's a side dish, as in this version. I originally got the recipe from Mollie Katzen's delightful* The Enchanted Broccoli Forest, *one of the first cookbooks I ever owned, and over the years I've made some alterations to it. I always make this dish for Rosh Hashanah, and people always end up asking for the recipe. Here it is.*

SERVES 8 AS A SIDE DISH

- 4 medium sweet potatoes, peeled and chopped into 1-inch cubes
- 4 carrots, peeled and sliced into ½-inch rounds
- 1 Granny Smith apple, peeled and chopped into ½-inch cubes
- 1 onion, finely chopped
- 2 cups pitted prunes, chopped
- Juice of 2 lemons
- 1 cup orange juice
- 1 teaspoon salt
- ½ teaspoon ground cinnamon
- ¼ cup honey
- ¼ cup matzo meal or dried bread crumbs

1. Preheat the oven to 350 degrees.
2. Place all of the ingredients except the matzo meal or bread crumbs in a large bowl and stir until fully combined.
3. Pour the mixture into an ungreased 13- by 9-inch baking dish. Sprinkle the matzo meal or bread crumbs on top. Cover the dish with aluminum foil. Bake for 1 hour. Remove the foil and cook until the ingredients are very soft and the top is slightly browned, another 30 to 45 minutes. Serve warm.

TSIMMES WITH MARSALA AND DRIED FRUIT

Eudice Mesibov of Chestnut Ridge, New York, calls this recipe "Secret Tsimmes." Why? "A number of years ago," Eudice explains, "I visited an acquaintance in a distant place. She told me she was going to make the best tsimmes ever. At the supermarket, she ordered me to pick up the ingredients as she read them off an index card. When we got home, she called out the cooking and measuring instructions, all the while holding the card out of my sight. When I said, 'It'll go much faster if you put the card down where I can see the instructions,' she pushed the card against her chest and replied, 'No, no, this is a secret!' The next morning, as soon as I got into my plane seat, I wrote the recipe down. (I have a very good memory.) Over the years I have made changes. The dried fruits now include more varieties, and I soak them in sweet wine."

SERVES 8 AS A SIDE DISH

- ½ cup pitted prunes, halved
- ⅓ cup dried pitted dates, halved
- ⅓ cup dried figs, quartered
- ¼ cup raisins
- ¼ cup dried cranberries
- ¼ cup dried apricots, halved
- About 1 cup Marsala wine (mixed with a little brandy, if desired)
- 6 carrots, peeled and cut into ½-inch rounds
- 6 sweet potatoes, peeled and cut into ½-inch cubes
- 1 cup orange juice, plus more if needed
- ¼ cup honey
- 1 teaspoon ground cinnamon

1. Place the dried fruit in a medium bowl and stir to combine. Cover with the Marsala and (if using) brandy. Let steep for 1 hour.

2. Preheat the oven to 350 degrees. Lightly grease a 13- by 9-inch baking dish

3. Place the carrots and sweet potatoes in the prepared baking dish, stirring to combine. In a small bowl, stir together the orange juice and honey and pour the mixture over the sweet potatoes and carrots. Sprinkle the cinnamon over them. Add the dried fruits, including the soaking liquid, and stir to combine.

3. Bake, uncovered, until the vegetables are very tender, 1½ to 2 hours. If the mixture starts to dry out, add a little more orange juice. Serve warm.

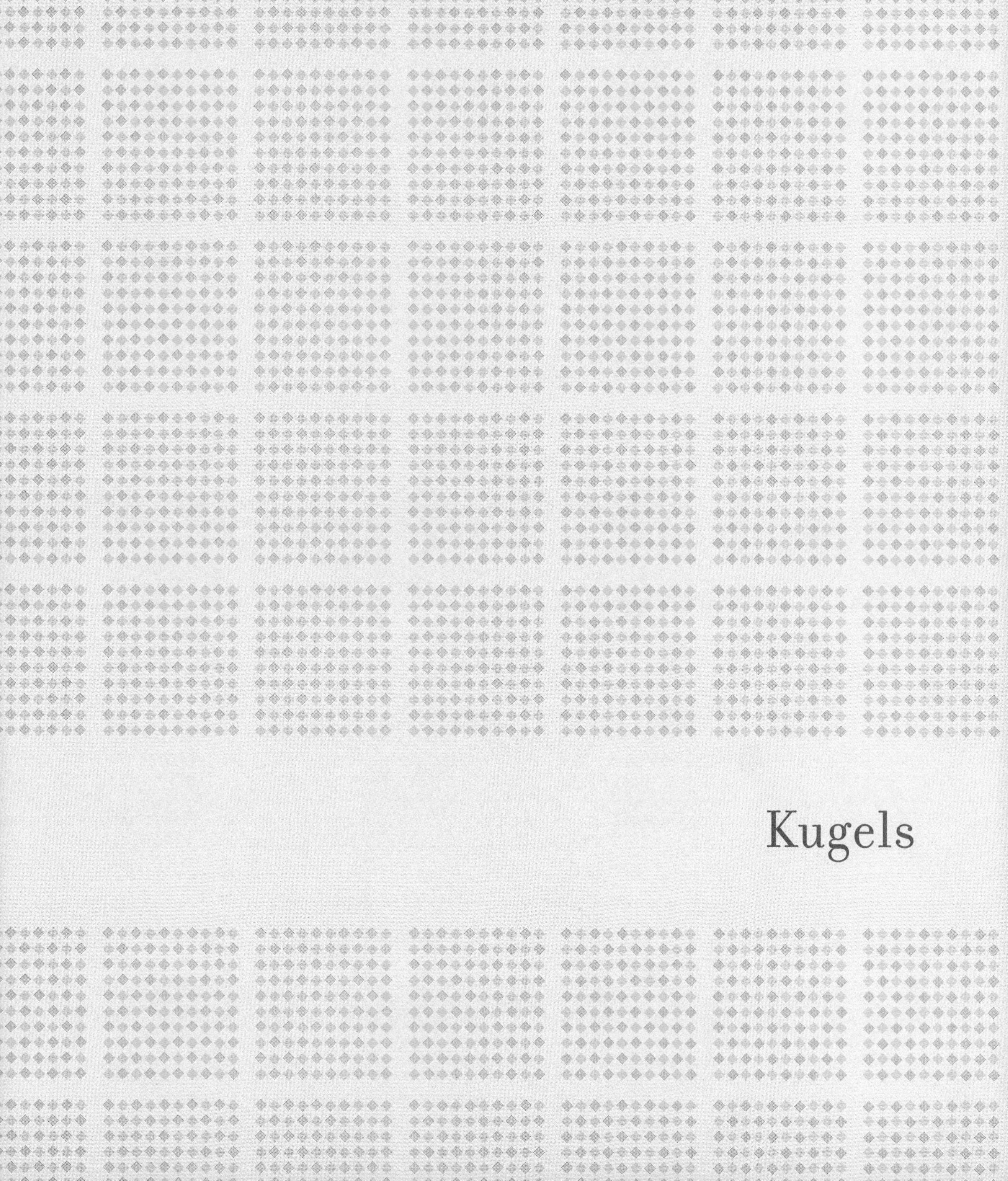

Kugels

DISHES: Kugel

It was Henry James who suggested that the two loveliest words in the English language are "summer afternoon." I'd like to propose these two as an alternative: "noodle kugel." Admittedly, this might not have quite the same universal appeal. The word *kugel*, after all, has only recently entered the English language, and its penetration, even now, could hardly be called widespread. It comes to us by way of Yiddish, having been derived from the German *Kugel*, meaning a ball or globe, though most often it is translated into English as pudding.

Essentially, a kugel is a baked casserole, bound with eggs and moistened with chicken fat, oil, or milk. Kugel is an admirably flexible food, which may be made either sweet or savory, and which can be served as a main course, side dish, or, depending on its preparation, even as a dessert. There are just about as many types of kugel as there are ingredients that can be cut up, mixed, and baked. To cite but one example, *The Jewish American Cook Book* (published by the *Jewish Daily Forward* in 1946) contains fully 114 recipes for kugel, including everything from carrot and steamed fruit to pineapple-matzo and veal brain.

Still, as anyone who knows about kugel already knows, two starchy types have long been preeminent: the aforementioned noodle (known often by the Yiddish *lokshn*) and potato. Like the category of kugel, noodle kugel can be either sweet or savory. The more widespread version is sweet, in which wide egg noodles are mixed with a blend of dairy products (most often curd cheese, sour cream, butter, and eggs), raisins, and sometimes apples, and flavored with sugar and cinnamon. The sweet noodle kugel is invariably a dairy dish, while the savory version often contains meat, most commonly through the use of rendered chicken fat, and sometimes chopped chicken livers.

Potato kugel, on the other hand, is almost always savory; I've seen recipes for dessert potato kugel, but they're unusual. Making potato kugel is about as simple as can be: You just peel potatoes, grate them, then mix them up with chopped onions, eggs, and a healthy—or, depending on your perspective, unhealthy—dollop of chicken fat before baking. A somewhat different method of preparation uses mashed instead of grated potatoes, resulting in a dish that is softer though, to my mind, a bit heavier.

Kugel is a perfect example of how a delicious, nutritious food can be created from a proper mixture of inexpensive ingredients, and as such it's long been one of the staples of Ashkenazic cookery. Like brisket, it often appears as part of the Friday-night dinner, a joy-giving aliment to help welcome the arrival of the Sabbath. In that regard, the Hebraicists of the nineteenth century—those who advocated making Hebrew the Jewish national language, as a way of creating a new, more modern kind of Jew—scornfully derided Yiddish as *kugel loshn*, or "kugel language." This was clearly a reference to how Yiddish draws upon elements from many different languages, as kugels incorporate a variety of ingredients, but I think it also speaks forcefully to how closely kugel was identified with traditional Jewish life in Eastern Europe. Perhaps no expression captures this reality quite as forcefully as the Yiddish saying used to describe someone as looking Jewish: *Der kugel ligt im af dem ponim*, or "The kugel lies on his face."

As it happens, there are quite a few Yiddish expressions involving kugel, which is probably as good an indication as any of its importance to traditional Jewish life. Another one is *Az me est Shabbes kugel, iz men di gantseh vokh zat*, or "If you eat kugel on Shabbos, you'll be full all week." The saying has, of course, a literal meaning: Most kugels are dense and caloric affairs, the sort of food that causes you to push the chair a bit farther away from the table when you've finished eating; after a good meal of kugel, you likely won't want another one right away (that is, unless it's more kugel). To paraphrase Shakespeare on alcohol, kugel provokes the desire to dance but takes away the performance. Which calls to mind a somewhat more spiritual interpretation of that saying as well: To eat a delicious kugel on Shabbos will fill you with a sense of warmth, comfort, and joy—a feeling that, ideally, will remain with you until the next Shabbos, and the next kugel, arrives again. Lovely, no?

NOODLE KUGEL

This recipe was given to my mother by her friend Roz Snow of Great Neck, New York, to whom it had been passed down by her own mother. It's been my mother's favorite kugel for many years—she is a great food lover, but I think I've never heard her speak quite so rhapsodically about any food as she does about this kugel—and the one that I knew and loved growing up. In the division between sweet and savory noodle kugels, this one falls unabashedly into the sweet camp. It's like a big-screen fantasy of kugel, with a crisp, flavory crust, and buttery noodles suspended in a lush, soft custard. This kugel is guaranteed to make your guests want seconds; but if you're lucky, they won't ask for thirds, because it happens to be just as good the next day, eaten cold for breakfast.

SERVES 8

- 1 pound wide egg noodles
- 8 tablespoons (1 stick) butter
- 8 ounces whipped cream cheese
- 8 ounces cottage cheese
- 1/3 cup sour cream
- 5 eggs, lightly beaten
- 4 cups milk
- 3/4 cup sugar
- 1/2 cup golden raisins
- 1 teaspoon ground cinnamon
- 1/2 teaspoon salt
- 1 cup crumbled corn flakes
- 1/4 cup slivered almonds

1. Bring a large pot of salted water to a boil. Add the noodles and cook until they are firm but tender, about 7 minutes. Drain.
2. Add 2 tablespoons of the butter to the noodles and mix well. Set aside.
3. Preheat the oven to 375 degrees. Butter a 13- by 9-inch baking dish.
4. Melt the remaining 6 tablespoons of butter and let cool.
5. In a large bowl, combine the melted butter with the cream cheese, cottage cheese, sour cream, eggs, milk, sugar, raisins, cinnamon, and salt and mix well. Add the noodles and mix until fully combined.
6. Pour the kugel mixture into the prepared dish and smooth the top. Sprinkle the top with the crumbled corn flakes and slivered almonds. Bake until the top is brown and crisp and the kugel has completely set, about 1 hour. Let cool slightly. Serve warm.

POTATO KUGEL

This kugel is excellent as a side dish for a meat course, or as the centerpiece of a lighter meal with applesauce and a salad on the side. In contrast to potato latkes, when making potato kugel I think that the potatoes and onion can be grated in a food processor rather than by hand. As with my recipe for chopped liver (see page 35), I augment the raw onion with caramelized onions for additional taste and moisture. Using a wide baking dish rather than a loaf pan creates more of the crisply browned crust that everyone loves best.

SERVES 8

3 large onions

½ cup vegetable oil

3 pounds (about 5 medium) russet potatoes, peeled

3 eggs, lightly beaten

½ cup matzo meal

2 teaspoons salt

Freshly ground black pepper

1. Thinly slice 2 of the onions.
2. Heat 3 tablespoons of the oil in a large skillet over medium-low heat. Add the sliced onions and cook, stirring often, until lightly caramelized, about 30 minutes. Remove from the heat and set aside.
3. Preheat the oven to 400 degrees. Lightly grease a 13- by 9-inch baking dish.
4. Grate the potatoes and the remaining onion in a food processor equipped with a shredding disk or by hand. Transfer them in a large bowl. Stir in the remaining 5 tablespoons of oil, the caramelized onions, eggs, and matzo meal, and season with the salt and pepper. Pour the mixture into the prepared baking dish and smooth the top.
5. Bake until the kugel is well browned on top, about 55 minutes. Let cool slightly. Serve warm.

SWEET POTATO KUGEL

This is a great alternative to traditional potato kugel, with lots of interesting, surprising flavors.

SERVES 8

- 6 tablespoons vegetable oil
- 3 large onions, thinly sliced
- 2 pounds (about 3 large) sweet potatoes, peeled
- 1 pound (about 2 medium) russet potatoes, peeled
- 3 eggs, lightly beaten
- 2 tablespoons maple syrup or honey
- ¾ cup matzo meal
- ½ teaspoon cayenne
- ½ teaspoon ground cumin
- ¼ teaspoon freshly grated nutmeg
- 2 teaspoons salt

1. Heat 3 tablespoons of the oil in a large skillet over medium-low heat. Add the onions and cook, stirring often, until soft and lightly colored. Remove from the heat and set aside.
2. Preheat the oven to 400 degrees. Lightly grease a 13- by 9-inch baking dish.
3. Grate the sweet potatoes and russet potatoes by hand or in a food processor equipped with a shredding disk. Transfer them in a large bowl. Add the remaining 3 tablespoons of oil, the cooked onions, eggs, maple syrup or honey, matzo meal, cayenne, cumin, nutmeg, and salt and stir to combine. Pour the mixture into the prepared baking dish and smooth the top.
4. Bake until the kugel is well browned on top, about 1 hour. Let cool for 10 minutes. Serve warm.

CARROT KUGEL

Just as latkes can be made with many vegetables other than potatoes, so too can kugels stretch well beyond the typical potato and noodle varieties. This kugel is sweet, moist, and surprisingly light, a lovely accompaniment for beef or chicken.

SERVES 6 AS A SIDE DISH

- 2 pounds carrots, peeled and grated
- 1/3 cup lightly packed brown sugar
- 4 tablespoons (1/2 stick) butter, melted and cooled (or 4 tablespoons vegetable oil)
- 3 eggs, lightly beaten
- 1/2 cup matzo meal
- 1/4 teaspoon vanilla extract
- 1/2 teaspoon ground cinnamon
- 1 teaspoon baking powder
- 1/2 teaspoon salt

1. Preheat the oven to 350 degrees. Grease a 9-inch square glass baking dish.
2. Place all of the ingredients in a large bowl and stir until fully combined. Pour the mixture into the prepared baking dish and smooth the top.
3. Bake until the kugel is well browned on top, about 55 minutes. Let cool for 10 minutes. Serve warm.

APPLE KUGEL

The recipe for this kugel, which is beautifully light, delicately sweet, and floral, was passed down to Sue London of Burlington, Vermont, by her father's aunt, Bess London Goldman. The kugel is kosher for Passover, and Sue London recalls many Passover-season meals at which it was served. (It's perfect with just a simple green salad on the side.) The Londons came to Burlington from Lithuania shortly after the Civil War and were a founding family of the town's Jewish community. One well-remembered family member was Aaron Hillel London, an itinerant peddler who once bought a horse that had belonged to the town's fire company to pull his cart—an incident recounted in the children's book Firehorse Max, *written by Sue London's daughter, Sara.*

SERVES 6

3 eggs, separated

½ cup sugar

2 cups grated peeled apples

⅓ cup matzo meal

Grated zest of 1 lemon

¼ teaspoon salt

1 tablespoon slivovitz (plum brandy) or kirschwasser (cherry brandy)

⅓ cup finely chopped pecans

1. Preheat the oven to 350 degrees. Grease the bottom and sides of a 9-inch springform pan.
2. In the bowl of a standing electric mixer, beat the egg yolks and sugar until pale and creamy. Add the apples, matzo meal, lemon zest, salt, and brandy and beat until fully combined.
3. In a separate bowl, beat the egg whites until they are stiff but not dry. Gently fold the egg whites into the apple mixture, working to maintain the lightness of the mixture. Pour the mixture into the prepared pan and sprinkle the pecans on top.
4. Bake until the top is browned and the center is fully set, about 40 minutes. Let cool slightly before removing the sides of the pan. Serve warm.

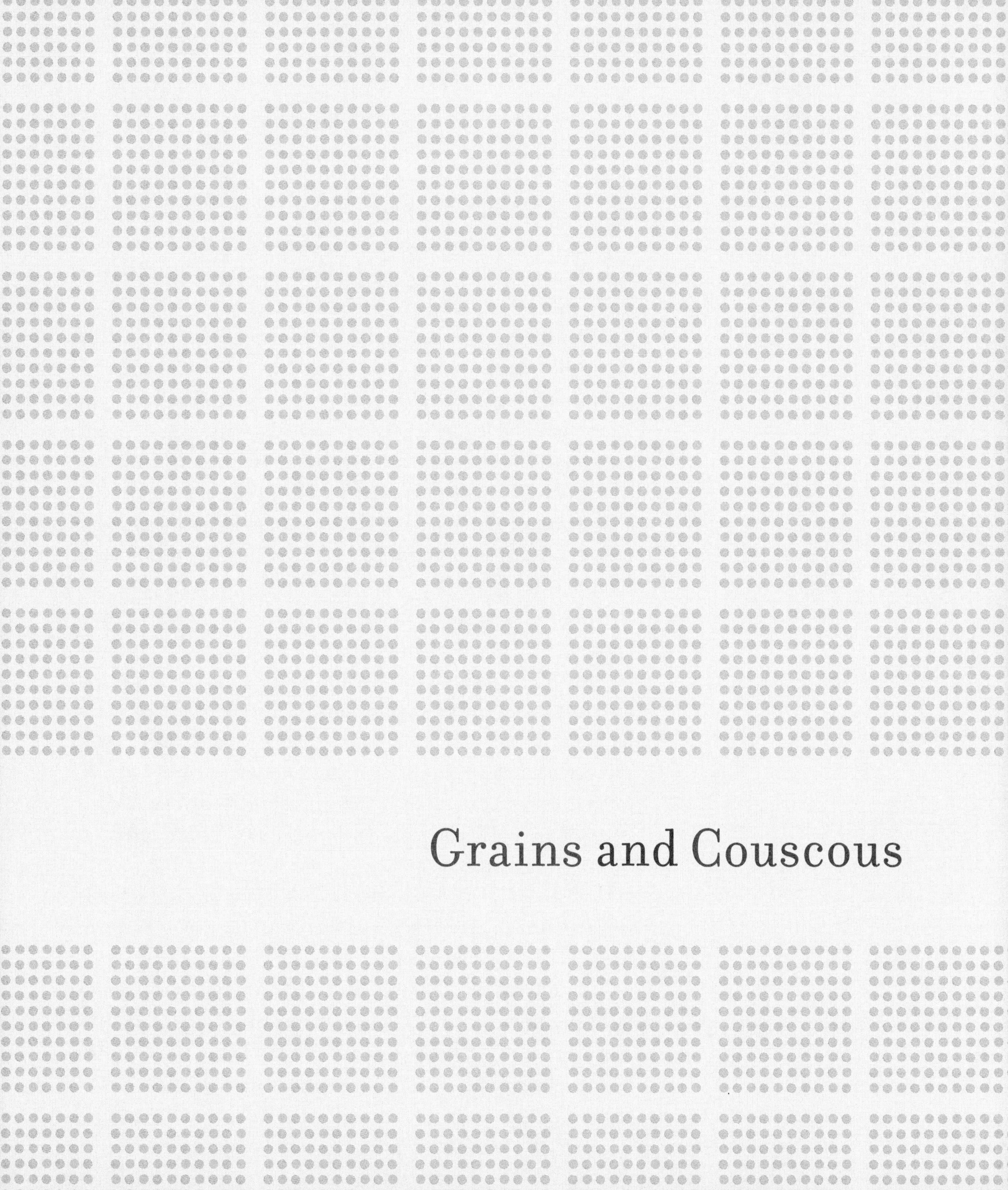

Grains and Couscous

Barley and wheat are indigenous to the Middle East and are mentioned numerous times in the Bible. ("Your belly," says the lover in the Song of Songs, "is a mound of wheat edged with lilies.") Jews likely first encountered rice during the Babylonian exile, and since that time it has become the staple grain of Jewish communities from the Near East to Central Asia and India.

Rice was little known among the Jews of Eastern Europe, where for centuries barley and buckwheat were the staple grains. By the nineteenth century these had been displaced by the potato, but they still retained an important place in the cuisine, as in *kasha varnishkes*—buckwheat groats with bow-tie noodles—a nutritious, wonderfully earthy dish that functions equally well as a side dish or main course.

Couscous is actually a semolina pasta and not, as many people believe, a grain. For millennia it has been the staple starch of the Jews of North Africa, and a mainstay at celebrations from weddings and bar mitzvahs to Sabbaths and holidays. In North Africa, couscous functions as a sort of blank canvas welcoming just about any form of culinary art. It is served with beef and lamb and chicken and fish, with turnips and carrots and pumpkin and fennel and fava beans; it's made spicy with chili peppers, fragrant with cilantro and mint, sweet with cinnamon and sugar.

In the United States, couscous is mostly sold in precooked boxed versions that require only the addition of boiling water. These are fine when you're looking for a quick and effortless side dish. Still, with instant couscous, as with instant coffee, what is saved in time is more than lost in flavor. If it is to be the centerpiece of the meal (as with the recipes in this chapter), you're much better off buying the loose couscous sold in natural-foods and Middle Eastern shops.

On the day that you read this, and on every other day of your lifetime, the majority of the world's people will have gained their main sustenance by eating rice. Indeed, in all of human history, only water, the very foundation of life, can match rice's importance in preserving the species. This is because rice possesses singular advantages that justify the huge outlay of concentrated labor—from building irrigation systems to seeding and harvesting—that it demands among societies that cultivate it on a massive scale. Rice gives higher and more reliable yields than most other grains, it stores well, is among the most nutritious and digestible of all foods (unlike wheat, almost no one is allergic to rice) and does not have to be ground into flour to be consumed; most importantly, people seem never to tire of its taste, even when they eat it every single day. So it's no surprise that, as food anthropologist Margaret Visser has noted, in some cultures the word for rice is synonymous with food in general, and even for life itself.

Though various theories have been propounded about where and when rice originated, the most recent scholarship suggests that the birthplace was in Southeast Asia, more than 5,000 years ago. Over the next millennium rice spread into China and India, and later into Japan as well as the Middle East. Rice seems to have made its first appearance in the Jewish world in Babylonia (what is today Iraq), during the time of the Persian Empire. Aramaic was the language spoken there, and rice was known as *ourouzza;* it was in Babylonia that Arab traders first encountered rice, and they began to call it *arozz.*

The Arab conquest of Sicily in the ninth century introduced the Jews there to rice. Later Sicily came under Spanish rule, and when Sicilian Jews fled into Italy after the Spanish expulsion they brought their knowledge of rice with them, along with eggplants, artichokes, and other important ingredients. The Jews of Italy have long enjoyed an abundance of rice dishes, but two especially deserve mention: one, a saffron-flavored rice cooked in broth, is a long-time Sabbath favorite (it is known as *riso del sabato*), while a risotto made with artichokes has traditionally been a first course for the Passover meal.

Italian Jews, like Sephardim generally, are allowed to eat rice during the Passover season, a practice traditionally forbidden by Ashkenazic rabbis. This isn't any special hardship, for Ashkenazim have never been very big rice eaters. For Sephardic Jews, though, and especially those of the Near East, India, and Central Asia, rice has been nothing short of a staple food. Among the Jews of Persia (now Iran), for instance, where it has been known since the time of Alexander the Great, rice is a fixture at meals from weekday dinners to Shabbat and holidays. The most commonly prepared rice dishes are Chelou (page 279), which features a delicious golden-brown crust at the bottom of the pot, and *polo*, crusty rice mixed with chopped meat or vegetables. (*Polo* is the modern pronunciation of the medieval Persian word *pulaw*, from which was also derived the Indian *pilau* and the Turkish pilaf.) Of course, rice is nowhere more important than in Asia, and among the Jews of Bukhara, in Central Asia, rice is the centerpiece of the defining Bukharan dish, known as *palov*. *Palov* is served at every ceremonial occasion, from holidays to weddings and bar mitzvahs; it features chicken and grated carrots, and often barberries or raisins, on a bed of carefully fluffed long-grain rice. Elsewhere in Asia, in the Bene Israel community of Bombay, rice is turned into sweet coconut-flavored puddings, though most often it is prepared in *pilaus* that are abundantly spiced with cardamom, cumin, cinnamon, and turmeric. The enthusiasm for rice is shared by the Baghdadi Jews of Calcutta, for whom rice was a staple of both their former and adopted homelands.

The fact that rice is not generally thought of as a Jewish food—at least in the United States, is due to the overwhelming preponderance of Ashkenazim here, who traditionally have encountered rice only inside a stuffed cabbage or as an alternative to noodles in chicken soup. This is a loss, but one that need not remain so. The great children's author Maurice Sendak once rhapsodized that "All seasons of the year are nice / for eating chicken soup with rice." But why cannot the same be true / of *polo*, *pilau*, and *chelou*?

CHELOU

IRANIAN CRUSTY RICE

Rice has long been the staple of the Persian (today Iranian) diet. In ancient times, Persian cooks designed a process for preparing rice, called chelou, *so that its grains remain separate. To begin, the rice is washed thoroughly, to remove surface starch that might cause the grains to cling; the rice is partially cooked by boiling it in a large pot of water, and then, after draining, it is cooked slowly in a small amount of water and oil. This second cooking creates a golden-brown crust on the bottom, known as the* tah dig *(literally, bottom of the pot). Among Iranians, the* tah dig *is universally considered the tastiest part of the dish, and some hosts even serve it on a separate platter for their guests. This is the* chelou *made by Mrs. Molook Ahdoot of Potomac, Maryland, who emigrated from Iran in 1972.*

SERVES 6 AS A SIDE DISH

- 6 cups plus 1/4 cup water
- 2 tablespoons salt
- 2 cups basmati or other long-grain rice, well washed
- 1/4 cup vegetable oil
- 1/4 teaspoon turmeric

1. In a Dutch oven or other large, heavy pot, bring the 6 cups water and the salt to a boil. Add the rice and cook, stirring occasionally, for 10 minutes. Drain and rinse briefly under cold running water.
2. Heat the oil in a small skillet over low heat. Stir in the turmeric, add the remaining 1/4 cup water, and set aside.
3. Return the rice to the pot. Slowly pour the oil and water mixture all over the rice. Cover the pot and cook over low heat (though not too low, or the crust will not form) until the rice is tender and the bottom is crusty, about 35 minutes. Using a large spoon to scrape the bottom, invert the rice onto a large serving platter. Use a fork to fluff the grains. Serve hot.

PILAU KISHMISH BADAM

INDIAN RICE WITH ALMONDS AND RAISINS

Calcutta Jewish cuisine features numerous variations of pilau; *this version is considered especially festive, and is served at celebratory occasions such as weddings and holidays.*

SERVES 6 TO 8 AS A SIDE DISH

3 tablespoons vegetable oil
1 onion, chopped
3 cloves
4 cardamom pods
1 cinnamon stick
2 bay leaves
2 cups basmati rice, well washed
1/4 teaspoon saffron threads, crumbled
3 cups hot water
1 teaspoon salt
1/4 cup slivered almonds
1/4 cup raisins
1 tablespoon chopped fresh cilantro

1. In a large, deep saucepan or pot with a cover, heat 2 tablespoons of the oil over medium heat. Add the onion and cook, stirring often, until soft and translucent. Add the cloves, cardamom pods, cinnamon stick, and bay leaves and cook, stirring regularly, for 2 minutes. Add the rice and continue to cook, stirring regularly, for 5 minutes.
2. Dissolve the saffron threads in 1 cup of hot water. Pour the saffron water over the rice. Add the remaining 2 cups hot water and the salt. Cover the pan, raise the heat, and bring to a boil. Reduce the heat to very low and simmer gently for 7 minutes. Stir and continue cooking until the water is absorbed and the rice is tender, about another 5 minutes. (If the rice still appears too firm, add another couple of tablespoons of water and keep cooking.) Cook for another minute. Turn off the heat and allow the rice to sit in the covered pan for 10 minutes.
3. While the rice is resting, heat the remaining 1 tablespoon oil in a small skillet over low heat. Add the slivered almonds and cook until golden brown, about 3 minutes. Remove and drain on paper towels. Put the raisins in the pan, adding a bit more oil if necessary, and cook until they plump up, about 2 minutes. Remove and mix in with the almonds.
4. Remove the cloves, cardamom pods, cinnamon stick, and bay leaves from the rice. Transfer the rice to a serving platter, fluffing the grains with a fork. Top with the almond and raisin mixture. Sprinkle the cilantro on top. Serve warm.

JEERA BAHAT

BOMBAY CUMIN RICE

In the Marathi language spoken by the Bene Israel Jews of Bombay, jeera *means cumin. This rice is often served on Friday nights, or on any other occasion when something a bit more special than plain rice is called for.*

SERVES 6 AS A SIDE DISH

- 2 cups basmati or other long-grain rice
- 2 tablespoons vegetable oil
- 1 small onion, chopped
- 1 cinnamon stick
- 2 teaspoons cumin seeds
- 3 cardamom pods
- 4 cups water

1. Rinse the rice very well under cold running water and set aside. In a medium pot, heat the oil over medium-low heat. Add the onion and cook, stirring often, until soft and translucent. Add the cinnamon stick, cumin seeds, and cardamom pods and cook for another minute.
2. Add the rice and water to the pot. Cover and bring to a boil. Reduce the heat to very low and simmer gently, covered, until the rice is tender, about 20 minutes. Turn off the heat and allow the rice to sit in the covered pan for 10 minutes. Transfer to a large serving platter. Serve warm.

COMMUNITIES: Bukhara

It is difficult to imagine New York without bagels—it's possible, I suppose, but painful to do—for bagels have become, with pizza and hot dogs, an all-embracing street food, and bagel bakeries a fixed feature of the landscape of the city, in Jewish and non-Jewish neighborhoods alike. In certain distinctly Jewish neighborhoods, though, many of the kosher bakeries produce nary a bagel, with no outcry from the crowds who gather there. Instead, domed tandor ovens turn out endless loaves of *lepeshka*, a delicious crusty round bread, something like a king-sized version of the Eastern European bialy. Nearby shops offer canned caviar and porcelain tea sets; the lettering on the signs in the windows is Cyrillic. These are the city's newest Jewish immigrants, who have emigrated by the tens of thousands from the Central Asian lands known collectively as Bukhara. The Queens neighborhoods of Forest Hills, Kew Gardens, and Rego Park now possess a Central Asian flavor as distinctive and unmistakable as the *Yiddishkayt* that a century ago marked the Lower East Side.

Though Bukhara is only one of the important cities of the region, the term *Bukharan* applies to any of the Jewish communities spread out across what are today the independent republics of Uzbekistan, Kazakhstan, Tajikistan, Turkmenistan, and Kyrgyzstan. (Many Americans first took notice of this region as a result of the nearby war against terrorism in Afghanistan; Uzbekistan in particular gave significant logistical support to U.S. forces.) The Jewish presence in Bukhara is said to have begun some 2,500 years ago. Jewish tradition has it that Bukhara is the Habor mentioned in 2 Kings 17:6, where the king of Assyria exiled the ten tribes of Israel. In the twelfth century, the historian Benjamin of Tudela wrote of a Jewish community in the city of Samarkand numbering 50,000. Then under Mongol rule, many Bukharan Jews made their living as merchants in the burgeoning silk trade with the East, or from the weaving and dyeing of textiles; it was said that a Bukharan Jew could be recognized anywhere by his purple-dyed hands. In the nineteenth century Bukhara was annexed by Russia, and under the Russians the traditional Bukharan language—a Persian dialect known as Judeo-Tajik, or Bukharic—eventually gave way to the colonial one. The twentieth century brought a further decline in traditional Bukharan life, owing both to the arrival of the railroad (allowing for the importation of cheap mass-produced goods rather than handmade silk) and to Soviet restrictions on religious observances.

With the breakup of the Soviet Union in the early 1990s, thousands of Bukharan Jews emigrated to the West, almost all of them either to Israel or the United States, where most took up residence in New York City. According to Boris Kandov, president of the Congress of Bukharan Jews of the USA and Canada, in 1980 about 2,000 Bukharan Jews lived in New York; today that number is closer to 50,000. In contrast, Mr. Kandov estimates that fewer than 35,000 Jews still reside in Central Asia, only about 8,000 of them of original Bukharan ancestry. The rest are Russian Jews, who fled there during the World War II.

Among the Bukharan émigrés to New York was Amnun Kimyagarov, who left Samarkand (now in Uzbekistan) with his family in 1993. "I came," he says simply, "because I wanted freedom for my children." A small man in his late-middle years, Kimyagarov wears a black fedora outside the house and is as likely as not to be found with a lit cigarette in his hand. Like so many first-generation immigrants, he is downwardly mobile, at least in an immediate economic sense. Trained as an engineer and once a university lecturer on food-processing technology (he holds thirteen Soviet-era patents), today he works as a salesman for a Canadian wallpaper company. One of his daughters is an accountant for the New York Philharmonic; the other is a pharmacist. "America is better for my children," he says with a shrug, "but not for me." Among his other achievements, Kimyagarov is also the co-author of a Russian-language cookbook—its title is translated as *The Cuisine and Lifestyles of the Bukharan Jews*—published in 1996 by a small Jewish press in New York. The book contains some 200 recipes, which he collected from his mother, his grandmother, and other Bukharan women living in New York in an effort to preserve the traditional dishes of the community. It is the world's only comprehensive cookbook of Bukharan Jewish cuisine.

As it happens, that cuisine is an especially fascinating one. The fabled Silk Road ran directly through Bukhara, and the food bears the hallmarks of the Central Asian crossroads. From China, for instance, came a variety of noodle soups, among them *lagman*, consisting of a tomatoey, peppery broth with thin noodles and chunks of beef. Savory pastries are known as *samosas*, as in Indian cookery, while the steamed meat dumplings called *kaskoni* are very similar to the Uzbek *manti*. Grilled kebabs are a Persian contribution, including lamb, beef, and chicken; one very delicious variety is made of sweetbreads.

As the above indicates, Bukharan cuisine is largely, even overwhelmingly, meat-based. Soup broths, for instance, are made with meat, as is the case with *lagman* as well as *pelmeni*, a lamb broth festooned with beef-filled ravioli. *Pelmeni* is often flavored with dill, which is one of the common flavorings of the cuisine, along with cilantro, cumin, and garlic. Sometimes, as with the boiled meat and chicken called *yakhni*, the meat is served alone, but more often it is wrapped in some type of dough or, most festively, used as a garnish atop the cuisine's other mainstay ingredient, rice.

Though they both include meat, the two most beloved dishes in the Bukharan Jewish repertoire are really rice dishes. In one, called *bahsh*, long-grain rice is cooked with chopped meat and liver and several handfuls of chopped cilantro. Traditionally the *bahsh* is prepared in a linen bag submerged in boiling water; sometimes the bag is left out overnight, and the *bahsh* eaten cold for Saturday lunch. The most beloved dish in the cuisine, though, is *palov*—soft, aromatic rice garnished with a layer of julienned carrots and either diced chicken or beef—which is served on all celebratory occasions, from weddings to bar mitzvahs and Shabbat dinners.

The Bukharan Shabbat dinner is a lavish meal, comprising several separate courses. Invariably it begins with fried fish in a strongly flavored garlic and cilantro sauce, followed by a variety of fresh and pickled vegetable salads including tomatoes, carrots, and cucumbers—this is about the only time vegetables appear in any significant way in the cuisine. Then comes *yakhni*, followed by the exclamation point of *bahsh* or *palov*; the meal winds down with a course of fresh fruit, which is pretty much all that Bukharans ever eat for dessert. Accompanying the meal are pots of green or black tea, or—the Russian influence—vodka. For his part, Amnun Kimyagarov prefers cognac, which reminds him of *arak*, a liqueur Bukharan families distilled at home from raisins.

Bukharan Jewish life managed to survive Turkish, Mongol, and Soviet rule, and now, in the United States, it still survives, in those bustling neighborhoods around Queens Boulevard. The cuisine survives, too, in the Beautiful Bukhara bakery and many others like it, in restaurants such as Salut and the Uzbekistan Cultural Center, and in Amnun Kimyagarov's cookbook for home kitchens. The Bukharan Jews live now in enclaves, but they will not forever; and as they become more widely assimilated, it is inevitable that their foods, like other Jewish foods before them, will also begin to penetrate the wider society. The bagel seems far too firmly entrenched ever to be overthrown, but will *lepeshka* be the new bialy?

OSHI SABO

BUKHARAN RICE WITH FRUIT

Among Bukharan Jews, oshi sabo *is often prepared on Friday and then cooked overnight at a very low heat, to be served warm on Saturday. Sometimes a half pound or so of chopped beef or lamb is added as well. This is a much simpler and less time-consuming version. The recipe comes from Amnun Kimyagarov, who emigrated to New York from Samarkand in 1993.*

SERVES 6

- 3 tablespoons vegetable oil
- 1 large onion, chopped
- 3 tomatoes, chopped
- 3 cups water
- 2 quinces
- 1 Granny Smith apple
- 2 cups basmati or other long-grain rice, well washed
- ½ cup pitted prunes, chopped
- 1½ teaspoons salt
- Freshly ground black pepper

1. Heat the oil in a Dutch oven or other large, heavy pot over medium heat. Add the onion and cook, stirring often, until soft and translucent.
2. Add the chopped tomatoes and 2 cups of the water. Cover and bring to a boil. Lower the heat and simmer, covered, for 30 minutes.
3. Preheat the oven to 350 degrees. Peel, core, and chop the quinces and the apple.
4. Add the rice, prunes, cut-up quinces and apple, and the remaining 1 cup water to the pot. Season with the salt and pepper. Cover and bring to a boil. Transfer the pot to the oven and bake until the rice and fruit are very soft, 1½ to 2 hours. Turn out onto a large serving platter. Serve hot.

KITCHREE

RED LENTILS WITH RICE

Among the Jews of Iraq and the Baghdadi Jews of Calcutta, this simple and filling dish was commonly served as part of the Thursday-night dairy meal, which was generally a lighter meal in anticipation of the Shabbat dinner the following night.

SERVES 4

- 2 tablespoons vegetable oil
- 3 garlic cloves, chopped
- 1 tablespoon tomato paste
- 1 teaspoon ground cumin
- ¼ teaspoon turmeric
- 1 cup basmati or other long-grain rice, well washed
- ½ cup red lentils
- 1 teaspoon salt
- Freshly ground black pepper
- 3 cups water
- 2 to 3 tablespoons butter, in pieces (optional)
- Plain yogurt for topping

1. Heat the oil in a large saucepan over medium heat. Add the garlic and cook just until golden. Add the tomato paste, cumin, and turmeric and cook for another minute.
2. Add the rice, lentils, salt, pepper, and water. If desired, dot the top with butter. Cover the pan and bring to a boil, then lower the heat and simmer gently, covered, until the rice and lentils are very soft, about 30 minutes. Serve hot, each serving topped with a dollop of yogurt.

KASHA VARNISHKES

BUCKWHEAT GROATS WITH BOW-TIE NOODLES

Kasha *derives from a Russian word meaning cereal, and it originally referred to any grain cooked with water, milk, or broth. Over time, however, it came to mean only buckwheat. In fact, kasha is not a grain at all, but rather a part of buckwheat's fruiting seed. To make kasha, the seed's husk is dried and split, so that the inner kernel, called the groat, can be extracted. The groats are then roasted until they become dark; this step turns buckwheat groats into kasha. Kasha was indispensible to the Jewish peasants of Eastern Europe, because the buckwheat plant grows in poor soil and difficult weather while providing an excellent source of fiber and cheap protein. Kasha has served as the filling for a wide variety of Jewish foods, but is most widely known for its role in* kasha varnishkes. *When I make this dish, I like to add mushrooms, which, like kasha, have a rich earthiness. I also add chopped nuts for a bit of crunch. Served with a salad, this is a perfectly hearty winter dinner.*

SERVES 6 TO 8

- 8 ounces (about 3½ cups) bow-tie noodles
- Vegetable oil for drizzling, plus 2 tablespoons
- 2 onions, sliced
- 2 cups sliced wild mushrooms, such as cremini or shiitake
- 1 cup kasha (whole granulation)
- 1 egg white, lightly beaten
- 2¼ cups water or chicken stock
- Salt
- Freshly ground black pepper
- ⅓ cup walnuts (optional)

1. Bring a large pot of salted water to a boil. Add the noodles and cook until firm but tender. Drain and remove to a bowl. Drizzle generously with oil and toss to combine.
2. Heat the 2 tablespoons oil in a large skillet over medium heat. Add the onions and cook, stirring often, until soft and lightly colored. Add the mushrooms and cook, stirring often, until the onions are light brown and the mushrooms are soft, about 5 minutes more. Remove to a plate.
3. Place the kasha in a small mixing bowl. Add the beaten egg white and mix well, so that all the grains are coated with egg. Place the kasha in the skillet, raise the heat to medium-high, and cook, stirring often, until the grains have dried and become lightly toasted, about 4 minutes. Season generously with salt and pepper.

4. Add the mushrooms, onions, and water or stock. Cover and simmer over low heat until the liquid is absorbed and the kasha is tender, about 10 minutes. (If the kasha is not tender at the end of the cooking time, add a bit more liquid, cover, and continue cooking until done.)

5. If desired, place the walnuts in a small dry skillet and cook over low heat, stirring continually, until lightly toasted, about 3 minutes. Let cool, then finely chop.

6. When the kasha is cooked, add the noodles and (if using) the chopped walnuts and combine well. Taste and adjust for seasoning. Transfer to a large serving platter. Serve hot.

CUSCUSÚ

MOROCCAN COUSCOUS WITH BEEF AND GLAZED VEGETABLES

Among the Jaquetia-speaking Jews of northern Morocco, this couscous was a fixture for Rosh Hashanah, Hanukkah, Sukkot, and Shavuot, as well as weddings, bar mitzvahs, family reunions, and all other festive occasions. Make sure to use the loose couscous sold in natural-foods and Middle Eastern shops rather than the instant version in boxes at the supermarket.

SERVES 8

- ½ cup dried chickpeas
- 1 pound (about 2½ cups) couscous
- 10 cups water
- 2 tablespoons olive oil
- 2 pounds brisket or chuck roast
- Salt
- Freshly ground black pepper
- 4 carrots, peeled and cut into 2-inch pieces
- 3 turnips, peeled and cut into 1½-inch chunks
- 2 sweet potatoes, peeled and cut into 1½-inch chunks
- 1 medium butternut squash, peeled, seeded, and cut into 1½-inch chunks
- ½ teaspoon ground cinnamon
- ¼ cup brown sugar
- 1 cup blanched whole almonds

1. Place the chickpeas in a large pot and cover with at least 2 inches of water. Let soak overnight. The next morning, drain the chickpeas thoroughly and set them aside in a covered pot until ready to use.
2. Place the couscous in a large bowl. Cover with 2 cups of the water and let stand until the water is absorbed, about 15 minutes. Drizzle the olive oil over the couscous while stirring with a wooden spoon. Cover with a towel and set aside.
3. Season the meat generously with salt and pepper. Place the meat in a soup pot and add the remaining 8 cups water along with additional salt and pepper. Cover and bring to a boil, skimming off any foam that may develop on the surface. Lower the heat and simmer for 1½ hours. Add the chickpeas and continue simmering.
4. Preheat the oven to 350 degrees.
5. Place the carrots, turnips, sweet potatoes, and squash in a roasting pan. Sprinkle the cinnamon and 3 tablespoons of the brown sugar over the vegetables. Moisten the vegetables with 1 cup of the cooking liquid from the pot. Place the pan in the oven and cook until the vegetables are tender, about 1 hour.
6. While the meat is simmering, place the couscous in a a fine-meshed colander lined with a single layer of cheesecloth. Place the colander over the simmering broth. Cover the colander with a

towel. Simmer until the couscous is tender, about 30 minutes. Set the couscous aside, keeping it covered with the towel, until ready to serve.

7. To serve, transfer the couscous to a large serving platter. Fluff the couscous grains with a fork or your fingers. Sprinkle the couscous with the remaining 1 tablespoon brown sugar, the almonds, and the chickpeas, removed from the pot with a slotted spoon.

8. Remove the meat from the pot and slice it thinly against the grain. Place it on a second serving platter and arrange the roasted vegetables alongside. Serve some of the cooking broth in a bowl to spoon over the couscous, meat, and vegetables.

COUSCOUS AUX LÉGUMES VERTS

ALGERIAN COUSCOUS WITH LAMB AND GREEN VEGETABLES

This recipe, given to me by Eva Bertoin of Paris, was passed down to Eva by her mother Semha Choukroun, who, like many Jews, came to France from Algeria in the early 1960s. Traditionally, of course, this couscous would include only fresh vegetables, but Eva often substitutes frozen. This, she notes, has the advantage of cutting preparation time and allows for serving the dish year round. Fresh or frozen, fava beans are often difficult to come by, so leave them out if you can't find them. Make sure to use the loose couscous sold in natural-foods and Middle Eastern shops rather than the instant version from boxes.

SERVES 8

FOR THE COUSCOUS

1 pound (about 2½ cups) couscous

2 cups water

2 tablespoons olive oil

½ teaspoon ground cumin

FOR THE SOUP

2 tablespoons olive oil

2 pounds bone-in lamb neck, cut into 1½-inch cubes

Salt

Freshly ground black pepper

3 onions, chopped

1 pound fresh or frozen peas

1 cup fresh shelled or frozen fava beans (optional)

8 canned, frozen, or fresh artichoke hearts, quartered

1. Prepare the couscous: Bring a large pot of water to a boil. Line a fine-meshed colander with a single layer of cheesecloth. Put the couscous in the colander and place the colander over the boiling water, so that the couscous can steam. (Make sure that none of the couscous is submerged in the water. If it is, remove some of the water.) Cover the colander with a towel and cook for 10 minutes.

2. Place the couscous in a large bowl. Stir with a fork while adding 1 cup of the water. Place the couscous back in the cheesecloth-lined colander. Cook, covered, for another 10 minutes. Return it to the bowl. Stir in the remaining 1 cup water, the oil, and cumin. Stir with a fork or your hands until no lumps remain. Cover the couscous with a towel and set aside.

3. Make the soup: Pour out the water from the large pot and dry the pot with a towel. Add the oil and heat over medium-high heat.

4. Season the lamb with salt and pepper. Cook the lamb, in batches, until well browned on all sides. Remove it to a plate. Lower the heat to medium, add the onions, and cook, stirring often, until soft and translucent.

5. Return the lamb to the pot. Add the peas, fava beans (if using), artichoke hearts, cumin, turmeric, salt and pepper, and water to cover by about 1 inch. Bring to a boil, skimming off any foam that develops on the surface. Lower the heat and simmer, covered, for 1 hour.

6. Add the zucchini and cilantro and simmer until the lamb is fully tender, at least 30 minutes. About 20 minutes before serving, return the couscous to the cheesecloth-lined colander and steam it, covered with the towel, the simmering liquid.

7. To serve, place the couscous on a serving platter, fluffing it with a fork or your hands. Place the meat, vegetables, and cooking liquid in a large serving bowl. Serve hot.

1 teaspoon ground cumin

1 teaspoon turmeric

3 zucchini, halved lengthwise and cut crosswise into 1-inch pieces

1/4 cup fresh chopped cilantro

MAMALIGA

ROMANIAN CORNMEAL PORRIDGE WITH CHEESE AND SAGE

In Romania, the cornmeal porridge known as mamaliga *(the name is derived from* malai, *meaning millet, long a staple grain of the region) was so beloved by the local Jewish peasantry that some Lithuanian Jews scornfully referred to Romanian Jews as* mamaliges. *Depending on the preparation,* mamaliga *could be served as part of either dairy or meat meals, and it was often served at breakfast, lunch, and dinner. It was the centerpiece of the morning ritual of the Romanian Jewish housewife, who awoke at dawn to begin making the* mamaliga, *tossing handfuls of cornmeal into the cooking pot and then stirring with great vigor for an hour or more. The arduousness of this task gave rise to the Yiddish expression,* Mamalige misht men mit a drik, men shnaydt zi mit a shtrik, un dernokh bensht men vi a flig *("You mix mamaliga with strain, you cut it with a string, and afterward, you bless it with the strength of a fly").*

My variation on the basic mamaliga recipe features kashkaval, a sheep's-milk cheese made throughout the Balkans, including in Romania. Kashkaval is available in cheese and other specialty shops, especially those featuring Eastern European products, but if you can't find kashkaval you can replace it with a mild cheese of your liking. Sage, native to the northern Mediterranean, provides strong flavoring, while the onion adds sweetness and texture.

SERVES 4 TO 6 AS A SIDE DISH

- 2 tablespoons butter
- 1 onion, chopped
- 3 cups water
- 1 teaspoon salt
- 1 cup yellow cornmeal
- 1 tablespoon finely chopped fresh sage
- ½ cup firmly packed grated kashkaval cheese

1. Heat the butter in a medium skillet over medium heat. Add the onion and cook, stirring often, until soft and lightly colored. Set aside.
2. Bring the water and salt to a boil in a large saucepan. Slowly pour the cornmeal into the boiling water, vigorously whisking to prevent lumps from forming. Lower the heat and simmer for at least 30 minutes, until very thick, stirring often with a wooden spoon. Use a spatter guard or a loosely covered lid when not stirring.
3. Add the onion and sage to the cornmeal mixture. Mix in the cheese, stirring until it is completely melted. Transfer to a serving bowl. Serve hot.

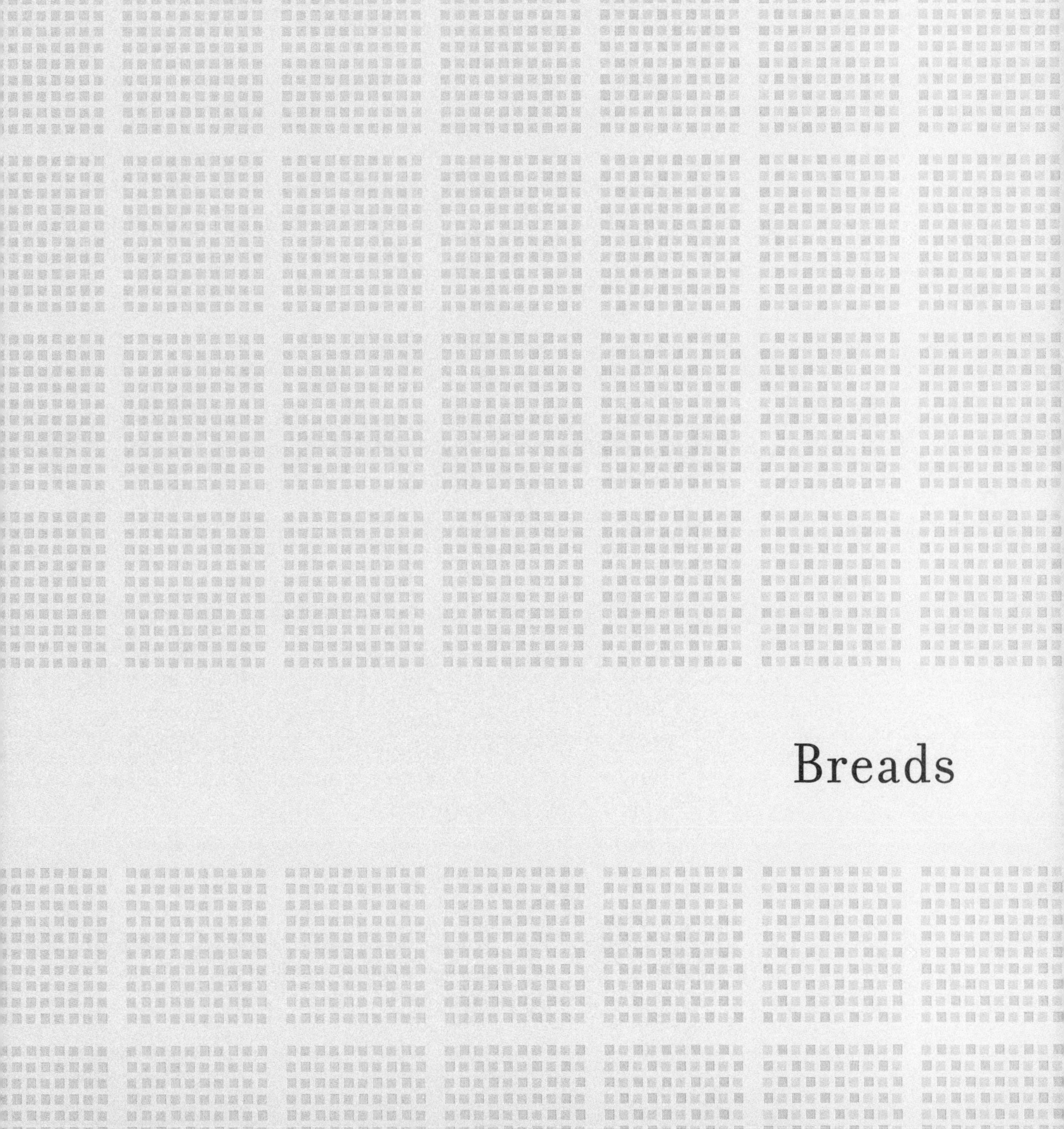

Breads

"If you have bread and butter," goes the old Yiddish saying, "you have good luck." This is especially true if the bread happens to be challah, the glossily crusted, luxuriously rich egg bread that has long been a staple of Ashkenazic Sabbath and holiday meals. There may be no bread more splendid, with butter or without—or, better yet, with butter and honey. If you have a slice of freshly baked challah spread with butter and honey, you have become very lucky indeed.

The name *challah* first appeared in the Bible, where it meant Sabbath bread. That was a simple flat bread, a far cry from the challah we know today; much closer is the pita-like flat bread known as *salouf*. Among Yemenite Jews, *salouf* is served at almost every meal; it's perfect for dipping in spreads, dunking in soups, or sopping up sauces. (It also makes for a tasty breakfast, lightly fried and then sprinkled with sugar and drizzled with lemon juice.)

A different sort of flat bread is the Eastern European *pletzlach*—chewy, crusty rounds topped with chopped onions and poppy seeds. Once a fixture in Jewish bakeries in the United States, in recent decades *pletzlach* have become less and less common. This is a regrettable trend, but also perhaps a reversible one: *Pletzlach* are not very difficult or time-consuming to make and are a guaranteed crowd-pleaser.

Part of the decline of *pletzlach* must surely be due to the astonishing popularity of the bagel. Bagels are now ubiquitous, but in almost every case these are pillowy-soft, insipid pretenders to the name. If you want bagels the way they used to be—dense, chewy, and wonderfully flavorful—you have to make them yourself. Unlike *pletzlach*, bagels are rather time-consuming to make at home, and it's not likely something that you'll do on a regular basis. Still, homemade bagels are unquestionably superior to any you can find in a store, and once in a while—say, for a Sunday brunch with family and friends—they're more than worth the trouble. "Love is sweet," goes another Yiddish saying, "but it's nice to have bread with it." Or, now and then, real bagels.

DISHES: Challah

The name *challah* comes from the Bible, where it refers both to Sabbath bread and to the portion of risen dough that the Jews of the Temple period gave each week to their priests, after God's commandment to Moses in Numbers 15:17–21. (Since the destruction of the Temple, female bakers have traditionally pinched off a one-ounce piece of the dough—this is known as "taking challah"—to be burned in the oven, as a symbol of the priest's portion; to do so is a *mitzvah* specifically reserved for women.) The challah of biblical times was a simple flat loaf; the kind with which we are familiar today could hardly be more different, and originated among German Jews of the Middle Ages, who modeled their Sabbath loaf on a popular German braided bread and called it *berches*. According to Jewish-food historian John Cooper, the etymology of this word is a subject of some dispute: At least one scholar has asserted that the braided loaf represented interlocked arms, and so the name *berches* was likely derived from the High German word for arms, *bergita*. A more widely held approach locates the origin in the German fertility goddess Berchta (also known as Perchta), for whom German women baked braided loaves of bread meant to resemble plaited hair. However, more recent scholarship points to the Hebrew *birkat* (blessing), a word often engraved on the knives used to cut the Sabbath bread. In Austria, the braided Sabbath loaf was commonly referred to by the biblical name *challah*, and this is the name by which it was known as it spread eastward, with the Jewish migration, into Poland and throughout Eastern Europe. In Germany, *berches* had the pronounced sourdough taste common among Central European breads, but like so many other Jewish foods it was made sweeter in Poland; the dough was additionally enriched with eggs, which in combination with the abundant sugar and oil gives challah its soft, fine, almost cakey crumb.

The braiding of the bread has a Germanic origin, but over time, as this version of challah became integral to Jewish observance, its shape accrued new symbolic meanings. Many Jewish bakers braided their challah to have six humps, which, when served in the traditional two loaves (representing the double portion of manna gathered before the Sabbath, so that no work was required on the day of rest), would represent the twelve tribes of Israel; or, instead, they used additional strands of dough to create intricately braided loaves with twelve humps apiece. In the Ukraine, loaves for the pre-Yom Kippur meal were fashioned into the shape of birds ("May our sins fly away like birds," Isaiah 31:5) and ladders, symbolizing the ascension to Heaven. For the Shabbat after Passover, key-shaped loaves expressed the hope of opening the heavenly gates.

For Rosh Hashanah, loaves of challah are traditionally formed into spirals rather than braids, signifying the continuity of life. On that sweet holiday the challah is dipped in honey, while on the Sabbath it is sprinkled with salt, reminiscent of the Temple altar, where salt was used in sacrifices. On top of the challah, poppy or sesame seeds symbolize the manna that fell from Heaven to feed the Jewish people during their years of wandering in the desert. The loaves (two of them, representing the double portion of manna gathered before the Sabbath, so that no work was required on the day of rest) are placed on a wooden board and covered with a cloth, as the manna was said to be protected by a layer of dew.

Beneath waits the shining challah, yeastily light, heavy with meaning.

CHALLAH

EASTERN EUROPEAN EGG BREAD

This rendition of challah, from Michael Rosen of Oberlin, Ohio, uses mashed potato to help create its wonderfully soft and firm texture. If you are serving the challah for Rosh Hashanah, you can make a round loaf by forming each dough half into a rope that is 20 inches long, about 3 inches wide on one end and tapering down to about 1 inch wide on the other. Place the wider end at the center of a baking sheet and coil the dough around it in a spiral, pinching the end together under the loaf. (If you prefer, you can replace the butter in the recipe with vegetable oil.)

MAKES 2 LOAVES

- 1 medium russet potato (about 8 ounces), peeled and quartered
- 8 tablespoons (1 stick) butter, cut into 4 pieces
- 3 tablespoons honey
- 1 tablespoon salt
- 1 package (about 2½ teaspoons) active dry yeast
- ¼ cup warm water
- 1 teaspoon sugar
- ¼ cup unbleached all-purpose flour, plus 6 cups
- Pinch of saffron threads, crumbled
- 2 tablespoons boiling water
- 3 eggs plus 2 egg yolks

1. Bring a pot of salted water to a boil. Add the potato and cook until soft. Drain and mash well. Reserve the cooking water. Place the mashed potato in a large liquid measuring container and add the butter, honey, salt, and enough of the potato cooking water to equal a total of 2½ cups. (The cooking water will melt the butter and liquify the honey.) Set aside and let cool.
2. In a small bowl, combine the yeast, warm water, sugar, and the ¼ cup flour. Mix well and let stand for 30 minutes.
3. Place the saffron in a small bowl and add the boiling water. Let stand for 15 minutes, then add to the potato mixture. Beat the eggs and egg yolks together and add them to the potato mixture.
4. Put the remaining 6 cups flour on a clean surface or in a large mixing bowl and form a well in the center. Add the yeast mixture and slowly begin to incorporate the flour. Then add the potato mixture, slowly incorporating more of the flour until all of the liquid is incorporated into the flour. If using raisins, add them to the dough. Knead the dough until it is smooth and elastic, about 10 minutes, adding more flour as necessary to keep it from sticking.

5. Place the dough in a large, lightly oiled bowl, turning once to coat. Cover with a towel and let rise in a warm place until doubled in volume, 1 to 1½ hours.

6. Grease 2 baking sheets or line them with parchment paper. When the dough has risen, punch it down and divide it in two. Knead each ball for a few minutes to firm up the dough. Set one ball aside and cover it with a towel. Divide the other ball into 3 pieces, rolling each piece into a rope about 1½ inches thick and 14 inches long. Place the 3 ropes side by side. Pinch together one end of the 3 ropes. With the pinched end away from you, bring the left-hand rope over the center rope. Next, bring the right-hand rope over what is now the center rope and pull the ropes tight. Continue braiding in this manner until all of the dough is braided. Pinch the 3 ends together. Put the formed loaf on one of the prepared baking sheets. Braid the other dough ball in the same manner.

7. Put a towel over each of the loaves and let them rise in a warm place for 30 minutes.

8. Preheat the oven to 425 degrees.

9. Using a pastry brush, brush the loaves with the egg wash. If desired, sprinkle the loaves with the poppy or sesame seeds. Bake for 20 minutes. Lower the heat to 375 degrees and continue baking until well browned, 20 to 25 minutes. Transfer to wire cooling racks. Let cool to room temperature before cutting.

1 cup raisins, soaked in water to plump for 15 minutes and drained (optional)

1 egg beaten lightly with 1 tablespoon water for egg wash

About 2 teaspoons poppy or sesame seeds for sprinkling (optional)

SWEET CHALLAH

This sweet, almost cake-like challah was made by my friend Chana Pollack's grandmother Rosie in the town of Ostrovtse, southeast of Warsaw. (Many dishes, such as challah, gefilte fish, and borscht, were sweeter in Poland than elsewhere.) She shaped the dough into a square, adding to its cake-like quality, but it can also be made in a round or braid.

MAKES 1 LOAF

2 tablespoons raisins

¼ cup boiling water

1 package (about 2½ teaspoons) active dry yeast

¼ cup sugar

½ cup warm water

⅓ cup vegetable oil

2 eggs, lightly beaten

1 teaspoon salt

About 4 cups unbleached all-purpose flour, sifted

1 egg beaten lightly with 1 tablespoon water for egg wash

About 1 teaspoon poppy or sesame seeds for sprinkling (optional)

1. Steep the raisins in the boiling water for 15 minutes. Remove the raisins (they can be discarded or reserved) and reserve the water for the dough.
2. Combine the yeast, 1 tablespoon of the sugar, and the warm water in a bowl. Let stand until the mixture begins to bubble, about 5 minutes.
3. Combine the yeast mixture, the remaining 3 tablespoons sugar, oil, eggs, salt, the reserved raisin soaking water, raisins (if using), and half of the flour in the bowl of a standing electric mixer and beat until fully combined. Slowly add the remaining flour, beating to create a soft, sticky dough that pulls away from the sides of the bowl. Cover the bowl and let stand for 10 minutes.
4. Turn the dough out onto a lightly floured surface. Knead until smooth and elastic, about 10 minutes, adding flour as necessary to keep the dough from sticking. Place the dough in a large, lightly oiled bowl, turning once to coat. Cover with a towel and let rise in a warm place until doubled in volume, about 2 hours.
5. Grease a large baking sheet or line it with parchment paper. Punch down the dough and form it into a square about 9 inches in diameter. Place the loaf on the prepared baking sheet. Cover with a towel and let rise in a warm place for 30 minutes.
6. Preheat the oven to 375 degrees. Using a pastry brush, brush the challah with the egg wash. If desired, sprinkle the top with the poppy or sesame seeds. Bake until well browned, about 30 minutes. Transfer to a wire cooling rack and let cool to room temperature before cutting.

PLETZLACH

EASTERN EUROPEAN FLAT BREADS

A pletzel—*it rhymes with pretzel—is a crusty flat bread, something like the Italian focaccia, that is topped with onions and often poppy seeds. The name comes from the Yiddish word for board, and in English, the bread is often known as an onion board. Like their Eastern European cousins bagels and bialys, good* pletzlach *are chewy and flavorful and best when eaten warm. I've adapted this recipe from one in* Crisco Recipes for the Jewish Housewife, *a Procter & Gamble recipe pamphlet published—in English and Yiddish, and running from back to front—in 1933. If you prefer, you can fry the onions before sprinkling them on the dough.*

MAKES 8

- 2 teaspoons salt
- 2 teaspoons sugar
- 2 tablespoons vegetable oil
- 1 cup hot water
- 1 package (about 2½ teaspoons) active dry yeast
- 1 egg, lightly beaten
- About 4 cups unbleached all-purpose flour
- 1 egg beaten lightly with 1 tablespoon water for egg wash
- 2 large onions, finely chopped
- About 1 tablespoon poppy seeds for sprinkling
- Salt for sprinkling

1. Combine the salt, sugar, oil, and hot water in a medium bowl. When the water cools to lukewarm, add the yeast and let stand until the mixture begins to bubble, about 5 minutes.
2. Pour the yeast mixture in the bowl of a standing electric mixer. Add the egg and beat to combine. Gradually add the flour, beating to create a soft dough that pulls away from the sides of the bowl. Turn the dough out onto a lightly floured surface and knead for 10 minutes, until smooth and elastic, adding flour as necessary to keep the dough from sticking.
3. Place the dough in a lightly oiled bowl, turning once to coat. Cover with a towel and let rise in a warm place until nearly doubled in volume, about 2 hours.
4. Preheat the oven to 350 degrees. Lightly grease 2 large baking sheets or line them with parchment paper.
5. Punch down the dough and divide it into 8 pieces. On a lightly floured surface, roll each piece into a round about 5 inches in diameter. With your fingertips, press down gently in the center

(continued)

of each round, creating a slight indentation with a raised rim about ½ inch wide around.

6. Place the rounds on the prepared baking sheets. Brush them with the egg wash, then top them with the chopped onions. Sprinkle with the poppy seeds and salt.

7. Bake until the crusts are crisp and golden brown, about 35 minutes. Transfer the breads to wire cooling racks. Serve warm or at room temperature.

SALOUF

YEMENITE FLAT BREAD

The round, pita-like bread known as salouf *is the mainstay of Yemenite breads, served at almost every meal. Instead of being baked, rounds of* salouf *can be fried in oil and then served with the spicy chili paste* Z'houg *(page 361). Alternatively, the fried rounds can be drizzled with lemon juice and sprinkled with sugar; these make a lovely breakfast. This recipe comes from Shoshana Sharabi Garber of Valley Stream, Long Island. Her grandparents were the proprietors of a dry-goods business in Sanaa, Yemen; they immigrated (on foot) to Palestine in the late nineteenth century.*

MAKES 4 LOAVES

- 2 cups warm water
- 1 package (about 2½ teaspoons) active dry yeast
- 1 teaspoon sugar
- 4½ cups unbleached all-purpose flour, plus additional for kneading and rolling
- 1 teaspoon salt

1. Put the warm water in a large bowl. Add the yeast and sugar and let stand until the mixture begins to bubble, about 5 minutes. Slowly add the flour and salt and stir until fully incorporated.
2. Turn the dough out onto a lightly floured surface and knead until it is smooth and elastic but still moist and slightly sticky, about 10 minutes, adding flour as necessary to keep the dough from sticking. Place the dough in a large, oiled bowl, turning once to coat. Cover with a towel and let rise in a warm place until nearly doubled in volume, about 1 hour.
3. When the dough has risen, punch it down, cover again, and let it rise for another 30 minutes.
4. Preheat the oven to 375 degrees. Lightly grease 2 baking sheets or line them with parchment paper.
5. Spread some flour on a large plate. Slice the dough into quarters. Roll each quarter into a ball, and roll the balls in the flour until they are lightly covered. Let them rest on the plate, covered with a towel, for 20 minutes.
6. On a lightly floured surface, stretch each dough ball into a round about 10 inches in diameter. Place 2 rounds on each of the prepared baking sheets and bake until golden brown, 15 to 20 minutes. Serve warm or at room temperature.

DISHES: Bagels

The origins of the bagel, like those of so many Old World foods, are today obscure to us. According to an oft-repeated tale, the bagel was born in Vienna in 1683, as a tribute to the Polish cavalry that had helped save the city from the invading Turks. In honor of the cavalry's efforts, so goes the story, a Viennese baker produced a roll in the shape of a horse's stirrup, known in German as a *Steigbügel*. The idea of this seems reasonable enough, but as it happens, a strikingly similar story has also been told about the birth of the French croissant. In this account, a baker heard the sound of Turks tunneling beneath the city's walls, and by alerting the local troops, saved Vienna; as thanks, the baker was granted the exclusive rights to bake a roll commemorating the event, in the shape of the crescent, the symbol of Islam. As has been noted by, among others, Alan Davidson in *The Oxford Companion to Food*, the legend of the vigilant Viennese baker is an especially enduring bit of culinary mythology (the croissant cannot be traced back any further than the late nineteenth century), and indeed, that same creation story—baker, siege, crescent-shaped pastry—has been told to explain the birth of a very different baked good, the Jewish rugelach. (How gastronomically propitious was this siege!)

More problematic still is the fact that bagels are referred to in the ordinances of the Jewish community of Krakow in 1610. In his scholarly Yiddish-language work *Yidishe Maykholim* (Jewish Food), Mortkhe Kosover reported that the bagels were "amongst the gifts that were sent solely to 'the midwives and the women who would be there at the midwife'"—that is, women about to give birth. So the origins of the bagel obviously predate the siege of Vienna, and its ring shape would seem to have had a more prosaic purpose, likely allowing a baker to carry them in bulk on a stick. The name itself, however, does seem to be derived from German, either from the word for stirrup, or from the verb *biegen* (to bend), or alternatively, from the Middle High German *bügel*, meaning a ring or bracelet. In any case, from

Germany the bagel traveled to Eastern Europe during the Middle Ages, where it became a staple as a quick and handy snack at work or school. The bagels of the time were small, dense, and chewy, with a hard crust formed by briefly boiling the bagel before placing it in the oven; with a single exception (the ring-shaped roll known as the *ri-oute,* a specialty of the Rhône Valley), this procedure—boiling before baking—is unique to the bagel.

From Eastern Europe the bagel made its way to the United States with the mass Jewish immigration of the late nineteenth and early twentieth centuries. As with pizza, another contemporary mass-market food, bagels existed in America for decades as a purely ethnic phenomenon, virtually unknown to the society at large. The bagels were made by hand, from exactly five ingredients: flour, water, yeast, salt, and malt. Though the bagels produced by different bakeries may have varied somewhat, the essential recipe had remained unchanged since the time of the immigrants, and likely long before that. So it was until the early 1960s, when came the revolution: the advent of the automated bagel machine (first employed by the Lender's company to help them produce their new line of frozen bagels), which set into motion a series of changes that resulted, by the end, in bagels that earlier generations would scarcely have recognized.

The traditional bagel dough, using high-gluten flour and relatively little water—necessary to create the bagel's dense, chewy texture—was extremely stiff, requiring lots of difficult, tiring kneading, which ultimately proved too tough for machines. Confronted by such a demanding dough, electric mixers burned out and extruders clogged up. The solution the bakeries hit upon was to add more water; this thinned the dough out, softening it up, so that it would run more smoothly through the machines. By the early 1970s, newer models were coming along that stored the bagel dough in huge hoppers. Unfortunately, the dough tended to stick to the sides of the hoppers, and so bakeries began adding oil as a lubricant, making the dough softer still.

An even more profound alteration came later in the decade, with the introduction of so-called dough conditioners. In the past, bagel dough had been left to ferment for several hours before baking, both to relax the dough (this creates a more uniform rounding in the bagels) and to build flavor. As any baker knows, long fermentation is essential for creating a full depth of flavor in yeast breads, and particularly one with such an austere ingredient list as has the bagel. By relaxing the dough right away, the conditioners eliminated the need for fermentation, and so allowed the baker to proceed directly from mixing to baking. As such, they were a boon to bakeries looking to simplify their process and reduce production time, but for the taste of the bagels they proved nothing short of catastrophic. Today, in the estimate of Tom Lehmann, Director of Bakery Assistance at the American Institute of Baking, "dough conditioners are used by at least 50 percent of the bagel shops out there." The new flavor—or lack of it—has become the industry standard; it is, in other words, what most people now grow up believing bagels taste like.

By the 1980s bagel shops had become a fixture on the American landscape, open from morning to night, and this is when owners of the shops began to recognize that the true growth potential of bagels lay not in their role as a breakfast item, with a prime selling period of only a couple of hours a day, but rather as a base for sandwiches, which could be served around the clock. There was, however, yet another problem that had to be overcome: The bagels would have to be made less crusty, because, it was felt, no one wants to have to work that hard to eat their sandwich. And so came perhaps the sorriest moment in the history of bagel baking, when in overwhelming numbers bakeries abandoned the step of preboiling—culinarily, the bagel's defining characteristic—replacing kettles with steam-injected ovens. Instead of a two-minute plunge into boiling water, the bagels received a mere twenty or thirty seconds of oven-steaming. Where once had been a thick, hardy crust, now there was only a sadly pale, flimsy lamina. The bagel had become, in the lament of the traditionalists, a roll with a hole.

Finally, in the manner of the rest of America's fast-food industry, came that perhaps inevitable step: supersizing. Just as there are no more small soda cups or servings of French fries, there are no more small bagels. At one time a bagel was made with about two-and-a-half ounces of dough; now it is, at a minimum, four ounces, with some behemoths—known in the industry as "bull" bagels—made from more than five ounces, or about one third the amount of dough used to make an entire loaf of bread.

So the transformation was complete. The bagel, which had once been small, flavorful, dense, and crusty, was now precisely the opposite—huge, insipid, and pillowy-soft. Within the span of two generations, the bagel had become as American as apple pie, and far more common. Bagels, frozen and fresh alike, can now be found in virtually every supermarket, and there is scarcely an American city that does not have at least one shop devoted to them. As had earlier happened with the doughnut and the muffin, a vast array of flavor varieties began to appear, the better to satisfy the demands of a large, diverse public. Initially, observed historian Donna R. Gabaccia, these were "flavors associated with desserts and breakfast cereals—honey, raisin, blueberry, cinnamon," but the 1990s also brought new savory flavors such as jalapeño, pesto, rosemary, cheddar cheese, and sun-dried tomato, the definitive yuppie ingredient of the day.

Lender's, for six decades a family business, was purchased by Kraft Foods in 1984 for $60 million; in 1996, Kellogg's paid $455 million for the company. That same year Dunkin' Donuts began selling bagels in all of its shops, the largest product introduction in the company's history. In 2000, Pillsbury launched its "Toaster Bagel Shoppe" line, consisting of a rectangular pastry, with no center hole, filled with fruit-flavored cream cheese. ("Putting cream cheese and jelly on a bagel isn't hard, but it takes time and it is messy," said a company spokesman. "Toaster Bagel Shoppe makes it hassle-free.") But perhaps the crowning moment in the bagel's mainstreaming had already arrived the previous year, when McDonald's announced that participating locations would now offer "bagel breakfast sandwiches": steam-baked bagels featuring a variety of fillings, among them egg, ham, and cheese, topped with a special "breakfast sauce."

"What a horror it is for a whole nation to be developing without the sense of beauty, & eating bananas for breakfast," wrote Edith Wharton in 1904. Surely the same might be said about ham and cheese on a steamed McBagel?

BAGELS

This is it: the five-ingredient real deal, the kind of crusty, chewy, flavorful bagel that in only a couple of generations has become an endangered species. Malt syrup and high-gluten flour can be purchased from King Arthur Flour at (800) 827-6836 or www.kingarthurflour.com.

MAKES 10

1½ cups warm water

1 package (about 2½ teaspoons) active dry yeast

2 teaspoons salt

1 teaspoon malt syrup

about 4½ cups high-gluten flour

Poppy seeds or sesame seeds for topping (optional)

1. In a small bowl, combine the warm water and yeast and let stand until the mixture begins to bubble, about 5 minutes.
2. Combine the yeast mixture, salt, and malt syrup in the bowl of a standing electric mixer and beat to blend. Slowly add the flour, beating to create a thick, crumbly dough that holds together well.
3. Turn the dough out onto a lightly floured surface and knead (the dough will seem very stiff) until smooth and elastic, 10 to 15 minutes. Cover the dough with a towel and let stand for 20 minutes.
4. Line 2 baking sheets with parchment paper. Divide the dough into 10 pieces, covering them with a towel while you knead and shape each piece. Roll each piece into a rope 10 inches long, tapered slightly at the ends. Attach the ends of the rope to form a circle, overlapping the ends by about 1 inch. Place the bagel on one of the parchment-lined baking sheets, gently pressing it down on top to flatten. Repeat the process with the remaining dough pieces.
5. Cover the baking sheets with plastic wrap and let stand for 15 minutes. Refrigerate for at least 6 hours or overnight.
6. Preheat the oven to 450 degrees. Line 2 baking sheets with parchment paper. Bring a large pot of water to a rolling boil. Working in small batches, drop the bagels into the water and boil for 45 seconds, then turn them over and boil for another 45 seconds. With a slotted spoon, transfer the bagels to wire racks and let drain completely.
7. Transfer the bagels to the parchment-lined baking sheets, leaving at least 2 inches between them. If desired, sprinkle each bagel with poppy or sesame seeds. Bake until brown, about 16 minutes. Transfer to wire cooling racks. Serve warm or at room temperature.

KAAK

ANISE-FLAVORED SESAME RINGS

Born in Brooklyn, Stanley Sultan is now a writer and professor of English at Clark University in Worcester, Massachusetts. His mother's side of the family was Ashkenazic, while his father's came from Aleppo, Syria. This recipe for the Syrian pretzel-like treats called kaak *comes from his aunt, Molly Sultan of Miami Beach. "She cooked like an angel," he says. "You never knew how good food could be until you had Aunt Molly's food."*

MAKES ABOUT 40

- ½ package (about 1¼ teaspoons) active dry yeast
- ½ cup warm water, plus more as needed
- 1 teaspoon sugar
- 2½ cups unbleached all-purpose flour, sifted, plus additional for kneading
- 1½ teaspoons salt
- ¼ cup vegetable oil
- 2 tablespoons anise seeds
- 1 egg beaten lightly with 1 tablespoon water for egg wash
- ¼ cup sesame seeds for topping

1. In a small bowl, combine the yeast, warm water, and sugar and let stand until the mixture begins to bubble, about 5 minutes.
2. Place the flour and salt in the bowl of a standing electric mixer. Add the yeast mixture, oil, and anise seeds and beat to combine. Add water, by tablespoons, beating to form a soft dough that holds together (2 to 3 tablespoons or so).
3. Turn the dough out onto a lightly floured surface and knead until it is smooth and elastic, about 5 minutes, adding flour as necessary to keep it from sticking. Place the dough in a large, lightly oiled bowl, turning once. Cover with a towel and let rise for 1 hour.
4. Preheat the oven to 400 degrees. Punch down the dough and divide it into quarters. On a lightly floured surface, roll out each dough quarter into a cylinder about 2 inches wide and 5 inches long. Slice the cylinders crosswise into ½-inch pieces. Roll each piece to a length of about 7 inches. Shape each one into a circle, overlapping the ends slightly and pressing down to seal. Brush with the egg wash, and dip the egg-covered top into the sesame seeds.
5. Place the *kaak*, sesame side up, at least 1 inch apart on 2 ungreased baking sheets. Bake until they just start to rise, about 5 minutes. Lower the heat to 250 degrees and continue baking until they are golden brown and crisp, about another 40 minutes. Transfer to wire cooling racks and let cool completely.

SHTRITZLACH

TORONTO BLUEBERRY BUNS

Blueberry buns are to Jewish Toronto what, say, smoked meat is to Jewish Montreal: one of those rare foods that manage to be at once vitally important to a specific community and almost unknown outside of it. It's not easy to come up with an analogy to describe blueberry buns. They are not injected with a glob of filling, as are jelly doughnuts; rather, the dough is first rolled out, the blueberry filling is poured on top, and the dough folded over and pinched closed. The dough itself is yeasty and light, a bit like that of a Danish pastry, though less rich; on the other hand, it's far richer than that of a traditional bun, and the crust is egg washed and sugary.

Blueberry buns were once commonly baked at home, but now they are almost exclusively a store-bought item. What may be the city's best can be found at the Open Window Bakery, which has been in operation since 1957. I've adapted this recipe from the one used by the Open Window.

MAKES 8

FOR THE FILLING

1½ cups fresh or thawed frozen blueberries

¼ cup sugar

1 tablespoon cornstarch dissolved in ¼ cup water

¼ teaspoon salt

FOR THE DOUGH

1 package (about 2½ teaspoons) active dry yeast

½ cup warm water

⅓ cup sugar

1. Make the filling: Combine all the ingredients in a medium saucepan over medium heat and bring to a boil. Lower the heat and simmer, uncovered, for 5 minutes, stirring occasionally, until the mixture thickens to a jelly-like consistency. Remove from heat and let cool.

2. Make the dough: In a small bowl, combine the yeast and warm water with ½ teaspoon of the sugar. Let stand until the mixture begins to bubble, about 5 minutes.

3. Combine the flour, the remaining sugar, and the salt in the bowl of a standing electric mixer. Mix briefly to combine. Add the shortening, the yeast mixture, and the eggs, and beat to form a soft dough that pulls away from the sides of the bowl. On a lightly floured surface, knead the dough just until smooth, about 2 min-

utes. Divide the dough in half and roll into 2 balls. Cover the balls with a towel and let stand at room temperature for 45 minutes.

4. Make the blueberry buns: Set out a bowl of cold water. On a lightly floured surface, roll out each dough ball into a 12- by 10-inch rectangle. Cut the rectangles into quarters (cutting first crosswise and then lengthwise), creating 4 pieces, each 6 inches by 5 inches. Place a heaping tablespoon of the filling in the center of each piece. Moisten the edges of the dough with water, fold the short end of the dough over (creating a 3- by 5-inch bun), and pinch the edges tightly closed.

5. Preheat the oven to 375 degrees. Grease 2 baking sheets or line them with parchment paper. Place the buns on the prepared sheets and cover them with towels. Let stand for 30 minutes.

6. Brush the buns with the egg wash and sprinkle the tops with sugar. Bake until browned, about 15 minutes. Transfer to wire cooling racks. Serve warm or at room temperature.

3 cups unbleached all-purpose flour, sifted

1 teaspoon salt

3 tablespoons vegetable shortening

2 eggs

1 egg lightly beaten with 1 tablespoon water for eggwash

Sugar for sprinkling

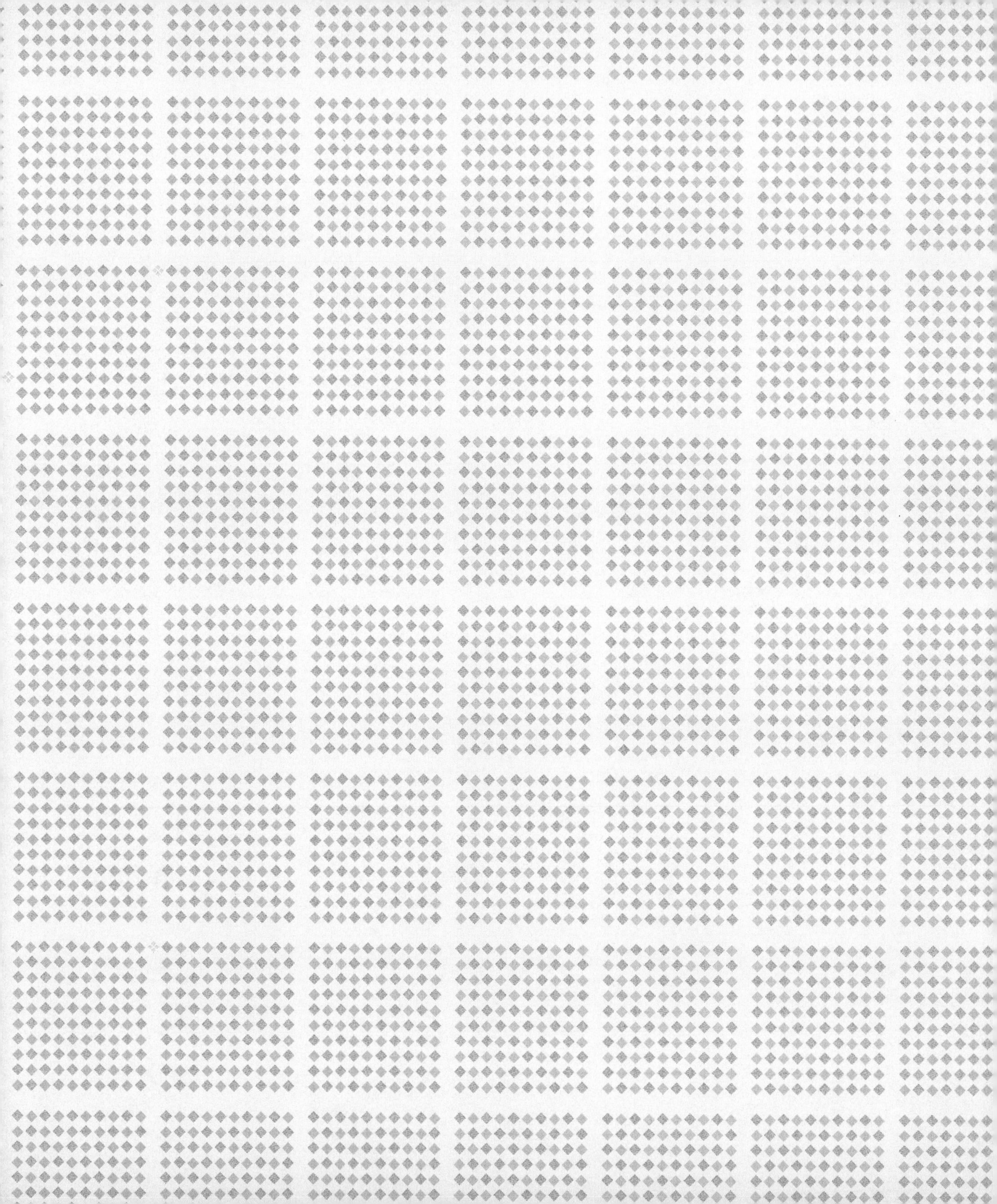

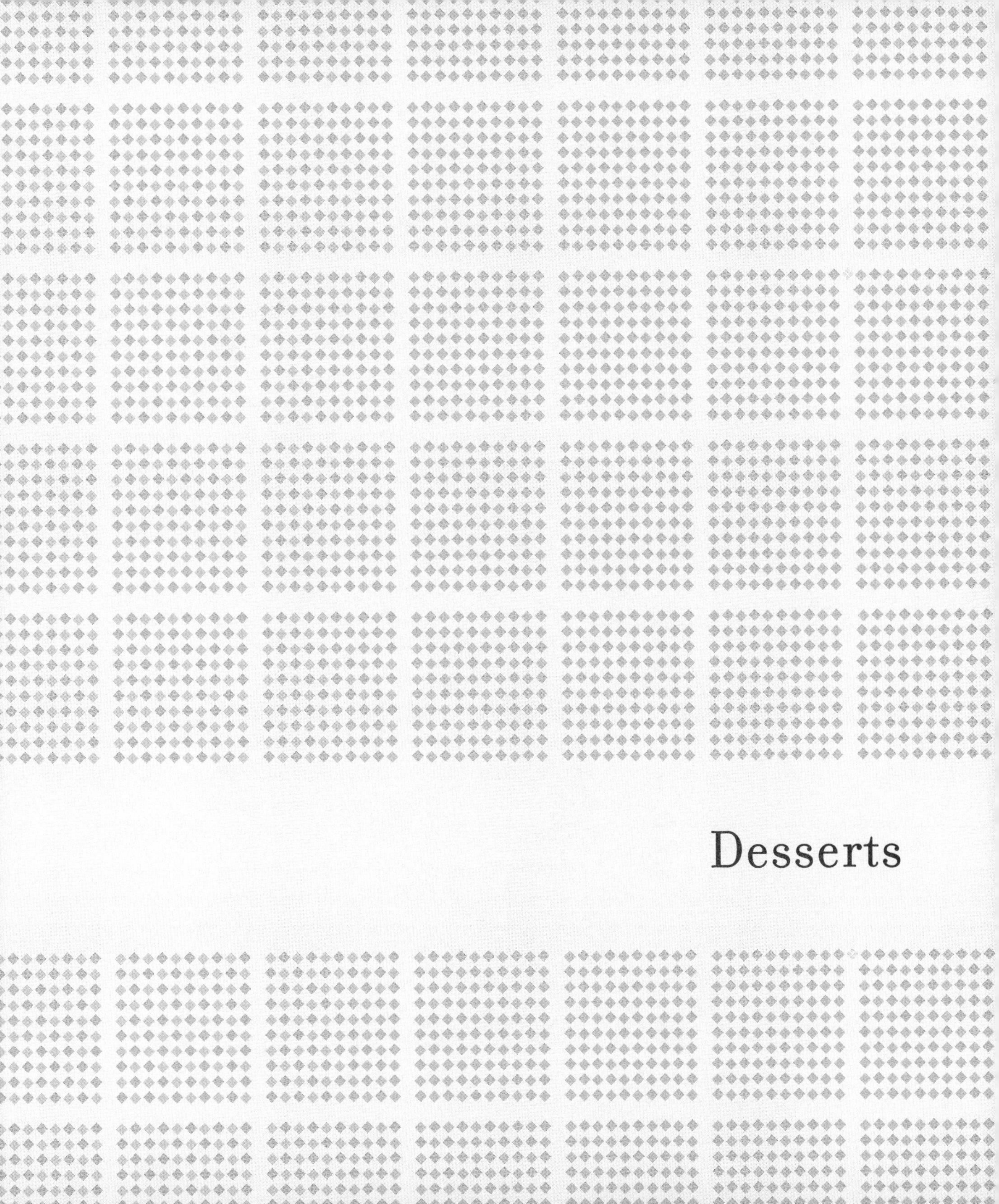

Desserts

Jewish tradition has always associated sweetness with joy and celebration, and it has long been customary to serve sweet foods on festive occasions such as Sabbaths and holidays. Over the centuries, certain of these sweet foods have come to be inextricably linked with particular holidays. Among Ashkenazic Jews, for instance, cheesecake is traditional for the springtime holiday of Shavuot, when dairy foods are served; it is difficult to imagine a more festive holiday, or one to be more happily observed, than that which encourages the eating of cheesecake.

Another springtime holiday, Purim, has for centuries featured the little triangle-shaped cookies called hamantashen, and macaroons, with their ground-almond base, are indispensable during Passover. (Macaroons are Ashkenazic, but Sephardic communities have their own Passover nut cookies, among them an ethereal Middle Eastern variety made with pistachios and rosewater.) On Passover, when the use of flour is forbidden, Jewish cooks also turn to tortes or sponge cakes, the leavening for which is provided by beaten egg whites. Italian Jews make matzo fritters on Passover, which are topped with a cinnamon-flavored honey syrup. Honey is also the topping for the yeast-raised fritters called *loukomades*, a Hanukkah treat in Greece; these are much like *bimuelos*, the sweet fritters popular throughout the Sephardic world, the topping for which is not honey but instead a citrus-flavored sugar syrup. Versions of that aromatic syrup—a legacy of medieval Spain, where sugar was first introduced to the West—sweeten many other Sephardic desserts as well, including *galaktoboureko*, a custard-filled filo pastry that Greek Jews have traditionally used to break the Yom Kippur fast.

Around the world, Jewish kitchens have turned out a remarkable array of cakes, pastries, puddings, fritters, cookies, and confections, of which the recipes in this chapter can of necessity be only a tiny sampling. Many, like the ones mentioned above, are holiday treats, but of course you don't need to save them only for then. Macaroons all year round: Now there's a truly festive idea.

DISHES: Cheesecake

We have the ancient Greeks to thank for cheesecake, for they made it first. The Greeks adored cheesecake and produced it in many varieties, including one especially decadent rendition in which the cake was deep fried and then swathed in honey. Cookbook author Evelyn Rose surmised that Jews first encountered cheesecake during the Greek occupation of Palestine beginning in the third century B.C.E., and this seems likely enough; what is unquestionable is that since ancient times Jews have baked cheesecakes for Shavuot, the late-spring holiday that celebrates the giving of the Torah on Sinai, on which it is traditional to serve dairy foods.

Cheesecake was a favorite delicacy of Eastern European Jews, who made it with curd cheeses such as farmer's cheese. When they emigrated to the United States, they brought their recipes for cheesecake with them, thus setting the stage for what would be the great revolution in modern cheesecake making. That revolution—what the authors of *The Joy of Cheesecake* call "the technological breakthrough that ushered in the Modern Age of Cheesecakes"—took place entirely by accident. In upstate New York in 1872 dairymen were experimenting with a cheese that they hoped would duplicate the popular Neufchâtel cheese of France. The cheese that resulted turned out, unexpectedly, to be far creamier than Neufchâtel, and they dubbed it "cream cheese." Cream cheese, however, spoiled quickly, and for all its obvious appeal it had limited use until James L. Kraft, founder of Kraft Foods, invented a method of pasteurizing cheese in 1912. Even then, cream cheese remained basically a specialty item until about 1920, when the Breakstone Company (formed in the 1880s by Joseph and Isaac Breakstone, né Breghstein, two Jewish immigrants from Lithuania) began mass-marketing their Downsville Cream Cheese. Before the decade was out, cream cheese had become a staple of groceries throughout the country and it was for the first time beginning to appear in the fillings of cheesecakes.

These cheesecakes—from what we might call the "early modern" period—were made from a combination of cream cheese and, after the Eastern European Jewish style, softer curd cheeses. Curd cheeses, though, could not compete with the sheer richness of cream cheese, and eventually they fell away and cream cheese reigned supreme, resulting in what has since come to be known, no matter where it is produced, as "New York" cheesecake. It is cream cheese, well beaten, that gives the New York cheesecake its perfect interplay of textural opposites—firm but soft, dense but creamy—cream cheese that gives the cake its glamorous gloss.

When aficionados speak in reverential tones about the New York cheesecake of the old days, the one they are referring to was likely made at Lindy's, the legendary late-night hangout for Broadway stars and hangers-on, mobsters and molls, the Runyonesque characters immortalized in the musical *Guys and Dolls*. Lindy's cheesecake is virtually the archetype of the New York style; its recipe calls for heavy cream, lots of eggs and sugar, vanilla extract, and lemon zest in both the filling and the crust, and no less than 2½ pounds of cream cheese, about twice the amount used in comparable cakes today.

These days, the sky's the limit when it comes to cheesecake, as bakers, like Vegas architects, compete for attention through sheer excess. Cheesecake fillings are flavored with ginger and marzipan and coconut and peppermint and whiskey, marbled with chocolate and pumpkin and caramel, studded with raisins and pralines and toffee; toppings can include peanut brittle, candied cherries, chocolate chips, chopped-up Snickers bars, and anything else, it seems, the baker happened to have stashed away on the back of the pantry shelf. With very few exceptions, all of this is sheer lily-gilding. For me, nothing beats a simple slice of well-made cheesecake, sweet and creamy and delicately scented, and gently drizzled with fruit compote for a bit of contrast in taste and texture. There may be no purer experience of bliss. Like those two other Greek contributions to our world—drama and democracy—cheesecake is rarely done right, but when it is, it is sublime.

NEW YORK CHEESECAKE

Making cheesecake at home can seem a daunting proposition, but it's actually very simple, as long as you obey one essential commandment: Thou shalt not overbake. Overbaking is the enemy of cheesecakes, because it causes them to dry out and—the bane of every cheesecake maker—to crack on top. It's best to remove the cheesecake from the oven when it's still slightly wobbly in the center; it will finish cooking as it cools. Too-rapid cooling, the other primary cause of cracking in cheesecakes, can be prevented by allowing the cake to cool partway in the oven with the heat turned off and the door ajar. Then, when the cake is out, make sure to run a thin knife around the crust; the cake will contract slightly as it cools, and any crust sticking to the side of the pan can also cause cracking.

This fabulous rendition of New York cheesecake comes from Marty and Irma Shore of (where else?) New York. My favorite serving method is to drizzle individual slices, depending on the season, with strawberry compote (see page 130) or sour cherry compote (see page 122).

SERVES 10 TO 12

FOR THE CRUST

1½ cups graham cracker crumbs (from about 10 graham crackers)

6 tablespoons (¾ stick) butter, melted

2 tablespoons sugar

FOR THE FILLING

1¼ pounds (20 ounces) cream cheese

1 cup sugar

½ teaspoon salt

4 eggs

1. Make the crust: Generously butter the bottom and sides of a 9-inch springform pan. Combine the graham cracker crumbs, sugar, and butter in a medium bowl and mix well. Press the mixture into the bottom and slightly up the sides of the prepared pan. Place the pan in the freezer until the crust is firm, 5 to 10 minutes.

2. Preheat the oven to 300 degrees.

3. Make the filling: In the bowl of a standing electric mixer, beat together the cream cheese, sugar, and salt at low speed until smooth. Add the eggs, 1 at a time, letting each become fully incorporated before adding the next. Beat in the sour cream, vanilla, and lemon juice and mix until very smooth, making sure to regularly scrape down the sides of the bowl with a rubber spatula.

- 1½ cups (about 1 pound) sour cream
- 1 teaspoon vanilla
- 2 teaspoons lemon juice
- Strawberry or sour cherry compote for topping (optional)

4. Pour the filling into the crust. Place the springform pan in a large baking pan, to catch any drips. Bake for 1 hour, then turn off the oven and allow the cake to bake in the turned-off oven for an additional 30 minutes.
5. Open the oven door. Allow the cake to cool for 30 minutes in the oven with the door ajar. Remove and carefully run a thin knife around the edge of the cake to loosen. Place the springform pan on a wire cooling rack to cool completely. When cool, cover with plastic wrap or aluminum foil and refrigerate at least 6 hours or overnight.
6. Remove the sides of the pan and transfer the cake to a serving platter. If desired, drizzle individual slices with fruit compote.

COFFEE CHEESECAKE

Coffee, I have always felt, is a natural for cheesecake; its bitter edge plays beautifully against the sweet creaminess of the cake. How good is this cheesecake? Listen: The first person for whom I ever made it took one bite and began literally to weep from happiness. Your results, of course, may vary.

SERVES 10 TO 12

FOR THE CRUST

1½ cups graham cracker crumbs

5 tablespoons sugar

8 tablespoons (1 stick) butter, melted

FOR THE FILLING

1½ pounds (three 8-ounce packages) cream cheese

¾ cup sugar

½ teaspoon salt

3 eggs

½ cup cold, very strong black coffee

1 teaspoon vanilla

⅓ cup heavy cream

2 teaspoons dark rum

Cocoa powder for dusting

Sliced fresh strawberries (optional)

1. Make the crust: Generously butter the bottom and sides of a 9-inch springform pan. Combine the graham cracker crumbs, sugar, and butter in a medium bowl and mix well. Press the mixture into the bottom and slightly up the sides of the prepared pan. Place the pan in the freezer until the crust is firm, 5 to 10 minutes.
2. Preheat the oven to 350 degrees.
3. Make the filling: In the bowl of a standing electric mixer, beat together the cream cheese, sugar, and salt at low speed until smooth. Add the eggs, 1 at a time, letting each become fully incorporated before adding the next. Beat in the coffee, vanilla, heavy cream, and rum, and mix until very smooth, making sure to regularly scrape down the sides of the bowl with a rubber spatula.
4. Pour the filling into the crust. Place the springform pan inside a larger baking pan, to catch any drips. Bake until the cake is nearly set, about 55 minutes. It should still be slightly wobbly in the center.
5. Turn off the oven, and let the cake cool for 30 minutes in the turned-off oven with the door ajar. Run a thin knife around the edge of the cake to loosen. Place the pan on a wire cooling rack to cool completely. When cool, cover with plastic wrap or aluminum foil and refrigerate at least 6 hours or overnight.
6. Remove the sides of the pan and transfer the cake to a serving platter. Dust with cocoa powder. If desired, serve with sliced strawberries.

SOUR CREAM COFFEE CAKE

Known in Yiddish as smeteneh, *sour cream was long a central ingredient in Russian Jewish cookery, used with everything from* borscht *and* schav *to blintzes and baked potatoes. Sour cream provided tanginess as well as vitamins A and D to a relatively stodgy diet lacking in both. The ingredient is also featured in coffee cake, which is, along with bagels and lox, one of the staples of the Jewish American brunch. This is an easy and scrumptious sour cream coffee cake, striped with two layers of cinnamon, sugar, and chopped nuts.*

SERVES 10

FOR THE FILLING

1 cup finely chopped walnuts

1/3 cup sugar

1 tablespoon ground cinnamon

FOR THE BATTER

8 tablespoons (1 stick) butter, softened

1 cup sugar

2 eggs

1 teaspoon vanilla

2 cups unbleached all-purpose flour

1 teaspoon baking soda

1/4 teaspoon salt

1 cup sour cream

Confectioners' sugar for dusting

1. Preheat the oven to 350 degrees. Butter and flour a 10-inch Bundt pan.
2. Make the filling: In a small bowl, mix together the walnuts, sugar, and cinnamon.
3. Make the batter: In the bowl of a standing electric mixer, beat together the butter and sugar until the mixture is pale and creamy. Add the eggs and vanilla and beat until fully incorporated.
4. Sift together the flour, baking soda, and salt. Add the dry ingredients to the batter in two additions, alternating with the sour cream, beginning and ending with the dry ingredients. Mix until the batter is smooth.
5. Spoon one-third of the batter into the prepared pan and smooth it. Sprinkle the batter with half of the walnut filling. Next, cover the filling with another third of the batter and smooth it. Top with the remaining filling. Spoon the remaining batter on top and smooth it.
6. Bake until the top of the cake is golden brown and a cake tester inserted in the middle comes out dry, 40 to 45 minutes. Let the cake cool slightly in the pan. Remove it from the pan by inverting it onto a wire cooling rack. When completely cool, dust with confectioners' sugar.

PAN DI SPAGNA

SPONGE CAKE

Sponge cakes—the leavening for which comes from beaten egg whites—are a staple of Jewish bakers during Passover season, when the use of flour and yeast is prohibited. Though sponge cakes are made by both Ashkenazic and Sephardic Jews, perhaps the best-known variety is the Sephardic pan de España; *the name literally means bread of Spain, which points to the cake's origins in pre-Inquisition Spain. When the Jews were expelled at the end of the fifteenth century they carried their sponge cake recipes throughout the continent, notably to Italy, where the cake is still known as* pan di Spagna.

In Italy the cake is served in a number of ways. For breakfast, pieces can be topped with fruit preserves. Or, when the cake is no longer fresh, it can be cut into slices and toasted. During Passover, pieces of pan di Spagna *are also sometimes topped with leftover* charoset *(see page 365). If you can't find matzo cake meal, you can grind regular matzo meal in a coffee grinder.*

SERVES 10

½ cup matzo cake meal
½ cup potato starch
8 eggs, separated
10 tablespoons sugar
¼ teaspoon salt
1 teaspoon vanilla
Grated zest from 1 lemon
1 tablespoon lemon juice

1. Preheat the oven to 350 degrees. Combine the matzo cake meal and potato starch in a medium bowl, then sift them together.
2. Place the egg yolks, sugar, salt, vanilla, lemon zest, and lemon juice in the bowl of a standing electric mixer and beat at medium speed until the mixture is thick and pale.
3. In a medium bowl, beat the egg whites until stiff but not dry. Gently fold them into the yolk mixture, working to retain the overall lightness of the mixture. Finally, fold in the matzo cake meal and potato starch mixture.
4. Pour the batter into an ungreased 10-inch tube pan, smoothing the top. Gently tap the pan a few times against the counter to remove any air bubbles. Bake until the cake is a deep brown and feels firm and springy when lightly pressed, about 50 minutes.

Invert the cake onto a wire cooling rack and let it cool completely.

5. When the cake is cool, run a thin knife around the edge of the pan and invert the cake onto a serving platter. (If you are using a two-piece tube pan, run a long knife under the cake before inverting it onto the platter.) Use a serrated knife to cut.

ORANGE-GLAZED SPONGE LAYER CAKE

Selma Cherkas's aunt, Essie Barist, brought this sponge cake recipe to the United States from her shtetl, *Rezhnivka, in the Ukraine. With its orange glaze and filling, it's a good deal more festive than an ordinary sponge cake and must have been considered quite the treat, as oranges were a scarce commodity there. Confectioners' sugar, an ingredient in the glaze, contains cornstarch and as such is not kosher for Passover. If you choose, you can make this cake without the glaze.*

SERVES 10

FOR THE CAKE

8 eggs, separated

½ cup sugar

Juice and grated zest of 1 lemon

Grated zest of 1 orange

½ cup matzo meal

½ cup potato starch

¼ teaspoon salt

FOR THE FILLING

2¼ tablespoons potato starch

½ cup sugar

1 cup orange juice

Grated zest of 1 orange

½ cup water

1 egg yolk, lightly beaten

1. Preheat the oven to 350 degrees. Line the bottom of a 9- or 10-inch springform pan with parchment paper and lightly grease the paper and the sides of the pan.

2. Make the cake: In the bowl of a standing electric mixer, beat together the egg yolks and sugar until they are pale and creamy. Add the lemon juice, lemon zest, and orange zest and beat to combine.

3. In a separate bowl, beat the egg whites until stiff but not dry. Gently fold the egg whites into the egg and sugar mixture, working to retain the overall lightness of the mixture.

4. In a small bowl, mix together the matzo meal, potato starch, and salt. Gently fold into the batter, working to retain the overall lightness of the mixture.

5. Spoon the batter into the prepared pan and smooth the top. Gently tap the pan a few times against the counter to remove any air bubbles. Bake until the cake is a deep brown and feels firm and springy when lightly pressed, about 50 minutes. Transfer to a wire cooling rack and let cool completely. Remove the sides and bottom of the pan.

6. Make the filling: Combine the potato starch and the sugar in a medium saucepan over low heat. Stir in the orange juice, zest, and

water, and then the beaten egg yolk. Bring to a gentle simmer, and then cook, stirring regularly, until the mixture thickens to a curd-like consistency, about 10 minutes. Remove from the heat and let cool.

7. Use a serrated knife to cut the cooled cake in half horizontally to make two layers. Spread the filling on the cut side of the bottom layer. Place the top layer over the filling.

8. Make the glaze: Combine the confectioners' sugar and orange zest in a medium bowl. Gradually add the orange juice, whisking until the glaze is smooth. Drizzle the glaze on the cake. Let the glaze harden completely before serving.

FOR THE GLAZE

1½ cups confectioners' sugar, sifted

Grated zest of ½ orange

About ¼ cup orange juice

ÖZGERINC

HUNGARIAN CHOCOLATE ALMOND TORTE

Tortes—cakes in which ground nuts substitute for flour and beaten egg whites provide the leavening—are a Jewish standard during Passover, when flour and yeast are forbidden. This recipe comes from Susan Meschel of Chicago, who recalls the torte being made by her mother Magda Patai. Born in Budapest in 1936, Susan graduated from Anna Frank Gymnasium, at the time the only Jewish high school in Eastern Europe. Like many Jews she fled Hungary after the aborted 1956 uprising, settling in the United States. Today she is a research scientist in metallurgy at the University of Chicago.

SERVES 10

FOR THE CAKE

8 eggs, separated

3/4 cup sugar

Grated zest of 1 lemon

1/2 teaspoon vanilla

1/4 cup matzo meal or flour

1/4 cup unsweetened cocoa powder

Pinch of salt

8 ounces (about 1 1/2 cups) unblanched almonds, finely ground

FOR THE FROSTING

12 ounces semisweet chocolate morsels

4 tablespoons (1/2 stick) butter, in small pieces

2 tablespoons brandy or dark rum

1. Preheat the oven to 350 degrees. Butter a 9-inch springform pan.
2. Make the cake: Place the egg yolks and sugar in the bowl of a standing electric mixer and beat until pale and creamy. Add the lemon zest, vanilla, matzo meal or flour, cocoa, and salt and beat until fully combined. Beat in the ground almonds.
3. In a separate bowl, beat the egg whites until stiff but not dry. Gently fold the egg whites into the nut mixture, working to maintain the overall lightness of the mixture.
4. Pour the batter into the prepared pan. Bake until the cake is well browned and feels firm and springy when lightly pressed, 60 to 70 minutes. Place on a wire cooling rack and let cool completely. Remove the sides of the pan.
5. Make the frosting: Place the chocolate in the top of a double boiler over boiling water. Heat until the chocolate is melted. Add the butter and brandy or rum and mix until fully combined. Let cool, then cover and refrigerate for 30 minutes. Spread the frosting over the top and sides of the cake.

INGREDIENTS: Honey

All foods are, in a sense, miraculous: gifts freely offered up by the world to preserve the life that dwells within it. In all of creation, though, there may be no food quite so miraculous as honey, for it is the only one that comes to us having been manufactured by other animals. Honey is, after all, a substance made by bees, in whose bodies the nectar of flowers is converted. Along with milk, honey is also our only food that has been produced by other animals to feed their young; thus these two are gifts imbued with special meaning, giving added resonance to the many biblical references to milk and honey.

Sweet, glistening, golden, syrupy, almost impossibly sexy: Is there anyone who can resist the allures of honey? It's no surprise that "honey" is a common term of endearment, nor that honey figures prominently in the greatest love poem ever written, the Song of Songs, where one of the lovers tells the other, "Your lips drip honey, honey and milk are under your tongue." The literary taste for honey has passed down to the writers of our own time. Nabokov, for instance, who in his chilly aristocratic way was a great romantic, made reference in his novel *Ada* to "the classical beauty of clover honey, smooth, pale, translucent, freely flowing from the spoon and soaking my love's bread and butter in liquid brass."

The Bible calls honey one of "the principal things necessary for the life of man." (The other foods cited are salt, bread, grapes, and oil.) The references to honey in the Torah, however, are not to the kind we know today, but rather to a thick syrup made from figs, grapes, and dates, a kind of syrup, called *halek*, that is still made by Jews of Iraqi descent. Some of the later books do refer to bee honey, however, as in the passage in Psalm 81 about "honey from the rock," and in Judges 14:9, where Samson eats honey from a swarm of bees found in the carcass of a lion.

Whenever it was that they first encountered it, at some point Jews had to determine whether bee-made honey was permitted under the

Jewish dietary laws. The laws of *kashrut* specifically cite insects as unclean animals, not to be eaten; the product of non-kosher animals is considered non-kosher as well. Honey, however, presents a unique situation, and in the end the sages ruled that honey was permissible, saying that although bees bring it into their bodies, it is not a product of their bodies. This seems to me to be faulty reasoning—in fact, bees bring nectar into their bodies, from which they produce honey—but in any case the ruling was a fortunate one, for without it the spiced honey cake known as Lekach (page 332) would never have been created, nor any other of the many honey-sweetened dishes found in Jewish cooking.

The use of honey in foods is actually much more prevalent among Ashkenazic than among Sephardic Jews, who have a far longer acquaintance with sugar, the sweetener that, from east to west, would eventually come to supplant it. Sugar was one of the many important crops introduced to the West by the Arabs; they established facilities for cultivating and refining sugar cane throughout their territories, including North Africa, Sicily, Greece, and Spain. In Spain, for example, sugar had become by the thirteenth century a major ingredient in the local cuisine, Jewish and non-Jewish alike. Indeed, sugar was featured to an astonishing degree, not just in desserts—such as marzipan-based confections and candied fruits—but also sprinkled atop savory dishes, often mixed with cinnamon.

In the non-Arab parts of Europe, on the other hand, sugar was available only through trade, and as a result was long a relatively rare and expensive item. Not until the nineteenth century, with the development of a technique for extracting sugar from beets, was sugar generally available even to the poorer classes. Among Jews (who were largely to be found in those classes) the use of sugar became most widespread in Poland, where many sugar beet refineries were in Jewish hands, and for the first time dishes such as challah, gefilte fish, stuffed cabbage, and borscht began to assume a sweeter tinge.

As for time-honored Jewish desserts, however, many of them were still made with honey, in Poland as elsewhere in Eastern Europe. In large part this is due to the many important symbolic connotations that honey has long had for Jews. Among the Jews of medieval Central Europe, for instance, on a child's first day of school he was shown a slate on which the Hebrew alphabet had been written and then smeared with honey; one by one, the teacher would recite the letters, to be repeated by the child, who then licked the honey from the slate—the purpose of which was, of course, to impart a lesson about the sweetness of religious learning. Often the child also received a gift of a honey cake, along with an egg with religious inscriptions written on its shell. According to an early-seventeenth-century source, Moses Henochs of Prague (cited in John Cooper's *Eat and Be Satisfied*), children there also received wafers dipped in honey from their parents before the first day of school.

Few of these traditions are still with us, but happily, many honeyed delicacies are, and especially so on Rosh Hashanah, the sweet holiday with which honey has long been associated. In Ashkenazic homes the main course of the Rosh Hashanah meal is often *tsimmes* (see page 174), a festive honey-sweetened stew made with meat, dried fruit such as prunes, and vegetables, including potatoes and carrots. (Carrots are another traditional Rosh Hashanah food, because their Yiddish name, *mern,* also means to multiply, and sliced carrots resemble golden coins, signifying abundance.) The meal will likely also conclude with a honey dessert, such as the aforementioned spiced honey cake called *lekach,* or *teyglach,* little nuggets of dough simmered in honey and nuts. And of course, honey is essential at the very beginning of the Rosh Hashanah meal, when bowls of it are served alongside challah and apples. Apples dipped in honey: There may be, culinarily speaking, no more powerful evocation of the lost Eden, and no more perfect food with which to welcome in the new year, offering fervent wishes that it might prove as sweet.

LEKACH

SPICED HONEY CAKE

Among Ashkenazic Jews, lekach *is served at all kinds of festive occasions, notably on Rosh Hashanah. The cake is usually flavored with sweet spices, coffee, perhaps a bit of whiskey or brandy, and of course lots of honey. This very delicious version comes from Bea Gitlin Abrams of West Hartford, Connecticut. Mrs. Abrams was born in 1913 in the formerly Jewish farming village of Colchester, Connecticut, where her family ran a dairy farm.*

SERVES 10 TO 12

3½ cups unbleached all-purpose flour

2½ teaspoons baking powder

1 teaspoon baking soda

½ teaspoon salt

1 teaspoon ground cinnamon

¼ teaspoon ground cloves

½ teaspoon powdered ginger

1⅓ cups honey

1⅓ cups hot strong coffee

¼ cup vegetable oil

2 tablespoons brandy (optional)

3 eggs, separated

1 cup sugar

1 cup golden raisins (optional)

1. Preheat the oven to 350 degrees. Grease a 10-inch tube pan.
2. Sift together the flour, baking powder, baking soda, salt, and spices.
3. In a medium bowl, combine the honey and the coffee and stir until the honey is dissolved. Add the oil and, if using, the brandy.
4. Place the egg yolks and sugar in the bowl of a standing electric mixer and beat until pale and creamy. Add about one third of the flour mixture and beat until fully combined, then beat in about one third of the honey mixture. Continue in this fashion until the flour mixture and honey mixtures have both been fully incorporated. Stir in the raisins (if using).
5. In another bowl, beat the egg whites until they are stiff but not dry. Gently fold the beaten egg whites into the batter, working to maintain the overall lightness of the mixture.
6. Pour the batter into the prepared tube pan. Bake until the cake is a deep brown and feels firm and springy when lightly pressed, about 60 minutes. Invert the cake onto a wire cooling rack and let it cool completely.
7. When the cake is cool, invert it onto a serving platter. Use a serrated knife to cut.

LOUKOMADES

GREEK FRIED PUFFS WITH HONEY

Loukomades *are the Greek version of* bimuelos, *the yeast-raised Hanukkah fritters made throughout the Sephardic world. Unlike* bimuelos, *which are usually topped with a sugar syrup,* loukomades *are dipped in warm honey and sprinkled with cinnamon. This recipe comes from* Come, Es Bueno!, *the Sephardic cookbook published by Congregation Etz Ahaim in New Brunswick, New Jersey. The puffs come out yeastily light, sweet, and crisp (not at all greasy, like so many fried pastries), and the warm honey imparts a golden shine. They're a guaranteed crowd pleaser.*

MAKES ABOUT 25

FOR THE DOUGH

- 1 package (about 2½ teaspoons) active dry yeast
- 1½ cups warm water
- ½ teaspoon sugar
- 3 cups unbleached all-purpose flour
- ½ teaspoon salt
- 1 egg, lightly beaten
- 1 tablespoon vegetable oil
- Vegetable oil for deep frying

- 2 cups (about 24 ounces) honey
- ¼ cup water
- Ground cinnamon for sprinkling

1. Make the dough: Place the yeast in ¼ cup of the warm water. Add the sugar and let stand until the mixture begins to bubble, about 5 minutes.
2. Sift the flour and salt into a large bowl. Make a well in the center. Pour the egg, oil, the remaining warm water, and the yeast mixture into the well and and stir until the mixture is smooth. Cover with a towel and let rise until doubled in volume, about 1½ hours.
3. In a Dutch oven or other large, heavy pot, heat at least 2 inches of oil to 375 degrees on a deep-fat thermometer. Dip a tablespoon into the oil, and use the oiled tablespoon to drop tablespoons of the dough into the oil. Fry in batches, turning as necessary, until golden brown on all sides, about 3 minutes total. Remove with a slotted spoon and drain on paper towels.
4. Combine the honey and water in a medium saucepan and heat over medium heat, stirring occasionally, until boiling. Dip the puffs into the warm honey and transfer to a large serving platter. Sprinkle with the cinnamon. Serve warm.

PIZZARELLE CON GIULEBBE

ITALIAN MATZO FRITTERS WITH HONEY SYRUP

As with many other dishes, the Roman version of matzo fritters is made distinctive by the addition of raisins and pine nuts. The lovely cinnamon-scented honey syrup known as giulebbe *is a topping for a variety of Italian Jewish desserts.*

MAKES ABOUT 25

FOR THE SYRUP

1 cup honey

½ cup water

2 teaspoons ground cinnamon

FOR THE FRITTERS

5 matzos, broken into small pieces

¼ cup sugar

¼ teaspoon vanilla

Pinch of salt

¼ cup raisins

¼ cup pine nuts

3 egg yolks, lightly beaten

2 egg whites

Vegetable oil for deep frying

1. Make the syrup: Combine the honey, water, and cinnamon in a small saucepan over medium heat. Cover and bring to a boil, then uncover, lower the heat, and simmer for 5 minutes, stirring regularly. Remove from heat and let cool. Pour into a serving bowl.
2. Make the batter: Place the matzo pieces in a bowl of cold water and soak until soft but not falling apart, 1 to 2 minutes. Drain in a colander and squeeze out any excess water. In a large bowl, mix together the matzo pieces, sugar, vanilla, salt, raisins, pine nuts, and egg yolks.
3. In a separate bowl, beat the egg whites until stiff but not dry. Gently fold the beaten egg whites into the matzo mixture.
4. Make the *pizzarelle:* In a Dutch oven or other large, heavy pot, heat at least 2 inches of oil to 375 degrees on a deep-fat thermometer. In small batches, drop heaping tablespoons of the matzo mixture into the oil. Fry in batches, turning as necessary, until they are a deep brown on all sides, about 5 minutes total. Remove with a slotted spoon and drain on paper towels. Serve warm or at room temperature, accompanied by the honey syrup.

APFEL FRITLACH

APPLE FRITTERS

This sophisticated version of the traditional Ashkenazic apple fritter comes from the cookbook Tabernacle Tastings, *published by the Hebrew Tabernacle Congregation in the Washington Heights section of New York City.*

MAKES ABOUT 16

FOR THE APPLES

4 medium apples, such as Fuji or Gala

¼ cup dry white wine

½ cup sugar

¼ teaspoon ground cinnamon

FOR THE BATTER

1 cup unbleached all-purpose flour

¼ teaspoon salt

½ cup milk

2 eggs, lightly beaten

4 tablespoons (½ stick) butter for frying, plus more as needed

Confectioners' sugar for dusting

1. Prepare the apples: Peel and core the apples, and slice them into rings about ½ inch thick. Place them in a medium bowl. In a small bowl, mix together the wine, sugar, and cinnamon and pour the mixture over the apples. Let stand at room temperature, turning the apples occasionally, for 1 hour.
2. Make the batter: Sift the flour and salt into a medium bowl. Add the milk and eggs and stir until the mixture is smooth. Let the batter stand at room temperature for 1 hour.
3. Preheat the oven to 200 degrees. Heat the butter in a large skillet over medium heat. In batches, dip the apple rings in the batter, shaking off any excess. Fry until golden brown on both sides, turning as necessary, about 10 minutes total. Add a bit more butter to the pan if necessary. Drain on paper towels. Place the fritters on a baking sheet and put the sheet in the oven until all of the apple rings have been fried. Just before serving, dust with confectioners' sugar. Serve warm.

GALAKTOBOUREKO

CUSTARD-FILLED FILO PASTRY WITH SYRUP

This filo dessert is light, custardy, and not overly sweet. (It's especially wonderful cold for breakfast.) In Ioannina, a piece of galaktoboureko *was often used to break the Yom Kippur fast, along with a glass of water mixed with ouzo, the anise-flavored liqueur.*

SERVES 15

FOR THE SYRUP

1 cup sugar

¾ cup water

2 cinnamon sticks

1 tablespoon lemon juice

FOR THE CUSTARD

¼ cup fine semolina or farina

4 cups milk

1½ teaspoons vanilla

4 tablespoons (½ stick) butter, melted

5 egg yolks

½ cup sugar

¼ teaspoon salt

16 frozen filo sheets, thawed

8 tablespoons (1 stick) butter, melted and cooled

1. Make the syrup: Combine the sugar, water, and cinnamon sticks in a medium saucepan. Cook over a low heat, stirring, until the sugar dissolves, about 3 minutes. Raise the heat to medium and boil until the syrup is thick enough to coat a spoon, another 5 to 10 minutes. Remove from heat. Remove the cinnamon sticks and stir in the lemon juice. Let cool.

2. Make the custard: Combine the semolina or farina, milk, vanilla, and butter in a large saucepan over medium heat. Bring to a boil, then lower the heat and simmer, stirring occasionally, until thick, about 15 minutes. Remove from the heat, let cool to room temperature, then refrigerate until cold.

3. Place the egg yolks, sugar, and salt in the bowl of a standing electric mixer and beat until thick. Add the semolina mixture and mix until fully combined.

4. Preheat the oven to 350 degrees. Butter a 13- by 9-inch baking dish.

5. Make the *galaktoboureko:* Set out the filo sheets in a stack. (Keep the filo covered with a damp towel when not in use, to keep it from drying out.) Place 2 sheets of filo on the bottom of the dish, cutting away the excess filo and brushing each with melted butter. Place 3 sheets of filo halfway in the dish, the other half draped outside it, brushing each with melted butter. (The sheets should all be facing in the same direction.) Place 3 more sheets halfway in the dish,

facing a second direction, brushing each of them with butter. Continue the process with 6 more filo sheets, so that each side of the dish has 3 half-sheets of filo draped outside it.

6. Pour the custard into the dish and smooth the top. Cover the filling with the draped half-sheets of filo, enclosing it like a packet. Brush the top with butter. Add 2 more filo sheets on top, cutting away the excess and brushing them with melted butter.

7. Bake until golden brown, 35 to 40 minutes. While the *galaktoboureko* is still hot, spoon the cooled syrup onto it. Let cool, then slice into squares or diamonds.

CASSOLA

ITALIAN BAKED RICOTTA PUDDING

This is a very old Roman dish. At one time, cassola *was saved for the spring, because that was when the ricotta was at its best. The sheep's milk, from which ricotta is made, was most available then, as this was the season when the lambs were being born, and the sheep were feeding on new grass and herbs, which made their milk taste the sweetest. Often the pudding is cooked on the stovetop and then browned under a broiler, but in this version, from Bruna Tedeschi of Rome, it is baked in the oven. It looks gorgeous when it is removed and makes a delightful finale to a festive dinner.*

SERVES 8 TO 10

- 2 pounds fresh ricotta cheese
- ¾ cup sugar
- 8 eggs
- 1 cup raisins
- ½ teaspoon vanilla
- ½ teaspoon ground cinnamon
- ¼ teaspoon salt
- Grated zest from 1 orange
- Grated zest from 1 lemon

1. Line a colander with a single layer of cheesecloth and spoon the ricotta into it. Place the colander over a large bowl and let the ricotta drain in the refrigerator for at least 2 hours.
2. Preheat the oven to 375 degrees. Lightly butter a 10-inch round deep-dish pie pan or casserole.
3. Place the drained ricotta in the bowl of a standing electric mixer. Add the sugar and beat at low speed to combine. Beat in the eggs, one by one, letting each incorporate before adding the next. Add the remaining ingredients and beat until fully combined.
4. Pour the ricotta mixture into the prepared pan and smooth the top. Bake until the edges are brown and the center has nearly set, 55 to 60 minutes. Transfer to a wire cooling rack. Serve warm or at room temperature.

PIZZA EBRAICA

ITALIAN FRUIT- AND NUT-FILLED PASTRIES

Along with the luscious ricotta torte with sour cherries, pizza ebraica *is one of the specialties of the Pasticceria Il Boccione, the kosher bakery located in the heart of Rome's Jewish Ghetto. The shortbread-like pastries are chock-filled with raisins, almonds, pine nuts, and candied fruit. At the Pasticceria Il Boccione, they're baked to a very deep brown, almost burnt, but most other versions don't cook them quite as long. They can be formed into separate little loaves before baking, or they can be sliced into rectangles after or—as in this recipe—midway through the baking. Candied citron can be purchased at specialty foods shops.*

MAKES 12

- 1 cup (2 sticks) butter
- 1 cup sugar
- 3½ cups unbleached all-purpose flour, sifted
- ½ cup almonds, coarsely chopped
- ½ cup pine nuts
- ½ cup raisins
- ⅓ cup chopped candied citron
- 1 teaspoon vanilla
- ¼ teaspoon salt
- About 7 tablespoons Marsala wine

1. Preheat the oven to 325 degrees. In the bowl of a standing electric mixer, combine the butter with the sugar and beat at low speed until pale and creamy. Gradually add the flour and beat until the dough resembles coarse meal. Add the almonds, pine nuts, raisins, candied citron, vanilla, and salt and beat until fully incorporated. Slowly beat in the wine to form a soft dough that holds together well.

2. Turn the dough out onto an ungreased baking sheet and form into a 12- by 8-inch rectangle. Bake for 25 minutes, then remove from the oven and, using a sharp knife or pizza cutter, cut into 2- by 4-inch rectangles, pushing the pastries slightly apart from each other. Return to the oven and cook until well browned, about another 15 minutes. Transfer to a wire rack and let cool.

RUGELACH

JAM- AND NUT-FILLED PASTRY HORNS

The word rugelach *is derived from the Slavic word* rog, *meaning horn; thus, rugelach are "little horns." In Eastern Europe the rugelach dough was made with butter or sour cream, but as with cheesecake, New World tastes preferred the unabashed luxury of cream cheese, which produces a dough that is exceedingly rich, flaky, and tender. This recipe, like the following one, is from rugelach maven Herb Schon of Santa Fe, New Mexico.*

MAKES 48

FOR THE DOUGH

1 egg yolk

1 tablespoon sour cream

4 ounces cream cheese

8 tablespoons (1 stick) butter, softened

1½ teaspoons vanilla

1¾ cups unbleached all-purpose flour

FOR THE FILLING

1 cup sugar

1½ cups finely chopped walnuts

1 tablespoon ground cinnamon

10 ounces apricot preserves

1. Make the dough: Place all of the dough ingredients except the flour in the bowl of a standing electric mixer and beat at medium speed until fully combined. Slowly add the flour, beating until the dough is smooth and cleans the sides of the bowl. Divide into 3 equal pieces, shape into disks, wrap in plastic, and refrigerate until firm, at least 1 hour.

2. Make the filling: In a medium bowl, combine the sugar, walnuts, and cinnamon.

3. Preheat the oven to 350 degrees. Grease 2 large baking sheets or line them with parchment paper.

4. Make the rugelach: On a lightly floured surface, roll one of the pastry disks into a 12-inch round; if necessary, cut around the edges of the pastry to create an even circle. (Keep the other 2 pastry disks in the refrigerator until ready to use.) Place one third of the preserves on the pastry round and spread evenly to within ½ inch of the edge. Sprinkle one third of the cinnamon-sugar mixture on the round and spread it evenly over the preserves.

5. Using a pizza cutter or sharp knife, cut the round into 16 triangles, slicing it like a pie. Starting at the outer edge, gently roll each triangle toward the center. Place the rugelach on one of the prepared

sheets. Make sure the point of the triangle faces down, so it will not unravel during baking. Repeat with the remaining 2 pastry disks and filling.

6. Bake until golden brown, 20 to 25 minutes. (Some preserves will ooze out during baking.) Let cool briefly, then transfer to wire cooling racks to cool completely. Store in an airtight container at room temperature or in the freezer.

CHOCOLATE-RASPBERRY RUGELACH

In 1921 Freda Orbach emigrated to the United States from Poland with her two daughters, settling in Newark. One of her favorite things to make was cinnamon-raisin rugelach; Freda's recipe was eventually written down by her daughter, and years later her grandson Herb Schon discovered it among his late mother's papers. When a bike accident kept him from working, he threw himself into baking rugelach, with such success that he eventually started his own business, Grandma's Recipe Rugelach—making not just his grandmother's traditional cinnamon-raisin rugelach, but a dozen other varieties of his own concoction, including peanut butter–chocolate, rum raisin, and this one, chocolate-raspberry.

MAKES 48

FOR THE DOUGH

1 egg yolk

1 tablespoon sour cream

4 ounces cream cheese

8 tablespoons (1 stick) butter, softened

1½ teaspoons vanilla

1¾ cups unbleached all-purpose flour

1 tablespoon unsweetened cocoa

FOR THE FILLING

¾ cup sugar

1 cup finely chopped walnuts

1 cup finely chopped semisweet chocolate bits

1 tablespoon ground cinnamon

1. Make the dough: Place all of the dough ingredients, except for the flour and cocoa, in the bowl of a standing electric mixer and beat at low speed until fully combined. Slowly add the flour, beating until the dough is smooth and cleans the sides of the bowl. Add the cocoa and pulse the machine several times. The cocoa should not be fully incorporated, but rather give the dough a marbleized look. Divide the dough into 3 equal pieces, shape into disks, wrap in plastic, and refrigerate until firm, at least 1 hour.

2. Make the filling: In a medium bowl, combine all of the filling ingredients except the preserves and mix well.

3. Preheat the oven to 350 degrees. Grease 2 large baking sheets or line them with parchment paper.

4. Make the rugelach: On a lightly floured surface, roll one of the pastry disks into a 12-inch round; if necessary, cut around the edges of the pastry to create an even circle. (Keep the other 2 pastry disks in the refrigerator until ready to use.) Place one third of the preserves on the pastry round and spread evenly to within ½ inch of the edge. Sprinkle 1 cup of the filling mixture on the round and spread it evenly over the preserves.

5. Using a pizza cutter or sharp knife, cut the round into 16 triangles, slicing it like a pie. Starting at the outer edge, gently roll each triangle toward the center. Place the rugelach on one of the prepared sheets. Make sure the point of the triangle faces down, so it will not unravel during baking. Repeat with the remaining 2 pastry disks and filling.

6. When all the rugelach have been rolled, lightly dust the tops with the cocoa-sugar mixture. Bake until golden brown, 20 to 25 minutes. (Some preserves will ooze out during baking.) Let cool briefly, then transfer to wire cooling racks to cool completely. Store in an airtight container at room temperature or in the freezer.

2 tablespoons unsweetened cocoa

10 ounces raspberry preserves

FOR THE TOPPING

1½ teaspoons unsweetened cocoa mixed with 2 tablespoons sugar

INGREDIENTS: Poppy Seeds

There is a connection between bagels and heroin, and it has nothing to do with the potentially addictive quality of each. It has to do instead with those unassuming little blue-gray specks—poppy seeds—that give the bagel's crust a nice extra crunch and get caught in your teeth so that your friends and co-workers know what you had for breakfast that day. If, on the other hand, you choose to plant those seeds rather than eat them, you will end up with poppy flowers, specifically the Breadseed Poppy, which happens to be a variety of the species *Papaver somniferum*, the unripe seed capsules of which are, when processed, the source of heroin (not to mention opium and morphine).

Though it is possible to grow drug-producing poppy flowers from grocery-bought poppy seeds, the seeds themselves are not narcotic. This can be attested to by anyone who, like me, has ever eaten too many poppy seed *hamantashen*, but as it happens, the point has been proven empirically by the Oregon State Police Crime Laboratory: In 1992 researchers from the laboratory tested the driving ability of several subjects who had consumed 25 grams of poppy seeds—baked into Bundt cakes, the lab's report charmingly notes—and found that driving ability was not impaired. However, those subjects did test positive for opium on a series of drug tests, and other scientific reports have confirmed that one will indeed "fail" a drug test after eating as little as two poppy seed bagels. *Seinfeld* cognoscenti will recall that this is precisely what happened to Elaine, a poppy seed bagel fan, on a drug test mandated by her employer Peterman.

Still, unless you happen to be in a situation like Elaine's, there is no reason why you should give up consumption of poppy seeds, on your bagel or anywhere else. In addition to their pleasing crunchiness, poppy seeds have a mildly nutty, sweet taste, and they have long been a welcome addition to a number of Ashkenazic Jewish dishes. As a topping, they're commonly sprinkled not just on bagels but also on challah, the yeasty egg bread that's a fixture on Sabbath tables. Poppy seeds are also featured in a number of sweet baked goods, and never more so than around Purim time.

The most joyous of Jewish holidays, Purim commemorates the bravery of Queen Esther, who interceded with her husband, the Persian ruler King Ahasuerus, thus thwarting the plans of the king's top advisor, Haman, to annihilate all the Jews of the kingdom. It is said that Esther fasted for three days, subsisting only on seeds and pulses, as she prayed to God to revoke the king's original misguided decree, and so today we're lucky enough to find many poppy seed delicacies served at Purim parties. Among the most popular are the buttery poppy seed cookies called *Mohn Kichel* (page 346), from the German and Yiddish word for poppy, *mohn*. (In the United States, these cookies are often colloquially known as "moon" cookies.) Certainly the most well-known of all Purim sweets, though, are the triangle-shaped cookies called *hamantashen* (see pages 347–348). These days you can find *hamantashen* filled with everything from prune or apricot jam to chocolate or cream cheese; the traditional filling, however, dating back to medieval times, was poppy seeds. *Tasche* is German for pocket or purse, which gives us the original name, *mohntaschen*, or pockets filled with poppy seeds. As these sweets came to be associated with Purim, *mohntaschen* evolved into *hamantashen*, which made special sense as a reference to the coat pockets in which Haman was supposed to have carried the lots, or *purim*, he cast to determine which day the Jews of his kingdom would die. (The idea that *hamantashen* are meant to resemble Haman's "three-cornered hat" is another popular misconception.)

Though *hamantashen* dough is sometimes made with yeast, which adds a certain delicacy to the preparation, none of these baked goods is especially difficult to make, and so success or failure depends almost entirely on the quality of your ingredients. As is true with other seeds and nuts, the flavor of poppy seeds can be intensified by toasting. Simply put the seeds in a dry skillet over a medium-low flame, and heat them until they start to crackle and you smell a nutty aroma; this should take about a minute. Stir the seeds regularly as you toast them, and be careful not to let them burn. Then use them just as the recipe directs. The results will undoubtedly prove delicious and make your loved ones very happy, which as everyone knows is the most potent high of all.

MOHN KICHEL

POPPY SEED COOKIES

This recipe was handed down to Anita Graber of North Bellmore, Long Island, by her mother, Fanny Wine. Mrs. Wine, who was born in 1906 in Providence but lived most of her life in Boston, learned how to make poppy seed cookies from her own mother, Eva Proctor, who had emigrated from the Ukraine in the late nineteenth century. Anita Graber remembers her grandmother serving these tender, not-too-sweet cookies on holidays and other special occasions, always accompanied by a glass of tea.

MAKES ABOUT 35

2½ cups unbleached all-purpose flour
1 teaspoon baking powder
¼ teaspoon baking soda
¼ teaspoon salt
8 tablespoons (1 stick) butter
½ cup sugar
1 egg
¼ cup sour cream
½ teaspoon vanilla extract
juice of ½ orange
¼ cup toasted poppy seeds

1. Preheat the oven to 375 degrees. Grease two baking sheets or line them with parchment paper.
2. Sift together the dry ingredients.
3. In the bowl of a standing mixer, beat the butter and sugar until the mixture is pale and creamy. Add the egg, sour cream, vanilla, and orange juice and beat until well combined. Slowly add the dry ingredients and beat until the dough is soft and smooth. Add the poppy seeds and mix to combine.
4. On a lightly floured surface, roll the dough out to about ¼-inch thickness. Using cookie cutters or the rim of a glass, cut the dough into 2-inch rounds and place them at least 1 inch apart on the prepared baking sheets.
5. Bake until golden brown, 15 to 20 minutes. Transfer the cookies to wire racks and let cool completely. Store in an airtight container at room temperature or in the freezer.

POPPY-PRUNE-APRICOT HAMANTASHEN

FILLED TRIANGLE COOKIES

Hamantashen *traditionally come with either a poppy, prune, or apricot filling. In this interesting variation from Selma Cherkas of Worcester, Massachusetts, you get all three at once. Poppy seeds can be purchased in bulk at many specialty stores, or by mail from Penzeys Spices at 800-741-7787 or www.penzeys.com.*

MAKES ABOUT 28

FOR THE DOUGH

2½ cups unbleached all-purpose flour

2 teaspoons baking powder

¼ teaspoon salt

⅓ cup vegetable oil

2 eggs, beaten

¼ cup honey

1 tablespoon lemon juice

1 teaspoon vanilla

FOR THE FILLING

½ cup water

½ cup poppy seeds

2 tablespoons honey

¼ cup finely chopped prunes

¼ cup finely chopped dried apricots

Grated zest of ½ lemon

2 teaspoons sweet red wine

1. Make the dough: Sift together the flour, baking powder, and salt. Place the dry ingredients in the bowl of a standing electric mixer. Add the oil and eggs and beat until the dough resembles coarse meal. Add the honey, lemon juice, and vanilla, and beat to form a soft, smooth dough that pulls away from the side of the bowl. Turn the dough out onto a lightly floured surface and knead for 3 minutes. Form the dough into 2 disks. Cover in plastic wrap and refrigerate for 1 hour.

2. Make the filling: Combine the water, poppy seeds, and honey in a medium saucepan over medium-low heat. Bring to a simmer and cook, stirring occasionally, until the mixture becomes soft and thick, about 10 minutes. Add the prunes, apricots, lemon zest, and red wine and cook for 5 minutes, stirring regularly. Set aside and let cool.

3. Preheat the oven to 350 degrees. Lightly grease 2 baking sheets or line them with parchment paper.

4. Make the *hamantashen*: On a lightly floured surface, roll out each dough disk to a thickness of about ⅛ inch. Using a cookie cutter or the rim of a glass, cut the dough into 3-inch rounds. Press each round out a little more thinly with your fingers before filling.

(continued)

5. Set out a bowl of cold water. Place 1 teaspoon of the filling in the center of a dough rounds. Moisten the rim of the round and then fold one end of the dough over the filling. Fold over a second side, pressing it together with the first fold to form one side of a triangle. Fold over a third side, pressing together the remaining edges to form a triangle with a small opening on top. Place it on one of the prepared baking sheets. Repeat with the remaining dough rounds and filling, leaving at least 1 inch between the pastries on the baking sheets.

7. Bake until golden, 12 to 15 minutes. Let cool slightly, then transfer to wire cooling racks to cool completely. Store in an airtight container at room temperature.

MANDLBROT

ALMOND SLICES

Mandlbrot is baked twice, first as a loaf and then in separate slices, and in this it resembles Italian biscotti. Indeed, mandlbrot is sometimes referred to as "Jewish biscotti." For me, it is one of those foods that acts, in Proust's great phrase, as an "inseparable paramour" of memory. With just a bite, I can close my eyes and find myself back on the Old World streets off Ocean Parkway, with their brown brick apartment houses and chained-in playgrounds and crammed tiny candy stores where we bought marbles and pink Spaldeens; back inside my grandparents' musty apartment, with its Chagall prints hanging over the plastic-covered furniture; back into the small kitchen, cluttered with newspapers and lists made out in my grandmother's spidery handwriting with pens hanging from strings, and where on the countertop often lay a plastic bag filled with mandlbrot, *which we always called "mandlbread."*

MAKES ABOUT 48

- 2 eggs
- 1 cup sugar
- 1 cup vegetable oil
- 1 teaspoon vanilla
- 1 cup coarsely chopped almonds
- 4 cups unbleached all-purpose flour
- 1 teaspoon baking powder
- 1/4 teaspoon salt

1. Preheat the oven to 325 degrees.
2. In the bowl of a standing electric mixer, beat the eggs and sugar until the mixture is pale and creamy. Add the oil, vanilla, and almonds and beat until fully combined.
3. Sift together the dry ingredients. Beat them into the wet mixture, 1 cup at a time, until the dough is soft, slightly oily, and able to hold its shape.
4. On a lightly floured surface, cut the dough into 4 equal pieces. Roll each piece into a ball, and then form the ball into a firm loaf about 6 by 3 inches and ½ inch high. Place the loaves at least 1 inch apart on a large ungreased baking sheet and bake until golden, 30 to 35 minutes. (They will still be slightly wet in the center.)
5. Using a serrated knife, cut the warm loaves crosswise into slices ½ inch thick. Turn the slices cut side up on the baking sheet and bake until lightly brown, about 15 minutes. Transfer to wire cooling racks and let cool completely. Store in an airtight container.

COCONUT MACAROONS

The word macaroon *comes from the medieval Venetian* macarone, *meaning fine paste, a reference to the almond paste that is its basic ingredient. The earliest account traces macaroons back to an eighth-century French monastery, where they were purportedly made in the shape of monks' navels (whether monks' navels are differently shaped than anyone else's is left out of the historical record). These days, most of us associate macaroons with those round tins that appear on supermarket shelves around Passover time. Those versions are certainly acceptable, but macaroons are far better when baked at home, by virtue of being fresh, warm (if, like me, you are impatient to sample the goods), and containing no artificial flavors or preservatives. Macaroons also happen to be remarkably easy to make. And best of all, if made at home, macaroons can be enjoyed not just at Passover season, but all year round.*

MAKES ABOUT 25

1½ cups (about 8 ounces) blanched almonds

1 cup sugar

1 cup (about 3½ ounces) sweetened shredded coconut

3 egg whites

1. Preheat the oven to 350 degrees. Grease 2 baking sheets or line them with parchment paper.
2. Grind the almonds with the sugar in the bowl of a food processor. Transfer the mixture to a large bowl. Add the coconut and mix well.
3. Beat the egg whites until stiff but not dry. Gently fold them into the almond mixture.
4. Drop the batter by heaping tablespoonfuls in balls onto the prepared baking sheets, leaving at least 1 inch between. Bake until lightly browned, 17 to 20 minutes. Let cool on the baking sheets for a few minutes, then transfer to wire racks to cool completely. Store in an airtight container at room temperature.

PISTACHIO MACAROONS

These are a delicious and couldn't-be-easier alternative to the more common coconut and almond varieties. They come out a beautiful brownish-green. Rosewater, which perfectly complements pistachios, can be purchased in many Middle Eastern and specialty shops.

MAKES ABOUT 30

- 3 cups (about 1 pound) shelled pistachios
- 1 cup sugar
- 3 egg whites
- 1½ teaspoons rosewater

1. Preheat the oven to 350 degrees. Grease 2 baking sheets or line them with parchment paper.
2. Grind the pistachios with the sugar in the bowl of a food processor, leaving some chunks for texture; transfer the mixture to a large bowl.
3. Beat the egg whites until stiff but not dry. Gently fold them, with the rosewater, into the pistachio mixture.
4. Drop the batter by heaping tablespoonfuls in balls onto the prepared baking sheets, leaving at least 1 inch between. Bake until lightly browned, 17 to 20 minutes. Let cool on the baking sheets for a few minutes, then transfer to wire racks to cool completely. Store in an airtight container at room temperature.

GOZINAKHI

GEORGIAN HONEY-NUT CLUSTERS

In Georgia, formerly a part of the Soviet Union and now an independent nation, the delicious (and very easy to make) honey and nut candy known as gozinakhi *is a mainstay of Rosh Hashanah celebrations, served with good thick coffee. Says Lea Chikashvili, who emigrated from Georgia to New York City in 1980, "Just as there's no Passover without matzo, there's no Rosh Hashanah without* gozinakhi.*" The traditional Georgian recipe calls for walnuts, but Lea prefers to use almonds, which are also native to Georgia.*

MAKES 15

1½ cups (about 8 ounces) blanched almonds
½ cup honey
1 teaspoon sugar
Nonstick cooking spray

1. Preheat the oven to 350 degrees.
2. Place the almonds on an ungreased baking sheet and toast, stirring every couple of minutes, until lightly colored, about 10 minutes. Remove from the oven and let cool.
3. In a medium saucepan, bring the honey to a boil, lower the heat, and simmer for 3 minutes, stirring regularly. Add the sugar and stir until dissolved. Add the almonds and simmer, stirring regularly, for another 5 minutes.
4. Coat a large wooden board or marble slab with nonstick cooking spray. Pour the honey-almond mixture onto the board and smooth it out with a wooden spoon into a rectangle about 10 by 6 inches. Let cool, then cut into 2-inch squares.
5. With moistened hands, form each square into a rounded cluster. Place the clusters on a layer of wax paper inside an airtight container. Keep refrigerated until ready to serve.

Spices and Condiments

It wouldn't have been altogether surprising had Jews traditionally avoided the use of garlic in cooking, if only for the bitter memories it evoked. Garlic, after all, was what the pharoahs fed the laborers who built the pyramids, as a way of maintaining their stamina under the most arduous working conditions. But the Jews of Egypt had long enjoyed garlic as a flavoring for stews and as a spread on bread, and the unpleasant business with the pyramids did not preclude these happy associations. In Numbers 11:5, the departing Israelites included it among the foods they grieved to leave behind: "We remember the fish, which we did eat in Egypt freely; the cucumbers, and the melons, and the leeks, and the onions, and the garlic."

Eventually garlic would come to be found in Jewish dishes in every corner of the Diaspora, from the chili pepper and garlic sauces of North Africa and Yemen to Eastern Europe's garlic dill pickles. Indeed, throughout much of Eastern Europe, garlic was the only savory spice used with any regularity—cinnamon was common in sweet foods—flavoring dishes ranging from pickles to pot roast and chicken soup.

Though as a rule Sephardic cooking uses more spices than does Ashkenazic, this is about the only generalization that can be made on the subject. There is a wide variance in the use of spices across the Sephardic world; in fact, it is often possible to differentiate specific cuisines not just by the local ingredients but by the favored spicings as well. In Morocco, for instance, the greatness of the cuisine comes in large part from a delicate balancing of spices including, among others, turmeric, ginger, cumin, paprika, coriander, and cinnamon. In nearby Tunisia there is less complex spicing, more emphasis on cumin and caraway, and the addition of heat with a red chili paste called *harissa.* Among the Jews of Yemen, the fiery-hot paste is called *Z'houg* (page 361), made from green chilies. The truly distinctive flavor of Yemenite cuisine, however, comes from the all-purpose spice mixture called *Hawaij* (page 360), which generally includes turmeric, black pepper, cumin, and cardamom. The garam masala spice mixture used by the Bene Israel Jews of Bombay comprises cardamom, cinnamon, and cloves, and sometimes other spices as well. In the Middle East, Syrians like to flavor meat dishes with cinnamon and allspice, while cardamom is more common in Iraq, and Iranian cooking is notable in large part for what it does *not* include—garlic.

INGREDIENTS: Spices

The first spice, according to the Bible, was found in the Garden of Eden. In Genesis 2:12, we are told of the land known as Havilah, "and the gold of that land is pure: bdellium and onyx stone are there." Bdellium (it is, in case you're wondering, the only word in the English language that begins with the letters *bd*) is an aromatic gum resin obtained by incising the bark of certain species of shrub-like trees. In his splendid *The Book of Spices*, Frederic Rosengarten informs us that the bdellium resin hardens into transparent little wax-like pellets ("resembling fragrant pearls," he notes), which women in ancient Egypt carried as perfume.

Though individual cases can get a bit tricky, spices are defined generally as the dried parts of aromatic plants—root, bark, seed, and so forth; the leaves and stalks are, instead, herbs. Spices are mentioned many times in the Bible, from the Genesis story of Joseph (his brothers sold him for 20 pieces of silver to spice traders carrying balm and myrrh to Gilead) to the numerous references in the Song of Songs ("Who is that rising from the desert," asks the lover, "more fragrant with myrrh and frankincense / than all the spices of the merchant!"). Dozens of varieties of spices are discussed in the Talmud, including many we would recognize today—ginger, cumin, mustard seed, black pepper—as well as more curious ones, such as the roots costus and dodder.

In the ancient world spices were used as a flavor enhancer, for medicinal purposes, and also for religious ritual. (To take an example from the Jewish tradition, in Exodus 30:22–24, God instructs Moses on Sinai on the preparation of the anointing oil for the tabernacle, going so far as to give precise proportions for the spices to be mixed in: 500 shekels of myrrh, 250 of cinnamon, 250 of calamus, 500 of cassia.) Most of the spices were imported from the East, and by the time of the Diaspora Jews were deeply involved in the flourishing spice trade. In the early centuries of the Common Era, the trade was carried on mainly by Jews and Syrians, but by the eighth century Syria had been conquered by the Arabs and the spice trade was subsequently controlled by Jewish merchants. Later, in the ninth and tenth centuries, these merchants came to play a key (and today, not widely appreciated) role in the very preservation of international commerce in Europe.

At the time—this is after the fall of Rome, which had earlier united all of Europe within a single empire—Europe was bitterly divided into two camps, Christian and Muslim. Virtually all trade channels between them had been shut down; by the year 800 it was no longer possible for a ship to sail from a Christian port to a Muslim one. The only traders tolerated by both Christians and Muslims, and who thus enjoyed freedom of movement, were the Jewish traveling merchants known as the Radanites.

That today anyone has even heard of the Radanites (the name may have come from the Persian *rah dan*, meaning "knows the way") is due to a single written source, a geography book written by one Ibn Khordadbeh, who served in the ninth century as the postmaster for the caliph of Baghdad. In *The Book of the Roads and the Kingdoms*, Ibn Khordadbeh tells of "Jewish Merchants called Radanites," fluent in several languages, who "journey from west to east, from east to west, partly on land, partly by sea." From the west, he reports, the Radanites brought cloth, furs, and swords, as well as eunuchs and female slaves for the harems of Asia; returning from the east, they carried back exotic spices.

The passage about the Radanites runs a scant two paragraphs, not much information to go on. Happily enough, though, in 1948 Rabbi Louis Rabinowitz of Johannesburg, South Africa, produced a fascinating little book called *Jewish Merchant Adventurers: A Study of the Radanites* that provides a full analysis of Ibn Khordadbeh's brief account and places it in historical context. According to Rabbi Rabinowitz, the Radanites plied four main trade routes stretching from Europe into North Africa and Asia. Along one of the routes, for instance, a Radanite trader would set out from France southward into Spain, then sail across the Mediterranean into Morocco, whence he traversed by camel caravan the entirety of North Africa into the Middle East, passed through the major cities of Baghdad and Basra, and made his way across India before finally arriving at the route's terminus in central China. That the Radanites could work such incredibly long trade routes was only possible because of a series of Jewish communities all along the way, from Spain at one end through, at the other, the Cochin and Bene Israel Jews of India and various settlements in China, including Hong Chou, Kaifeng, and Canton. These communities allowed the Radanites unrivaled access to the goods of the East, for they and the local Jewish merchants shared not merely a common religion, but also at least one language (Hebrew), a code of law, references for letters of introduction, and, perhaps most importantly, a well-developed system of commercial credit. As a result, a Jewish trader from France could, with a minimum of confusion, conduct business with a Jewish purveyor of goods in, say, Cairo or Baghdad.

In his account, Ibn Khordadbeh specifically mentioned only four spices traded by the Radanites—"musk, aloes, camphor, cinnamon"—subsuming everything else under the general phrase "other products of the East." These products may have included pearls and precious stones, but certainly numerous other spices as well, among them black pepper, cloves, nutmeg, ginger, and saffron. Rabbi Rabinowitz noted that spices constituted the most important commodity brought back by the Radanites from the East, for they readily fulfilled the three criteria necessitated by such an arduous journey: smallness of bulk, a ready market, and huge profits.

By the end of the tenth century, the Radanite monopoly was already being challenged by the ascendant merchants of Venice. By the end of the eleventh century, with the military successes of the Crusades, the blocked trade routes between East and West had been opened up again and the Radanites, now superfluous, fell into an obscurity that has lasted to the present day. (Still, how important were they during their own times? Simply consider this: For more than one hundred years, virtually every bit of spice that entered Christian Europe did so as a result of Radanite trade.) At the beginning of the sixteenth century, another group of Jewish traders rose to prominence when Portugal opened a direct sea route with East India. Sephardic spice merchants plied their trade in Lisbon and, to the north, in Antwerp—in northern Europe, Jews controlled a large part of the market for pepper and other spices and later, with the ascension of the Dutch armada, in Amsterdam as well. According to contemporaneous accounts, of the sixteen major spice importers in Amsterdam in 1612, eleven were Sephardic Jews.

Undoubtedly, the overwhelming percentage of the buyers of these spices were not Jewish; however, the Jews of the Middle East and North

Africa had been adding spices to their food since ancient times, and over time this continued to be true throughout much of the modern Diaspora, though by no means all of it. The use of spices was far more prevalent among the Sephardim than the Ashkenazim, for whom most spices were prohibitively rare and expensive. Garlic was about the only one used to any extent in the Eastern European Jewish kitchen, although farther south, in Hungary and Romania, paprika and certain other spices could be found as well. Compare this with the profusion of spices used by the Bene Israel Jews of western India, where spice plants grow in abundance: all of the aromatic "C" spices—cinnamon, cloves, cardamom, coriander, cumin—plus turmeric, nutmeg, ginger, garlic, and a host of others.

Salt, of course, does not come from a plant—it is not vegetable but mineral—and so cannot be considered a spice. Still, as the most prevalent seasoning agent the world over, among Jewish and non-Jewish cooks alike, it deserves at least a brief mention in this context. There are many varieties of salt, from sea salt to iodized table salt. The one generally associated with Jewish cooking is known as kosher salt, although this is something of a misnomer, as all salt is kosher. Rather, this variety should be called "koshering salt," since its relatively coarse crystals aid in drawing out blood from slaughtered meat, a prerequisite for kosher cookery. Not only is salt useful in koshering, but in earlier times, before refrigeration, it was essential in the preservation of meat and fish. The preservative power of salt also functions symbolically in the so-called covenant of salt made between God and the Israelites in Numbers 18:19, a covenant that is said will last "for ever."

Even earlier, when the Israelites escaped from Pharaoh's Egypt, the only food they carried with them was matzo, plain unleavened bread. It has long been said that this was because in their flight, they did not have time to let the bread rise. In his comprehensive *Salt: A World History*, Mark Kurlansky suggests an alternative explanation: that the recourse to matzo was "a conscious rejection of Egyptian culture and the luxuries of the slave owners. Raised bread and salt curing were emblematic of the high-living Egyptians." Salt, then, played a doubly indispensable role in the early establishment of the Jewish people, in its presence and absence alike.

HAWAIJ

YEMENITE SPICE MIXTURE

Hawaij *is the most popular of the Yemenite spice mixtures, used in all manner of dishes, from chicken soup to poached fish to broiled meat, imparting to all of them that distinctively aromatic Yemenite flavor.*

MAKES ABOUT ½ CUP

3 tablespoons cumin seeds

4 teaspoons black peppercorns

4 tablespoons turmeric

6 cloves

7 cardamom pods

Place all of the ingredients in an electric spice grinder or coffee grinder. Grind until finely ground. Store in a tightly closed container.

Z'HOUG

YEMENITE GREEN CHILI PASTE

This fiery-hot paste is essential to Yemenite cuisine and is added as a flavoring to stews or served as an accompaniment with grilled fish and meats or with the many varieties of Yemenite bread.

MAKES ABOUT 2 CUPS

- 1 cup fresh cilantro or flat-leaf parsley leaves
- 3 teaspoons cumin seeds
- 4 teaspoons black peppercorns
- 1 teaspoon caraway seeds
- 8 cloves
- 8 cardamom pods
- 1 teaspoon salt
- 8 garlic cloves
- 1/4 pound green chili peppers, such as jalapeño or serrano
- 3 tablespoons olive oil

Combine all of the ingredients in a blender or food processor and process to a rough paste. Transfer to a tightly closed jar and refrigerate until ready to use. It will keep in the refrigerator for several weeks.

DISHES: Charoset

Its name derived from the Hebrew word for clay, *chres*, *charoset* is a sweet paste made from chopped fruit, usually combined with nuts and red wine. In the Passover seder, it symbolizes the mortar used by Israelite slaves during the Egyptian captivity. During the seder, the bitter herb known as *maror* (among Ashkenazic Jews, this is generally horseradish, while Sephardim more often use escarole or other bitter greens) is dipped into the *charoset*; the sweetness of the *charoset* thus counteracts the bitterness of the *maror*, representing the Jews' eternal optimism in the face of oppression. The *charoset* is also eaten with *maror* and matzo in the "Hillel sandwich," so called because the sage Hillel believed that these foods were eaten together during Temple times.

Though *charoset* itself is shared by every Jewish community, each one has its own version—or, more accurately, versions. (I once asked Laura Supino, a consultant to the Museo Ebraico in Rome, if there was an Italian-style *charoset*; she just threw back her head and laughed. "Do you want ten recipes, or one hundred?" she asked. "Every Jewish family in Rome has its own, and they all consider theirs to be the best.") Still, even granting latitude for individual variation, it is possible to make certain geographic generalizations.

The *charoset* best known among American Jews is relatively simple, comprising just chopped apples and walnuts, which are then sweetened with honey or sugar, spiced with cinnamon, and loosened up with a bit of sweet red wine. This is the traditional *charoset* of Eastern European Jewry, who used apples because they are a biblical-era fruit (important for an Exodus-based holiday), one of the few hardy enough to survive in the forbidding soil of the region. Elsewhere, though, Jews were not so limited in their choices, and in Sephardic *charoset* we see a broader range of fruits, especially those grown in biblical Israel: dates, figs, raisins, and pomegranates. Among Syrian Jews, for instance, *charoset* is made with dried dates mixed with walnuts and red wine; Turkish Jews traditionally add apples and figs to the dates, as well as the grated zest of an orange. (In both of these versions, as with most Sephardic *charoset*, the dried fruit is first simmered in water to soften.) Yemenite Jews put together a remarkably complex *charoset*, which can include apples, dates, figs, raisins, almonds, pine nuts, pomegranate seeds, bananas, sesame seeds, matzo meal, and red wine; the Yemenites, who like their foods spicy, also add ground ginger and sometimes black pepper. Pistachio nuts are a fixture in the *charoset* of Iranian Jews—Iran is one of the world's leading producers of pistachios—while pine nuts commonly appear in *charoset* from Greece. Almonds are often the nut of choice in Italy—in northern regions, chestnuts are also very common—and the fresh fruits include not just apples, but also oranges and pears.

Across the Mediterranean, in Morocco, the *charoset* is sometimes rolled into little balls. This may be a legacy of Spanish practice: In *A Drizzle of Honey*, David Gitlitz and Linda Kay Davidson present a medieval Spanish recipe for *charoset* balls made from apples, dried fruit, almonds, and cooked chestnuts and sweetened with sugar and cinnamon. Unlike most versions of *charoset*, this one contained no red wine. Instead, the rolled balls were drizzled with white vinegar just before serving.

Among Iraqi Jews, the *charoset* is neither paste nor balls, but something else entirely. Its foundation is the date syrup called *halek* (the name likely derives from *hallec*, a Roman fish sauce), made from boiling dates and, after straining the liquid, reducing it over a low flame until thick. *Halek* is a genuinely ancient food, one of the earliest of all sweeteners; the biblical description of Israel as a "land flowing with milk and honey" actually refers not to bee honey (which does not appear in the Bible until later), but to *halek*. For Passover, Iraqi Jews—as well as the Jews of Calcutta, who descend in large part from Iraqis—simply add chopped walnuts or almonds to the date syrup, thus producing their own unique version of *charoset*.

Though less complex in its taste than other versions of *charoset*, the color and texture of *halek* is perhaps most comparable to the Nile silt used by the ancient Israelites for their mortar. And so it vividly calls to mind the food's original meaning, and reminds us, once again, that all *charoset*, no matter where it comes from or with what ingredients it is made, is indescribably sweet.

EASTERN EUROPEAN CHAROSET

This is the variety of charoset *with which most American Jews are familiar. The recipe comes from Susan Friedland, my editor, and was first published in her excellent book* The Passover Table. *As she says, "Make enough so that people can eat it with the meal—it's that good."*

MAKES ABOUT 4 CUPS

- 2 large red apples, such as Fuji or Gala (about 1 pound total)
- 1¼ cups shelled walnuts
- 2 teaspoons ground cinnamon, or to taste
- 3 to 5 tablespoons sweet red wine, to taste

1. Peel and core the apples. Finely chop the apples and the walnuts by hand, or place them in the bowl of a food processor and pulse until the mixture is finely chopped.
2. Transfer the apple-walnut mixture to a medium bowl. Add the cinnamon and wine and stir until the mixture comes together as a coarse paste. Taste and add cinnamon or wine, as desired.

ITALIAN CHAROSET

This is my very favorite charoset. *A slightly different version replaces the dates with ½ cup of sugar, but I much prefer this one.*

MAKES ABOUT 4½ CUPS

- 2½ cups blanched almonds
- 1½ cups pitted dried dates
- ½ large red apple, such as Fuji or Gala
- ½ large pear
- Juice of 2 oranges
- 3 tablespoons sweet red wine, or to taste
- Ground cinnamon (optional)

1. Finely chop the almonds and dates by hand or in the bowl of a food processor fitted with the metal blade. Grate the apple and pear by hand on a box grater or in a food processor equipped with a shredding disk.
2. Place the almonds, dates, apple, and pear in a large bowl. Add the orange juice, red wine, and cinnamon (if using) and stir to combine.

YEMENITE CHAROSET

A fresh pomegranate is often difficult to find around Passover season, and its seeds are not strictly necessary here. You might also stir in a spoonful or two of sesame seeds, and for more spice, a few grinds of black pepper.

MAKES ABOUT 2½ CUPS

- 1 cup pitted dried dates
- ⅔ cup shelled walnuts
- ⅓ cup pine nuts
- ⅓ cup blanched almonds
- 1 large red apple, such as Fuji or Gala, peeled and chopped
- Seeds of ½ pomegranate (optional)
- 1 teaspoon ground cinnamon
- ½ to ¾ teaspoon powdered ginger
- ¼ cup sweet red wine, or to taste

1. Place the dates in a medium saucepan and add water to cover. Bring to a boil, lower the heat, and simmer until soft, about 10 minutes. Drain in a colander and let cool.
2. Place the dates in the bowl of a food processor. Add the remaining ingredients, except the wine, and pulse until coarsely ground. Transfer the mixture to a medium bowl. Stir in the wine until the mixture reaches the desired consistency. Taste and adjust for seasoning.

CHREYN

FRESH HORSERADISH WITH BEETS

Horseradish is a plant native to Eastern Europe and Western Asia. Its root, which is long and whitish yellow in color, is notorious for being eye-tearingly, sinus-clearingly pungent, although this is only the case when it is cut: the intact root is virtually odorless. As a result, the Jews of Eastern Europe and Russia, and their descendants, have long used grated horseradish as the maror, *the bitter herb of the Passover seder. Grated horseradish is also commonly mixed with beets, the sweetness of which helps to subdue the root's fire. It is the best possible topping for gefilte fish.*

MAKES ABOUT 1 CUP

½ pound horseradish root, peeled and cut into 1-inch pieces

2 beets, peeled and quartered

1 teaspoon salt

2 teaspoons sugar

2 to 3 tablespoons white or apple cider vinegar

1. Place the horseradish root and the beets in the bowl of a food processor and process until smooth. Remove the lid of the processor and let the mixture stand for 30 minutes.
2. Transfer the mixture to a medium bowl. Add the salt, sugar, and just enough vinegar to moisten and stir to combine. Taste and adjust for seasoning. Spoon into a tightly covered jar and refrigerate until ready to serve.

Selected Bibliography

Abramowicz, Hirsz. *Profiles of a Lost World.* Detroit: Wayne State University Press, 1999.

Algar, Ayla. *Classical Turkish Cooking.* New York: HarperCollins, 1991.

Bellin, Mildred Grosberg. *The Jewish Cook Book.* New York: Bloch, 1941.

Bernstein, Ignatz. *Yidishe Shprikhverter.* 1912. New York: Alvetlekher Yidisher Kultur-Kongres, 1983.

Bolens, Lucie. *La Cuisine Andalouse, Un Art de Vivre: XIe-XIIIe Siècle.* Paris: Albin Michel, 1990.

Bovbjerg, Dana, and Jeremy Iggers. *The Joy of Cheesecake.* Hauppauge, N.Y.: Barron's, 1980.

Cooper, John. *Eat and Be Satisfied: A Social History of Jewish Food.* London: Jason Aronson, 1993.

Crisco Recipes for the Jewish Housewife. Cincinnati: Procter & Gamble, 1933.

Davidson, Alan. *The Oxford Companion to Food.* New York: Oxford University Press, 1999.

De Pomiane, Edouard. *The Jews of Poland: Recollections and Recipes.* 1929. Translated by Josephine Bacon. Garden Grove, Calif.: Pholiota Press, 1985.

Denker, Joel. *The World on a Plate.* Boulder, Co.: Westview Press, 2003.

Diner, Hasia R. *Hungering for America: Italian, Irish, and Jewish Foodways in the Age of Migration.* Cambridge, Mass: Harvard University Press, 2001.

Fisher, M. F. K. *The Art of Eating.* New York: Macmillan, 1990.

Flandrin, Jean-Louis, and Massimo Montanari, editors. *Food: A Culinary History.* English edition by Albert Sonnenfeld. New York: Columbia University Press, 1999.

Friedland, Susan R. *The Passover Table.* New York: HarperCollins, 1994.

Frishwasser, Regina. *Jewish American Cook Book.* New York: Forward Association, 1946.

Gabaccia, Donna R. *We Are What We Eat: Ethnic Food and the Making of Americans.* Cambridge, Mass.: Harvard University Press, 1988.

Geller, Ruth Liliana. *Roma Ebraica.* Rome, Italy: Viella, 1984.

Gerber, Jane. *The Jews of Spain.* New York: The Free Press, 1992.

Gitlitz, David M., and Linda Kay Davidson. *A Drizzle of Honey: The Lives and Recipes of Spain's Secret Jews.* New York: St. Martin's, 1999.

Gotein, S. D. *From the Land of Sheba.* New York: Schocken, 1973.

Grossinger, Jennie. *The Art of Jewish Cooking.* New York: Bantam Books, 1960.

Herzog, Marvin I. *The Yiddish Language in Northern Poland.* The Hague: Mouton, 1965.

Herzog, Marvin I., Wita Ravid, and Uriel Weinreich. *The Field of Yiddish: Studies in Language, Folklore, and Literature.* The Hague: Mouton, 1969.

Hyman, Mavis. *Indian-Jewish Cooking.* London: Hyman Publishers, 1992.

Katz, Nathan. *Who Are the Jews of India?* Berkeley: University of California Press, 2000.

Kazzaz, David. *Mother of the Pound.* Brooklyn, N.Y.: Sepher-Hermon Press, 1999.

Kiple, Kenneth F., and Kriemhild Coneè Ornelas. *The Cambridge World History of Food.* Volumes 1 and 2. New York: Cambridge University Press, 2000.

Klein, Maggie Blyth. *Feast of the Olive.* San Francisco: Chronicle Books, 1994.

Koronyo, Viki, and Sima Ovadyo. *Sefarad Yemekleri.* Istanbul: Society of Assistance to Old People, 1990.

Kosover, Mortkhe. *Yidishe Maykholim: A Shtudye in Kultur, Geshikhte un Shprakhforshung.* New York: YIVO Institute of Jewish Research, 1958.

Kurlansky, Mark. *Salt: A World History.* New York: Walker and Company, 2002.

Levy, Esther. *Jewish Cookery Book.* 1871. Cambridge, Mass.: Applewood Books, 1988.

Machlin, Edda Servi. *The Classic Cuisine of the Italian Jews.* Croton on Hudson, N.Y.: Giro Press, 1993.

McGee, Harold. *The Curious Cook.* New York: Wiley, 1990.

Nathan, Joan. *Jewish Cooking in America.* New York: Alfred A. Knopf, 1994.

Paris, Erna. *The End of Days.* Amherst, N.Y.: Prometheus Books, 1995.

Rabinowitz, Louis. *Jewish Merchant Adventurers: A Study of the Radanites.* London: Edward Goldston, 1948.

Roden, Claudia. *The Book of Jewish Food.* New York: Alfred A. Knopf, 1996.

Roland, Joan G. *The Jewish Communities of India.* New Brunswick, N.J.: Transaction Publishers, 1998.

Root, Waverly. *Food.* New York: Smithmark, 1980.

Rosengarten, Frederic. *The Book of Spices.* New York: Pyramid Books, 1973.

Schwartz, Oded. *In Search of Plenty: A History of Jewish Food.* London: Kyle Cathie, 1992.

Shaida, Margaret. *The Legendary Cuisine of Persia.* London: Lieuse, 1992.

Shortridge, Barbara G., and James R. Shortridge, editors. *The Taste of American Place.* Lanham, Md.: Rowman & Littlefield, 1998.

Shosteck, Patti. *A Lexicon of Jewish Cooking.* Chicago: Contemporary Books, 1979.

Stan, Anisoara. *The Romanian Cook Book.* Secaucus, N.J.: Castle, 1951.

Stavroulakis, Nicholas. *Cookbook of the Jews of Greece.* Port Jefferson, N.Y.: Cadmus Press, 1986.

———. *Salonika: Jews and Dervishes.* Athens: Talos Press, 1993.

Trager, James. *The Food Chronology.* New York: Henry Holt, 1995.

Visser, Margaret. *Much Depends on Dinner.* New York: Macmillan, 1986.

Ward, Susie, Claire Clifton, and Jenny Stacey. *The Gourmet Atlas.* New York: Macmillan, 1997.

Weinreich, Max. *History of the Yiddish Language.* Translated by Shlomo Noble. Chicago: 1973. Reprint, University of Chicago Press, 1980.

Index